Reflections in AMERICAN POLITICAL THOUGHT

Readings from PAST AND PRESENT

PHILIP ABBOTT
Wayne State University

MICHAEL P. RICCARDS
State University of New York
College at Buffalo

CHANDLER PUBLISHING COMPANY
An Intext Publisher
New York and London

*To Patricia Abbott and
Patrick, Margaret, and Diana Riccards*

Copyright © 1973 by Intext Press, Inc.

All rights reserved. No part of this book may be reprinted, reproduced, or utilized in any form or by any electronic, mechanical, or other means, now known or hereafter invented, including photocopying and recording, or in any information storage and retrieval system, without permission in writing from the Publisher.

Library of Congress Cataloging in Publication Data

Abbott, Philip, comp.
    Reflections in American political thought.

    1. Political science—History—United States—Addresses, essays, lectures. I. Riccards, Michael P., joint comp. II. Title.
JA84.U5A615   320.9'73   72-13666
ISBN 0-8102-0469-X

Chandler Publishing Company
257 Park Avenue South
New York, New York 10010

CONTENTS

Preface   vii

Introduction   1

I. The Origin of Politics   7

   1. Human Nature and Politics   7

      John Cotton, Limitation of Government   9
      Thomas Paine, Common Sense   11
      John Adams, Letter to John Taylor of Caroline   17
      Reinhold Neibuhr, Moral Man and Immoral Society   23
      John Dewey, Democracy and Human Nature   29

   2. Justifying Government—The Consent Model   37

      Declaration of Independence   39
      Joseph Tussman, Obligation and the Body Politic   42
      Hanna Pitkin, Obligation and Consent—I   49
      Philip Abbott, Moral Duty, Political Obligation, and the Doctrine of Consent   65

II. The Limits of Politics   85

   1. Natural Rights   85

      Thomas Paine, Rights of Man   87
      William Channing, Slavery   89
      William Graham Sumner, Some Natural Rights   95
      Edward Bellamy, The Parable of the Water Tank   98
      William J. Wainwright, Natural Rights   104

   2. The Morality of Resistance   115

      Thomas Jefferson, Notes on Revolution   117
      Henry David Thoreau, A Plea for Captain John Brown   118
      Robert Paul Wolff, On Violence   123
      Jeffrie G. Murphy, Punishment for Looters?   136
      Philip Abbott, Revolutionary Ethics   140
      National Commission on the Causes and Prevention of Violence, Civil Disobedience   148

III. The Problems of Self-Government   163

1. Class and Faction   163

James Madison, The Federalist Papers, Number 10   165
James Madison, The Federalist Papers, Number 51   170
John C. Calhoun, The Concurrent Majority   174
Robert A. Dahl, American Pluralism   182
Willmore Kendall and George W. Carey, The Intensity Problem and Democratic Theory   190
Theodore Lowi, Pluralism as an Ideology   197

2. The American as Citizen   208

Alexis de Tocqueville, The Philosophical Method and Beliefs of Americans   210
Michael P. Riccards, The Socialization of Civic Virtue   216
V.O. Key, Jr., Public Opinion and Democratic Politics   223
Michael Walzer, A Day in the Life of a Socialist Citizen   230

IV. The Search for Authentic Freedom   237

1. Liberty and Political Restraint   237

Thomas Jefferson, The First Inaugural Address   239
Mark Twain, As Regards Patriotism   242
Mark Twain, The War Prayer   243
Louis D. Brandeis and Samuel D. Warren, The Right to Privacy   246
Friedrich Hayek, Planning and Democracy   250

2. The Illusions of "Free" Men   257

Frederick Douglass, What to the Slave Is the Fourth of July?   259
Students for a Democratic Society, Port Huron Statement   262
S. M. Lipset, Working Class Authoritarianism   268
Murray Edelman, The Symbolic Nature of Politics   272
Martin Luther King, Jr., Letter From Birmingham Jail   278

Index of Persons Cited   293

PREFACE

Our purpose in producing yet another anthology is to challenge two almost universally accepted axioms of contemporary political thought. One contends that political theory can be understood only within a rigid historical framework. The other grieves (or rejoices) at the belief that Americans simply have no tradition of political theory. In teaching courses in political thought, both the authors have become increasingly dissatisfied with these assertions. Clearly there is an incongruity in announcing to the class that there is no American political thought and then in proceeding to spend months unraveling the theories of Winthrop, Williams, Paine, Jefferson, Madison, Channing, Fitzhugh, Calhoun, Royce, Dewey, Veblen, Beard, Parrington, Dahl, Rawls, and Galbraith. We could think of no better way to challenge these beliefs than to present American political thinkers in an analytic context, which contrasts past and present statements on enduring issues, and let the student judge for himself if Americans had failed as political theorists.

Originally, we intended to devote Parts I and II to "normative" issues and Parts III and IV to "empirical" ones, but we were not surprised to find that the distinction was not very meaningful, and we abandoned it. Instead the first two parts are on the origin and limits of politics, the second two on the problems of self-government and the search for authentic freedom. Philip Abbott assumed primary responsibility for the first two parts of the book and Michael P. Riccards for the second two, but we found that even working 300 miles apart, it was not difficult to sustain the book as a cohesive whole.

We offer here selections of some length so that the substance of a writer's views will be fairly presented and will be comprehensible to the student. This strategy results in fewer selections, but we feel that anthologies need not be encyclopedic. We also have tried to keep our own remarks informal. The bibliographical notes at the end of each section are intended to allow the student to pursue his interests either in an individual thinker or in a particular problem.

We trust that this anthology will persuade both students and their instructors that American political thought is as varied, as complex, and as vibrant as the nation itself.

In putting this work together, we became indebted to many people for their assistance—especially to those authors and publishers who consented to having parts of their works represented here. We also are grateful to Barbara

Riccards for her translation of Tocqueville and to Jonathan Sharp and Victor Jones for their editorial friendship. Several colleagues have been most helpful: Gordon J. Schochet, Howard Park, Charles Parrish, Murray Seidler, Martin Kotch, and R. E. Johnston. Reviews of our manuscript were done for Chandler Publishing Company by Richard E. Ashcraft, UCLA; Philip W. Dyer, University of Nebraska; Paul N. Goldstene, California State University, Sacramento; and James P. Young, State University of New York, Binghamton—all of whom made valuable suggestions.

Finally, a word of thanks to our wives, who graciously put up with both us and these clippings for a year.

Reflections in
AMERICAN POLITICAL THOUGHT

INTRODUCTION

In the university today, the commitment to studying and teaching American political thought is justified in the same way one would acknowledge his obligation to care for a hopelessly ill child. American academics have not prided themselves as theoreticians, and they have contended that in this respect they sit comfortably by their ancestors. Yet, despite the near universal agreement that Americans are second-rate political thinkers, there is a curious absence of consensus regarding the nature and source of this assessment.

It is difficult to accept the proposition that a nation which fought a long guerilla war of independence, survived a major civil war only to face a rapid and cruel industrial revolution, tripled its size, absorbed millions of immigrants, and fought two world wars separated by a devastating economic depression, should fail to produce a tradition of political thought. Incredible as this might seem, it is this position which has been offered by Daniel Boorstin in his *The Genius of American Politics*. The genius that Boorstin admires is the absence of men like Plato, Aristotle, Hobbes, Locke, and Rousseau in American life. In his words: "The United States has never produced a political philosopher of their stature or a systematic theoretical work to rank with theirs. . . . No nation has ever been less interested in political philosophy or produced less in the way of theory." This failure, however, is not the result of any intellectual disability but actually a mark of higher wisdom. Those nations which have produced political philosophers may pride themselves in their intellectual heritage, but they soon find they have opened a Pandora's box. Political theory becomes idolatry when it provides statesmen or people with a blueprint of their society. For Boorstin the "tyrannies of our age"—Nazism, Fascism, and Communism—are the result of some academic's well-meaning prose. The circumstances which have prevented the existence of such blueprints for America are "the hallmark of a decent, free, and God-fearing society." In place of political theory Americans have gotten by with a sense of "givenness" which Boorstin defines as an appreciation of the "accumulating wisdom of tradition and institutions."

Shortly after Boorstin's book was published, another interpretation of American political thought was to arrive at a startlingly different conclusion. Louis Hartz in *The Liberal Tradition in America* argued that the apparent absence of a tradition of political thought in America was not quite accurate. Americans do have a political theory—liberalism. While Hartz is annoyingly vague about what he regards as the central tenets of liberalism, one finds that it does involve a commitment to rationalism, constitutionalism, individualism, and laissez faire capitalism. Hartz freely admits that the grip of this "Lockean tyranny" on America can be explained by a single factor theory. American political history can be understood by reference to its origins. In a new land peopled by the "fragment culture" of the seventeenth-century English middle class, there was no possibility for the construction of a feudal society. Without a golden age of aristocracy to look back on, no genuine conservatism could develop in America. Similarly, without a sense of the rigid inequalities fostered by feudalism, no socialist interpretation of politics could make itself relevant to the American experience. Deprived of both a viable political right and left, the ideological spectrum in America has been inordinately narrow. A basic agreement on political and economic institutions founded upon liberal principles has made effective radical dissent nearly impossible. Hartz concludes his book by noting that the allegiance to liberal principles has been so deeply held that Americans are virtually unable to understand any other way of life. This has hampered creative action in America's relations with other nations and has contributed to an hysterical reaction toward dissenters at home. In general then, the pragmatism of which Americans are so proud operates only within the context of a very narrow range of acceptable alternatives.

For yet another interpretation of American political thought we need to move back more than a century and consider Alexis de Tocqueville's *Democracy in America*. When Tocqueville came to study nineteenth-century America first-hand, he was struck by the manner in which Americans were unable to relate ideals and practice. The American mind oscillated almost uncontrollably between ideas which were "all either extremely minute and clear" and those "extremely general and vague." Tocqueville ascribed this "democratic" quality of mind to two factors. The absence of an aristocracy invariably meant that there could be no shared body of opinions, habits, and allegiances which guaranteed a measure of intellectual as well as political stability in society. In a democracy each citizen was his own philosopher. When he looked higher than himself he only saw "the immense form of society at large or the still more imposing aspect of mankind." The tradition of Calvinism with its insistence upon a direct relationship between the individual and God and its Manichean world view also contributed to the disjointed character of American thought. While Tocqueville saw certain clear advantages in democracy, he feared that the dualist thought patterns it produced would lead to a great confusion in philosophy, morals, and politics. Fortunately for the democratic citizen, there is a variety of social, economic, and political groups with which he can identify and from which he can receive some traditions and standards. In one sense, groups in a democratic society perform some of the same functions as the old aristocracy.

However, many political scientists—like Tocqueville—have emphasized the incoherencies and instabilities of American public opinion. They have argued that the reason why America has not produced great theorists is not because we have a preference for muddling through or because we have long since settled on a satisfactory political theory. Instead they maintain that America has failed to produce a tradition of political thought because democracies simply do not possess the requisite stable social and economic institutions which permit an opportunity for systematic reflection on where society has been or where it is going. Armed with a few precious political axioms and some principles of political practice, the American has been frantically juggling both for two hundred years. Terrified that either may fall, he has not had the luxury of thinking about their worth.

While these critiques clearly differ, it is possible to trace their positions to a single cause. None of them are neutral observations of American political history. Since they are in varying degrees ideological statements, they are subject to analysis from the perspective of the sociology of knowledge. Boorstin wrote against the background of World War II, the Cold War, and the experience of McCarthyism. Like many writers in this period, Boorstin connected the conflicts in Europe which gave rise to Hitler, Mussolini, and Stalin with the emergence of chiliastic ideologies of that period. According to this reasoning, broad-gauge belief systems which appeal to the masses produce an irrational and violent politics that can only lead to the rise of brutal demagogues. In Boorstin's mind any coherent, systematic approach to politics is dangerous and must be avoided. The 1950s anti-Communist paranoia fostered by Joseph McCarthy also seemed to arouse the interest and support of the masses and challenged the normal political process. To the extent that writers could convince others that "ideological" thinking was un-American they felt that they might avoid the severe economic and political polarization which seemed to result in the European debacle only a decade before. In a sense, Boorstin's work is a piece of political theory in its own right. For by indicating that a constitution and elections are not themselves a guarantee of political stability, Boorstin is revising the tenets of classical liberalism. In fact, Boorstin's contention that Americans have rejected political theorizing is more a plea than an observation.

What Nazism and Communism meant for Boorstin, the French revolution meant for Tocqueville. Tocqueville's reservations about democracy were clear, and while he did not disguise his pleasure over the fact that America had developed a democratic political system without the sort of revolution with which the French had been burdened, he projected his fears of a late-blooming Jacobin reign of terror upon his description of a schizoid American mind.

Yet even granting the ideological foundation of these works, it is necessary to consider them at their face value. Two persistent claims are still made about American political thought in the universities today: (1) even if Americans should be more conscious of the foundations of their political system, they have not seriously engaged in political theory; (2) when they have done political thought it has not been uniquely American but essentially borrowed from the predominant political theories of Europe. Both these assertions are too sweeping to be adequately questioned in this introduction and only a few remarks will be offered here. First, we must remember America as a nation is less than three hundred years old. If we exclude the rare bursts of political thought that occurred in fifth-century Athens or seventeenth-century England, how many political theorists of first rank can a nation produce in a few centuries? One cannot help but harbor the suspicion that the sense of inferiority Americans have always felt when they compared themselves to Europe has extended to the evaluation of our political theorists. Moreover, the sort of architectonic political theory which offered its epistemology, psychology, and political inquiry as a logical whole was becoming more rare by the eighteenth century and nearly obsolete by the end of the nineteenth. Yet America is judged by a model of political thought which flourished when its settlers were clearing forests.

The argument that Americans have been astute imitators of European political thought also begins to falter upon closer scrutiny. The fact of the matter is that until 1750 or even 1763 Americans *were* Europeans in many of their customs and ideas. Yet even if we grant this, it is important to note that many of the New England Puritan conceptions of government were being developed before or simultaneously with the writings of Sidney and Locke. Moreover, the works of Williams, Madison, Calhoun, Thoreau, Emerson, Godkin, Royce, Veblen, Arnold, and Pound, to mention only a few at random, can hardly be passed off as imitations without the most careful historical analysis.

Finally (and with full recognition that this is tantamount to heresy), although no American theorist is represented in any major textbook on the history of political thought, was Williams' *Bloody Tenet* less effective than Milton's *Areopagitica* or Mills' *On Liberty?* Is Madison's contribution to the Federalist papers really inferior to Aristotle's *Politics,* or Bellamy's *Looking Backward* less insightful than Harrington's *Oceana* or More's *Utopia,* or Dewey's *The Public and its Problems* and *Reconstruction in Philosophy* less imposing than T. H. Green's *Principles of Political Obligation?* The standards for the evaluation of political theories are not fixed, but however one may choose to employ them, Americans have had their share of journeymen.

If we return now to Louis Hartz's thesis we will find that it can best be described as an exaggeration rather than an error. No one can deny that liberalism has held a decisive hegemony over other forms of American political thought. Whether it has ever been seriously challenged is a subject of legitimate contention. More than likely, we can say that its influence has ebbed at the more turbulent periods of American history only to rise again in periods of relative calm. Yet despite the general accuracy of Hartz's argument, it misses a good deal about American history. Hartz fails to note the significant variations within liberal political thought and misconceives the sources of political conflict in American history. The student cannot fail to note that the liberalism of William Graham Sumner is very different from the liberalism of Reinhold Neibuhr or Robert Dahl. These differences cannot even be totally accounted for by drawing a distinction between classical and modern liberalism. The bitter dispute between John Dewey and Randolph Bourne over the justification of American participation in World War I was not an economic one nor was it limited to a disagreement over means. Liberalism is as varied and complex a tradition as Marxism. And just as we cannot treat the battles of Communists as lovers' spats we cannot overlook the severe schisms within liberal political thought.

Furthermore, if we reduce the source of variety in political thought to the existence of economic class, then we miss the meaning of most of America's political theories. While it is certainly correct to say that the absence of feudalism has served to diminish class politics in America, one must also note that the issues which have nearly torn America apart have not been directly economic issues at all. There have been two major sources of political instability in America: the conflict between liberal and democratic beliefs as they relate to positions on political problems and the conflict between ethnic groups and races. Both of these arenas of conflict have clear economic roots, but they cannot be totally explained by an economic reduction. Liberal political thought has managed to absorb many of the tenets of democratic ideology. But individuals who have a commitment to some aspects of liberalism may be fearful, to some extent, of mass political participation as well as economic and political centralization. The always uneasy coalition of liberal and democratic values has fallen apart at the turn of the century and in the 1930s and 1960s. The pieces have been and will probably now be picked up again, but there is no guarantee that these values can continue to coexist.

The issue of race has been a part of our political life since the eighteenth century and has remained since with only a few moments of quiet. It consumed most of the time of the colonial legislatures, and was a source of conflict even when Americans saw the need for unity on the eve of the revolution. Before the Civil War, much of the discussion over governmental power and states rights really involved the question of race.

Some critics have noted that Calhoun, the foremost political thinker of the period, was seeking to find a justification for feudal aristocracy in America. Yet if one examines Calhoun's arguments closely and without reference to European politics, it is clear that this was not his purpose. Calhoun's concurrent majority was an attempt to insure racial supremacy through the use of liberal principles. Calhoun did not need to beckon to an age of a benevolent land-holding aristocracy; liberalism provided a much more effective model for his purposes. Thus even liberalism is a much broader tradition that is generally recognized.

This volume then assumes not only that American political thought exists, but that it is worthy of attention and study. The selections that follow are a varied collection that is meant to introduce the reader to some of the major political problems that Americans have discussed and considered important.

I. THE ORIGIN OF POLITICS

1. Human Nature and Politics

Nothing is more crucial to the subsequent recommendations of a political theorist than his account of human nature. Although the concept itself is ambiguous and has many variations, it is usually taken to mean an assessment of man's propensities in a wide range of situations. The concept of human nature is purposely designed to be a very high-level generalization. When we say it is human nature to cheat on our income tax, we are saying that social class, intelligence, moral training, and temptation are all factors which influence our actions but that, *ceteris paribus,* the inclination of men is to cheat. For those writers who employ it, human nature becomes a separate variable in their calculations of how men will act. Most theorists have contended that those who ignore it, especially in politics, are bound to err in their estimates of situations.

While human nature is frequently treated as an ethical consideration (Are men basically good or evil?), it often involves an assessment of men's propensity for violence and ambition, and their level of native intelligence. Important as these judgments are, perhaps more crucial are two other considerations. Let us say, for instance, that most men are incapable of making more than the most simple decisions and that only a few men have the ability, perseverance, and foresight to sensibly select alternatives. The next question we will want to ask is, How do we find the few intelligent men and separate them from the mass? We might conclude that these few are easy to find—they all are ordained priests, all have university degrees, or all have red hair. When we offer our judgments about how to organize a good society, we would naturally devise a political system which would make use of our criteria. If, however, we have concluded that very few men are capable of making rational decisions, but they are randomly dispersed throughout the population, we would recommend a very different political system.

Another consideration frequently associated with a discussion of human nature is the malleability of these clusters of personality traits. If it is in men's nature to resolve conflicts by violence, is it possible to alter that inclination by placing men in an entirely different social or economic setting?

The following essays reflect the preoccupation of American political theorists with the darker side of human existence. For them the purpose of politics is to limit and harness those impulses. For John Cotton, man's ambition makes government necessary but at the same time poses a clear threat to liberty. Cotton's remarks were written in 1655 as part of a sermon on the Apocalypse and indicate how the Puritans came to respect the principle of limited government.

The selection by Thomas Paine is a classic of liberal political thought. Written only months before the outbreak of the American revolution, this pamphlet contends that governments arise from the "inability of moral virtue to govern the world." While Paine's historical sense appears incredibly naive to us today, his plea for simplicity as a standard for judging political institutions is not an irrelevant notion.

John Adams was the black sheep of the early days of the American republic. His *Defense of the Constitutions,* written in 1787 frankly admitted both the likelihood and desirability of elites within a democracy. The selection offered here is a response to John Taylor's criticism of his position. His comments are even sharper than those in his original work. While Adams' beliefs in a natural aristocracy were treasonous to the Jeffersonian democrats, his remarks bear a remarkable similarity to the positions taken by contemporary American political scientists. (See the selections by V. O. Key, Robert Dahl, and Seymour Lipset in Parts III and IV of this book.)

The works of Reinhold Niebuhr are an attempt to combine Protestant theology and social science to reach an assessment of human nature. In this selection Niebuhr argues that as men conceive of themselves as members of larger and larger groups, their sense of moral restraint diminishes correspondingly. In an age characterized by massive organization, Niebuhr's remarks are foreboding.

John Dewey contends that theories of human nature have been rationalizations for challenged and challenging social and economic groups in society. Dewey would have us treat human nature as a moral ideal and place it in the service of the advancement of democracy. If we were to subject America's foremost philosopher to the standards of his own analysis, we might question whether his conception of human nature is also a rationalization of some socioeconomic group.

LIMITATION OF GOVERNMENT
John Cotton

... This may serve to teach us the danger of allowing to any mortall man an inordinate measure of power to speak great things, to allow to any man uncontrollablenesse of speech, you see the desperate danger of it: Let all the world learn to give mortall men no greater power then they are content they shall use, for use it they will: and unlesse they be better taught of God, they will use it ever and anon, it may be make it the passage of their proceeding to speake what they will: And they that have liberty to speak great things, you will finde it to be true, they will speak great blasphemies. No man would think what desperate deceit and wickednesse there is in the hearts of men: And that was the reason why the Beast did speak such great things, hee might speak, and no body might controll him. *What,* saith the Lord in Jer. 3.5. *Thou hast spoken and done evill things as thou couldst.* If a Church or head of a Church could have done worse, he would have done it: This is one of the straines of nature, it affects boundlesse liberty, and to runne to the utmost extent: What ever power he hath received, he hath a corrupt nature that will improve it in one thing or other; if he have liberty, he will think why may he not use it. Set up the Pope as Lord Paramount over Kings and Princes, and they shall know that he hath power over them, he will take liberty to depose one, and set up another. Give him power to make Laws, and he will approve, and disprove as he list; what he approves is Canonicall, what hee disproves is rejected: Give him that power, and he will so order it at length, he will make such a State of Religion, that he that so lives and dyes shall never be saved, and all this springs from the vast power that is given to him, and from the deep depravation of nature. Hee will open his mouth, *His tongue is his owne, who is Lord over him,* Psal. 12. 3, 4. It is therefore most wholsome for Magistrates and Officers in Church and Common-wealth, never to affect more liberty and authority then will do them good, and the People good; for what ever transcendant power is given, will certainly over-run those that give it, and those that receive it: There is a straine in a mans heart that will sometime or other runne out to excesse, unlesse the Lord restraine it, but it is not good to venture it: It is necessary therefore, that all power that is on earth be limited, Church-power or other: If there be power given to speak great things, then look for great blasphemies, look for a licentious abuse of it. It is counted a matter of danger to the State to limit Prerogatives; but it is a further danger, not to have

From Puritan Political Ideas, *edited by Edmund S. Morgan, copyright © 1965, by the Bobbs-Merrill Company, Inc.; reprinted by permission of the publisher.*

them limited: They will be like a Tempest, if they be not limited: A Prince himselfe cannot tell where hee will confine himselfe, nor can the people tell: But if he have liberty to speak great things, then he will make and unmake, say and unsay, and undertake such things as are neither for his owne honour, nor for the safety of the State. It is therefore fit for every man to be studious of the bounds which the Lord hath set: and for the People, in whom fundamentally all power lyes, to give as much power as God in his word gives to men: And it is meet that Magistrates in the Common-wealth, and so Officers in Churches should desire to know the utmost bounds of their own power, and it is safe for both: All intrenchment upon the bounds which God hath not given, they are not enlargements, but burdens and snares; They will certainly lead the spirit of a man out of his way sooner or later. It is wholsome and safe to be dealt withall as God deales with the vast Sea; *Hitherto shalt thou come, but there shalt thou stay thy proud waves:* and therefore if they be but banks of simple sand, they will be good enough to check the vast roaring Sea. And so for Imperiall Monarchies, it is safe to know how far their power extends; and then if it be but banks of sand, which is most slippery, it will serve, as well as any brazen wall. If you pinch the Sea of its liberty, though it be walls of stone or brasse, it will beate them downe: So it is with Magistrates, stint them where God hath not stinted them, and if they were walls of brasse, they would beate them downe, and it is meet they should: but give them the liberty God allows, and if it be but a wall of sand it will keep them: As this liquid Ayre in which we breath, God hath set it for the waters of the Clouds to the Earth; It is a Firmament, it is the Clouds, yet it stands firme enough, because it keeps the Climate where they are, it shall stand like walls of brasse: So let there be due bounds set, and I may apply it to Families; it is good for the Wife to acknowledge all power and authority to the Husband, and for the Husband to acknowledg honour to the Wife, but still give them that which God hath given them, and no more nor lesse: Give them the full latitude that God hath given, else you will finde you dig pits, and lay snares, and cumber their spirits, if you give them lesse: there is never peace where full liberty is not given, nor never stable peace where more then full liberty is granted: Let them be duely observed, and give men no more liberty then God doth, nor women, for they will abuse it: The Devill will draw them, and Gods providence leade them thereunto, therefore give them no more than God gives. And so for children; and servants, or any others you are to deale with, give them the liberty and authority you would have them use, and beyond that stretch not the tether, it will not tend to their good nor yours: And also from hence gather, and goe home with this meditation; That certainly here is this distemper in our natures, that we cannot tell how to use liberty, but wee shall very readily corrupt our selves: Oh the bottomlesse depth of sandy earth! of a corrupt spirit, that breaks over all bounds, and loves inordinate vastnesse; that is it we ought to be careful of. . . .

COMMON SENSE
Thomas Paine

Some writers have so confounded society with government, as to leave little or no distinction between them; whereas they are not only different, but have different origins. Society is produced by our wants, and government by our wickedness; the former promotes our happiness *possitively* by uniting our affections, the latter *negatively* by restraining our vices. The one encourages intercourse, the other creates distinctions. The first is a patron, the last a punisher.

Society in every state is a blessing, but Government, even in its best state, is but a necessary evil; in its worst state an intolerable one: for when we suffer, or are exposed to the same miseries *by a Government,* which we might expect in a country *without Government,* our calamity is heightened by reflecting that we furnish the means by which we suffer. Government, like dress, is the badge of lost innocence; the palaces of kings are built upon the ruins of the bowers of paradise. For were the impulses of conscience clear, uniform and irresistibly obeyed, man would need no other law-giver; but that not being the case, he finds it necessary to surrender up a part of his property to furnish means for the protection of the rest; and this he is induced to do by the same prudence which in every other case advises him, out of two evils to choose the least. Wherefore, security being the true design and end of government, it unanswerably follows that whatever form thereof appears most likely to ensure it to us, with the least expence and greatest benefit, is preferable to all others.

In order to gain a clear and just idea of the design and end of government, let us suppose a small number of persons settled in some sequestered part of the earth, unconnected with the rest; they will then represent the first peopling of any country, or of the world. In this state of natural liberty, society will be their first thought. A thousand motives will excite them thereto; the strength of one man is so unequal to his wants, and his mind so unfitted for perpetual solitude, that he is soon obliged to seek assistance and relief of another, who in his turn requires the same. Four or five united would be able to raise a tolerable dwelling in the midst of a wilderness, but one man might labour out the common period of life without accomplishing any thing; when he had felled his timber he could not remove it, nor erect it after it was removed; hunger in the mean time would urge him to quit his work, and every different want would call him a different way. Disease, nay even misfortune, would be death; for though neither might be mortal, yet either would disable him from living,

From The Writings of Thomas Paine. *Copyright by G. P. Putnam's Sons, 1894.*

and reduce him to a state in which he might rather be said to perish than to die.

Thus necessity, like a gravitating power, would soon form our newly arrived emigrants into society, the reciprocal blessings of which would supercede, and render the obligations of law and government unnecessary while they remained perfectly just to each other; but as nothing but Heaven is impregnable to vice, it will unavoidably happen that in proportion as they surmount the first difficulties of emigration, which bound them together in a common cause, they will begin to relax in their duty and attachment to each other: and this remissness will point out the necessity of establishing some form of government to supply the defect of moral virtue.

Some convenient tree will afford them a State House, under the branches of which the whole Colony may assemble to deliberate on public matters. It is more than probable that their first laws will have the title only on Regulations and be enforced by no other penalty than public disesteem. In this first parliament every man by natural right will have a seat.

But as the Colony encreases, the public concerns will encrease likewise, and the distance at which the members may be separated, will render it too inconvenient for all of them to meet on every occasion as at first, when their number was small, their habitations near, and the public concerns few and trifling. This will point out the convenience of their consenting to leave the legislative part to be managed by a select number chosen from the whole body, who are supposed to have the same concerns at stake which those have who appointed them, and who will act in the same manner as the whole body would act were they present. If the colony continue encreasing, it will become necessary to augment the number of representatives, and that the interest of every part of the colony may be attended to, it will be found best to divide the whole into convenient parts, each part sending its proper number: and that the *elected* might never form to themselves an interest separate from the *electors,* prudence will point out the propriety of having elections often: because as the *elected* might by that means return and mix again with the general body of the *electors* in a few months, their fidelity to the public will be secured by the prudent reflection of not making a rod for themselves. And as this frequent interchange will establish a common interest with every part of the community, they will mutually and naturally support each other, and on this, (not on the unmeaning name of king,) depends the *strength of government, and the happiness of the governed.*

Here then is the origin and rise of government; namely, a mode rendered necessary by the inability of moral virtue to govern the world; here too is the design and end of government, viz. Freedom and security. And however our eyes may be dazzled with show, or our ears deceived by sound; however prejudice may warp our wills, or interest darken our understanding, the simple voice of nature and reason will say, 'tis right.

I draw my idea of the form of government from a principle in nature which no art can overturn, viz. that the more simple any thing is, the less liable it is to be disordered, and the easier repaired when disordered; and with this maxim in view I offer a few remarks on the so much boasted constitution of England. That it was noble for the dark and slavish times in which it was erected, is granted. When the world was overrun with tyranny the least remove therefrom was a glorious rescue. But that it is imperfect, subject to convulsions, and incapable of producing what it seems to promise, is easily demonstrated.

Absolute governments, (tho' the disgrace of human nature) have this advantage with them, they are simple; if the people suffer, they know the head from which their suffering springs; know likewise the remedy; and are not bewildered by a variety of causes and cures. But the constitution of England is so exceedingly complex, that the nation may suffer for years together without being able to discover in which part the fault lies; some will say in one and some in another, and every political physician will advise a different medicine.

I know it is difficult to get over local or long standing prejudices, yet if we will suffer ourselves to examine the component parts of the English constitution, we shall find them to be the base remains of two ancient tyrannies, compounded with some new Republican materials.

First.—The remains of Monarchical tyranny in the person of the King.

Secondly.—The remains of Aristocratical tyranny in the persons of the Peers.

Thirdly.—The new Republican materials, in the persons of the Commons, on whose virtue depends the freedom of England.

The two first, by being hereditary, are independant of the People; wherefore in a *constitutional sense* they contribute nothing towards the freedom of the State.

To say that the constitution of England is an *union* of three powers, reciprocally *checking* each other, is farcical; either the words have no meaning, or they are flat contradictions. . . .

To the evil of monarchy we have added that of hereditary succession; and as the first is a degradation and lessening of ourselves, so the second, claimed as a matter of right, is an insult and imposition on posterity. For all men being originally equals, no one by birth could have a right to set up his own family in perpetual preference to all others for ever, and tho' himself might deserve some decent degree of honours of his cotemporaries, yet his descendants might be far too unworthy to inherit them. One of the strongest natural proofs of the folly of hereditary right in Kings, is that nature disapproves it, otherwise she would not so frequently turn it into ridicule, by giving mankind an *Ass for a Lion.*

Secondly, as no man at first could possess any other public honors than were bestowed upon him, so the givers of those honors could have no power to give away the right of posterity, and though they might say "We choose you for your head," they could not wihout manifest injustice to their children say "that your children and your children's children shall reign over ours forever." Because such an unwise, unjust, unnatural compact might (perhaps) in the next succession put them under the government of a rogue or a fool. Most wise men in their private sentiments have ever treated hereditary right with contempt; yet it is one of those evils which when once established is not easily removed: many submit from fear, others from superstition, and the more powerful part shares with the king the plunder of the rest.

This is supposing the present race of kings in the world to have had an honorable origin: whereas it is more than probable, that, could we take off the dark covering of antiquity and trace them to their first rise, we should find the first of them nothing better than the principal ruffian of some restless gang, whose savage manners or pre-eminence in subtilty obtained him the title of chief among plunderers: and who by increasing in power and extending his depredations, overawed the quiet and defenceless to purchase their safety by frequent contributions. Yet his electors could have no idea of giving hereditary right to his descendants, because such a perpetual exclusion of themselves was incompatible with the free and unrestrained principles they professed to live by. Wherefore, hereditary succession in the early ages of monarchy could not take place as a matter of claim, but as something casual or complemental; but as few or no records were extant in those days, and traditionary history stuff'd with fables, it was very easy, after the lapse of a few generations, to trump up some superstitious tale conveniently timed, Mahomet-like, to cram hereditary right down the throats of the vulgar. Perhaps the disorders which threatened, or seemed to threaten, on the decease of a leader and the choice of a new one (for elections among ruffians could not be very orderly) induced many at first to favour hereditary pretensions; by which means it happened, as it hath happened since, that what at first was submitted to as a convenience was afterwards claimed as a right.

England since the conquest hath known some few good monarchs, but groaned beneath a much larger number of bad ones: yet no man in his senses can say that their claim under William the Conqueror is a very honourable one. A French bastard landing with an armed Banditti and establishing himself king of England against the consent of the natives, is in plain terms a very paltry rascally original. It certainly hath no divinity in it. However it is needless to spend much time in exposing the folly of hereditary right; if there are any so weak as to believe it, let them promiscuously worship the Ass and the Lion, and welcome. I shall neither copy their humility, nor disturb their devotion.

Yet I should be glad to ask how they suppose kings came at first? The question admits but of three answers, viz. either by lot, by election, or by usurpation. If the first king was taken by lot, it establishes a precedent for the next, which excludes hereditary succession. Saul was by lot, yet the succession was not hereditary, neither does it appear from that transaction that there was any intention it ever should. If the first king of any country was by election, that likewise establishes a precedent for the next; for to say, that the right of all future generations is taken away, by the act of the first electors, in their choice not only of a king but of a family of kings for ever, hath no parallel in or out of scripture but the doctrine of original sin, which supposes the free will of all men lost in Adam; and from such comparison, and it will admit of no other, hereditary succession can derive no glory. For as in Adam all sinned, and as in the first electors all men obeyed; as in the one all mankind were subjected to Satan, and in the other to sovereignty; as our innocence was lost in the first, and our authority in the last; and as both disable us from reassuming some former state and privilege, it unanswerably follows that original sin and hereditary succession are parallels. Dishonourable rank! inglorious connection! yet the most subtle sophist cannot produce a juster simile.

As to usurpation, no man will be so hardy as to defend it; and that William the Conqueror was an usurper is a fact not to be contradicted. The plain truth is, that the antiquity of English monarchy will not bear looking into.

But it is not so much the absurdity as the evil of hereditary succession which concerns mankind. Did it ensure a race of good and wise men it would have the seal of divine authority, but as it opens a door to the *foolish,* the *wicked,* and the *improper,* it hath in it the nature of oppression. Men who look upon themselves born to reign, and others to obey, soon grow insolent. Selected from the rest of mankind, their minds are early poisoned by importance; and the world they act in differs so materially from the world at large, that they have but little opportunity of knowing its true interests, and when they succeed to the government are frequently the most ignorant and unfit of any throughout the dominions.

Another evil which attends hereditary succession is, that the throne is subject to be possessed by a minor at any age; all which time the regency acting under the cover of a king have every opportunity and inducement to betray their trust. The same national misfortune happens when a king worn out with age and infirmity enters the last stage of human weakness. In both these cases the public becomes a prey to every miscreant who can tamper successfully with the follies either of age or infancy.

The most plausible plea which hath ever been offered in favor of hereditary succession is, that it preserves a nation from civil wars; and were this true, it would be weighty; whereas it is the most bare-faced falsity ever imposed upon mankind. The whole history of England disowns the fact. Thirty kings and two minors have reigned in that distracted kingdom since the conquest, in which time there has been (including the revolution) no less than eight civil wars and nineteen Rebellions. Wherefore instead of making for peace, it makes against it and destroys the very foundation it seems to stand upon.

The contest for monarchy and succession, between the houses of York and Lancaster, laid England in a scene of blood for many years. Twelve pitched battles besides skirmishes and sieges were fought between Henry and Edward. Twice was Henry prisoner to Edward, who in his turn was prisoner to Henry. And so uncertain is the fate of war and the temper of a nation, when nothing but personal matters are the ground of a quarrel, that Henry was taken in triumph from a prison to a palace, and Edward obliged to fly from a palace to a foreign land; yet, as sudden transitions of temper are seldom lasting, Henry in his turn was driven from the throne, and Edward re-called to succeed him. The parliament always following the strongest side.

This contest began in the reign of Henry the Sixth, and was not entirely extinguished till Henry the Seventh, in whom the families were united. Including a period of 67 years, viz. from 1422 to 1489.

In short, monarchy and succession have laid (not this or that kingdom only) but the world in blood and ashes. 'Tis a form of government which the word of God bears testimony against, and blood will attend it.

If we enquire into the business of a King, we shall find that in some countries they may have none; and after sauntering away their lives without pleasure to themselves or advantage to the nation, withdraw from the scene, and leave their successors to tread the same idle round. In absolute monarchies the whole weight of business civil and military lies on the King; the children of Israel in their request for a king urged this plea, "that he may judge us, and go out before us and fight our battles." But in countries where he is neither a Judge nor a General, as in England, a man would be puzzled to know what *is* his business.

The nearer any government approaches to a Republic, the less business there is for a King. It is somewhat difficult to find a proper name for the government of England. Sir William Meredith calls it a Republic; but in its present state it is unworthy of the name, because the corrupt influence of the Crown, by having all the places in its disposal, hath so effectually swallowed up the power, and eaten out the virtue of the House of Commons (the Republican part in the constitution) that the government of England is nearly as monarchical as that of France or Spain. Men fall out with names without understanding them. For 'tis the Republican and not the Monarchical part of the constitution of England which Englishmen glory in, viz. the liberty of choosing an House of Commons from out of their own body—and it is easy to see that when Republican virtues fails, slavery ensues. Why is the constitution of England sickly, but because monarchy hath poisoned the Republic; the Crown hath engrossed the Commons.

In England a King hath little more to do than to make war and give away places; which, in plain terms, is to empoverish the nation and set it together by the ears. A pretty business indeed for a man to be allowed eight hundred thousand sterling a year for, and worshipped into the bargain! Of more worth is one honest man to society, and in the sight of God, than all the crowned ruffians that ever lived.

LETTER TO JOHN TAYLOR OF CAROLINE
John Adams

Sir,—I have received your *Inquiry* in a large volume neatly bound. Though I have not read it in course, yet, upon an application to it of the *Sortes Virgilianæ*, scarce a page has been found in which my name is not mentioned, and some public sentiment or expression of mine examined. Revived as these subjects are, in this manner, in the recollection of the public, after an oblivion of so many years, by a gentleman of your high rank, ample fortune, learned education, and powerful connections, I flatter myself it will not be thought improper in me to solicit your attention to a few explanations and justifications of a book that has been misunderstood, misrepresented, and abused, more than any other, except the Bible, that I have ever read. . . .

There is no necessity of "confronting Mr. Adams's opinion, that aristocracy is natural, and therefore unavoidable, with the other, that it is artificial or factitius, and therefore avoidable," because the opinions are both true and perfectly consistent with each other.

By *natural aristocracy,* in general, may be understood those superiorities of influence in society which grow out of the constitution of human nature. By *artificial aristocracy,* those inequalities of weight and superiorities of influence which are created and established by civil laws. Terms must be defined before we can reason. By aristocracy, I understand all those men who can command, influence, or procure more than an average of votes; by an aristocrat, every man who can and will influence one man to vote besides himself. Few men will deny that there is a natural aristocracy of virtues and talents in every nation and in every party, in every city and village. Inequalities are a part of the natural history of man.

I believe that none but Helvetius will affirm, that all children are born with equal genius.

None will pretend, that all are born of dispositions exactly alike,—of equal weight; equal strength; equal length; equal delicacy of nerves; equal elasticity of muscles; equal complexions; equal figure, grace, or beauty.

I have seen, in the Hospital of Foundlings, the *"Enfans Trouvés,"* at Paris, fifty babes in one room;—all under four days old; all in cradles alike; all nursed and attended alike; all dressed alike; all equally neat. I went from one end to the other of the whole row, and attentively observed all their

From The Works of John Adams, *(Vol. VI).* Copyright Charles C. Little and James Brown, 1851.

countenances. And I never saw a greater variety, or more striking inequalities, in the streets of Paris or London. Some had every sign of grief, sorrow, and despair; others had joy and gayety in their faces. Some were sinking in the arms of death; others looked as if they might live to fourscore. Some were as ugly and others as beautiful, as children or adults ever are; these were stupid; those sensible. These were all born to equal rights, but to very different fortunes; to very different success and influence in life.

The world would not contain the books, if one should produce all the examples that reading and experience would furnish. One or two permit me to hint.

Will any man say, would Helvetius say, that all men are born equal in strength? Was Hercules no stronger than his neighbors? How many nations, for how many ages, have been governed by his strength, and by the reputation and renown of it by his posterity? If you have lately read Hume, Robertson or the Scottish Chiefs, let me ask you, if Sir William Wallace was no more than equal in strength to the average of Scotchmen? and whether Wallace could have done what he did without that extraordinary strength?

Will Helvetius or Rousseau say that all men and women are born equal in beauty? Will any philosopher say, that beauty has no influence in human society? If he does, let him read the histories of Eve, Judith, Helen, the fair Gabrielle, Diana of Poitiers, Pompadour, Du Barry, Susanna, Abigail, Lady Hamilton, Mrs. Clark, and a million others. Are not despots, monarchs, aristocrats, and democrats, equally liable to be seduced by beauty to confer favors and influence suffrages? . . .

That all men are born to equal rights is true. Every being has a right to his own, as clear, as moral, as sacred, as any other being has. This is as indubitable as a moral government in the universe. But to teach that all men are born with equal powers and faculties, to equal influence in society, to equal property and advantages through life, is as gross a fraud, as glaring an imposition on the credulity of the people, as ever was practised by monks, by Druids, by Brahmins, by priests of the immortal Lama, or by the self-styled philosophers of the French revolution. For honor's sake, Mr. Taylor, for truth and virtue's sake, let American philosophers and politicians despise it . . .

That aristocracies, both ancient and modern, have been "variable and artificial," as well as natural and unchangeable, Mr. Adams knows as well as Mr. Taylor, and has never denied or doubted. That "they have all proceeded from moral causes," is not so clear, since many of them appear to proceed from physical causes, many from immoral causes, many from pharisaical, jesuitical, and Machiavelian villany; many from sacerdotal and despotic fraud, and as many as all the rest, from democratical dupery, credulity, adulation, corruption, adoration, superstition, and enthusiasm. If all these cannot be regulated by political laws, and controlled, checked, or balanced by constitutional energies, I am willing Mr. Taylor should say of them what Bishop Burnet said of the hierarchy, or the severest things he can express or imagine. . . .

Take the first hundred men you meet in the streets of a city, or on a turnpike road in the country, and constitute them a democratical republic. In my next, you may have some conjectures of what will appear in your new democracy.

When your new democratical republic meets, you will find half a dozen men of independent fortunes; half a dozen, of more eloquence; half a dozen, with more learning; half a dozen, with eloquence, learning, and fortune.

Let me see. We have now four-and-twenty; to these we may add six more, who will have more art, cunning, and intrigue, than learning, eloquence, or fortune. These will infallibly soon unite with the twenty-four. Thus we make thirty. The remaining seventy are composed of farmers, shopkeepers, merchants, tradesmen, and laborers. Now, if each of these thirty can, by any means, influence one vote besides his own, the whole thirty can carry sixty votes,—a decided and uncontrolled majority of the hundred. These thirty I mean by aristocrats; and they will instantly convert your democracy of ONE HUNDRED into an aristocracy of THIRTY.

Take at random, or select with your utmost prudence, one hundred of your most faithful and capable domestics from your own numerous plantations, and make them a democratical republic. You will immediately perceive the same inequalities, and the same democratical republic, in a very few of the first sessions, transformed into an aristocratical republic; as complete and perfect an aristocracy as the senate of Rome, and much more so. Some will be beloved and followed, others hated and avoided by their fellows.

It would be easy to quote Greek and Latin, to produce a hundred authorities to show the original signification of the word *aristocracy* and its infinite variations and application in the history of ages. But this would be all waste water. Once for all, I give you notice, that whenever I use the word *aristocrat,* I mean a citizen who can command or govern two votes or more in society, whether by his virtues, his talents, his learning, his loquacity, his taciturnity, his frankness, his reserve, his face, figure, eloquence, grace, air, attitude, movements, wealth, birth, art, address, intrigue, good fellowship, drunkenness, debauchery, fraud, perjury, violence, treachery, pyrrhonism, deism, or atheism; for by every one of these instruments have votes been obtained and will be obtained. You seem to think aristocracy consists altogether in artificial titles, tinsel decorations of stars, garters, ribbons, golden eagles and golden fleeces, crosses and roses and lilies, exclusive privileges, hereditary descents, established by kings or by positive laws of society. No such thing! Aristocracy was, from the beginning, now is, and ever will be, world without end, independent of all these artificial regulations, as really and as efficaciously as with them!

Let me say a word more. Your democratical republic picked in the streets, and your democratical African republic, or your domestic republic, call it which you will, in its first session, will become an aristocratical republic. In the second session it will become an oligarchical republic; because the seventy-four democrats and the twenty-six aristocrats will, by this time, discover that thirteen of the aristocrats can command four votes each; these thirteen will now command the majority, and, consequently, will be sovereign. The thirteen will then be an oligarchy. In the third session, it will be found that among these thirteen oligarchs there are seven, each of whom can command eight votes, equal in all to fifty-six, a decided majority. In the fourth session, it will be found that there are among these seven oligarchs four who can command thirteen votes apiece. The republic then becomes an oligarchy, whose sovereignty is in four individuals. In the fifth session, it will be discovered that two of the four can command six-and-twenty votes each. Then two will have the command of the sovereign oligarchy. In the sixth session, there will be a sharp contention between the two which shall have the command of the fifty-two votes. Here will commence the squabble of Danton and Robespierre, of Julius and Pompey, of Anthony and Augustus, of the white rose and the red rose, of Jefferson and Adams, of Burr and Jefferson, of Clinton and Madison, or, if you will, of Napoleon and Alexander.

This, my dear sir, is the history of mankind, past, present, and to come.

In the third page of your "Inquiry," is an assertion which Mr. Adams has a right to regret, as a gross and egregious misrepresentation. He cannot believe it to have been intentional. He imputes it to haste; to ardor of temper; to defect of memory; to any thing rather than design. It is in these words,— "Mr. Adams asserts, 'that every society naturally produces an order of men, which it is impossible to confine to an equality of RIGHTS.'" This pretended quotation, marked as it is by inverted commas, is totally and absolutely unfounded. No such expression ever fell from his lips; no such language was ever written by his pen; no such principle was ever approved or credited by his understanding, no such sentiment was ever felt without abhorrence in his heart. On the contrary, he has through life asserted the moral equality of all mankind. His system of government, which is the system of Massachusetts, as well as the system of the United States, which are the same as much as an original and a copy are the same, was calculated and framed for the express purpose of securing to all men equal laws and equal rights. Physical inequalities are proclaimed aloud by God Almighty through all his works. Mr. Adams must have been destitute of senses, not to have perceived them in men from their births to their deaths; and, at the same time, not to have perceived that they were incurable and inevitable, by human wisdom, goodness, or power. All that men can do, is to modify, organize, and arrange the powers of human society, that is to say, the physical strength and force of men, in the best manner to protect, secure, and cherish the moral, which are all the natural rights of mankind. . . .

Suppose another case, which is not without examples,—a family of six daughters. Four of them are not only beautiful, but serious and discreet women. Two of them are not only ugly, but ill tempered and immodest. Will either of the two have an equal chance with any one of the four to attract the attention of a suitor, and obtain a husband of worth, respectability, and consideration in the world?

Such, and many other natural and acquired and habitual inequalities are visible, and palpable, and audible, every day, in every village, and in every family, in the whole world. The imagination, therefore, of a government, of a democratical republic, in which every man and every woman shall have an equal weight in society, is a chimera. They have all equal rights; but cannot, and ought not to have equal power.

Unhappily, the cases before stated are too often reversed, and four or five out of six sons, are unwise, and only one or two praiseworthy; and four or five out of six daughters, are mere triflers, and only one or two whose "price is above rubies." And may I not ask, whether there are no instances, in which the whole of six sons and daughters are found wanting; and instead of maintaining their single vote, and their independence, become all dependent on others? Nay, there are examples of whole families wasted and totally lost by vice and folly. Can these, while any of them existed, have maintained an equality of consideration in Society, with other families of equal numbers, but of virtuous and considerate characters?

Matrimony, then, Mr. Taylor, I have a right to consider as another source of natural aristocracy. . . .

I will be bolder still, Mr. Taylor. Would Washington have ever been commander of the revolutionary army or president of the United States, if he had not married the rich widow of Mr. Custis? Would Jefferson ever have been president of the United States if he had not married the daughter of Mr. Wales? . . .

In this fourth page you say, that "Mr. Adams's system tells us that the art of government can never change." I have said no such thing, Mr. Taylor! I know the art of government has changed, and probably will change, as often as the arts of architecture, painting, sculpture, music, poetry, agriculture, horticulture, medicine; and that is to say, almost as often as the weather or the fashion in dress.

But all these arts are founded in certain general principles of nature, which have never been known to change; and it is the duty of philosophers, legislators, and artists to study these principles; and the nearer they approach to them, the greater perfection will they attain in their arts. There may be principles in nature, not yet observed, that will improve all these arts; and nothing hinders any man from making experiments and pursuing researches, to investigate such principles and make such improvements. But America has made no discoveries of principles of government that have not been long known. Morality and liberty, and "moral liberty," too, whatever it may mean, have been known from the creation. Cain knew it when he killed Abel, and knew that he violated it.

You say, sir, that I have gravely counted up several victims "of popular rage, as proofs that democracy is more pernicious than monarchy or aristocracy." This is not my doctrine, Mr. Taylor. My opinion is, and always has been, that absolute power intoxicates alike despots, monarchs, aristocrats, and democrats, and jacobins, and *sans culottes*. I cannot say that democracy has been more pernicious, on the whole, than any of the others. Its atrocities have been more transient; those of the others have been more permanent. The history of all ages shows that the caprice, cruelties, and horrors of democracy have soon disgusted, alarmed, and terrified themselves. They soon cry, "this will not do; we have gone too far! We are all in the wrong! We are none of us safe! We must unite in some clever fellow, who can protect us all,—Caesar, Bonaparte, who you will! Though we distrust, hate, and abhor them all; yet we must submit to one or another of them, stand by him, cry him up to the skies, and swear that he is the greatest, best, and finest man that every lived!"

It has been my fortune, good or bad, to live in Europe ten years, from 1778 to 1788, in a public character. This destiny, singular in America, forced upon my attention the course of events in France, Holland, Geneva, and Switzerland, among many other nations; and this has irresistibly attracted my thoughts more than has been for my interest. The subject cannot have escaped you. What has been the conduct of the democratic parties in all those nations? How horribly bloody in some! Has it been steady, consistent, uniform, in any? Has it not leaped from democracy to aristocracy, to oligarchy, to military despotism, and back again to monarchy, as often, and as easily, as the birds fly to the lower, the middle, or the upper limbs of a tree, or leap from branch to branch, or hop from spray to spray?

Democracy, nevertheless, must not be disgraced; democracy must not be despised. Democracy must be respected; democracy must be honored; democracy must be cherished; democracy must be an essential, an integral part of the sovereignty, and have a control over the whole government, or moral liberty cannot exist, or any other liberty. I have been always grieved by the gross abuses of this respectable word. One party speak of it as the most amiable, venerable, indeed, as the sole object of its adoration; the other, as the sole object of its scorn, abhorrence, and execration. Neither party, in my opinion, know what they say. Some of them care not what they say, provided they can accomplish their own selfish purposes. These ought not to be forgiven.

You triumphantly demand: "What motives of preference between forms of government remain?" Is there no difference between a government of laws and a government of men? Between a government according to fixed laws, concerted by three branches of the legislature, composed of the most experienced men of a nation, established, recorded, promulgated to every individual, as the rule of his conduct, and a government according to the will of one man, or to a vote of a few men, or to a vote of a single assembly, whether of a nation or its representatives?

It is not Mr. Adams's system which can "arrest our efforts or appall our hopes in pursuit of political good." Other causes have obstructed and still embarrass the progress of the science of legislation.

MORAL MAN AND IMMORAL SOCIETY
Reinhold Niebuhr

Human beings are endowed by nature with both selfish and unselfish impulses. The individual is a nucleus of energy which is organically related from the very beginning with other energy, but which maintains, nevertheless, its own discreet existence. Every type of energy in nature seeks to preserve and pereptuate itself and to gain fulfillment within terms of its unique genius. The energy of human life does not differ in this from the whole world of nature. It differs only in the degree of reason which directs the energy. Man is the only creature which is fully self-conscious. His reason endows him with a capacity for self-transcendence. He sees himself in relation to his environment and in relation to other life. Reason enables him, within limits, to direct his energy so that it will flow in harmony, and not in conflict, with other life. Reason is not the sole basis of moral virtue in man. His social impulses are more deeply rooted than his rational life. Reason may extend and stabilise, but it does not create, the capacity to affirm other life than his own. Nature endows him with a sex impulse which seeks the perpetuity of his kind with the same degree of energy with which he seeks the preservation of his own life. So basic is this impulse that Freudian psychology is able to interpret the *libido* entirely in its terms. Even if we should adopt the more plausible theory of Adler, that the *libido* expresses itself chiefly in terms of the will-to-power, or that of Jung, which makes the *libido* an undifferentiated energy from which sexuality, the will-to-power and their various derivatives arise, it is obvious that man does not express himself in terms of pure self-assertion, even before conscious purpose begins to qualify egoistic impulse. His natural impulses prompt him not only to the perpetuation of life beyond himself but to some achievement of harmony with other life. Whatever the theory of instincts which we may adopt, whether we regard them as discreet and underived, or whether we think they are sharply defined only after they are socially conditioned, it is obvious that man not only shares a gregarious impulse with the lower creatures but that a specific impulse of pity bids him fly to aid of stricken members of his community. Rationalistic moralists, as for instance Stoics and Kantians, who derive man's moral capacities purely from his reason and consequently set the mind at war with the impulses, are therefore always driven to the absurdity of depreciating the moral quality of social impulses, which are undeniably

Reprinted by permission of Charles Scribner's Sons from Moral Man and Immoral Society, *pages 25–34 and 47–50, by Reinhold Niebuhr. Copyright 1932 Charles Scirbner's Sons; renewal copyright © 1960 Reinhold Niebuhr.*

good but obviously rooted in instinct and nature. Thus the Stoics abhorred pity and Kant scorned sympathy if it did not flow from a sense of duty.

Reason, inasfar as it is able to survey the whole field of life, analyses the various forces in their relation to each other and, gauging their consequences in terms of the total welfare, it inevitably places the stamp of its approval upon those impulses which affirm life in its most inclusive terms. Practically every moral theory, whether utilitarian or intuitional, insists on the goodness of benevolence, justice, kindness and unselfishness. Even when economic self-seeking is approved, as in the political morality of Adam Smith, the criterion of judgment is the good of the whole. The utilitarians may insist that the goodness of altruism is established by its social utility, and they may distinguish themselves from more rigorous moralists by assigning social utility and moral worth to egoism as well. But, in spite of these differences, the function of reason for every moralist is to support those impulses which carry life beyond itself, and to extend the measure and degree of their sociality. It is fair, therefore, to assume that growing rationality is a guarantee of man's growing morality.

The measure of our rationality determines the degree of vividness with which we appreciate the needs of other life, the extent to which we become conscious of the real character of our own motives and impulses, the ability to harmonise conflicting impulses in our own life and in society, and the capacity to choose adequate means for approved ends. In each instance a development of reason may increase the moral capacity.

The intelligent man, who exploits available resources for knowledge of the needs and wants of his fellows, will be more inclined to adjust his conduct to their needs than those who are less intelligent. He will feel sympathy for misery, not only when it comes immediately into his field of vision, but when it is geographically remote. A famine in China, a disaster in Europe, a cry for help from the ends of the earth, will excite his sympathy and prompt remedial action. No man will ever be so intelligent as to see the needs of others as vividly as he recognises his own, or to be as quick in his aid to remote as to immediately revealed necessities. Nevertheless it is impossible for an astute social pedagogy to increase the range of human sympathy. Social agencies in large urban communities, where individual need is easily obscured in the mass, have evolved stereotyped methods of individualising need by the choice of significant and vivid single examples of general social conditions. Thus they keep social sympathy, which might perish amid the indirect relationships of a large city, alive. The failure of even the wisest type of social pedagogy to prompt benevolences as generous as those which a more intimate community naturally evolves, suggests that ethical attitudes are more dependent upon personal, intimate and organic contacts than social technicians are inclined to assume. The dependence of ethical attitudes upon personal contacts and direct relations contributes to the moral chaos of a civilisation, in which life is related to life mechanically and not organically, and in which mutual responsibilities increase and personal contacts decrease.

The ability to consider, or even to prefer, the interests of others to our own, is not dependent upon the capacity for sympathy. Harmonious social relations depend upon the sense of justice as much as, or even more than, upon the sentiment of benevolence. This sense of justice is a product of the mind and not of the heart. It is the result of reason's insistence upon consistency. One of Immanuel Kant's two moral axioms: "Act in conformity with that maxim and that maxim only which you can at the same time will to be universal law" is simply the application to problems of conduct of reason's desire for consistency. As truth is judged by its harmonious relation to a previously discovered system of truths, so the morality of an action is judged by the possibility of conforming it to a universal scheme of consistent moral actions. This means, in terms of conduct, that the satisfaction of an impulse can be called good only if it can be related in terms of inner consistency with a total harmony of impulses. Unreason may approve the satisfaction of an impulse in the self and disapprove the same impulse in another. But the reasonable man is bound to judge his actions, in some degree, in terms of the total necessities of a social situation. Thus reason tends to check selfish impulses and to grant the satisfaction of legitimate impulses in others.

It is a question whether reason is ever sufficiently powerful to achieve, or even to approximate, a complete harmony and consistency between what is demanded for the self and what is granted to the other; but it works to that end. Its first task is to harmonise the various impulses of the self and to bring order out of the chaos of impulses with which nature has endowed man. For nature has not established the same degree of order in the human as in the lower creature. In the animal, impulses are related to each other in a pre-established harmony. But instincts are not as fully formed in human life, and natural impulses may therefore be so enlarged and extended that the satisfaction of one impulse interferes with the satisfaction of another. "All mind," declares Santayana, "is naturally synthetic. . . . In the mindful person the passions have spontaneously acquired a responsibility toward each other; or if they still allow themselves to make merry separately—for liveliness in the parts is a good without which the whole would be lifeless—yet the whole possesses, or aspires to possess, a unity of direction in which all parts may conspire, even if unwittingly." It is naturally easier to bring order into the individual life than to establish a synthesis between it and other life. The force of reason is frequently exhausted in the first task and never essays the second. Yet the rational man is bound to recognise the claims made by others and to see the necessity of arriving at some working harmony for the total body of human impulse. Reason ultimately makes for social as well as for internal order.

The force of reason makes for justice, not only by placing inner restraints upon the desires of the self in the interest of social harmony, but by judging the claims and assertions of individuals from the perspective of the intelligence of the total community. An irrational society accepts injustice because it does not analyse the pretensions made by the powerful and privileged groups of society. Even that portion of society which suffers most from injustice may hold the power, responsible for it, in reverence. A growing rationality in society destroys the uncritical acceptance of injustice. It may destroy the morale of dominant groups by making them more conscious of the hollowness of their pretensions, so that they will be unable to assert their interests and protect their special privileges with the same degree of self-deception. It may furthermore destroy their social prestige in the community by revealing the relation between their special privileges and the misery of the underprivileged. It may also make those who suffer from injustice more conscious of their rights in society and persuade them to assert their rights more energetically. The resulting social conflict makes for a political rather than a rational justice. But all justice in the less intimate human relations is political as well as rational, that is, it is established by the assertion of power against power as well as by the rational comprehension of, and arbitration between, conflicting rights. The justice which results from such a process may not belong in the category of morally created social values, if morality be defined purely from the perspective of the individual. From the viewpoint of society itself it does represent a moral achievement. It means that the total society, and each constituent group, judges social relations not according to custom and tradition, but according to a rational ideal of justice. The partial perspective of each group makes the achievement of social harmony without conflict impossible. But a rational ideal of justice, operates both in initiating, and in resolving, conflict.

The development of reason and the growth of mind makes for increasingly just relations not only by bringing all impulses in society into reference with, and under the control of, an inclusive social ideal, but also by increasing the penetration with which all factors in the social situation are analysed. The psychological sciences discover and analyse the intricate web of motivation, which lies at the base of all human actions. The social sciences trace the consequences of human behavior into the farthest reaches of social life. They are specialised and yet typical efforts of a growing human intelligence, to come into possession of all facts relevant to human conduct. If the psychological scientist aids men in analysing their true motives, and in separating their inevitable pretensions from the actual desires, which they are intended to hide, he may increase the purity of social morality. If the social scientist is able to point out that traditional and customary social policies do not have the results, intended or pretended by those who champion them, honest social intentions will find more adequate instruments for the attainment of their ends, and dishonest pretensions will be unmasked.

Thus, for instance, a *laissez faire* economic theory is maintained in an industrial era through the ignorant belief that the general welfare is best served by placing the least possible political restraints upon economic activity. The history of the past hundred years is a refutation of the theory; but it is still maintained, or is dying a too lingering death, particularly in nations as politically incompetent as our own. Its survival is due to the ignorance of those who suffer injustice from the application of this theory to modern industrial life but fail to attribute their difficulties to the social anarchy and political irresponsibility which the theory sanctions. Their ignorance permits the beneficiaries of the present anarchic industrial system to make dishonest use of the waning prestige of *laissez faire* economics. The men of power in modern industry would not, of course, capitulate simply because the social philosophy by which they justify their policies had been discredited. When power is robbed of the shining armor of political, moral and philosophical theories, by which it defends itself, it will fight on without armor; but it will be more vulnerable, and the strength of its enemies is increased.

When economic power desires to be left alone its uses the philosophy of *laissez faire* to discourage political restraint upon economic freedom. When it wants to make use of the police power of the state to subdue rebellions and discontent in the ranks of its helots, it justifies the use of political coercion and the resulting suppression of liberties by insisting that peace is more precious than freedom and that its only desire is social peace. A rational analysis of social facts easily punctures this pretension also. It proves that the police power of the state is usually used prematurely; before an effort has been made to eliminate the causes of discontent, and that it therefore tends to perpetuate injustice and the consequent social disaffections. Social intelligence may, in short, eliminate many abortive means to socially approved ends, whether they have been proposed honestly or dishonestly, and may therefore contribute to a higher measure of social morality. If psychological and social scientists overestimate the possibilities of improving social relations by the development of intelligence, that may be regarded as an understandable *naïveté* of rationalists, who naturally incline to attribute too much power to reason and to recognise its limits too grudgingly. Men will not cease to be dishonest, merely because their dishonesties have been revealed or because they have discovered their own deceptions. Wherever men hold unequal power in society, they will strive to maintain it. They will use whatever means are most convenient to that end and will seek to justify them by the most plausible arguments they are able to devise. . . . The larger social groups above the family, communities, classes, races and nations all present men with the same twofold opportunity for self-denial and self-aggrandisement; and both possibilities are usually exploited. Patriotism is a high form of altruism, when compared with lesser and more parochial loyalties; but from an absolute perspective it is simply another form of selfishness. The larger the group the more certainly will it express itself selfishly in the total human community. It will be more powerful and therefore more able to defy any social restraints which might be devised. It will also be less subject to internal moral restraints. The larger the group the more difficult it is to achieve a common mind and purpose and the more inevitably will it be unified by momentary impulses and immediate and unreflective purposes. The increasing size of the group increases the difficulties of achieving a group self-consciousness, except as it comes in conflict with other groups and is unified by perils and passions of war. It is a rather pathetic aspect of human social life that conflict is a seemingly unavoidable prerequisite of group solidarity. Furthermore the greater the strength and the wider the dominion of a community, the more will it seem to represent universal values from the perspective of the individual. There is something to be said for Treitschke's logic, which made the nation the ultimate community of significant loyalty, on the ground that smaller units were too small to deserve, and larger units too vague and ephemeral to be able to exact, man's supreme loyalty. Treitschke was wrong only in glorying in this moral difficulty.

Try as he will, man seems incapable of forming an international community, with power and prestige great enough to bring social restraint upon collective egoism. He has not even succeeded in disciplining anti-social group egoism within the nation. The very extension of human sympathies has therefore resulted in the creation of larger units of conflict without abolishing conflict. So civilization has become a device for delegating the vices of individuals to larger and larger communities. The device gives men the illusion that they are moral; but the illusion is not lasting. A technological civilisation has created an international community, so interdependent as to require, even if not powerful or astute enough to achieve, ultimate social harmony. While there are halting efforts to create an international mind and conscience, capable of coping with this social situation, modern man has progressed only a little beyond his fathers in extending his ethical attitudes beyond the group to which he is organic and which possesses symbols, vivid enough to excite his social sympathies. His group is larger than that of his fathers, but whatever moral gain may be ascribed to that development is partially lost by the greater heterogeneity and the diminished mutuality of this larger group. The modern nation is divided into classes and the classes exhibit a greater disproportion of power and privilege than in the primitive community. This social inequality leads not only to internal strife but to conflict between various national communities, by prompting the more privileged and powerful classes to seek advantages at the expense of other nations so that they may consolidate the privileges which they have won at the expense of their own nationals. Thus modern life is involved in both class and international conflict; and it may be that class privileges cannot be abolished or diminished until they have reduced the whole of modern society to international and intra-national chaos. The growing intelligence of mankind seems not to be growing rapidly enough to achieve mastery over the social problems, which the advances of technology create.

DEMOCRACY AND HUMAN NATURE
John Dewey

... The popular view of the constitution of human nature at any given time is a reflex of social movements which have either become institutionalized or else are showing themselves against opposing social odds and hence need intellectual and moral formulation to increase their power. I may seem to be going far afield if I refer to Plato's statement of the way by which to determine the constituents of human nature. The proper method, he said, was to look at the version of human nature written in large and legible letters in the organization of classes in society, before trying to make it out in the dim petty edition found in individuals. And so on the basis of the social organization with which he was acquainted he found that since in society there was a laboring class toiling to find the means of satisfying the appetitites, a citizen soldiery class loyal even to death to the laws of the state, and a legislative class, so the human soul must be composed of appetitite at the base—in both significations of "base"—of generous spirited impulses which looked beyond personal enjoyment, while appetite was engaged only in taking in and absorbing for its own satisfaction, and finally reason, the legislative power.

Having found these three things in the composition of human nature, he had no difficulty in going back to social organization and proving that there was one class which had to be kept in order by rules and laws imposed from above, since otherwise its action was without limits, and would in the name of liberty destroy harmony and order; another class, whose inclinations were all towards obedience and loyalty to law, towards right beliefs, although itself incapable of discovering the ends from which laws are derived; and at the apex, in any well-ordered organization, the rule of those whose predominant natural qualities were reason, after that faculty had been suitably formed by education.

It would be hard to find a better illustration of the fact that any movement purporting to discover the psychological causes and sources of social phenomena is in fact a reverse movement, in which current social tendencies are read back into the structure of human nature; and are then used to explain the very things from which they are deduced. It was then "natural" for the men who reflected the new movement of industry and commerce to erect the appetites, treated by Plato as a kind of necessary evil, into the cornerstone of

---

Reprinted by permission of G. P. Putnam's Sons from Freedom and Culture *by John Dewey. Copyright 1939 by John Dewey, renewed 1967 by Mrs. John Dewey.*

social well-being and progress. Something of the same kind exists at present when love of power is put forward to play the role taken a century ago by self-interest as the dominant "motive"—and if I put the word motive in quotations marks, it is for the reason just given. What are called motives turn out upon critical examination to be complex attitudes patterned under cultural conditions, rather than simple elements in human nature.

Even when we refer to tendencies and impulses that actually are genuine elements in human nature we find, unless we swallow whole some current opinion, that of themselves they explain nothing about social phenomena. For they produce consequences only as they are shaped into acquired dispositions by interaction with environing cultural conditions. Hobbes, who was the first of the moderns to identify the "state of nature" and its laws—the classic background of all political theories—with the raw uneducated state of human nature, may be called witness. According to Hobbes, "In the nature of man we find three principal causes of quarrel. First competition, secondly diffidence, thirdly glory. The first maketh men invade for gain; the second for safety; and the third for reputation. The first use violence to make themselves the masters of other persons; the second to defend them; the third for trifles as a word, a smile, a different opinion or any other sign of undervalue, either direct in their persons or by reflection in their kindred, their friends, their nation."

That the qualities mentioned by Hobbes actually exist in human nature and that they may generate "quarrel," that is, conflict and war between states and civil war within a nation—the chronic state of affairs when Hobbes lived — is not denied. Insofar, Hobbes' account of the natural psychology which prevents the state of security which is a pre-requisite for civilized communities shows more insight than many attempts made today to list the traits of raw human nature that are supposed to cause social phenomena. Hobbes thought that the entire natural state of men in their relations to one another was a war of all against all, man being naturally to man "as a wolf." The intent of Hobbes was thus a glorification of deliberately instituted relations, authoritative laws and regulations which should rule not just overt actions, but the impulses and ideas which cause men to hold up certain things as ends or goods. Hobbes himself thought of this authority as a political sovereign. But it would be in the spirit of his treatment to regard it as glorification of culture over against raw human nature, and more than one writer has pointed out the likeness between his Leviathan and the Nazi totalitarian state.

There are more than one instructive parallelisms that may be drawn between the period in which Hobbes lived and the present time, especially as to insecurity and conflict between nations and classes. The point here pertinent, however, is that the qualities Hobbes selected as the causes of disorders making the life of mankind "brutish and nasty," are the very "motives" that have been selected by others as the cause of *beneficient* social effects; namely, harmony, prosperity, and indefinite progress. The position taken by Hobbes about competition as love of gain was completely reversed in the British social philosophy of the nineteenth century. Instead of being a source of war, it was taken to be the means by which individuals found the occupation for which they were best fitted; by which needed goods reached the consumer at least cost, and by which a state of ultimate harmonious interdependence would be produced—provided only competition were allowed to operate without "artificial" restriction. Even today one reads articles and hears speeches in which the cause of our present economic troubles is laid to political interference with the beneficent workings of private competitive effort for gain.

The object of alluding to these two very different conceptions of this component in human nature is not to decide or discuss which is right. The point is that both are guilty of the same fallacy. In itself, the impulse (or whatever name be given it) is neither socially maleficent nor beneficent. Its significance depends upon consequences actually produced; and these depend upon the conditions under which it operates and with which it interacts. The conditions are set by tradition, by custom, by law, by the kind of public approvals and disapprovals; by all conditions constituting the environment. These conditions are so pluralized even in one and the same country at the same period that love of gain (regarded as a trait of human nature) may be both socially useful and socially harmful. And, in spite of the tendency to set up cooperative impulses as thoroughly beneficial, the same thing is true of them—regarded simply as components of human nature. Neither competition nor cooperation can be judged as traits of human nature. They are names for certain relations among the actions of individuals as the relations actually obtain in a community.

This would be true even if there were tendencies in human nature so definitely marked off from one another as to merit the names given them and even if human nature were as fixed as it is sometimes said to be. For even in that case, human nature operates in a multitude of different environing conditions, and it is interaction with the latter that determines the consequences and the social significance and value, positive or negative, of the tendencies. The alleged fixity of the structure of human nature does not explain in the least the differences that mark off one tribe, family, people, from another—which is to say that in and of itself it explains no state of society whatever. It issues no advice as to what policies it is advantageous to follow. It does not even justify conservatism as against radicalism.

But the alleged unchangeableness of human nature cannot be admitted. For while certain needs in human nature are constant, the consequences they produce (because of the existing state of culture—of science, morals, religion, art, industry, legal rules) react back into the original components of human nature to shape them into new forms. The total pattern is thereby modified. The futility of exclusive appeal to psychological factors both to explain what takes place and to form policies as to what *should* take place, would be evident to everybody—had it not proved to be a convenient device for "rationalizing" policies thar are urged on other grounds by some group or faction. While the case of "competition" urging men both to war and to beneficent social progress is most obviously instructive in this respect, examination of the other elements of Hobbes supports the same conclusion.

There have been communities, for example, in which regard for the honor of one's self, one's family, one's class, has been the chief conservator of all worth while social values. It has always been the chief virtue of an aristocratic class, civil or military. While its value has often been exaggerated, it is folly to deny that in interaction with certain cultural conditions, it has had valuable consequences. "Diffidence" or fear as a motive is an even more ambiguous and meaningless term as far as its consequences are concerned. It takes any form, from craven cowardice to prudence, caution, and the circumspection without which no intelligent foresight is possible. It may become reverence—which has been exaggerated in the abstract at times but which may be attached to the kind of objects which render it supremely desirable. "Love of power," to which it is now fashionable to appeal, has a meaning only when it applies to everything in general and hence explains nothing in particular.

Discussion up to this point has been intended to elicit two principles. One of them is that the views about human nature that are popular at a given time are usually derived from contemporary social currents; currents so conspicuous as to stand out or else less marked and less effective social movements which a special group believes *should* become dominant:—as for example, in the case of the legislative reason with Plato, and of competitive love of gain with classical economists. The other principle is that reference to components of original human nature, even if they actually exist, explains no social occurrence whatever and gives no advice or direction as to what policies it is better to adopt. This does not mean that reference to them must necessarily be of a "rationalizing" concealed apologetic type. It means that whenever it occurs with practical significance it has *moral* not psychological import. For, whether brought forward from the side of conserving what already exists or from that of producing change, it is an expression of valuation, and of purpose determined by estimate of values. When a trait of human nature is put forward on this basis, it is in its proper context and is subject to intelligent examination. . . .

While this brief exposition of the reaction against the individualistic theory of human nature suggests the ground pattern of National Socialism, it also throws some light upon the predicament in which democratic countries find themselves. The fact that the individualistic theory was used a century and more ago to justify political self-government and then aided promotion of its cause does not constitute the theory a present trustworthy guide of democratic action. It is profitable to read today the bitterly vivid denunciations of Carlyle on the theory as it was originally put forth. He denounced with equal fierceness the attempt to erect political authority upon the basis of self-interest and private morals upon the exercise of sympathy. The latter was sentimentalism run riot and the former was "Anarchy plus the Constable"—the latter being needed to preserve even a semblance of outward order. His plea for discipline and order included even a plea for leadership by select persons.

The present predicament may be stated as follows: Democracy does involve a belief that political institutions and law be such as to take fundamental account of human nature. They must give it freer play than any non-democratic institutions. At the same time, the theory, legalistic and moralistic, about human nature that has been used to expound and justify this reliance upon human nature has proved inadequate. Upon the legal and political side, during the nineteenth century it was progressively overloaded with ideas and practices which have more to do with business carried on for profit than with democracy. On the moralistic side, it has tended to substitute emotional exhortation to act in accord with the Golden Rule for the discipline and the control afforded by incorporation of democratic ideals into *all* the relations of life. Because of lack of an adequate theory of human nature in its relations to democracy, attachment to democratic ends and methods has tended to become a matter of tradition and habit—an excellent thing as far as it goes, but when it becomes routine is easily undermined when change of conditions changes other habits.

Were I to say that democracy needs a new psychology of human nature, one adequate to the heavy demands put upon it by foreign and domestic conditions, I might be taken to utter an academic irrelevancy. But if the remark is understood to mean that democracy has always been allied with humanism, with faith in the potentialities of human nature, and that the present need is vigorous reassertion of this faith, developed in relevant ideas and manifested in practical attitudes, it but continues the American tradition. For belief in the "common man" has no significance save as an expression of belief in the intimate and vital connection of democracy and human nature.

We cannot continue the idea that human nature when left to itself, when freed from external arbitrary restrictions, will tend to the production of democratic institutions that work successfully. We have now to state the issue from the other side. We have to see that democracy means the belief that humanistic culture *should* prevail; we should be frank and open in our recognition that the proposition is a moral one—like any idea that concerns what *should* be. . . .

The greatest practical inconsistency that would be revealed by searching our own habitual attitudes is probably one between the democratic method of forming opinions in political matters and the methods in common use in forming beliefs in other subjects. In theory, the democratic method is persuasion through public discussion carried on not only in legislative halls but in the press, private conversations and public assemblies. The substitution of ballots for bullets, of the right to vote for the lash, is an expression of the will to substitute the method of discussion for the method of coercion. With all its defects and partialities in determination of political decisions, it has worked to keep factional disputes within bounds, to an extent that was incredible a century or more ago. While Carlyle could bring his gift of satire into play in ridiculing the notion that men by talking to and at each other in an assembly hall can settle what is true in social affairs any more than they can settle what is true in the multiplication table, he failed to see that if men had been using clubs to maim and kill one another to decide the product of 7 times 7, there would have been sound reasons for appealing to discussion and persuasion even in the latter case. The fundamental reply is that social "truths" are so unlike mathematical truths that unanimity of uniform belief is possible in respect to the former only when a dictator has the power to tell others what they must believe—or profess they believe. The adjustment of interests demands that diverse interests have a chance to articulate themselves.

The real trouble is that there is an intrinsic split in our habitual attitudes when we profess to depend upon discussion and persuasion in politics and then systematically depend upon other methods in reaching conclusions in matters of morals and religion, or in anything where we depend upon a person or group possessed of "authority." We do not have to go to theological matters to find examples. In homes and in schools, the places where the essentials of character are supposed to be formed, the usual procedure is settlement of issues, intellectual and moral, by appeal to the "authority" of parent, teacher, or textbook. Dispositions formed under such conditions are so inconsistent with the democratic method that in a crisis they may be aroused to act in positively anti-democratic ways for anti-democratic ends; just as resort to coercive force and suppression of civil liberties are readily palliated in nominally democratic communities when the cry is raised that "law and order" are threatened.

It is no easy matter to find adequate authority for action in the demand, characteristic of democracy, that conditions be such as will enable the potentialities of human nature to reach fruition. Because it is not easy the democratic road is the hard one to take. It is the road which places the greatest burden of responsibility upon the greatest number of human beings. Backsets and deviations occur and will continue to occur. But that which is its weakness at particular times is its strength in the long course of human history. Just because the cause of democratic freedom is the cause of the fullest possible realization of human potentialities, the latter when they are suppressed and oppressed will in time rebel and demand an opportunity for manifestation. With the founders of American democracy, the claims of democracy were inherently one with the demands of a just and equal morality. We cannot now well use their vocabulary. Changes in knowledge have outlawed the significations of the words they commonly used. But in spite of the unsuitability of much of their language for present use, what they asserted was that self-governing institutions are the means by which human nature can secure its fullest realization in the greatest number of persons. The question of what is involved in self-governing methods is now much more complex. But for this very reason, the task of those who retain belief in democracy is to revive and maintain in full vigor the original conviction of the intrinsic moral nature of democracy, now stated in ways congruous with present conditions of culture. We have advanced far enough to say that democracy is a way of life. We have yet to realize that it is a way of personal life and one which provides a moral standard for personal conduct.

BIBLIOGRAPHICAL NOTE

Whether the result of revulsion or fascination or a little of both, the Puritan mind has held the interest of scholars for centuries. The Puritans themselves deserve no small credit for their attention. They were prolific writers in nearly all fields of thought—science, literature, and history, as well as theology and politics. Perry Miller's and Thomas H. Johnson's two-volume anthology, *The Puritans*, illustrates the breadth of Puritan scholarship. Edmond Morgan's *Puritan Political Ideas* contains a number of previously inaccessible statements of Puritan political theory. Perry Miller's three-volume study of the American Puritans, *The New England Mind*, is unmatched for its detail and insight. Ralph Barton Perry has combined historical and analytical approaches in a sympathetic portrayal of the Puritan heritage in *Puritanism and Democracy*. Max Weber's *Protestantism and the Rise of Capitalism* is particularly revealing in light of American political development. Michael Walzer has presented a novel interpretation of the English Puritans in *The Revolution of the Saints*.

Although John Cotton wrote over thirty works, extant copies are very rare. There are two major works on Cotton. Larzer Ziff, *The Career of John Cotton*, and Everett H. Emerson, *John Cotton*, do reproduce sizable excerpts from his writings. Since the reputation that Cotton does enjoy results from his conflict with Roger Williams, the student may wish to tackle the latter's *The Bloody Tenet of Persecution*.

Thomas Paine's *The Rights of Man*, a response to Burke's *Reflections on the Revolution in France*, offers an extended treatment of man and society. (See Part II of this book.) Paine's *The American Crisis*, a set of pamphlets written during the American revolution are classic examples of nationalist propaganda. Paine's most ambitious work, *The Age of Reason*, led to his exhumation by his irate American countrymen.

John Adams' writings were faithfully preserved by his nephew, Charles Francis, in a ten-volume set. For one with a more casual interest is Lester Cappon's two-volume collection of the Adams-Jefferson letters. While political enemies throughout most of their lives, Adams and Jefferson mellowed in later years. If the student has the patience to ignore the complaints of two old men, these letters are well worth the effort. The correspondence contains reminiscences of past political conflict and speculations about the future of America. While Adams complained that no monuments would be built for him, he has been resurrected by some contemporary conservatives. See Clinton Rossiter, *Conservatism in America*, and Russell Kirk, *The Conservative Mind*.

Reinhold Niebuhr's books include *Christianity and Power Politics; The Nature and Destiny of Man; The Children of Light and the Children of Darkness* and *The Irony of American History*. Niebuhr's "realistic," anticommunist liberalism was accepted and secularized by many writers in the 1950s. See especially Arthur M. Schlesinger, Jr., *The Vital Center*. For critiques see Morton White's revised edition of *Social Thought in America* and Charles Frankel's *The Case for Modern Man*.

For John Dewey's major contributions in political theory see his *Individualism Old and New*, *The Public and Its Problems* and *Liberalism and Social Action*. Dewey also was a prolific pamphleteer. Many of his *New Republic* articles are reprinted in *Characters and Events*, ed. Joseph Ratner. For attacks on Dewey from different perspectives see Randolph Bourne, "Twilight of the Idols" in *Untimely Papers;* William Y. Elliot, *The Pragmatic Revolt in Politics;* Aurthur Ekrich, *The Decline of Liberalism*.

There are, of course, important views on the relationship between human nature and political action not represented in this volume. The concept of human nature is crucial for the anarchist. See, for instance, Emma Goldman, *Anarchism and Other Essays* and Benjamin Tucker, *Instead of a Book*. For the application of Freudian psychology to politics, see Harold Lasswell's *Politics: Who Gets, What, When and How* and *Psychopathology and Politics*, and Bruno Bettelheim, *The Informed Heart*. B. F. Skinner has, in the view of some critics, ruthlessly applied the techniques of behaviorist psychology to political problems in *Walden II* and *Beyond Freedom and Dignity*.

2. Justifying Government— The Consent Model

Few statements about social practice can be made unequivocally. One of the precious few which can be is that all societies advance a theory of political obligation. Whether the question, "Why should I obey political authority?" is answered with reference to magic, ancestry, divine right, or simply security, men have found that they have not been able (or not been willing) to live together without providing a reason more impelling than force.

If theories of political obligation have generally attempted to tell men why they morally ought to obey the state, no account has been more successful than consent theory. Simply stated, consent theory contends that you are obligated to obey only that government to which you have consented. It would appear that this theory would provide only for a justification of limited government with authority resting with the people. This was precisely the intention of many seventeenth-century English writers such as Sidney and Locke, who used consent theory to argue for increased powers for the Parliament over the Crown. Yet the same doctrine was employed for precisely the opposite purposes by other philosophers, the most notable of whom was Thomas Hobbes. In point of fact, consent theory, broadly conceived, has no built-in prejudice in favor of any form of government. By defining what consent is, what counts as consent (mere residence or "meaningful" political participation), and what men consent to, a writer can devise a justification of government just short of anarchy or the most comprehensive tyranny.

The first selection offered here is a document known by every American schoolboy. Yet perhaps because it is part of our received tradition it is not studied as the controversial document it was meant to be. The selection reprinted is the version after it was revised by the Continental Congress from Thomas Jefferson's draft. Jefferson's hope was that the Declaration was "an expression of the American mind" and history has more than fulfilled his intentions.

Few American writers have rejected the consent account of political obligation in principle. They have, however, spent great effort attempting to fill in some of the theory's failings. One of these has always been the problem of establishing what shall be taken as evidence of consent. The Declaration notes that governments derive their "just powers from the consent of the governed" and lists a set of grievances against King George without explicitly answering the question we have posed. In the second selection, Joseph Tussman attempts to restate consent theory while admitting that there are those who have not thought about consenting. In the first part of a now famous article, Hanna Pitkin criticizes the implications of the child-bride theory (one consents or he is placed in tutelage until he consents) and offers a theory of "hypothetical consent." Philip Abbott takes an even more critical position, asking if, as Pitkin suggests, we owe allegiance to a government that we would consent to if we had the opportunity, then why justify obedience on the basis of consent at all?

Adam Smith, a writer not unsympathetic to the principle of limited government, once said that the consent theory of government amounts to dragging a man aboard a ship and, when well out to sea, telling him he has a duty to remain aboard because he consented. Yet despite the enormous problems in basing political legitimacy upon consent, Americans are reluctant to discard it. Not the least of reasons perhaps is that it is difficult to imagine a theory which could replace it.

DECLARATION OF INDEPENDENCE

When in the course of human events, it becomes necessary for one people to dissolve the political bands which have connected them with another, and to assume among the Powers of the earth, the separate and equal station to which the Laws of Nature and of Nature's God entitle them, a decent respect to the opinions of mankind requires that they should declare the causes which impel them to the separation.

We hold these truths to be self-evident, that all men are created equal, that they are endowed by their Creator with certain unalienable Rights, that among these are Life, Liberty, and the pursuit of Happiness. That to secure these rights, Governments are instituted among Men, deriving their just powers from the consent of the governed; That whenever any Form of Government becomes destructive of these ends, it is the Right of the People to alter or to abolish it, and to institute new Government, laying its foundation on such principles and organizing its powers in such form, as to them shall seem most likely to effect their Safety and Happiness. Prudence, indeed, will dictate that Governments long established should not be changed for light and transient causes; and accordingly all experience hath shown, that mankind are more disposed to suffer, while evils are sufferable, than to right themselves by abolishing the forms to which they are accustomed. But when a long train of abuses and usurpations, pursuing invariably the same Object evinces a design to reduce them under absolute Despotism, it is their right, it is their duty, to throw off such Government, and to provide new Guards for their future security.—Such has been the patient sufferance of these Colonies; and such is now the necessity which constrains them to alter their former Systems of Government. The history of the present King of Great Britain is a history of repeated injuries and usurpations, all having in direct object the establishment of an absolute Tyranny over these States. To prove this, let Facts be submitted to a candid world.

He has refused his Assent to Laws, the most wholesome and necessary for the public good.

He has forbidden his Governors to pass Laws of immediate and pressing importance, unless suspended in their operation till his Assent should be obtained; and when so suspended, he has utterly neglected to attend to them.

He has refused to pass other Laws for the accommodation of large districts of people, unless those people would relinquish the right of Representation in the Legislature, a right inestimable to them and formidable to tyrants only.

He has called together legislative bodies at places unusual, uncomfortable, and distant from the depository of their Public Records, for the sole purpose of fatiguing them into compliance with his measures.

He has dissolved Representative Houses repeatedly, for opposing with manly firmness his invasions on the rights of the people.

He has refused for a long time, after such dissolutions, to cause others to be elected; whereby the Legislative Powers, incapable of Annihilation, have returned to the People at large for their exercise; the State remaining in the meantime exposed to all the dangers of invasion from without, and convulsions within.

He has endeavoured to prevent the population of these States; for that purpose obstructing the Laws of Naturalization of Foreigners; refusing to pass others to encourage their migration hither, and raising the conditions of new Appropriations of Lands.

He has obstructed the Administration of Justice, by refusing his Assent to Laws for establishing Judiciary Powers.

He has made Judges dependent on his Will alone, for the Tenure of their Offices, and the Amount and Payment of their Salaries.

He has erected a multitude of new Offices, and sent hither Swarms of Officers to harrass our People, and eat out their Substance.

He has kept among us, in Times of Peace, Standing Armies, without the consent of our Legislatures.

He has affected to render the Military independent of and superior to the Civil Power.

He has combined with others to subject us to a Jurisdiction foreign to our Constitution, and unacknowledged by our Laws; giving his Assent to their Acts of pretended Legislation:

For quartering large Bodies of Armed Troops among us:

For protecting them, by a mock Trial, from Punishment for any Murders which they should commit on the Inhabitants of these States:

For cutting off our Trade with all Parts of the World:

For imposing Taxes on us without our Consent:

For depriving us, in many Cases, of the Benefits of Trial by Jury:

For transporting us beyond the Seas to be tried for pretended Offences:

For abolishing the free System of English Laws in a neighbouring Province, establishing therein an arbitrary Government, and enlarging its Boundaries, so as to render it at once an Example and fit Instrument for introducing the same absolute Rule into these Colonies:

For taking away our Charters, abolishing our most valuable Laws, and altering fundamentally the Forms of our Governments:

For suspending our own Legislatures, and declaring themselves invested with Power to legislate for us in all Cases whatsoever.

He has abdicated Government here, by declaring us out of his Protection and waging War against us.

He has plundered our Seas, ravaged our Coasts, burnt our Towns, and destroyed the Lives of our People.

He is at this time transporting large armies of foreign mercenaries to compleat the works of death, desolation and tyranny, already begun with circumstances of Cruelty & perfidy scarcely paralleled in the most barbarous ages, and totally unworthy the Head of a civilized nation.

He has constrained our fellow Citizens taken Captive on the high Seas to bear Arms against their Country, to become the executioners of their friends and Brethren, or to fall themselves by their Hands.

He has excited domestic insurrections amongst us, and has endeavoured to bring on the inhabitants of our frontiers, the merciless Indian Savages, whose known rule of warfare, is an undistinguished destruction of all ages, sexes and conditions.

In every stage of these Oppressions We have Petitioned for Redress in the most humble terms: Our repeated Petitions have been answered only by repeated injury. A Prince, whose character is thus marked by every act which may define a Tyrant, is unfit to be the ruler of a free People.

Nor have We been wanting in attention to our British brethren. We have warned them from time to time of attempts by their legislature to extend an unwarrantable jurisdiction over us. We have reminded them of the circumstances of our emigration and settlement here. We have appealed to their native justice and magnanimity, and we have conjured them by the ties of our common kindred to disavow these usurpations, which would inevitably interrupt our connections and correspondence. They too have been deaf to the voice of justice and of consanguinity. We must, therefore, acquiesce in the necessity, which denounces our Separation, and hold them, as we hold the rest of mankind, Enemies in War, in Peace Friends.

We, therefore, the Representatives of the united States of America, in General Congress, Assembled, appealing to the Supreme Judge of the world for the rectitude of our intentions, do, in the Name, and by Authority of the good People of these Colonies, solemnly publish and declare, That these United Colonies are, and of Right ought to be Free and Independent States; that they are Absolved from all Allegiance to the British Crown, and that all political connection between them and the State of Great Britain, is and ought to be totally dissolved; and that as Free and Independent States, they have full Power to levy War, conclude Peace, contract Alliances, establish Commerce ,and to do all other Acts and Things which Independent States may of right do. And for the support of this Declaration, with a firm reliance on the Protection of Divine Providence, we mutually pledge to each other our Lives, our Fortunes and our sacred Honor.

OBLIGATION AND THE BODY POLITIC
Joseph Tussman

"The consent of the governed" is an expression laden with significance for political life, but its apparent simplicity conceals many difficulties. Its meaning is not exhausted by saying that the ship of state floats on a sea of popular sentiment, that suffering and acquiesence have limits, that government cannot be both intolerable and enduring. For we are also told that governments derive 'their just powers from the consent of the governed,' and this reminds us of the relation between consent and legitimacy. Consent has not always been regarded as a necessary basis for the claim to political authority, but for the last three hundred years every other basis has been so badly shaken that there is hardly a government which does not claim, however fraudulently, to rest upon it.

There are two aspects of this fundamental consent which traditionally have been distinguished. First, the demand for consent is the demand that the government must be more than self-appointed and must, in some significant way, be the chosen instrument through which the body politic or community acts; the ruler, in short, must be authorized by the ruled. And second, the demand for consent is the demand that membership be distinguishable from captivity. It must in some meaningful sense be voluntary.

The fact that consent is sometimes discussed with reference to the relation of government to the body politic and at other times with reference to the relation of the individual to the body politic is itself a cause of some confusion and controversy. Thus it is possible to hold that membership in a body politic is not voluntary but that the demand for consent is satisfied if the government is authorized by some consent-giving process. It may also be held that government need not be authorized but that the demand for consent is satisfied if membership in the body politic is voluntarily acquired and voluntarily relinquishable. And it may, of course, be insisted that consent is lacking unless membership is voluntary *and* the government is properly authorized.

The possibility of thus distinguishing voluntary adherence from the authorization of government has led theorists to distinguish between a 'pact of association' and a 'pact of government'—the former, an agreement which transforms a multitude or aggregate of individuals into a single community or organization; the latter, an agreement by which the community establishes its

From Obligation and the Body Politic *by Joseph Tussman. Copyright © 1960 by Oxford University Press, Inc. Reprinted by permission.*

government. But to separate distinguishable aspects into two distinct acts is not only to multiply entities needlessly, it is to obscure the whole point. The act which creates a body politic out of a multitude is precisely the act by which a number of individuals establish a common decision-making authority; the act by which one acquires membership is the act of accepting the authority of the government. Thus, for example, the ratification of the Constitution which created our Federal Union involved for each state the acceptance of the authority of the proposed government. That single act created both a new body politic and the new governing authority. The agreement which makes one a member is the agreement to be governed in a particular way.

It is easy to forget that the consent of the governed, upon which we insist, is consent to be governed. If it is a voluntary act it is nevertheless an act of voluntary subordination. A body politic is not a state of anarchy in which sovereign individuals confront each other; it is an organization in which individuals are sovereign neither in theory nor in practice but are related as members or parts of a system. The consent which is seen as the necessary basis of a body politic is precisely the acceptance by the individual of the status of 'member.' And this involves a significant twofold subordination.

The first aspect of subordination is that by which one acknowledges himself bound by a decision other than his own—the subordination of private judgment to public judgment. This may sound rather offensive to our independent ears, but it is really one of the most familiar features of political life.

Consider, for example, a political caucus. A number of individuals faced with the necessity for agreement upon a concerted course of action bind themselves to act upon the decision of the caucus, determined, let us suppose, by a majority vote. This is done with full awareness that participation in the caucus involves binding oneself to act upon a decision which one may, in fact, vote against. To enter a caucus is thus to acknowledge the authority of a decision other than one's own. It is obvious that adhering to or being a member of a caucus is a matter of voluntary decision, that *every* member is a party to the caucus agreement, that no one would be considered a member who would insist on a veto power, thus claiming to be bound only by a decision with which he agrees, and that no one is bound by the decision who is not a member of the caucus or at least represented at it.

It is generally assumed or expected that the caucus decision will not be unanimous; for if unanimity is required the caucus agreement is pointless. It is precisely the failure of unanimity which makes the caucus necessary. There is thus both a presupposition of unanimity and a deliberate rejection of the demand for unanimity. The sense in which unanimity is presupposed is the sense in which everyone who is a member is a party to the agreement. But the unanimous agreement is to the bindingness of subsequent nonunanimous decisions and, in this form, to the subordination of individual judgment to group judgment and decision.

The real problem is that of getting away from the demand for unanimity as a condition of group action. This requires creating a situation in which the 'group' can be said to decide or to act not only in the face of non-concurrence by a portion of its members but with the understanding that the dissenters are bound to consider the decision as *theirs*. The voice of the majority, for example, is designated as the voice of the group. But this designation must be by each member, since there is nothing inherently authoritative about a majority. We are sometimes so impressed with the democratic aspect of majority rule that we forget that it does involve some abdication of autonomy and the subordination of private decision to the decision of the group. Without this subordination there would, in fact, be no caucus. To be a member is thus to subordinate oneself.

What is so dramatically apparent in the caucus, the unanimous agreement to transcend the demand for unanimity, is an essential feature of any situation in which voting is significantly involved. It may, in fact, be said to be the crucial invention of the political mind. We are so familiar with it that, as with the wheel, we seldom think of it as an achievement. But where would we be without it? How much concerted, group action would there be if we always needed unanimity? Considering this, it is hardly surprising that the agreement to waive unanimity should come to be regarded as *the* social compact.

Whether it be described as the delegation of decision-making authority or the authorization of a decision-making tribunal or the acceptance of the jurisdiction of a tribunal, what is involved is the voluntary waiving of autonomy, the voluntary subordination of private to public decision. 'To delegate,' 'to authorize,' 'to put oneself under the jurisdiction of' are, of necessity, voluntary acts; they are ways of giving consent. But its voluntary character must not obscure the hard fact that it is an act of subordination, giving precedence to public over private decision. A body politic, based on consent, is a group of individuals each of whom is a party to a basic agreement, making a common delegation of authority, acknowledging, within its proper scope, the subordination of private to public decision.

This is not the whole story. The act of subordination is not pointless or unbounded. It is a purposive act, and its purposive character brings us to another aspect of the subordination involved in membership—the subordination of priate to public purpose.

Familiar as it is, there is something fundamentally misleading about the slogan that the aim of government is 'the welfare of the individual.' It is hard to quarrel with the demand that the body politic provide or safeguard the conditions necessary for the fullest development of each of its members. And I do not intend to quarrel with it. But I do not think we can escape the distinction between the demands or interests of a particular individual and the demands of the system of interests which any individual's is only a part. The government's concern is, and must be, systemic. If it deals with some individual or individuals with hostility we condemn its action as discriminatory; if it treats some with special softness we accuse it of partiality. This recognition of the impropriety of discrimination and partiality testifies to the fact that the government's concern for the individual is not to be understood as special concern for *this* or *that* individual but rather as concern for all individuals. Government, that is to say, serves the welfare of the community. And if it be said here that the 'welfare of the community' means simply the welfare of the individuals who constitute it, that the general good is simply the sum of particular goods, the point still holds. For there is a very real difference between trying to maximize my private good and trying to maximize the whole system of private goods—as any Utilitarian faced with a pack of Hedonists will quickly realize. Even in individualistic terms, then, the distinction between a particular interest and the system, or complex, or collection of particular interests forces itself upon us in a way which requires us to state the government's concern as with the general or public good, with *ours* rather than with *mine*.

If, then, the agreement which constitutes a body politic involves the subordination of private judgment to public judgment, and if the public judgment is directed at the public interest, there is also a significant subordination of private interest to public interest. To be a member is to acknowledge that one's own interests are only a part of a broader system of interests, that other members have theirs as you have yours, and that it is the function of government to promote and safeguard the entire system, of which yours is a part but no more significant a part than any others. . . .

It is quite easy to ridicule the ridiculous notion of an original or aboriginal contract by which a collection of savages solemnly and at one stroke, tiring of the state of nature, invent civilization. This is not only a dead horse, it is an imaginary dead horse. But there is a real 'historical' question and we meet it in two forms. The difference is roughly the difference between becoming a charter member and becoming a member of a going concern, between forming a body politic and joining an already existing body politic. While I am chiefly concerned with the latter, the former should not be dismissed without a brief remark.

We are not unfamiliar with the process of creating a new body politic by explicit agreement. How else are we to describe the process of promulgating and ratifying the Constitution which created our Federal Union? A more recent example is the creation of the United Nations which, while lacking some of the necessary conditions of being a body politic, has some of its features. There is nothing in the discussions of the last decade about the United Nations which would be in the slightest degree strange or novel to Hobbes—sovereignty and veto power, enforcement problems, rights and duties under the charter, reservations about self-preservation, fear of mutual destruction—the whole story. It is of no special significance that the units involved are themselves states. The problem is that of creating a system of agreements, to which states are voluntary parties, with decision-making tribunals authorized to deal effectively with the problems whose existence makes the organization necessary. In this area we still move entirely within the basic analysis and concepts of social contract theory.

It should be noted that both the United States and the United Nations have members who are not charter members—who were not in on the formation of the organization—but who have become members of a going concern by becoming parties to the same system of agreements. Too much attention is given to the original agreement and not enough to the process by which one becomes a member of an already existing body politic. This is the form in which the question 'when did I agree?' presents itself to us.

Let us first consider the case of the person, not born a citizen of the United States, who, through the process of naturalization, becomes a member of the body politic in full standing. At the threshold of citizenship he is called upon to give and does give his explicit 'consent.' He agrees to recognize the authority of the governing institutions, the constitution, and the laws made pursuant to it. He makes his submission, pledges his allegiance, and is received as a member with the rights which go with that status. He is not required to 'agree' with every existing law. There may be laws in force which he might well have opposed had he had a voice in the matter and which he would like to have a hand in changing. But he acknowledges the authority of the whole system. In giving his consent he declares himself a party to the system of agreements which constitute the body politic.

For the naturalized citizen, therefore, the question 'when did I agree?' has a clear and easy answer. At a particular time and place he gave his express consent. But for the native citizen the problem seems more difficult. We commonly distinguish the minor from the adult citizen, but we seem to drift or grow into full citizenship without ceremony. Yet I wonder if we would really consider the difference between the naturalized and native citizen as the difference between one who has 'consented' and one who has not. We do sometimes speak of the one as a citizen 'by choice,' but do we mean by this to indicate that only the naturalized are governed by consent? I think not. We fall back rather, upon the familiar notion of tacit consent.

There are many occasions upon which the native citizen makes a formal, ceremonial pledge which could well be regarded as an express giving of consent. I mention this but I do not depend on it. I am intrigued, however, by the baffled and puzzled reaction of many persons when this is called to their attention and by their resistance to the suggestion that they have, in this form, 'consented.' Perhaps this attitude is the result of making the pledge of allegiance a schoolboy ritual, robbing it of any moral significance; perhaps it is a symptom of something even more disturbing. But I leave this matter unexplored and turn to the question of tacit consent.

The difference between express and tacit consent is not, I think, the difference between two kinds or degrees of consent. It is a difference in the way in which consent is given. There is really little point in insisting that the only way in which consent can be indicated or given is by the express utterance of 'I consent' or 'I pledge allegiance.' Not only may there be other verbal acts which can be interpreted as the giving of consent, but there may be non-verbal acts which have the same force. So that the question of tacit consent is the question of whether there are some actions, including perhaps, the failure to act, which can properly be regarded as the equivalent of the express consent given by the naturalized citizen.

That there are such acts has been the traditional view. Voting, for example, has generally been regarded as implying consent or allegiance; as has applying for a passport. It is not profitable, however, to argue abstractly about the acts which can be taken as a sign that one has become a party to the system of agreements constituting a body politic. Beyond insisting that there is little justification for the narrow demand that nothing but the signature on the dotted line will serve, there is one crucial point that needs to be made.

There is a necessary condition which must be satisfied *whatever* is proposed as a sign of tacit consent. That is, the act can only be properly taken as 'consent' if it is done 'knowingly,' if it is understood by the one performing the act that his action involves his acceptance of the obligations of membership. This condition seems to me so crucial that, in fact, it may even override the force of an explicit verbal expression of consent. That is why we take the child's pledge lightly. He says the magic words, but he does not know quite what he is saying. It is form without substance.

While this may involve complications, we cannot really regard 'entrapment' as possible here—as when a man performs a particular act and subsequently has it held up to him as evidence that he has agreed or consented and is thus caught in bonds he knew nothing of. Consent must be voluntary, not unconscious or accidental. We take good care that in naturalization the knowing quality of the act is preserved. Unfortunately we do not do as well with the native, and this is a grave failure in political education. It has disturbing consequences.

When we reflect upon what we mean when we describe ourselves as members of a body politic I think we come to accept the fact that it means we have agreed to something, that we are parties to a social compact. But we must accept it as a plain fact that many native 'citizens' have in no meaningful sense agreed to anything. They have never been asked and have never thought about it. They are political childbrides who have a status they do not understand and which they have not acquired by their own consent.

If it is true that 'American Citizen' includes some who have 'agreed' and some who have not, we seem to be in some difficulty. If it is insisted that only those who have consented are members of the body politic then the body politic may shrink alarmingly. But if all—those who have not consented as well as those who have—are regarded as members, then consent cannot be taken as a necessary condition of membership.

Confronted with these alternatives I conclude, with some reluctance, that some variant of the 'shrinkage' notion needs to be accepted. Or rather, it must be recognized that the class of minors, or others who for some reason are regarded as lacking full status, is larger than we think. Any description of a body politic, like the United States, would have to recognize that there are some, or many, 'citizens' who could not be described as having consented.

There is no point to resorting to fiction to conceal this fact. It makes more sense to speak of the social compact as an ideal which is never completely realized. Non-consenting adult citizens are, in effect, like minors who are governed without their own consent. The period of tutelage and dependence is unduly prolonged. And this, as I have suggested earlier, is a failure of political education.

Something should be said about the voluntary character of the act of becoming a party to the basic agreement. I have already spoken of its 'knowing' character. But it is sometimes said that membership is not voluntary because there is no real choice, no alternative to giving one's consent. We cannot, of course, have it both ways: we cannot assert on the one hand that government is based on consent, and on the other hand that membership, and the subordination it entails, is involuntary.

Only if we suppose that an act which is motivated is, therefore, involuntary is there any real difficulty; but this is to confuse reasonable with involuntary acts. Of course there are reasons for giving one's consent, and very good ones. But to have good reasons is not to be compelled or to have no alternative; it does not rob a deliberate choice of its voluntary character. There is a difference between an alternative's being inconvenient, hard, or unpleasant and its being impossible. The fact that the easier course is easier does not make the harder course impossible. There is considerable range before we come to the situation in which choice disappears because an alternative is really no alternative at all. 'Your money or your life!' may not really present you with a choice; but to say that consenting to the status of a member is involuntary because the alternative is not as pleasant or convenient is simply to confuse convenience with necessity. And if we have come to the point at which we find the inconvenient really impossible then we are beyond the help of political or moral theory and in need of psychiatric treatment. Difficult as the alternative to citizenship may be, there is sufficient alternative to preserve the voluntary character of the consent which creates membership.

To the extent that 'becoming a member' of a body politic involves the express or tacit giving of the consent by which one becomes a party to the agreements which constitute a structure of authority, the conception of the body politic as a voluntary group finds its embodiment in the real world. To this extent is it possible to speak meaningfully of government based on the consent of the governed. We must ask ourselves, then, whether it is not the case that we, as citizens, native as well as naturalized, have agreed to something. We must ask ourselves, when we claim to be free men, whether we are not asserting that we are voluntary parties to the social compact.

OBLIGATION AND CONSENT–I
Hanna Pitkin

One might suppose that if political theorists are by now clear about anything at all, they should be clear about the problem of political obligation and the solution to it most commonly offered, the doctrine of consent. The greatest modern political theorists took up this problem and formulated this answer. The resulting theories are deeply imbedded in our American political tradition; as a consequence we are already taught a sort of rudimentary consent theory in high school. And yet I want to suggest that we are not even now clear on what *"the* problem of political obligation" is, what sorts of "answers" are appropriate to it, what the consent answer really says, or whether it is a satisfactory answer. This essay is designed to point up the extent of our confusion, to explore some of the ground anew as best it can, and to invite further effort by others. That such effort is worthwhile, that such political theory is still worth considering and that it can be made genuinely relevant to our world, are the assumptions on which this essay rests and the larger message it is meant to convey.

I. THE PROBLEM OF POLITICAL OBLIGATION

The difficulties begin with the formulation of the problem itself. What exactly is the "problem of political obligation"? It is characteristic that we take it for granted there is a single problem to be defined here, and that nevertheless a dozen different formulations clamor for our attention. The classical theorists on the subject have treated it in varying ways; and even within the writings of a Hobbes, Locke or Rousseau it is difficult to say what the theorist's "basic problem" is, or indeed whether he has one. We tend, I think, to suppose that it does not matter very much how you phrase the problem, that the different formulations boil down to the same thing. But my first point will be that this attitude of arbitrariness or indifference should not be trusted. It is not, in fact, true that any formulation of the problem is equivalent to any other. Rather, this supposed single problem is a whole cluster of different questions—questions of quite various kind and scope. And though their answers *may* turn out to be related, so that an answer to one provides answers to the others also, it is by no means obvious that this must be so. Specifically, I suggest that most of the familiar answers to the problem are satisfactory responses to some of its questions but not to others, and that the answer adopted depends a good deal on the question stressed.

From the American Political Science Review, *XL (December, 1965), pp. 990–999. Copyright by the* American Political Science Review. *Reprinted by permission of publisher and author.*

For the purposes of this essay it will be useful to distinguish four questions, or rather, four clusters of questions, all of which are part of what bothers theorists about political obligation.[1] They range from a relatively concrete and practical political concern with what is to be done, through increasing theoretical abstractness, to a philosophical concern with the meanings of concepts and the paradoxes that arise out of them. Because we are used to treating them all as different versions of one problem, the reader may not at first see any significant differences among them; but the differences should emerge in the course of the discussion.

We are told often enough that the theorists of political obligation were not merely philosophers, but also practical men writing about the political needs of their times. They produced "not simply academic treatises, but essays in advocacy, adapted to the urgencies of a particular situation. Men rarely question the legitimacy of established authority when all is going well; the problem of political obligation is urgent when the state is sick, when someone is seriously contemplating disobedience or revolt on principle."[2] Thus we may begin with a cluster of questions centered around the *limits* of political obligation, the more or less practical concern with *when*, under what circumstances, resistance or revolution is justified. The theorist wants to promote or prevent a revolution, or he lives in a time when one is taking place, or he contemplates one in the recent past. So he seeks some fairly general, but still practically applicable principles to guide a man in deciding when (if ever) political obligation ends or ceases to bind. They must have a certain degree of generality in order to be principles rather than *ad hoc* considerations in one particular situation, in order to be recognized by us as *theory*. But they are also fairly directly tied to what Tussman has called the question "what should I do?"[3] They are guidelines to action.

At other times the same practical concern tends to take a slightly different form: "Whom am I obligated to obey? Which of the persons (or groups) claiming to command me actually has authority to do so?" Put this second way, the problem seems to be one of rival authorities, sometimes identified in political theory as the problem of the locus of sovereignty. The former question tends to arise in situations of potential civil disobedience or nascent revolution, where the individual is relatively alone in his confrontation of a government. The latter question is more likely to come up in situations of civil war or when a revolution is more advanced, when the individual is already confronted by two "sides" between which he must choose.

But as the theorist tries to formulate general principles to guide such a choice, he may be led to a more abstract version of his problem. He may be struck by the seeming arbitrariness or conventionality of human authority: how is it that some men have the right to command, and others are obligated to obey? And so the theorist looks for the general difference between legitimate authority on the one hand, and illegitimate, naked coercive force on the other. He begins to wonder whether there is really any difference in principle between a legitimate government and a highway robber, pirate, or slave-owner. He begins to suspect that terms like "legitimate," "authority," "obligation" may be parts of an elaborate social swindle, used to clothe those highway robbers who have the approval of society with a deceptive mantle of moralistic sanctity. Essentially, he begins to ask whether men are ever truly obligated to obey, or only coerced. "Strength is a physical attribute," says Rousseau, "and I fail to see how any moral sanction can attach to its effects. To yield to the strong is an act of necessity, not of will. At most it is the result of a dictate of prudence. How, then, can it become a duty?"[4] Such questions are no longer merely guides to action; they are attempts to describe and classify parts of the social world. Instead of focussing on the individual's "what should I do?" they focus outward, on the (real or alleged) authority: "what is legitimate authority like?"

Finally, behind even this more abstract question, lies what is essentially a philosophical problem, a cluster of questions centering around the *justification* of obligation: *why* are you obligated to obey even a legitimate government? Why is anyone ever obligated to obey any authority at all? How can such a thing be rationalized, explained, defended, justified? What can account for the binding nature of valid law and legitimate authority? I call these questions philosophical problems because they no longer seek distinctions or guides to action, but arise out of puzzlement over the nature of law, government, obligation as such. They are categorical questions to which the theorist is led, characteristically, after an extended abstract contemplation of the concepts he has been using. They are reminiscent of other philosophical puzzles, like "do we ever really know anything?" or "do other people really exist?"

We have, then, four clusters of questions, any or all of which are sometimes taken to define the problem of political obligation:

1. The limits of obligation (*"When* are you obligated to obey, and when not?")
2. The locus of sovereignty (*"Whom* are you obligated to obey?")
3. The difference between legitimate authority and mere coercion ("Is there *really* any difference; are you ever *really* obligated?")
4. The justification of obligation (*"Why* are you ever obligated to obey even a legitimate authority?")

Obviously the answers to these questions may be connected. If, for example, one answers question three in terms of the reductionist realism of a Thrasymachus or of vulgar Marxism: "there is no difference," then the other questions become essentially irrelevant. But we should not take it for granted that any answer to one of these questions will automatically provide consistent answers to the rest; we should look to see how familiar answers in fact perform. Our prime interest is, of course, the consent answer, but before examining it, we might look briefly at very abstract, ideal-typicalized versions of some of its major rivals. Their brief treatment here would not allow, and is not meant to be a balanced assessment of their merits. It is meant only to explore a little of the complexity of political obligation, and the difficulty of providing a consistent treatment of it.

Theories of Divine Right or the will of God, for example, seem much better designed to cope with some of our questions than with others. Saying, with St. Paul, that "the powers that be are ordained of God," seems a decisive answer (at least for a believer) to our question four. Granted only that there is a God (in the full sense of the word), the fact that he commands certain actions is surely a decisive justification for our obligation to perform them. But applied to our other questions the doctrine is ambiguous. Taken one way, it seems to imply that there is no difference between mere coercive force and legitimate authority, since all power comes from God. Then resistance is never justified, even against a heretical ruler who attacks religion. For times when power is in flux, as in cases of civil war, this version of the theory seems to provide very little guidance for action. Taking the doctrine a different way, some divine right theorists have wanted to argue that there is nevertheless a distinction to be made between divinely ordained power and illegitimate power, and that there are times when certain kinds of power must be resisted.

Prescription, another familiar response to the problem of obligation, seems more directly designed to give an unequivocal answer to questions one and perhaps three. It teaches that old, established power is legitimate in every case, and there are no limits on our obligation to obey it. But this again is no guide in times of successful revolution; is it obedience or counterrevolution that is then required? And what of occasions when an old, established government begins to act in new and tyrannical ways? Even Burke was sympathetic to the American Revolution. Further, this doctrine has real difficulties with our question four; a government's age, and our habitual obedience to it, do not seem to *justify* an obligation to obey. At most the connection can only be made through a number of additional assumptions concerning human reason and the nature of society, and adding up to the thesis that old, accepted government is most likely to be good government.

A third, equally well known response to our problem, that of Utilitarianism, is perhaps an even better illustration of the complexities involved. The utilitarian theorist argues that you are obligated to obey if and only if the consequences of obedience will be best on the whole, in terms of a calculus of pains and pleasures. There are, of course, familiar difficulties over the manner of calculation and whether all pains and pleasures are to count equally. But even beyond these, there is a fundamental question left unclear, namely, *whose* pains and pleasures are to count: your own personal ones, or those of the (majority of) people in your society. Bentham himself says that it is

> allowable to, if not incumbent on every man . . . to enter into measures of resistance . . . when the probable mischiefs of resistance (speaking with respect to the community in general) appear less to him than the probable mischiefs of obedience.[5]

But the phrase in the parentheses is, of course, the crux of the matter. The Utilitarians are notoriously inconsistent on precisely this point, saying one thing when they speak of personal ethics and personal decision, and quite another on the subject of legislation and public policy. So it will be well for us to consider both possibilities.

First, there is what might be called individualistic utilitarianism. Such a theory argues that you are obligated when the consequences of obedience are best on the whole in terms of your personal pleasure and pain. As a response to our question four, this argument has a certain appeal: you are obligated *because* it is best for you in terms of your own pleasure and pain. But the implications for the other questions are more strange. For they are that each individual is obligated to obey only while it is best for him, and becomes obligated to resist when that would promote his personal welfare. Thus the same government will be a legitimate authority for some of its subjects but naked illegitimate power to others. And anyone is free to disobey or resist whenever it benefits him to do so; he can have no obligation to the contrary. Indeed, the sum total of such a doctrine is that you have no obligation at all, or none except the pursuit of your own welfare. If that happens at one point to entail obeying the law, you should do so; if not, not. And in precisely the same way, if it happens at one point to entail obeying a highway robber, you are "obligated" to do that. Thus, as an answer to question three, individualistic utilitarianism essentially denies the existence of authority altogether.

The second alternative is what we might call social utilitarianism. This position argues that you are obligated to obey if and only if the consequences of your doing so will be best on the whole, in terms of the pains and pleasures of the people in your society—in terms of the greatest good for the greatest number. Unlike individualistic utilitarianism, this seems a fairly reasonable, conventional answer to questions one and two. You must obey while that promotes the welfare of society, even if it hurts you; and you must resist when that is socially best, even if it hurts you. The answer to question three is less obvious but not, on the face of it, irrational. A legitimate government is one that promotes the greatest good for the greatest number; and if a highway robber does that, then he becomes thereby a legitimate authority entitled to your obedience. A selfish or (on the whole) harmful robber or government may or must be resisted. But as an answer to question four, social utilitarianism seems less successful. For it teaches that you are obligated *because* your obedience will promote the greatest good for the greatest number. But if you are bothered about political obligation, *that* is just the problem: why should that criterion mean anything to you? Why should it be any easier to accept *that* obligation than to accept the obligation to obey law and authority?

Sometimes, of course, the utilitarians assume that there is no problem about individualistic *versus* social utilitarianism, that the two criteria are essentially the same because of the invisible hand, because individual welfare is (in sum) social welfare. When they write about economics, particularly, this solution tempts them. But in political life, concerning legislation or concerning political obligation, they are fairly well aware that this is not the case. Private interest must be *made* to coincide with public interest by wise legislation. And instructions to resist when it is best for society will often produce quite different results than instructions to resist when it is best for you personally. There are bound to be occasions when the public welfare requires serious sacrifices (perhaps even of life) by some individuals. To suppose otherwise seems incredibly unrealistic.

The theorist founding political obligation in consent responds to our four questions in this way: you are obligated to obey if and only if you have consented. Thus your consent defines the limits of your obligation as well as the person or persons to whom it is owed. Legitimate authority is distinguished from mere coercive power precisely by the consent of those subject to it. And the justification for your obligation to obey is your own consent to it; because you have agreed, it is right for you to have an obligation. But the seeming harmonious simplicity of these answers is deceptive; when consent theory is worked out in detail, it answers to some of our questions begin to interfere with its answers to others.

In the first place, there is the problem of exactly whose consent is to count. We have all known, at least since Hume—if it was not already obvious before him—that the historical origins of society are essentially irrelevant to the consent argument. The consent of our ancestors does not settle the problem about our obligation today. Or rather, someone who seriously argues that the consent of our ancestors does settle this problem, is arguing more from prescription than from consent, and is probably not very troubled about political obligation anyway.

But even if it is the consent of those now subject to power (or authority) that matters, there are still several alternatives: is it to be the individual's personal consent that determines his obligation, or the consent of all (or most) of those subject to the government? And is it to be his or their present consent, or consent given in the past? Let us consider the possibilities.

1. You are obligated only insofar as you personally consent right now. Where your consenting ends, there ends also your obligation. What this presumably means is that as long as you accept the government it is wrong for you to disobey it, and right for it to punish any disobedience by you. But as soon as you withdraw your consent, you become free to disobey, and no attempt to punish you can be justified. This doctrine would have the peculiar consequence that you can never violate your obligation; for as soon as you decide the time has come for revolution (withdraw your consent), your obligation disappears. It also means that you can never be mistaken about your obligation, for what you think defines it. This answer comes to much the same thing as individualistic utilitarianism, except that it demands no rational calculation, looking to your will rather than to your welfare.

2. You are obligated only insofar as you personally have *in the past* consented. This is closer to traditional contract theory. You gave your word, and so you are bound for the future, unless (of course) the government changes

and becomes tyrannical. But this position seems to allow the possibility of becoming obligated to a tyrannical government, if you expressly consent to one that was already corrupt. One can avoid that problem by saying such promises are invalid, that you *cannot* expressly consent to become a slave; but then the argument is already moving away from a consent theory. Then your obligation is no longer merely a matter of your having consented (tried to consent, intended to consent).

Further, there seems to be a real problem about why and whether your past promise should bind you now. The classical contract theorists provide a law of nature to take care of this difficulty: it is a law of nature that promises oblige. But why should it seem so obvious and "natural" and self-evident that your promises oblige you, when it is so doubtful and problematic and un-"natural" that law and authority oblige you?

3. You are obligated only insofar as your fellow-subjects consent. One consequence of this position is that the matter is no longer left up to you; you can sometimes be obligated to obey even against your will and your private judgment, and without ever having consented or been consulted. But, if so, how many of your fellow-subjects must consent? All? That is surely impossible. A majority? But that implies that the way to decide whether you are obligated, or whether you should start a revolution, is to take a public opinion poll. And can majorities never be wrong? Are there no occasions in the history of mankind when it was right for a dedicated minority to begin agitating for a revolution, or even to lead or make a revolution? And finally, *why* should what the majority (or any other proportion) of your fellow-subjects think be binding on you? What justification is there for that? Why should that obligation seem more basic or natural or self-evident than the obligation to obey laws and authority? Because you have consented to majority rule? But then the whole cycle of difficulties begins again.

Besides the matter of whose consent is to count, consent theory is also much troubled by the difficulty of showing that you, or a majority of your fellow-citizens (as the case may be) have in fact consented. Most of us have not signed any contract with our government or our society or our fellow-citizens. There is no such contract for us to sign. And while we political theorists may be enlightened about our obligations, we realize that the largest proportion of our fellow-citizens has never contemplated this sort of question at all. If they have consented, it comes as news to most of them. Of course, these facts need not invalidate the consent argument. Perhaps most of us are not really obligated in modern, apathetic mass society; perhaps our government is not really legitimate. But such conclusions seem to fly in the face of common sense. Surely, one feels, if the present government of the United States is not a legitimate authority, no government has ever been. And surely it is absurd to adopt a theory according to which only those people who are most educated and aware of their obligations, most moral and sensitive, are obligated to obey the law. Surely it is absurd to suppose that all the rest are free to do whatever they please, whatever they can get away with. A more common move at this stage in the argument is the introduction of some notion of "tacit consent", demonstrating that even the unaware masses have consented after all. But it appears to be extremely difficult to formulate a notion of tacit consent strong enough to create the required obligation, yet not so strong as to destroy the very substance and meaning of consent.

Let us now examine in more detail how these difficulties are encountered and treated in two consent arguments: the most famous one of the tradition, made by John Locke, and a recent attempt at revision by Joseph Tussman. What should emerge from a review of their arguments is a somewhat unexpected and different doctrine of political obligation: perhaps a new interpretation of consent theory, perhaps a new rival to it.

II. LOCKE ON CONSENT

Locke tells us in the preface to his *Two Treatises* that he wants both to "make good" the title of William III to the English throne "in the consent of the People" and also "to justifie to the World, the people of England, whose love of their Just and Natural Rights, with their Resolution to preserve them, saved the Nation when it was on the very brink of Slavery and Ruine."[6] Apart from the exegetic problems of how much of the *Treatises* may have been written before the Glorious Revolution and for quite other purposes, the thrust of Locke's argument makes clear enough that this dual orientation does pervade the work.[7] He seeks both to defend the obligation to obey legitimate authority (which is authority based on consent), and to defend the right to resist coercive force in the absence of authority. But Locke moves easily, and seemingly without awareness, from one to another of our four questions about obligation and back again. Often when the going gets difficult on one, he switches to another.

Legitimate authority, for Locke, comes from the consent of those subject to it, never from mere conquest (force); and even a consent extracted by coercion is invalid.[8] Thus the limits of a government's authority are defined by the social contract on which it is based. Strictly speaking, of course, Locke's contract sets up *society* and government is established by society as a trust.[9] There is no contract with the government. But the government gets its powers (in trust) from "the society", acting by majority vote. And "the society" has only such powers to give, as it has itself received from the separate contracting individuals. Thus, even for Locke, it is the contract which ultimately determines what powers the government can have. He himself makes this assumption and I shall follow suit, since it simplifies the argument.[10]

Although Locke sometimes seems to take contract seriously as an account of the historical origins of society, he is nevertheless quite explicit about the requirement that no person is obligated to obey today unless he has himself consented.[11] Most of us have not consented expressly? Ah, but there is tacit consent, and its scope turns out to be very wide indeed. Although a father may not consent for his son, he can make consent to the community a condition on inheritance of the property he leaves behind; then in accepting the property the son tacitly consents to obey the government.[12] But the final definition of tacit consent is even wider, for land is not the only form of property, and property not the only form of right that men enjoy:

> Every man that hath any possession or enjoyment of any part of the dominions of any government doth thereby give his tacit consent, and is as far forth obliged to obedience to the laws of that government, during such enjoyment, as any one under it, whether this his possession be of land to him and his heirs forever, or a lodging only for a week; or whether it be barely traveling freely on the highway; and, in effect, it reaches as far as the very being of anyone within the territories of that government.[13]

Just as Locke maintained earlier in the *Treatise* that men have tacitly consented to all inequalities in property, simply by accepting and using money as a medium of exchange; so in the political realm he argues that men have tacitly consented to obey a government, simply by remaining within its territory.[14] But now there no longer seems to be much power in the concept of consent, nor any difference between legitimate government and mere coercion. Being within the territory of the worst tyranny in the world seems to constitute tacit consent to it and create an obligation to obey it. Only physical withdrawal—emigration—and the abandoning of all property frees you from that obligation; there is no such thing as tacit *dissent*.

At this point we are likely to feel cheated by Locke's argument: why all the stress on consent if it is to include everything we do; why go through the whole social contract argument if it turns out in the end that everyone is automatically obligated? It seems that in his eagerness to save the consent answer to our question four (because only your own consent *can* justify your obligation), Locke has been forced so to widen the definition of consent as to make it almost unrecognizable. He has been forced to abandon his answers to our other questions as well as one of his own initial purposes: the justification of an (occasional) right of revolution.

But clearly this is not Locke's real position. I have developed it this way only because the corrections we must now make are so revealing about consent theory. For despite his doctrine of tacit consent, Locke does not want to abandon either the right of revolution or the distinction between legitimate authority and coercive power. His position is not, in fact, that living within the territory of a tyrannical government or holding property under it constitutes tacit consent to it.

Suppose that we ask: *to what* have you consented when you live in a country and use its highways? Unfortunately, Locke is less than clear on this question. What he says explicitly in the crucial section on tacit consent is that you have "consented," period; he does not say to what.[15] But apparently, what you consent to is a kind of associate membership in the commonwealth. Full membership, achieved only be express consent, is an indissoluble bond for life. The obligation of a tacit consenter, however, terminates if he leaves the country and gives up his property there.[16] Locke also variously describes tacit consent as a joining oneself to a society, putting oneself under a commonwealth and submitting to a government. Sometimes he simply equates its "joining up" aspects with submission to a government; at other times he regards submission as an immediate consequence of joining.[17]

But in the context of the problems we have encountered, a better interpretation of Locke's intention here would be this: what you consent to tacitly is *the terms of the original contract which the founders of the commonwealth made,* no more and no less. You append your "signature," as it were, to the original "document." Then if you live or use the roads or hold property under a government which is violating its trust, exceeding its authority, taking property without due compensation, "altering the legislative," or generally acting in a tyrannical manner, you have consented to none of these things. You are not obligated to obey one inch beyond the limits of the original contract, any more than its original signatories were. You retain the right of revolution, as they did, in case the government oversteps the limits of its authority.

So we seem to be led to the position that you are obligated to obey not really because you have consented; your consent is virtually automatic. Rather, you are obligated to obey because of certain characteristics of the government—that it is acting within the bounds of a trusteeship based on an original contract. And here it seems to me that interpreters of Locke have given far too little attention to the degree to which he regards the terms of the original contract as inevitably determined. In truth, the original contract could not have read any otherwise than it did, and the powers it gave and limits it placed can be logically deduced from the laws of nature and conditions in the state of nature. Not only does Locke himself confidently deduce them in this way, sure that he can tell us what the terms of that original contract were, *must* have been; but he says explicitly that they could not have been otherwise. For men had to give up sufficient of their rights to make an effective government possible, to allow a government to remedy the "inconveniences" of the state of nature. Nothing short of this would create a society, a government. "There, and there only, is political society, where everyone of the members" has given up the powers necessary to a society.[18]

Whosoever therefore out of a state of nature unite into a community, must be understood to give up all the power necessary to the needs for which they unite into society. . . .[19]

More power than this, on the other hand, men cannot be supposed to have given; and, indeed, they are forbidden by the law of nature to give more. When the limits of authority are to be defined, Locke invokes the purpose for which the contract was made, the intention which those making it must have had:

But though men when they enter into society give up the equality, liberty and executive power they had in the state of nature into the hands of the society, to be so far disposed of by the legislative as the good of society shall require, yet it being only with an intention in everyone the better to preserve himself, his liberty and his property *(for no rational creature can be supposed to change his condition with an intention to the worse)*, the power of the society or legislative constituted by them *can never be supposed to extend farther* than the common good, but is obliged to secure everyone's property by providing against those three defects above-mentioned that made the state of nature so unsafe and uneasy.[20]

Thus men cannot sell themselves into slavery "for nobody has an absolute arbitrary power over himself" to give to another; he *"cannot* subject himself to the arbitrary power of another."[21] Arbitrary or absolute power can never be legitimate, consented to, because "God and Nature" do not allow "a man so to abandon himself as to neglect his own preservation."[22] "Thus," says Locke, "the law of nature stands as an eternal rule to all men, legislators as well as others."[23]

If the terms of the original contract are, as I am arguing, "self-evident" truths to Locke, which could not be or have been otherwise, then the historical veracity of the contract theory becomes in a new and more profound sense irrelevant. For now the Lockean doctrine becomes this: your personal consent is essentially irrelevant to your obligation to obey, or its absence. Your obligation to obey depends on the character of the government—whether it is acting within the bounds of *the* (only possible) contract. If it is, and you are in its territory, you must obey. If it is not, then no amount of personal consent from you, no matter how explicit, can create an obligation to obey it. No matter how often you pledge allegiance to a tyranny, those pledges *cannot* constitute a valid obligation, because they violate the law of nature. So, not only is your personal consent irrelevant, but it actually no longer matters whether this government or any government was really founded by a group of men deciding to leave the state of nature by means of a contract. As long as a government's actions are within the bounds of what such a contract hypothetically *would have* provided, would have *had* to provide, those living within its territory must obey. This is the true significance of what we have all learned to say in political theory: that the historical accuracy of the contract doctrine is basically irrelevant—that the contract is a logical construct. The only "consent" that is relevant is the hypothetical consent imputed to hypothetical, timeless, abstract, rational men.

III. TUSSMAN ON CONSENT

A more modern version of the story is told by Joseph Tussman in his excellent and provocative book, *Obligation and the Body Politic.* Tussman, too, seeks to found political obligation in the consent of the governed. Only on that basis, he maintains, is political obligation "distinguishable from captivity," for "obligations are, or even must be voluntarily assumed."[24] Tussman acknowledges the rarity of express consent except in the case of naturalized citizens who take an oath of citizenship. But, like Locke, he introduces a notion of tacit consent.

Unlike Locke's, however, Tussman's tacit consent does not include merely walking on a country's highway; he insists that even tacit consent must be "knowing," made with awareness of what one is doing and of its significance.[25] A great many different actions, done with awareness and intent, can constitute such tacit consent: pledging allegiance to the flag, voting in an election, and so on. But even this doctrine, as Tussman admits, produces only a relatively small number of persons who can be said to have consented. Reluctantly he accepts this conclusion, which he calls the notion of "shrinkage."

> If it is insisted that only those who have consented are members of the body politic then the body politic may shrink alarmingly. . . . [But] any description of a body politic, like the United States, would have to recognize that there are some, or many, "citizens" who could not be described as having consented. There is no point to resorting to fiction to conceal this fact.[26]

Thus it is Tussman's position that only those who have consented (perhaps tacitly, but knowingly) are truly members, and that these may be relatively small proportion of the population.[27] But, of course, he is not willing to conclude that only those few consenting members are bound to obey the laws and accept the actions of the government as authoritative. He takes it for granted that everyone must obey, is obligated to obey, ought to be punished for disobeying—even the man who has never given government or obligation a single thought. Tussman allows for the possibility of withdrawal, emigration, as an express refusal to consent; but (as with Locke) there is no such thing as tacit dissent. The clods who merely live in a country without ever being sufficiently aware of public life to consent even tacitly, are not members of the body politic, but they are nevertheless bound to obey the law. The clods are obligated, Tussman says, like children. "Non-consenting-adult citizens are, in effect, like minors who are governed without their own consent. The period of tutelage and dependence is unduly prolonged."[28]

The interesting thing is that this doctrine does not seem to bother Tussman; he sees no inconsistency in it. He is not disturbed by saying on the one hand that membership in a body politic can only be distinguished from mere captivity if it is voluntary, and on the other hand that large masses of people must obey though they have not consented and are consequently not members. He does not seem to be bothered by saying that great masses of adults are obligated like children; he does not discuss why or how children are obligated, how their obligation—let alone its continuation into adult life—can be *justified*. To be sure, he obviously regrets the state of affairs that makes so large a proportion of our population clods who are not truly members. In a sense his whole book is written to advocate a more adequate system of political education, which would make more people aware of morality and public life, so that they would truly consent.

This is his ideal; but we have a right to ask what happens in the meantime, and how satisfactorily Tussman's account explains political obligation in the meantime. And when we do, we have the same feeling of betrayal as with Locke: why all the liberal protestations at the outset about the need for voluntary consent, if the net result in the end is that everyone has to obey anyway? In Locke the betrayal seems to center in the way he stretches the notion of tacit consent; Tussman avoids this, but instead introduces a second, childlike kind of obligation.

Now, there are good reasons why Tussman's argument proceeds as it does, why he does not seem to see these difficulties. For, although his book purports to be about obligation (as the title indeed indicates) the primary thrust of its argument, the question Tussman really seems to have asked himself, is about *membership* in a body politic. He takes it for granted that exploring the nature of membership will also produce answers about political obligation. At the outset of the book, confronting the question of what membership in a body politic is like, Tussman suggests three alternative possibilities: that membership be construed as subordination to a single coercive power; or as sharing in a common set of habits or customs; or as being party to (consenting to) a system of agreements on the model of a voluntary association. Given these three alternatives, he opts for the last one, because only if membership rests on consent can it be related to concepts like legitimacy and obligation. " 'I have a duty to . . .' seems to follow from 'I have agreed to' in a way that it does not follow from 'I am forced to' or 'I am in the habit of.' "[29]

In terms of our classification, Tussman directs his inquiry at question three, the difference between legitimate authority and coercive power. As an answer to that question, as an account of membership, his theory surely is very compelling. Confronted with unaware, nonconsenting clods, it seems reasonable then to say that not everyone is truly a member; that no body politic is entirely legitimate, based on the consent of every single subject; that political education might make our nation a better, truer political association in the future. But approached from our question four, for instance, the theory seems arbitrary and inadequate. If "obligations are, or even must be voluntarily assumed," then how can one consistently maintain that children or the nonconsenting clods are obligated to obey the law? How is their situation different from captivity, and how can it be justified? Tussman is not interested in our question four. Or perhaps that statement is not strong enough; he refuses to consider the question, because he regards it as "a symptom of moral disorder."[30]

Tussman is right to be suspicious of the question; there is something strange about it, as we shall later see. But it is a symptom less of moral disorder than of philosophical disorder; and it needs to be considered, not rejected. For although Tussman explicitly rejects the question, he is already profoundly committed to one particular answer to it: that only consent can justify obligation, distinguish it from captivity. And this commitment conflicts with his treatment of the clods in society. As a result, Tussman's theory also has difficulties with our questions one and two, concerning the limits and location of authority.

For Tussman wants to maintain that all persons in a country—consenting members and clods alike—are obligated to obey law and government, *except when occasions for revolution arise.* He recognizes that there are occasions and situations when revolution is justified, that there is a right of revolution. He talks about the need to "exhaust the remedies" available within a system, about what happens when there are only "corrupt tribunals" left to appeal to; and he says "where government is based on force, forceful opposition needs no special permit."[31] Thus we may legitimately ask him, *who* has the right to revolt when the occasion for revolution arises. The members presumably do. Surely they never consented to tyranny, and a tyrannical government is acting *ultra vires,* beyond any consent they have given. But surely, too, the clods, who have never consented, ought also to be morally free to resist a "government" that has become a tyranny. Though they may ordinarily be obligated to obey as children are, yet surely Tussman cannot mean that they continue to be obligated no matter what the government does or how it degenerates. Surely a clod who suddenly awakens to moral awareness under a Hitler government is right to resist it.

But why, when, how does their childlike obligation come to an end? Tussman does not tell us, because he does not consider the question. He seems, thus, to be saying: you are obligated to obey a government that is legitimate authority, *whether you personally consented to it or not.* If you have consented, you are obligated as a member; if not, as a child. In either case your obligation ends if the government abuses its power or ceases to be a legitimate authority. And what defines a legitimate authority? Why, consent, of course. Then we are all of us obligated to obey a government based on our consent, whether or not we have consented to it.

Though he never makes it explicit, the position that Tussman really seems to want to take is that we are all obligated to obey a government based on the consent *of the aware elite,* the true members, whether or not we ourselves have consented. A government is legitimate when those who are aware consent to it, and it then becomes legitimate for *all* its subjects; a government is tyrannical if it lacks this consent of the aware ones, or oversteps the limits of it. And then *all* its former subjects are released from their obligation. Some evidence for the contention that this is what Tussman means to say may be drawn from his treatment of the child's obligation. For he says "Non-consenting adult citizens are, in effect, like minors who are governed without *their own* consent."[32]

But again Tussman fails to tell us who does consent for minors, how and why the consent of some can legitimately be taken to bind others. Thus saying that the aware few consent for the rest is by no means a satisfactory answer, but from it I believe a more satisfactory answer can be reached by one further step. We must ask Tussman whether the aware few *could conceivably* consent to a tyranny, whether such consent would *count,* would be binding on them or the clods. I think clearly Tussman would want to say no, that such an action would not be a genuine consent, that an attempt to consent to tyranny does not create valid obligation either for the aware few or for the many clods for whom they are said to act. Thus a different doctrine begins to emerge between the lines of Tussman's book, as it did with Locke. It is not so much your consent nor even the consent of a majority of the aware few in your society that obligates you. You do not consent to be obligated, but rather are obligated to consent, if the government is just. Your obligation has something to do with the objective characteristics of the government—whether, for example, its "tribunals" are or are not "corrupt." Again the relevant consent seems to be best interpreted as hypothetical or constructive—the abstract consent that would be given by rational men. Like Locke, Tussman can be pushed back to this position: you are obligated neither by your own consent nor by that of the majority, but by the consent rational men in a hypothetical "state of nature" would have to give. A government acting within the bounds of such a hypothetical consent is legitimate and we are all obligated to obey it. A government systematically violating those limits is tyrannical, and we are free to resist it.

Both Locke's and Tussman's argument, then lead us to a somewhat surprising new doctrine: that your obligation to obey depends not on any special relationship (consent) between you and your government, but on the nature of that government itself. If it is a good, just government doing what a government should, then you must obey it; if it is a tyrannical, unjust government trying to do what no government should, then you have no such obligation. In one sense this "nature of the government" theory is thus a substitute for the doctrine of consent. But it may also be regarded as a new interpretation of consent theory, what we may call the doctrine of *hypothetical* consent. For a legitimate government, a true authority, one whose subjects are obligated to obey it, emerges as being one to which they *ought to consent*,[33] quite apart from whether they have done so. Legitimate government acts within the limits of the authority rational men would, abstractly and hypothetically, have to give a government they are founding. Legitimate government is government which *deserves* consent.

I do not mean to suggest that the "nature of the government" theory which thus emerges is really Locke's and Tussman's secret doctrine, which they hide from the casual reader and which has only now been unearthed. Probably neither of them saw that his argument was moving in this direction. Rather I suggest that this theory is a better response to the problem of political obligation from their own premises—that it is the truth toward which they were striving, but which they saw only indistinctly. Only in that sense is it "what they really meant to say," and of course both of them also say other things incompatible with it.

NOTES

1. No doubt the problem encompasses more than these four questions, and could be divided up in a number of different ways. Indeed, some aspects of it not covered by these four questions will emerge in the course of this discussion.

2. S. I. Benn and R. S. Peters, *Social Principles and the Democratic State* (London, George Allen & Unwin, 1959), pp. 299–300.

3. Joseph Tussman, *Obligation and the Body Politic* (New York, Oxford University Press, 1960), p. 12.

4. Jean-Jacques Rousseau, *The Social Contract*, in Sir Ernest Barker, ed., *The Social Contract* (New York, Oxford, 1960), Bk. I, iii.

5. Jeremy Bentham, *Fragment on Government*, ch. IV, par. 21.

6. Peter Laslett, ed., *John Locke, Two Treatises of Government* (Cambridge University Press, 1960) p. 155.

7. For a discussion of the evidence on when the *Treatises* were written, see *ibid.*, Introduction, esp. part III.

8. John Locke, *Second Treatise of Civil Government*, in Barker, *op. cit.*, par. 176.

9. *Ibid.*, pars. 132, 149, 199, 211.

10. For example, *ibid.*, par. 171: "political power" is spoken of as that power which every man has "in the state of Nature given up into the hands of the society, and therein to the governors whom the society hath set over it self...."

11. *Ibid.*, par. 116.

12. *Ibid.*, and also par. 73.

13. *Ibid.*, par. 119.

14. "But since gold and silver, being little useful to the life of man, in proportion to food, raiment, and carriage, has its value only from the consent of men, whereof labour yet makes in great part the measure, it is plain that the consent of men have agreed to a disproportionate and unequal possession of the earth...." *Ibid.*, par. 50.

15. *Ibid.*, par. 119.

16. *Ibid.*, par. 121.

17. *Ibid.*, pars. 73, 119, 120.

18. *Ibid.*, par. 87.

19. *Ibid.*, par. 99.

20. *Ibid.*, par. 131, italics mine. See also pars. 90, 135, 137, 149, 164.

21. *Ibid.*, pars. 135, 23.

22. *Ibid.*, pars. 90, 168.

23. *Ibid.*, par. 135; see also par. 142.

24. *Op. cit.*, pp. 24, 8. I hope it is clear, in spite of all the criticisms I make of Tussman's argument, how greatly this essay is indebted to his work.

25. *Ibid.*, p. 36.

26. *Ibid.*, p. 37.

27. *Ibid.*, p. 127.

28. *Ibid.*, pp. 37, 39–41.

29. *Ibid.*, p. 8.

30. *Ibid.*, p. 29.

31. *Ibid.*, p. 44.

32. *Ibid.*, p. 37, italics mine.

33. *Cf.* Benn and Peters, *op. cit.*, pp. 323, 329.

MORAL DUTY, POLITICAL OBLIGATION, AND THE DOCTRINE OF CONSENT*

Philip Abbott

The search for the moral justification of political authority has always been one of the central concerns of political philosophy. Somehow an answer to the question "Why should I obey the state?" which relies on prudence has always seemed unsatisfactory. Political philosophers (and rulers) have nearly always asked for more. (After all, it makes a good deal of difference to view resistance as immoral rather than as imprudent.) Theories of justice, utility tradition, divine right, gratitude, and natural law represent attempts to apply moral principles to political relationships. They have a long and complicated history. But consent theory is a relatively new justification for political authority. The notion that political authority rests upon some identifiable and voluntary act of the citizenry emerged from the political conflicts of the seventeenth and eighteenth centuries. Consent theory became increasingly connected with democratic government. Moreover, its premises were more than congenial to a world which viewed man as autonomous and rational and politics as conventional and artificial.

The doctrine of consent is now firmly imbedded in our vocabulary of politics. It is difficult for us to imagine a government deserving obedience which does not rest upon consent. Robert Dahl conveys conventional political wisdom when he says:

> ... government without one's consent can be an affront to human dignity and respect. We see this most vividly in extreme cases—the hapless victim in a concentration camp, who is subjected to the utmost humiliation, degradation, depravation, and torture, loses thereby a part of his humanity.[1]

Yet despite their unchallenged position (or perhaps because of it) consent theorists have yet to present us with a clear analysis of political obligation. They have insisted that the basis of obedience to the state rests with consent but they have been far from clear in telling us precisely what consent is, how it creates moral duty and how consent to a government creates a moral obligation to obey that government. John Plamenatz has remarked that John Locke, the most famous of the consent theorists, begins with a concept of consent too rigorous to allow for any legitimate government and ends with a

---

I wish to express my thanks to Gordon Schochet, Michael Riccards, and Martin Kotch for helpful comments on an earlier version of this essay.

notion so loose that any government would be justified simply by having power to put down attempts at rebellion. In point of fact, this paper will contend that all consent theories exhibit this curious elasticity. They veer alternately, often in the same work, toward both a justification of anarchy and of absolutism. The broader purpose of this essay then will be to do for consent theorists what they have failed to do for themselves—to determine what we mean when we say "I consent," to analyze what we might call the "structural apparatus of consent" (how consent obliges, how far it obliges and why it obliges), and to examine how we might determine what counts as consent to a government and how far that consent obliges one to obey a government.

Consent theorists are not a homogeneous lot. They offer readers numerous interpretations of what consent is, how it works, and how far it obliges. This would not be an insuperable problem if we were able to find a consistent and clear line of development within any particular consent theory. Unfortunately, this is a benefit we are rarely permitted to enjoy. Yet, it may be possible to outline various positions on consent and its relation to moral duty and political obligation. We will find that some consent theorists hold to more than one position despite the fact that the views on consent in each may well be mutually exclusive.

1. CONSENT AS APPROVAL: STRONG AND WEAK VERSIONS

This position sees consent as an expression of approval or recognition. There is some disagreement, however, over what should be taken as constituting recognition or approval. A strong version of this theory contends that approval is dependent either upon the existence of certain political institutions or, at least, upon individual judgments about the direction of government.

This is clearly the position taken by Hanna Pitkin in her recent attempt to relate anew consent and political obligation.[2] She contends that to consent is to "recognize (government) as an authority" but that traditional consent theory is defective:

> ... it directs a man's attention to the wrong place. It teaches him to look at himself (for his own consent) or at the people around him (for theirs), rather than at the merits of the government.[3]

Her doctrine, which she calls "hypothetical consent," contends that obligation depends not on whether you have consented but on whether the government is such that you ought to consent to it:

> ... your obligation depends not on any actual act of consenting, past or present, by yourself or your fellow citizens, but on the character of your government. If it is a good, just government doing what a government should, then you must obey it, if it is a tyrannical unjust government trying to do what no government may, then you have no such obligation.[4]

The second and weaker version of this position contains a much broader conception of approval in that acquiescence is regarded as evidence of consent. John Locke employs this version in at least two instances in his *Second Treatise*. First, he uses this position to justify inequality in property ownership:

> But since gold and silver, being little useful to the Life of Man in proportion to Food, Rayment and Carriage, has its value only from the consent of men, whereof Labour yet makes, in great part, the measure, it is plain, that Men have agreed to disproportionate and unequal possession of the Earth, they having by a tacit and voluntary consent found out a way, how a man may fairly possess more land than he himself can use the product of, by receiving in exchange for the overplus, gold and silver . . .[5]

Yet one is not in a position to ask "When did I consent?" to a coin exchange. Locke merely tells us that "Fancy or Agreement" led men to place value upon them.[6] Men simply do recognize money as exchange and Locke is willing to count this recognition as consent. Lest one fail to see the significance of the consequences of this application of consent, let him note Locke's position on labor relations. While Locke insists that a master may not take away a servant's life or "at pleasure, so much as maim him but the loss of an Eye or Tooth," a contract of "Drudgery" is clearly obligatory as is "the Subjection of the Needy Beggar . . . who preferred being his [Master's] subject to starving."[7]

Locke's use of consent to justify political authority is well known: "no one can be . . . subjected to the Political Power of another without his own consent." Yet when Locke asks "What shall be understood to be a sufficient Declaration of a Man's Consent, to make him subject to the laws of any government?"[8] he arrives at two distinct positions on consent. For those who "by actual Agreement, and . . . express Declaration" give their consent, Locke outlines a theory of consent which will be discussed in a moment. For those who have made "no Expressions of it at all," Locke offers a theory of tacit consent. One has consented (and is thereby obligated) if he owns property or even is "largely travelling freely on the Highway."[9] Locke even admits that tacit consent "reaches as far as the very being of any one within the Territories of that Government."[10]

Now this does indeed appear to be a strange doctrine. It asserts, in effect, that one is obligated because he consented or because, even though he didn't actually consent, he is obligated because he exists. This seems a far cry from the stringent individualism with which Locke is associated. What, after all does it mean to say that consent must be individually given and then to say that the mere occupation of space counts as consent? Thus John Plamenatz in his classic work on consent irately concludes "to live under the protection of a certain government does not constitute consent to the existence of that government. . . . It does not impose upon the protected person an obligation to obey them."[11] The point, however, is this:

precisely how does Locke's concept of tacit consent attempt to answer the question "Why should I obey the state?". Plamenatz is quite right in saying that living under the protection of a certain government does not constitute consent to the existence of that government nor an obligation to it. Living within a state does not presuppose the recognition of obligation to that government. It does, however, still permit one to ask the question "Why obey the law?" and possibly respond by saying that in lieu of continuing to enjoy certain privileges I will consent to obey what it commands. But it can easily work the other way also. Enjoying an estate and enjoying the use of a highway or even enjoying fresh air are very different privileges. The person benefiting from the latter may well see fit to answer that the continuation of breathing fresh air within a given territory is simply not worth consenting to this law. In any case, before this question is asked, and indeed answered in a certain way, consent has not been given. Ironically Locke's error lay in failing to distinguish the act of consent from the reasons which might move one to consent. The latter (what Locke called tacit consent) is not consent at all, but only a preliminary consideration to the question, "Why should I obey the law?". Locke clearly jumped the gun. He loaded the question by placing it within the consent apparatus.[12]

There are others, however, both within and outside academic circles who appear to accept this Lockean position without reservation.[13] I should like to speak of only one particular writer in this context—Joseph Tussman in his *Obligation and the Body Politic.*[14] Professor Tussman's book is ideal for our purpose since it sets out to systematically advance this position where others only treat it with a passing reference.

Professor Tussman begins with much the same purpose in mind as we have suggested. If we are to be able to account for political obligation in moral terms, then, given the fact that the notion of the state deprives each of us of a right to a whole range of actions we must offer an account that sees the individual's relation to the state as voluntary. This is Professor Tussman's point as well. The "body politic" may be seen in a variety of ways: (1) as a membership subordinate to a single coercive power; (2) as a membership sharing in a common set of habits; (3) as a membership party to a system of agreements on the model of a voluntary association.[15] Only in the last case can we speak of a relationship in which "I have a moral obligation" can apply. Professor Tussman proceeds to ask a crucial question: "Are we satisfied with the answer that accepting this subordination (of private judgment to public judgment) is what 'being moral' or 'being a good citizen' really means?"[16] The answer, for Mr. Tussman at least, lay in terms of series of decidedly naturalistic justifications. The voluntary character of membership in a body politic involves:

1. Some justification for the subordination in the light of the interests and purposes of the individual.
2. recognition of some *common* or shared concern

3. some recognition that one's own interests constitute only a subordinate part of a broader system of interests.[17]

Thus far our summary of Professor Tussman's position does not sound terribly unlike the "strong" interpretation of consent which we had noted earlier. Consent is conceived as recognition and recognition varies from approval of the character of a particular government to approval of the need for government. In fact, the above description of the "body politic" could be readily acceptable to a philosophical anarchist. But it is at this point that Tussman's position begins to show itself as a very loose conception of consent indeed and in addition (and more importantly for our purposes) begins to show how elusive is the concept of consent itself. The nature of obligation to the state is compared to the decision-making apparatus of a caucus:

It is generally assumed or expected that the caucus decision will not be unanimous; for if unanimity is required the caucus agreement is pointless. It is precisely the failure of unanimity which makes the caucus necessary. There is thus both a presupposition of unanimity and a deliberate repetition of the demand for unanimity. The sense in which unanimity is presupposed is the sense in which everyone who is a member is a party to the agreement. But the unanimous agreement is to the bindingness of subsequent non-unanimous decisions and, in this form, to the subordination of individual judgment to group judgment and decision.[18]

Professor Tussman concludes that "considering this it is hardly surprising that the agreement to waive unanimity should come to be regarded as *the* social compact."[19] These statements are indeed the core of all traditional consent theory and we should not be surprised if it is at this point that we find a Spaniard in the works.

Since Tussman is attempting to use consent as a vehicle for a theory of moral obligation to the state, he must convince us that the decision to agree unanimously to future nonunanimous decision-making is voluntary. But he then places himself in the position of having to contend that such a set of decisions actually do or did take place. It will not do for him to say that there are such things as moral obligations to the state and that they are derived from individual voluntary acts of recognition or agreement with the state but that these acts in fact never really took place. We simply cannot say that they could or can take place because until they have there is no consent and thus, on these terms, no moral obligation. Hypothetical reasoning, although it has many valid uses in terms of other moral concepts, cannot be used as a basis for *establishing* consent. While it is true that we can say that there can be no moral obligations to the state until one consents we must reserve our evaluation of whether such obligations exist until we actually decide if anyone has consented. To say that in any political system people should or would consent and thus have a moral obligation to the state is really to base moral obligation to the state upon an apparatus other than consent, simply because consent (by one's own admission) has not been given.

It is now easy to see why Professor Pitkin's reformulation of consent is really no longer consent at all. To say that if a government is good then you must obey it is completely irrelevant to consent.[20] Tussman, however, does not give up so easily. He sets out to do what consent theory has always said it could do—establish how the body politic actually does consent. Once we see how this is done we shall find that consent, even on Mr. Tussman's own terms becomes irrelevant to obligation, though in a very different way than Miss Pitkin's does.

Right on cue, Professor Tussman notes "the assertion that the citizen of a body politic is a party to a system of agreements inevitably evokes the surprised response—'when did I agree to any such thing?' "[21] Like so many consent theorists Tussman notes instances which indicate that consent has taken place: the creation of a new body politic by explicit agreement (the promulgation and ratification of the U.S. Constitution, the creation of the United Nations) and the naturalization of citizens. But then comes the rub. Tussman admits "We fall back . . . upon the familiar notion of tacit consent." The difference between tacit and express consent is not the difference between two kinds of consent. It is only the difference in the way consent is given:

Not only may there be other verbal acts which can be interpreted as the giving of consent, but there may be non-verbal acts which have the same force. So that the question of tacit consent is the question of whether there are some actions, including perhaps, the failure to act, which can properly be regarded as the equivalent of the express consent given by the naturalized citizen.[22]

Yet Professor Tussman hesitates at a most crucial juncture. He refuses to tell us what acts may be taken as tacit consent: "It is not profitable . . . to argue abstractly about the acts which can be taken as a sign that one has become a party to the system of agreements constituting a body politic."[23] The only condition for tacit consent that he will give us is that it must be done "knowingly." Consent and subsequent obligation do not revolve about particular institutions or practices and one's participation in them. Saluting the flag, registering for conscription, voting, filing one's income for taxes or even using a zip code on mail could all be taken as instances of consent if the citizen by performing these acts understands that he has incurred obligations to the state. Consent then is a radically individual personal action. One could do all the above things and simply not conceive them as consent. But even here a note of skepticism seeps in:

But we must accept it as a plain fact that many native 'citizens' have in no meaningful sense agreed to anything. They have never been asked and have never thought about it. They are political childbrides who have a status they do not understand and which they have not acquired by their own consent.[24]

There is by Tussman's own admission, a "shrinkage" in the body politic. The solution Tussman offers to this "shrinkage" is the only one available to him if he wishes to retain consent as a basis of moral obligation to the state. But it is also one, which on examination, ultimately wreaks havoc with the concept of consent:

> Non-consenting adult citizens are, in effect, like minors who are governed without their own consent. The period of tutelage and dependence is unduly prolonged.[25]

Mr. Tussman's theory is complete. When is one obligated to obey and when not? One is obligated when he consents, tacitly or expressly. If one does not give his consent he is obligated as a child. Whom is one obligated to obey? He is obligated to obey the legitimate authority presiding over the body politic. The legitimate authority is that government to which one has consented or refused to consent. The paradox is painfully clear. One either consents, or if he fails to consent, is placed under a moral tutelage until he does. In which case the absence of consent "as a failure of political education" exists in any political system. Or consent is somehow unrelated to obligations to the state since one is obligated whether he consents or does not.

Part of both Tussman's and Pitkin's problems with offering a viable account of consent lay in their failure to systematically evaluate the whole apparatus of consent, i.e., to ask what really does it mean to consent? We shall ask this question for ourselves shortly. But another part of their problem lay in choosing an inappropriate definition of consent. Our next task then is to look at two positions which see consent not as approval or recognition but as a far different sort of operation.

2. CONSENT AS PERMISSION—I

We are now about to begin upon a road toward the reconstruction of the concept of consent and again we will find that ironically John Locke can lead the way for us. The reader will recall that according to Locke, men in the State of Nature, are in a "state of perfect Freedom to order their Actions, and dispose of their Possessions and Persons as they think fit, within the bounds of the Law of Nature, without asking leave, or depending upon the Will of any other Man."[26] The only way this condition can be altered is through the act of consent:

> Men being, as has been said by Nature, all free, equal and independent, no one can be put out of his Estate, and subjected to the Political Power of another, without his own Consent. The only way whereby anyone divests himself of his Natural Liberty, and puts on the bounds of Civil Society is by agreeing with other Men to join and unite into a Community . . .[27]

Men born under existing government become obliged only when by some explicit act they give permission to a government:

And thus the Consent of Free-men, born under Government, which only makes them Members of it, being given separately in their turns, as each comes to be of Age, and not in a multitude together . . .[28]

Merely living under the jurisdiction of government may oblige one to the extent that one recognizes that others (by Locke's definition, members of Civil Society) have consented to it but such an obligation to submit to the government "begins and ends with the Enjoyment."[29] Nothing can make a man a subject or member of civil society save "his actually entering into it by positive Engagement, and express Promise and Compact."[30]

In the position on consent which we had previously stated, we indicated that in its strong version, consent was interpreted so exactingly that not only could no government live up to it but that the concept really involved no "consenting" at all. The weak version erred on the opposite side. It became impossible to envisage any subject-ruler relationship that could not be interpreted as being based upon consent. This part of Locke's formulation appears to avoid both these pitfalls. It does so, I think, because it incorporates certain basic features which the previous theories failed to realize. First, Locke, at least in this instance, does not treat the act of consent as an act of approval or as an act of recognition or agreement. Consent becomes an act of permission. We can safely call it such because Locke tells us that there are certain actions which the state may now undertake, especially in terms of the regulation of property, which it could not have previously legitimately undertaken. I may approve of state actions but the right of the state to pursue certain objectives as they relate to me is irrelevant to my approval. I may, be action or word, recognize the existence of the state but that recognition is independent of an act of permission. This is a very important distinction and Locke's concepts of express and tacit consent and his insistence that they oblige differently account for this (albeit, in a very oblique way).

The distinction between approval or recognition is so crucial to the concept of consent and to political theory in general that it is necessary at this point to expend some effort at clarification. Let me begin by using a very simple illustration. A friend takes my television set without my knowledge. Missing the set, I call him and ask him if he knows where it is. He tells me that he took it to repair it and in fact, that now it is in perfect working order. Faced with my consternation, he may ask "Didn't you want the set repaired? Aren't you glad it's fixed? Why are you so upset?" My reply might be that my pleasure with the set is not the point. The point is that no one had the right to take the set without my permission. Now we may contend that I am being unduly harsh with my friend. After all, his intentions were admirable, he is competent, and he does live just around the block. The intentions of the state, however, are not always as easily discernible, nor is its competence, nor are the individual's powers of retrieval as proximate. But we are getting a bit ahead of ourselves. We shall return to this question shortly.

Consent conceived as permission contains the same radical individualism as the weak version of the approval theory. The difference is that the language of permission forces us to consider the precise role that consent plays in terms of a transfer of moral rights. Heretofore the legitimacy of an action was related to my recognition of the rightness of the action or to my approval of its effects. Traditional consent theory then proceeds to limit this operation by placing consent in a particular time sequence in relation to the acts in question. One may explicitly recognize or approve of an action in time period T_1 and find that this recognition or approval binds him in T_2 for the same or even new actions. For example, Smith takes Jones' television set in order to repair it. Jones, even though he had no knowledge of Smith's action, recognizes and approves of it by accepting the set and saying "Thank you." Did Jones' recognition and approval bind him to loan his television set to Smith at any future time? Did it bind him to accept the television set if the second time it was returned it was damaged? How far, in short, does Jones' consent (as approval or recognition) to the first action bind him to submit to other actions (similar or dissimilar) in the future? Is Jones now bound to accept Smith's appropriation, temporary or permanent, of his dishwasher or his books or even his wife? At this point the reader might object. Surely Jones' original action bound him only to accept that particular set at that particular time or at most bound him to accept all of Smith's actions designed to meet Jones' wishes. Any more inclusive interpretation of Jones' consent, the reader might conclude, sounds ridiculous. Yet there are clear and substantial reasons why the larger interpretations of Jones' consent do indeed sound ridiculous. These reasons can be contained within a theory of consent. Yet they become muddled in traditional consent theory. How much different is it to say that men, by living in a particular society, thereby consent to that society's medium of economic exchange or to say that men by agreeing to be bound to the decisions of a caucus are henceforth bound to subsequent decisions of that body or to say that in voting one is thereby bound to accept the commands of the winner is it to say that Jones by consenting to Smith's appropriation of his television set is bound to accept Smith's appropriation of his wife?

The reason that the approval theory of consent fails to account for these questions is because its approach does not lead one to consider the relation between the act of consent and moral duty. Our discussion indicated two crucial questions about consent and moral duty: How far (both in terms of time and scope of action) does consent bind? Does consent rise from a nexus between an expression of desire or a wish and its fulfillment on the part of another? Traditional consent theory always answers yes to the second question and then always denies the relation between wish and fulfillment in later actions. Consent is born from a favorable conjunction of approval and fulfillment, but like Frankenstein's monster, it lives on long after that conjunction has dissipated. The reader will remember that we had said that the consent apparatus is a structure which enables obligations to occur within the context of the suspension of moral judgment. Therefore within the confines of a consent apparatus it is not a genuine argument to contend that "because you agreed" as an answer to the question "Why am I obligated?" is misplaced and should rather be "because it is right." The whole purpose of the consent apparatus is to shift the answer to "Why am I obligated?" away from the considerations of moral judgment. The failure of the approval theory of consent, however, is that it is unable to account for a plausible relationship with moral duty.

Both the approval and permission theories of consent focus upon the features and circumstances surrounding the original actions of the parties. In approval theory one asks did I "agree or approve" of the action in question in order to find what is a morally correct course of action? The permission theory asks did I give "permission" to the action in question? The difference is crucial to a plausible account of consent. In the former case, one's duty is determined by his actions or words in relation to another party. He either agreed to Smith's actions, or wished Smith would have done a particular action or he approved of Smith's action. These attitudes indicate how far he is bound to Smith's action. Nothing is said about how consent obliges apart from the notion that the conjunction between agreement, approval or wish and its fulfillment obliges. It sounds nonsensical for me to say that I have consented to my neighbor's mowing of his lawn because I agree or approve or wish that he would do so. Yet many accept without so much as a blink of an eyelash the assertion that because I approve of the President's policies or wish he would take a decision on an issue which he later does, I have consented to the policies or to the President or to both. I have approved of the policies but nowhere have I consented to them. The point that we are making is this: the approval theory of consent fails to make clear that the act of consent involves the transfer or creation of moral rights which could not otherwise exist. John Plamenatz has stated this position very succinctly: "The giving of consent is essentially the granting of permission, and there cannot be action by permission unless the right of the agent to act depends for its existence upon the granting of permission."[31] There are then all sorts of actions one might agree to. One may agree to have his daughter marry. Yet we cannot call this an act of consent until we are in a position to say that one's daughter could not, morally speaking, marry *without* her father's permission. The approval theory so neglects this aspect of consent that its pronouncements, at least in terms of political theory, often produce a "what's yours is mine and what's mine is mine" account of obligation.

There are a number of other features of the consent apparatus which must be discussed before we can safely say that we have provided an account of consent, but the permission theory, as indicated by Locke and as so clearly stated by Plamenatz, gives us our foundation. A theory of consent must apply to situations in which permission is necessary before an agent has the right to perform the action in question.

In summary then, the position regarding consent which we have just outlined is superior to both versions of the approval theory in that it emphasizes the significance of the act of consent in relation to the performance of specific actions. It does this by using language which emphasizes the enlargement of moral authority which takes place in a consenting act and by clarifying where moral rights lie before and after the act of consent. This interpretation of consent is particularly constraining when it is applied to political affairs and it should not surprise us to learn that few democratic theorists have been willing to accept it. For it contends in effect, that consent fails to provide for an adequate account of political obligation unless those holding office are unable to perform any action without the permission of the citizenry. Since even the most democratic political systems operate without this necessary qualification and only act as if they had met this prerequisite, one must reach the position that the rights of the governors exist independent of the consent of the governed or that the governors indeed have no rights at all. It is interesting to note that Locke, while using this notion of consent, never indicated how many of the governed had indeed expressly consented to the state and only assumed that they had when he later spoke of the justifications for revolt. John Plamenatz appears to be the only writer to have held this position and seen it to its logical conclusion.

We see then, that both under pure democracy and under representative democracy there is no such thing as government by the consent of all persons supposed to owe obedience to government. Under the very best possible conditions, so far as consent is concerned, it may be true that the rights of the governors depend upon the consent of a majority of governed, but never upon the consent of all persons who can rightly be said to be obliged to obey the law.[32]

3. CONSENT AS PERMISSION—II
There is, however, a third position on consent, one which continues to conceive of consent as permission but also is willing to count participation in, or the existence of, certain political practices as evidence of permission.[33] Here is a position which is so widely accepted in modern democratic theory that no one takes the trouble to attempt to justify it. One writer who has taken the trouble is, paradoxically, John Plamenatz. Professor Plamenatz in *Man and Society* and in his postscript to the second edition of *Consent, Freedom and Political Obligation* now admits that his "definition (of consent) was too narrow," that "where there is an established process of election to an office, then . . . anyone who takes part in the process consents to the authority of whoever is elected to the office."[34] His larger argument is contained below:

When you vote for a person or party that wins an election you directly consent to his or their authority, and you also consent indirectly to the system of government. Even when your vote is cast for persons who intend to change the system you consent until it is changed. For you make use of the system in order to change it . . . Even if you dislike the system and wish to change it, you put yourself by your vote under an obligation to obey whatever government comes legally to power under the system, and this can properly be called giving consent. For the purpose of an election is to give authority to the people who win it, and if you vote knowing what you are doing and without being compelled to do it, you voluntarily take part in the process which gives authority to those people. It does not matter what your motive is, any more than it matters what your motive is in making a promise.[35]

Plamenatz defends his correlation of voting with consent as one which makes "ordinary use of one of the most important terms in the political vocabulary."[36] Indeed, one of the most important points which is lost in this position is that consent belongs to a moral vocabulary and not a political one. But the reader has waited long enough for a systematic analysis of consent. The election position finally forces us to undertake such an analysis. For in order to judge whether voting establishes obligation via consent, we must ask how consent is precisely related to obligation. And since when one votes he is not consenting as such but in Plamenatz's words "can be said to consent," we must ask precisely what consent is with a view toward deciding how close voting is indeed to consenting.

We have already seen that a good deal of the confusion over consent theories of political obligation have been related to an inadequate examination of what consent really is. We will attempt to remedy this condition by analyzing what we might call the structural apparatus of consent. Statements in political thought such as "governments derive their just powers from the consent of the governed" or "political parties are the vehicles for consent in modern democracies" and phrases such as "express and tacit" consent and "direct and indirect" consent all depend upon a conception of the operation of consent for their intelligibility. Before, however, we are in a position to decide what counts as consent, if indeed anything can "count" as consent, we must discover both what it means to say "I consent" and what one actually *does* when he consents.

Consent has a number of features common to other sorts of apparatus which give rise to obligations. When one consents, as when one promises or contracts, he is engaged in some commitment to do, or forbear from, some future action. One simply cannot say "I promise to quit smoking last year" or "I contract with Jones to build a dam last month" just as one cannot say "I consent to your marriage last week." The past tenses of "promise," "contract," or "consent" are used solely to explain or justify one's present obligations. To say "You promised" or "You consented" is a way of saying your time is up; the pay-off is the performance of an obligation incurred in a previous time period. Promising, consenting and contracting are future-oriented acts when they take place. It is the obligations they incur which are explained in terms of past actions. Consenting also is a relational term. One consents to someone else, just as one promises someone else or contracts with someone else. While we do have a grammar which allows for an internal dialogue using these terms, such as "I promise myself" or "I have permitted myself (a piece of cake)," it is not altogether clear that it has any significance for moral philosophy.

Unlike contracting, however, consent, in terms of the obligations incurred, does not involve reciprocal relationships. If the reader will recall social contract theory, he will note that for Hobbes the agreement between "every man with every man" involves obligations on the part of all parties:

I Authorize and give up my Right of Governing myself, to this Man, or to this Assembly of men, on this condition, that thou give up thy Right to him, and Authorize all his in like manner.[37]

When an agent consents, however, he limits his actions while the recipient actually has his enlarged. When a father, for instance, consents to the marriage of his daughter, he incurs certain obligations. He not only must refrain from disrupting the ceremony, he must refrain from ordering his daughter about henceforth. The prospective husband, on the other hand, incurs no obligations, at least in terms of consent. On the contrary, he now has the *right* to perform actions otherwise unavailable to him. If I consent to have my television fixed, I incur obligations which arise from its repair. These may even include an obligation to pay for repairs I had not anticipated. The repairman, on the other hand, now has a right to repair my set. Again, he incurs no obligations toward me as a recipient of my consent. The point of all this is simply that both parties in a consenting act assume new moral roles. The agent is placed in a passive and obligatory role, while the recipient takes on an active (in the sense that the future action in question is his to "do") and claimant role.[38]

The consenting act then is a nonreciprocal one. The agent does not get something in return by consenting. Although he may have reciprocity in mind when he consents, the consenting act itself makes no demands in terms of mutual performance of action. It is certainly possible for one to say that he will consent to x, if the recipient consents to do y. But then we have two consenting acts being proposed here. This relationship is quite different from a contractual arrangement in that mutual obligation is part of the act in question. The contract's relation to moral duty, of course, need not necessarily prove to be any more clear-cut. One may have second thoughts about the moral correctness of the contract or he may find that the performance of the obligation of a contract violates obligations he has subsequently incurred toward others. Nevertheless, when one consents the demand for reciprocity as a payment for obligations is not a relevant argument.

The unique structural features of consent, its nonreciprocity and the unequal demands placed upon consenting parties and the incurring of obligations to action in the future, may damage its connection with moral duty when applied to the affairs of state. That is to say, these features of consent when applied to a context in which the agent is the citizen and the recipient the state may drastically accentuate the inequality of services and obligations which are already part of its structure. While consent theory has the merit of indicating that a government must somehow depend upon the governed for one to speak of obligations, the very apparatus which is employed to convey this position may work in the other direction. When one gives his consent to another person, we have seen that he has constricted his own moral autonomy. He has, in fact, transferred that autonomy to the recipient of his consent. When the recipient is the state, the individual's ability to retrieve or define his consent is limited in a way uncommon to personal relationships. The limitation is not merely the result of an existing system of legal sanctions in the hands of one of the parties to the consenting act. It is also limited by the resources available to the state as it defines its role as recipient of an obligation. Officials of the state are in a position to speak over the head of the agent to the whole citizenry. A citizenry cannot be expected to be disposed to readily accept the claims of an individual agent under the conditions of such an unequal forum. Should an agent ally himself with other like-minded agents to press their case, the state again is in a position to define what it considers the group claims to be. These are rarely placed in a favorable light. The point we must remember is that when the agent of consent, either an individual or a group, claims that permission was not granted on a policy of the government, the position of the state is such that it can effectively appeal to the rest of the citizenry by defining the contest of claims in its own terms. When the government speaks its voice is heard by more people and with more plausibility. This presents a significant problem in the application of the doctrine of consent to political theory. Democratic theory, in particular, attempts to save the doctrine by emphasizing the role of elections and the right to organize opposition. The election certainly may make the agents' task of withdrawing consent easier. Most of us would agree that the job of electing another person or party to office is a bit easier than engaging in successful revolution. Nevertheless, if elections are to be justified as a practice which affords the agent an opportunity to withdraw his consent from a government, the very participation in an election cannot also be made to count as consent. That is, a political system which affords its citizens the opportunity to change a government and/or its policies, does not necessarily mean that system is based upon consent. It may be true that free elections are necessary for one to be able to speak of government by consent in the sense that elections hold out the possibility for the agent to openly contest the claims of the state as recipient. But then the practice of elections in itself is not an act of consent. If it were, a citizen could not withdraw permission except by not voting. If he participates in the election process at all he is consenting. The practice of elections then does not contain the option of withdrawing consent. This interpretation shows its basic absurdity if we ask: what can a citizen do if he wishes to withhold or withdraw his consent to the government? He cannot vote for any opposition because the act of voting commits him to consent to the winner. Now if the incumbent's chances of success are greater than the insurgent's and if the citizen refuses to give consent to the incumbent, our advice to him is not to vote at all. This strategy hardly affords a justification of elections for democracies. The more intense the opposition to the incumbent, the more likely are the chances of an incumbent victory. Any voter who may feel intensely about the current government had best not vote at all.

Voting is only an activity to be undertaken when one is quite willing to see either party win or only has a slight preference for one over the other. In that case, elections remain a basis for consent but they hardly provide the role for which they are intended. They can no longer be a vehicle of change or opposition. Ironically, we find that if we insist that voting is consent, then opposition to a government becomes fundamentally the same sort of opposition that a citizen must undertake in an authoritarian state, extra-legal action. Our only other alternative is to contend that elections are relevant to consent in the sense that they provide the equivalent in politics of what we would call rational argument in moral disputes. That is, the election is a way in which the citizen as agent can "talk" to the government as recipient. But the consenting act itself must have occurred outside the structure of elections. Clearly voting is not the same as talking in many respects, the most significant of which is that in voting one has actually made a decision rather than merely talk about it. But then the fact that we allow the citizen to say only "no" or "yes" to the state is the price we must pay if we choose to rest political obligation upon consent.

We have yet one more question to answer, however, before we can ask if the price we must pay for consent is indeed too high. What precisely is the relationship between consent and moral duty? How far does consent oblige? We have just completed an examination of the structure of the consenting act. What we are about to do now is ask how far consent goes toward explaining one's moral duty. There are, I think, three important requirements that must be met for consent to give rise to obligation on the part of both the agent and recipient:

1. The recipient must receive some right which he would not be morally justified in asserting without the consent of the agent.
2. An agent must have existing moral authority over an object to give his consent to some use of it. One cannot consent to have another's property sold simply because it is not his to consent to.
3. Consent does not mean that standards of rightness become irrelevant to doing one's duty. The agent in a consenting act is not limited to consideration of whether he gave permission to the act in question. Although consent is an apparatus designed to eliminate contingency between moral agents, it may sometimes be necessary for an agent to ask questions other than "did I consent?" in determining duty. Returning a gun to whom one has subsequently learned is a psychopath, is not doing one's duty.

The reader can see that consent gives rise to moral duty only under certain circumstances: when an agent possessed moral rights, when a recipient can acquire those rights only by permission and when obligations assumed take place within the boundaries of moral rightness. Consent is irrelevant to moral duty when an agent has an obligation to perform an act simply because he (morally) ought to do so. Only certain classes of actions require permission to make them (morally) right for the recipient to do. Democratic theory has assumed the burden of contending that all obligations of the citizenry and all rights of the government are the result of consenting acts.[39] Nevertheless, it remains clear that consent explains moral duty only under certain circumstances. One can indeed ask, why should I consent to x, when I am already obliged because to do x is right? Consent is even more circumscribed when we consider that granting permission cannot be the final answer in the determination of moral duty. When Locke contended that men could give their consent to slavery, he was saying that giving permission cannot explain certain obligations. When one asserts that voting is consent he fails to take into account the objects of consent. Consent indeed is a procedure. But it is a procedure which gives rise to substantive obligations. The question "was I right to consent?" is a secondary question but it is a question which may need to be answered nonetheless. When it is, one must ask "what did I consent to?" with a view toward assessing the obligations he has incurred. If I have no obligation to respect my daughter's marriage to a psychopath even though I consented, then I have no obligation to obey a prime minister who makes a set of morally disastrous decisions even though I voted for him. Refusing to perform obligations incurred by consent is a solemn act but it may certainly be consistent with doing one's duty.

We are forced to conclude that while it is a relevant question to ask "what right have you to do x, I never consented?", the particular relationship between consent and moral duty, the inability to find practices which can "count" as consent in political systems, and the very structure of consent itself make it a very unlikely basis for an answer to "why should I obey the state?"

NOTES

1. Robert Dahl, *Pluralist Democracy in the United States: Conflict and Consent* (Chicago: Rand McNally, 1967), p. 15.
2. Hanna Pitkin, "Obligation and Consent - I & II", *American Political Science Review* LX (December, 1965), pp. 990–999, LXI (March, 1966), 39–52. The doctrine of "hypothetical consent" is also held by C.W. Cassinelli although his interpretation is closer to the weak version of this form of consent theory, not terribly unlike Locke's notion of tacit consent mentioned below. "The Consent of the Governed" *Western Political Quarterly* XII (1959), pp. 391–409.
3. Pitkin, "Obligation & Consent - II," pp. 39–40.
4. *Ibid.*, p. 40.
5. John Locke, *Two Treatises of Government,* Peter Laslett, ed., (New York: Mentor, 1965), II, 50, pp. 343–44; see also: II, 47, 343. Yet when he deals with the origin of government Locke rejects the argument that historical acquiescence provides the basis for normative theory. II, 103, pp. 379–380.
6. *Ibid.,* II, 46, p. 342.
7. *Ibid.,* II, 24, p. 326; I, 43, 206.
8. *Ibid.,* II, 119, p. 392.

9. *Ibid.*
10. *Ibid.*
11. John Plamenatz, *Consent, Freedom and Political Obligation,* rev. ed. (London: Oxford University Press, 1968), p. 24.
12. This error is also committed by Rousseau. *Social Contract and Discourses,* G. D. H. Cole, ed., (New York: E. P. Dutton, 1950), p. 33. Of the traditional contract theorists only Hobbes appears to have avoided this position by contending that when one has not consented he nevertheless owes obedience out of gratitude for benefits received. *Leviathan,* C. B. Macpherson, ed., (Baltimore: Penguin, 1968), Pt. I, Ch. XV, p. 209. On this point see Howard Warrender, *The Political Philosophy of Thomas Hobbes* (London: Oxford University Press, 1957), pp. 50–51.
13. H. B. Mayo, *An Introduction to Democratic Theory* (New York: Oxford University Press, 1960) p. 29; Yves Simon, *Philosophy of Democratic Government* (Chicago: University of Chicago Press, 1951); A. D. Lindsay, *The Modern Democratic State,* Vol. I (New York: Oxford University Press, 1962), p. 206; Leslie Lipson, *The Great Issues of Politics,* 2nd ed. (Englewood Cliffs, New Jersey: Prentice-Hall, 1960), pp. 76–78, 84–85; J. R. Lucas, *The Principles of Politics* (London: Oxford University Press, 1966), pp. 284–287; Charles Frankel, *The Democratic Prospect* (New York: Harper and Row, 1962), pp. 12–13, 24–29 (Frankel does, however, offer consent as consultation or influence at pp. 33–35); R. M. Hare, "The Lawful Government" in *Philosophy, Politics and Society,* 3rd series, Peter Laslett and W. G. Runciman, eds., (London: Basil Blackwell, 1967), pp. 157–172; Michael Walzer, *Obligations* (Cambridge: Harvard University Press, 1970), pp. IX–XVI. (Walzer softens his position by extending the doctrine of consent to groups and by speaking of "diminished" obligations).
14. New York: Oxford University Press, 1966.
15. *Ibid.,* pp. 3–7.
16. *Ibid.,* p. 29.
17. *Ibid.*
18. *Ibid.,* p. 26. A recent analysis of unanimous decision-making indicates that Tussman's position is by no means self-evident. Heinz Eulau, "Logic of Rationality in Unanimous Decision-Making" *Nomos VII: Rational Decision,* Carl Friederich, ed., (New York: Atherton, 1967), pp. 26–54.
19. *Ibid.,* p. 27.
20. This point is ably presented by Stanley Benn and Richard Peters in *Principles of Political Thought* (New York: Free Press, 1959), p. 355.
21. Tussman, *Obligation and the Body Politic,* p. 32.
22. *Ibid.,* p. 35.
23. *Ibid.,* p. 36.
24. *Ibid.,* pp. 36–37.
25. *Ibid.*
26. Locke, *Two Treatises,* II, 4, p. 309.
27. *Ibid.,* II, 95, pp. 374–375.
28. *Ibid.,* II, 117, p. 39.
29. *Ibid.,* II, 121, p. 393.
30. *Ibid.,* II, 122, p. 394.
31. Plamenatz, *Consent, Freedom and Political Obligation,* pp. 9–10.
32. *Ibid.,* p. 23.
33. For other recent statements of this position see: John J. Jenkins, "Political

Consent" *Philosophical Quarterly* XVIII (1968), pp. 60–66 and D. D. Raphael, *Problems in Political Philosophy* (New York: Praeger, 1971), pp. 94–99.

34. Plamenatz, *Consent, Freedom and Political Obligation,* p. 170. Desire and consent are reunited in Plamenatz's Postscript.

35. Plamenatz, *Man and Society,* vol. I (London: Longman's, 1966), pp. 239–241.

36. Plamenatz, *Consent, Freedom and Political Obligation,* pp. 170–171.

37. Thomas Hobbes, *Leviathan,* Ch. XIV.

38. It should be noted that I am using "agent" in its most general sense as "one who acts." This definition is not to be confused with a more specific, and perhaps more common, meaning of agent as "one who acts or does business for another."

39. Michael Walzer epitomizes what is surely a serious categorical error in democratic theory when he says "The paradigm form of consent theory is simply, I have committed myself (consented): I am committed (obligated)."

BIBLIOGRAPHICAL NOTE

The definitive historical account of social contract theory is John Gough's *The Social Contract: A Critical Study of Its Development.* The consent model is the basis of three masterpieces of modern political thought: Thomas Hobbes' *Leviathan,* John Locke's *Two Treatises on Government,* and Jean Jacques Rousseau's *Social Contract.* All three use the concept of consent to justify very different political systems.

While students of American political thought have been taught to consider Locke's influence on the founding fathers as axiomatic truth, this view has recently been persuasively challenged by John Dunn in his "The Politics of Locke in England and America in the Eighteenth Century," *John Locke: Problems and Perspectives,* ed. John W. Yolton. Dunn's thesis notwithstanding, an appreciation of Locke is central to understanding consent theory. Sympathetic, though not uncritical treatments of Locke can be found in volume one of John Plamenatz, *Man and Society;* G.E.G. Catlin, *The Principles of Politics;* Martin Seliger, *The Liberal Politics of John Locke* and Theodore Waldman, "A Note on Locke's Concept of Consent," *Ethics* (1957–1958). It is an understatement to say that critical accounts of Locke are caustic. See C. B. Macpherson, *The Theory of Possessive Individualism,* and Wilmore Kendall, *John Locke and the Doctrine of Majority Rule.* For more balanced accounts, although from divergent viewpoints, see Frank Marini, "John Locke and the Revision of Classical Liberalism," *Western Political Quarterly* (1969), and Gordon J. Schochet's introduction to *Life, Liberty and Property: Essays on Locke's Political Ideas.*

Carl Becker's *The Declaration of Independence: A Study in the History of Political Ideas* contains the numerous revised drafts of the Declaration and is a masterful analysis of this celebrated document. For an engaging account of the period in general see Clinton Rossiter's *Seedtime of the Republic.*

Consent theory has rarely been challenged in the history of American political thought. When it has, it has usually been in the context of the denial of the mainstream of the American political tradition. See, for instance, Lysander Spooner's bitter critique from the anarchist perspective in his *No Treason* and George Fitzhugh's attack in his defense of slavery, *Cannibals All!*

For contemporary justifications of consent theory not represented in this section see Michael Walzer, *Obligations;* John Rawls, *A Theory of Justice;* Robert Booth Fowler, "Political Obligation and the Draft" in *Obligation and Dissent,* ed. Hanson and Fowler; John R. Carnes, "Myths, Bliks, and the Social Contract," *Journal of Value Inquiry* (1970), and Chapter one of Robert Dahl, *Pluralist Democracy: Conflicts and Consent* (reprinted in Part III of this book).

II. THE LIMITS OF POLITICS

1. Natural Rights

At numerous points in history, men have seen the necessity of limiting the range of issues susceptible to political resolutions. But perhaps more than any other people, Americans have been fearful of resorting to the political system to resolve social conflict. The distinction between public and private is not an invention of American political theorists but few societies can claim to have elevated it to the status of religious principle.

A convenient and effective doctrine that expresses these convictions is the notion of natural rights. This concept is a variation of natural-law thought, which forms the core of Western political theory. Stated very briefly, a natural law is an eternal moral principle, transcendent of time and place, and obligatory for every man. Needless to say, writers have not agreed upon precisely what natural law obliges us to do, but principles like keeping promises and doing to others as we would have done to ourselves are frequently mentioned. In the seventeenth century, writers incorporated the notion of natural rights into the theory of natural law. They argued that if men had duties (usually interpreted as imposed by God), He must have granted rights as well.

Thomas Paine employed the doctrine of natural rights as a defense of the French Revolution against the criticisms of Edmund Burke. Thomas Copeland has rightly described the dialogue as the most crucial ideological debate ever carried on in English. In the *Rights of Man*, Paine derides Burke's devotion to incremental change and social convention by asking why men should be asked to suffer when the very essence of their existence is being denied by a class-ridden society. It was Paine's belief that the French revolutionaries were organizing a new society based upon man's natural right to comfort and happiness. In the next selection William Channing, a New England Unitarian minister, uses the doctrine of natural right to denounce the practice of slavery. He rejects the proslavery arguments of economic and political necessity by contending that national wealth "can have no value . . . until the supremacy of the Rights of the Individual is the first article of a nation's faith."

Despite its use as a defense of revolution and condemnation of slavery, the doctrine of natural right could have not found a more influential home than in its use as an apologia for unregulated capitalism. In the selection offered here, William Graham Sumner castigates those who he thinks use natural rights language too loosely. While Sumner toys with the idea that the right to appropriate capital is a natural right not subject to governmental scrutiny, it was the task of theorists like Carnegie and Spencer to enshrine the industrialist upon an altar of moral approbation. In a bitter satire, Edward Bellamy challenges these subsequent interpretations. Bellamy's version of socialism American style was very popular in the late nineteenth century and served as a powerful alternate model for the advancing capitalist society.

The closing essay by William J. Wainwright is an attempt to clarify the concept of natural right by submitting it to the rigor of philosophical analysis. The student may find it profitable to judge the earlier works on the basis of Wainwright's comments.

RIGHTS OF MAN
Thomas Paine

The duty of man is not a wilderness of turnpike gates, through which he is to pass by tickets from one to the other. It is plain and simple, and consists but of two points. His duty to God, which every man must feel; and with respect to his neighbor, to do as he would be done by. If those to whom power is delegated do well, they will be respected: of not, they will be despised; and with regard to those to whom no power is delegated, but who assume it, the rational world can know nothing of them.

Hitherto we have spoken only (and that but in part) of the natural rights of man. We have now to consider the civil rights of man, and to show how the one originates from the other. Man did not enter into society to become *worse* than he was before, nor to have fewer rights than he had before, but to have those rights better secured. His natural rights are the foundation of all his civil rights. But in order to pursue this distinction with more precision, it will be necessary to mark the different qualities of natural and civil rights.

A few words will explain this. Natural rights are those which appertain to man in right of his existence. Of this kind are all the intellectual rights, or rights of the mind, and also all those rights of acting as an individual for his own comfort and happiness, which are not injurious to the natural rights of others. Civil rights are those which appertain to man in right of his being a member of society. Every civil right has for its foundation some natural right pre-existing in the individual, but to the enjoyment of which his individual power is not, in all cases, sufficiently competent. Of this kind are all those which relate to security and protection.

From this short review it will be easy to distinguish between that class of natural rights which man retains after entering into society and those which he throws into the common stock as a member of society.

The natural rights which he retains are all those in which the *power* to execute is as perfect in the individual as the right itself. Among this class, as is before mentioned, are all the intellectual rights, or rights of the mind; consequently religion is one of those rights. The natural rights which are not retained, are all those in which, though the right is perfect in the individual, the power to execute them is defective. They answer not his purpose. A man, by natural right, has a right to judge in his own cause; and so far as the right of the mind is concerned, he never surrenders it. But what availeth it him to judge, if he has not power to redress? He therefore deposits this right in the

From The Writings of Thomas Paine. *Copyright by G. P. Putnam's Sons, 1894.*

common stock of society, and takes the arm of society, of which he is a part, in preference and in addition to his own. Society *grants* him nothing. Every man is a proprietor in society, and draws on the capital as a matter of right.

From these premisses two or three certain conclusions will follow:

First, That every civil right grows out of a natural right; or, in other words, is a natural right exchanged.

Secondly, That civil power properly considered as such is made up of the aggregate of that class of the natural rights of man, which becomes defective in the individual in point of power, and answers not his purpose, but when collected to a focus becomes competent to the purpose of every one.

Thirdly, That the power produced from the aggregate of natural rights, imperfect in power in the individual, cannot be applied to invade the natural rights which are retained in the individual, and in which the power to execute is as perfect as the right itself.

We have now, in a few words, traced man from a natural individual to a member of society, and shewn, or endeavoured to shew, the quality of the natural rights retained, and of those which are exchanged for civil rights. Let us now apply these principles to governments.

In casting our eyes over the world, it is extremely easy to distinguish the governments which have arisen out of society, or out of the social compact, from those which have not; but to place this in a clearer light than what a single glance may afford, it will be proper to take a review of the several sources from which governments have arisen and on which they have been founded.

They may be all comprehended under three heads. First, Susperstition. Secondly, Power. Thirdly, the common interest of society and the common rights of man.

The first was a government of priestcraft, the second of conquerors, and the third of reason.

When a set of artful men pretended, through the meduim of oracles, to hold intercourse with the Deity, as familiarly as they now march up the back-stairs in European courts, the world was completely under the government of superstition. The oracles were consulted, and whatever they were made to say became the law; and this sort of government lasted as long as this sort of superstition lasted.

After these a race of conquerors arose, whose government, like that of William the Conqueror, was founded in power, and the sword assumed the name of a sceptre. Governments thus established last as long as the power to support them lasts; but that they might avail themselves of every engine in their favor, they united fraud to force, and set up an idol which they called *Divine Right,* and which, in imitation of the Pope, who affects to be spiritual and temporal, and in contradiction to the Founder of the Christian religion, twisted itself afterwards into an idol of another shape, called *Church and State.* The key of St. Peter and the key of the Treasury became quartered on one another, and the wondering cheated multitude worshipped the invention.

When I contemplate the natural dignity of man, when I feel (for Nature has not been kind enough to me to blunt my feelings) for the honour and happiness of its character, I become irritated at the attempt to govern mankind by force and fraud, as if they were all knaves and fools, and can scarcely avoid disgust at those who are thus imposed upon.

We have now to review the governments which arise out of society, in contradistinction to those which arose out of superstition and conquest.

It has been thought a considerable advance towards establishing the principles of Freedom to say that Government is a compact between those who govern and those who are governed; but this cannot be true, because it is putting the effect before the cause; for as man must have existed before governments existed, there necessarily was a time when governments did not exist, and consequently there could originally exist no governors to form such a compact with.

The fact therefore must be that the *individuals themselves,* each in his own personal and sovereign right, *entered into a compact with each other* to produce a government: and this is the only mode in which governments have a right to arise, and the only principle on which they have a right to exist.

SLAVERY
William Channing

... I am to show, that man has sacred Rights, the gifts of God, and inseparable from human nature, which are violated by slavery. Some important principles, which belong to this head, were necessarily anticipated under the preceding; but they need a fuller exposition. The whole subject of Rights needs to be reconsidered. Speculations and reasonings about it have lately been given to the public, not only false, but dangerous to freedom, and there is a strong tendency to injurious views. Rights are made to depend on circumstances, so that pretences may easily be made or created for violating them successively, till none shall remain. Human rights have been represented as so modified and circumscribed by men's entrance into the social state, that only the shadows of them are left. They have been spoken of as absorbed in the public good; so that a man may be innocently enslaved, if the public good shall so require. To meet fully all these errors, for such I hold them, a larger work than the present is required. The nature of man, his relations to the state, the limits of civil government, the elements of the public good, and the degree to which the individual must be surrendered to this good, these are the topics which the present subject involves. I cannot enter into them particularly, but shall lay down what seem to me the great and true principles in regard to them. I shall

From The Works of William E. Channing, *Vol. II. Copyright by George G. Channing, 1849.*

show, that man has rights from his very nature, not the gifts of society, but of God; that they are not surrendered on entering the social state; that they must not be taken away under the plea of public good; that the Individual is never to be sacrificed to the Community; that the idea of Rights is to prevail above all the interests of the state.

Man has rights by nature. The disposition of some to deride abstract rights, as if all rights were uncertain, mutable, and conceded by society, shows a lamentable ignorance of human nature. Whoever understands this must see in it an immovable foundation of rights. These are gifts of the Creator, bound up indissolubly with our moral constitution. In the order of things, they precede society, lie at its foundation, constitute man's capacity for it, and are the great objects of social institutions. The consciousness of rights is not a creation of human art, a conventional sentiment, but essential to and inseparable from the human soul.

Man's rights belong to him as a Moral Being, as capable of perceiving moral distinctions, as a subject of moral obligation. As soon as he becomes conscious of Duty, a kindred consciousness springs up, that he has a Right to do what the sense of duty enjoins, and that no foreign will or power can obstruct his moral action without crime. He feels, that the sense of duty was given to him as a Law, that it makes him responsible for himself, that to exercise, unfold, and obey it is the end of his being, and that he has a right to exercise and obey it without hindrance or opposition. A consciousness of dignity, however obscure, belongs also to this divine principle; and, though he may want words to do justice to his thoughts, he feels that he has that within him which makes him essentially equal to all around him.

The sense of duty is the fountain of human rights. In other words, the same inward principle, which teaches the former, bears witness to the latter. Duties and Rights must stand or fall together. It has been too common to oppose them to one another; but they are indissolubly joined together. That same inward principle, which teaches a man what he is bound to do to others, teaches equally, and at the same instant, what others are bound to do to *him*. That same voice, which forbids him to injure a single fellow-creature, forbids every fellow-creature to do *him* harm. His conscience, in revealing the moral law, does not reveal a law for himself only, but speaks as a Universal Legislator. He has an intuitive conviction, that the obligations of this divine code press on others as truly as on himself. That principle, which teaches him that he sustains the relation of brotherhood to all human beings, teaches him that this relation is reciprocal, that it gives indestructible claims, as well as imposes solemn duties, and that what he owes to the members of this vast family, they owe to him in return. Thus the moral nature involves rights. These enter into its very essence. They are taught by the very voice which enjoins duty. Accordingly there is no deeper principle in human nature, than the consciousness of rights. So profound, so ineradicable is this sentiment, that the oppressions of ages have nowhere wholly stifled it.

Having shown the foundation of human rights in human nature, it may be asked what they are. Perhaps they do not admit very accurate definition, any more than human duties; for the Spiritual cannot be weighed and measured like the Material. Perhaps a minute criticism may find fault with the most guarded exposition of them; but they may easily be stated in language which the unsophisticated mind will recognise as the truth. Volumes could not do justice to them; and yet, perhaps they may be comprehended in one sentence. They may all be comprised in the right, which belongs to every rational being, to exercise his powers for the promotion of his own and others' Happiness and Virtue. These are the great purposes of his existence. For these his powers were given, and to these he is bound to devote them. He is bound to make himself and others better and happier, according to his ability. His ability for this work is a sacred trust from God, the greatest of all trusts. He must answer for the waste or abuse of it. He consequently suffers an unspeakable wrong, when stripped of it by others, or forbidden to employ it for the ends for which it is given; when the powers, which God has given for such generous uses, are impaired or destroyed by others, or the means for their action and growth are forcibly withheld. As every human being is bound to employ his faculties for his own and others' good, there is an obligation on each to leave all free for the accomplishment of this end; and whoever respects this obligation, whoever uses his own, without invading others' powers, or obstructing others' duties, has a sacred, indefeasible right to be unassailed, unobstructed, unharmed by all with whom he may be connected. Here is the grand, all-comprehending right of human nature. Every man should revere it, should assert it for himself and for all, and should bear solemn testimony agaisnt every infraction of it, by whomsoever made or endured.

Having considered the great fundamental right of human nature, particular rights may easily be deduced. Every man has a right to exercise and invigorate his intellect or the power of knowledge, for knowledge is the essential condition of successful effort for every good; and whoever obstructs or quenches the intellectual life in another, inflicts a grievous and irreparable wrong. Every man has a right to inquire into his duty, and conform himself to what he learns of it. Every man has a right to use the means, given by God and sanctioned by virtue, for bettering his condition. He has a right to be respected according to his moral worth; a right to be regarded as a member of the community to which he belongs, and to be protected by impartial laws; and a right to be exempted from coercion, stripes, and punishment, as long as he respects the rights of others. He has a right to an aquivalent for his labor, He has a right to sustain domestic relations, to discharge their duties, and to enjoy the happiness which flows from fidelity in these and other domestic relations. Such are a few of human rights; and if so, what a grievous wrong is slavery!

Perhaps nothing has done more to impair the sense of the reality and sacredness of human rights, and to sanction oppression, than loose ideas as to the change made in man's natural rights by his entrance into civil society. It is commonly said, that men part with a portion of these by becoming a community, a body politic; that government consists of powers surrendered by the individual; and it is said, "If certain rights and powers may be surrendered, why not others? why not all? what limit is to be set? The good of the community, to which a part is given up, may demand the whole; and in this good, all private rights are merged." This is the logic of despotism. We are grieved that it finds its way into republics, and that it sets down the great principles of freedom as abstractions and metaphysical theories, good enough for the cloister, but too refined for practical and real life.

Human rights, however, are not to be so reasoned away. They belong, as we have seen, to man as a moral being, and nothing can divest him of them but the destruction of his nature. They are not to be given up to society as a prey. On the contrary, the great end of civil society is to secure them. The great end of government is to repress *all wrong*. Its highest function is to protect the weak against the powerful, so that the obscurest human being may enjoy his rights in peace. Strange that an institution, built on the idea of Rights, should be used to unsettle this idea, to confuse our moral perceptions, to sanctify wrongs as means of general good!

It is said, that, in forming civil society, the individual surrenders a part of his rights. It would be more proper to say, that he adopts new modes of securing them. He consents, for example, to desist from self-defence, that he and all may be more effectually defended by the public force. He consents to submit his cause to an umpire or tribunal, that justice may be more impartially awarded, and that he and all may more certainly receive their due. He consents to part with a portion of his property in taxation, that his own and others' property may be the more secure. He submits to certain restraints, that he and others may enjoy more enduring freedom. He expects an equivalent for what he relinquishes, and insists on it as his right. He is wronged by partial laws, which compel him to contribute to the state beyond his proportion, his ability, and the measure of benefits which he receives. How absurd is it to suppose, that, by consenting to be protected by the state, and by yielding it the means, he surrenders the very rights which were the objects of his accession to the social compact!

The authority of the state to impose laws on its members I cheerfully allow; but this has limits, which are found to be more and more narrow in proportion to the progress of moral science. The state is equally restrained with individuals by the Moral Law. For example, it may not, must not, on any account, put an innocent man to death, or require of him a dishonorable or criminal service. It may demand allegiance, but only on the ground of the protection it affords. It may levy taxes, but only because it takes all property and all interests under its shield. It may pass laws, but only impartial ones, framed for the whole, and not for the few. It must not seize, by a special act, the property of the humblest individual, without making him an equivalent. It must regard every man, over whom it extends its authority, as a vital part of itself, as entitled to its care and to its provisions for liberty and happiness. If, in an emergency, its safety, which is the interest of each and all, may demand the imposition of peculiar restraints on one or many, it is bound to limit these restrictions to the precise point which its safety prescribes, to remove the necessity of them as far and as fast as possible, to compensate by peculiar protection such as it deprives of the ordinary means of protecting themselves, and, in general, to respect and provide for liberty in the very acts which for a time restrain it. The idea of Rights should be fundamental and supreme in civil institutions. Government becomes a nuisance and scourge, in proportion as it sacrifices these to the many or the few. Government, I repeat it, is equally bound with the individual by the Moral Law. The ideas of Justice and Rectitude, of what is due to man from his fellow-creatures, of the claims of every moral being, are far deeper and more primitive than Civil Polity. Government, far from originating them, owes to them its strength. Right is older than human law. Law ought to be its voice. It should be built on, and should correspond to, the principle of justice in the human breast, and its weakness is owing to nothing more than to its clashing with our indestructible moral convictions.

That government is most perfect, in which Policy is most entirely subjected to Justice, or in which the supreme and constant aim is to secure the rights of every human being. This is the beautiful idea of a free government, and no government is free but in proportion as it realizes this. Liberty must not be confounded with popular institutions. A representative government may be as despotic as an absolute monarchy. In as far as it tramples on the rights, whether of many or one, it is a despotism. The sovereign power, whether wielded by a single hand or several hands, by a king or a congress, which spoils one human being of the immunities and privileges bestowed on him by God, is so far a tyranny. The great argument in favor of representative institutions is, that a people's rights are safest in their own hands, and should never be surrendered to an irresponsible power. Rights, Rights, lie at the foundation of a popular government; and when this betrays them, the wrong is more aggravated than when they are crushed by despotism.

Still the question will be asked, "Is not the General Good the supreme law of the state? Are not all restraints of the individual just, which this demands? When the rights of the individual clash with this, must they not yield? Do they not, indeed, cease to be rights? Must not every thing give place to the General Good?" I have started this question in various forms, because I deem it worthy of particular examination. Public and private morality, the freedom and safety of our national institutions, are greatly concerned in settling the claims of the "General Good." In monarchies, the Divine Right of kings swallowed up all others. In republics, the General Good threatens the same evil. It is a shelter for the abuses and usurpations of government, for the profligacies of statesmen, for the vices of parties, for the wrongs of slavery. In considering this subject, I take the hazard of repeating principles already laid down; but this will be justified by the importance of reaching and determining the truth. Is the General Good, then, the supreme law, to which every thing must bow?

This question may be settled at once by proposing another. Suppose the public good to require, that a number of the members of a state, no matter how few, should perjure themselves, or should disclaim their faith in God and virtue. Would their right to follow conscience and God be annulled? Would they be bound to sin? Suppose a conqueror to menace a state with ruin, unless its members should insult their parents, and stain themselves with crimes at which nature revolts. Most the public good prevail over purity and our holiest affections? Do we not all feel that there are higher goods than even the safety of the state? that there is a higher law than that of mightiest empires? that the idea of Rectitude is deeper in human nature than that of private or public interest? and that this is to bear sway over all private and public acts?

The supreme law of a state is not its safety, its power, its prosperity, its affluence, the flourishing state of agriculture, commerce, and the arts. These objects, constituting what is commonly called the Public Good, are indeed proposed, and ought to be proposed, in the constitution and administration of states. But there is a higher law, even Virtue, Rectitude, the voice of Conscience, the Will of God. Justice is a greater good than property, not greater in degree, but in kind. Universal benevolence is infinitely superior to prosperity. Religion, the love of God, is worth incomparably more than all his outward gifts. A community, to secure or aggrandize itself, must never forsake the Right, the Holy, the Just.

Moral Good, Rectitude in all its branches, is the Supreme Good; by which I do not intend, that it is the surest means to the security and prosperity of the state. Such, indeed, it is, but this is too low a view. It must not be looked upon as a Means, an Instrument. It is the Supreme End, and states are bound to subject to it all their legislation, be the apparent loss of prosperity ever so great. National wealth is not the End. It derives all its worth from national virtue. . . .

In all ages the Individual has, in one form or another, been trodden in the dust. In monarchies and aristocracies, he has been sacrificed to One or to the Few; who, regarding government as an heirloom in their families, and thinking of the people as made only to live and die for their glory, have not dreamed that the sovereign power was designed to shield every man, without exception, from wrong. In the ancient Republics, the Glory of the State, especially Conquest, was the end to which the individual was expected to offer himself a victim, and in promoting which, no cruelty was to be declined, no human right revered. He was merged in a great whole, called the Commonwealth, to which his whole nature was to be immolated. It was the glory of the American people, that, in their Declaration of Independence, they took the ground of the indestructible rights of every human being. They declared all men to be essentially equal, and each born to be free. They did not, like the Greek or Roman, assert for themselves a liberty, which they burned to wrest from other states. They spoke in the name of humanity, as the representatives of the rights of the feeblest, as well as mightiest of their race. They published universal, everlasting principles, which are to work out the deliverance of every human being. Such was their glory. Let not the idea of Rights be erased from their children's minds by false ideas of public good. Let not the sacredness of Individual Man be forgotten in the feverish pursuit of property. It is more important that the Individual should respect himself, and be respected by others, than that the wealth of both worlds should be accumulated on our shores. National wealth is not the end of society. It may exist where large classes are depressed and wronged. It may undermine a nation's spirit, institutions, and independence. It can have no value and no sure foundation, until the supremacy of the Rights of the Individual is the first article of a nation's faith, and until reverence for them becomes the spirit of public men.

SOME NATURAL RIGHTS
William Graham Sumner

The mediæval notions about rights was that they were franchises or grants from the head of the state; each man started with just such ones, and so many of them as his ancestors had succeeded in getting out of the struggle of war and court intrigue. If his ancestors had not been successful in that struggle, he had none. The theoretical basis of the civil system was, therefore, the assumption that, in advance of actions by the civil authority, man as such had no rights. All must be assumed to be under the same constraints and restrictions, until, by franchises, privileges, and exemptions, each of which was capable of proof by legal evidence, documents, or tradition, some had emancipated themselves from the restrictions. As these franchises and privileges admitted of every variety, when compared with each other or combined with each other, there could be no equality. In the system, the fact that one man had obtained a certain charter was no reason why anybody else should have the same.

It will be found again and again in examining the political and social dogmas which were enunciated in the eighteenth century, and which have become commonplaces and catchwords in the nineteenth, that they had their origin in a just and true revolt against the doctrines of mediæval society, so that they are intelligible and valuable, when viewed in their historical connection, however doubtful they may be when taken as universal *a priori* dogmas.

In the case just stated, we have an instance of this. The eighteenth-century notion of "natural rights," or of the "rights of man," was a revolt against the notion that a man had nothing and was entitled to nothing until some other men had given him some rights here. The rights of man meant that

Reprinted by permission of the publisher from Essays of William Graham Sumner, *Albert Galloway Keller and Maurice R. Davie, eds., (New Haven: Yale University Press, 1934), Vol. I, pp. 363–368.*

a man, as a man, entered human society, not under servitude and constraint to other men, or to social traditions, but under a presumption of non-servitude and non-obligation to other men, or to social organization. Natural rights, as opposed to chartered rights, meant that the fundamental presumption must be changed, and that every man must, in the view of social order and obligation, be regarded as free and independent, until some necessity had been established for restraining him, instead of being held to be in complete subjection to social bonds, until he could prove that some established authority had emancipated him.

When so regarded, it is evident that the notion of natural rights is one of great value and importance. In the abuse of it, however, it has come to pass that this notion has become a doctrine which affords the most ample space for arbitrary dogmatism, and empty declamation. It has become one of the favorite methods of modern schemers, when they find it difficult to provide means by which men may get what they need in order to enjoy earthly comfort, to put all those necessary things among "natural rights." It then stands established, by easy deduction, that every man has a natural right to succeed in the struggle for existence, or to be happy. It is the duty of the state to secure natural rights. Therefore, if there is anything which a man wants, he is entitled to have it so long as there is any of it.

The notion that all men are equal is likewise reasonable and useful when taken in its historical setting. It meant, in contradiction to the mediaeval notion, that whatever rights the state might give to some, it should give to all, and that whatever burdens it laid on some, it should lay on all, without distinctions of persons or classes. No such thing has ever been realized or ever can be, and the doctrine would need modification and limitation to make it true, but, as a revolt against mediaevalism, it is intelligible. In its best form it is our modern "equality before the law"; but we are constantly striving to use the state to give privileges, and then to make the privileges equal, or to give them to everybody. Turn all such propositions as we will, they are only attempts to lift ourselves by our boot-straps, or to bring good things into existence by decree.

Ever since it has been accepted doctrine that there are natural rights, innumerable attempts have been made to formulate "declarations" of them, that is, to tell what they are. No such attempt has ever succeeded, and the history of the effort to define and specify what the rights of man are is instructive for the sense and value of the notion itself. At present this effort is prosecuted, not by parliaments and conventions, but by social philosophers. As these attempts go on, they develop more and more completely the futility of the notion, or its purely mischievous character as a delusion which draws us away from what might profit us.

Among the latest enunciations of the fundamental and universal rights of man, is that of "the right to the full product of labor." This has been declared, in the most intelligent exposition of it known to me,[1] to be the same as "the right to an existence." The two "rights" are in plain contradiction.

In the first place, the "right to the complete product of labor" contains one of the usual ambiguities. Is it meant that the man who does any manual labor in connection with, or contribution to the production of a thing, should have the whole of that thing? Or, is it meant that the man who contributes manual labor to the productive enterprise should have all that part of the thing which belongs to the labor element, in proportion to the capital, land, and other elements which contribute to production? If the former, then we are face to face with a proposition for robbery, with all the social consequences which must be anticipated. Furthermore, although it may seem a very simple thing to provide all that those who do the manual work shall have all the product, it is plain, so soon as we reflect upon the complicated combinations of labor which are involved in any case of production, and also upon the complicated character of modern "products" and the way in which they contribute to, and depend upon each other, that it would be impracticable to divide the products among those who have done the labor part of production.

If it is meant that the labor element shall have all the part of the product which is due to the labor element in it, the question arises, how is that element to be measured? How is its proportion to the whole to be determined? At present it is done by supply and demand, and until we have some standard of measurement provided, we cannot tell whether the present arrangement does not do just what is desired. There are constantly reiterated assertions that it does not. It is well worth noticing that no ground for these assertions is offered, and that there is no possibility of verifying them unless some standard of measurement can be proposed by which we can find out what the share ought to be, and compare it with what is.

In any case the right to the full product of labor would be contradictory to the right to an existence, for, if the full product of the labor of some falls short of what is necessary to maintain their existence, then they must encroach upon the full labor product of the others, that is, impair the right of the latter. The "right to an existence," however, has the advantage of putting the notion in a distinct and complete form; it covers the whole ground at once; it no longer spends energy in struggling for such means as the right to property, or labor, or liberty, or life. If dogmatic affirmation can do anything, why waste it on the means? Why not expend it at once upon the desired end? The real misery of mankind is the struggle for existence; why not "declare" that there ought not to be any struggle for existence, and that there shall not be any more? Let it be decreed that existence is a natural right, and let it be secured in that way.

If we attempt to execute this plan, it is plain that we shall not abolish the struggle for existence; we shall only bring it about that some men must fight that struggle for others.

Although the right of existence has the advantage of being broad and radical, it has the disadvantage of being abstract and impracticable. Another writer has recently given another formula, which, although less ambitious, is equally effective and far more practical; he affirms the natural right to capital. This must be regarded as the rational outcome, so far, of the attempt to formulate natural rights. All the good things which we want, and find so hard to get, depend on capital. Logically, it is less satisfactory to demand a means than to demand an end; but when the means is the one complete and only necessary one, that point is of little importance. If we could all have capital, we should have the great and only weapon for the struggle for existence. It is only a pity, however, that, in this case, as in all the others, so soon as we get a good formula, it turns out to be either a contradiction, a bathos, an impracticability, or an absurdity. So long as capital has to be brought into existence by human labor and self-denial, if we set up a right to capital in all men, we shall have to affirm that those who have not produced the capital have a right to have it, but that those who have produced it have not a right to have it, since from these latter we take it away.

THE PARABLE OF THE WATER TANK
Edward Bellamy

"That will do, George. We will close the session here. Our discussion, I find, has taken a broader range than I expected, and to complete the subject we shall need to have a brief session this afternoon.—And now, by way of concluding the morning, I propose to offer a little contribution of my own. The other day, at the museum, I was delving along the relics of literature of the great Revolution, with a view to finding something that might illustrate our theme. I came across a little pamphlet of the period, yellow and almost undecipherable, which, on examination, I found to be a rather amusing skit or satirical take-off on the profit system. It struck me that probably our lesson might prepare us to appreciate it, and I made a copy. It is entitled, 'The Parable of the Water Tank,' and runs this way:

" 'There was a certain very dry land, the people whereof were in sore need of water. And they did nothing but to seek after water from morning until night, and many perished because they could not find it.

" 'Howbeit, there were certain men in that land who were more crafty and diligent than the rest, and those had gathered stores of water where others could find none, and the name of these men was called capitalists. And it came to pass that the people of the land came unto the capitalists and prayed them that they would give them of the water they had gathered that they might drink, for their need was sore. But the capitalists answered them and said:

" ' "Go to, ye silly people! why should we give you of the water which we have gathered, for then we should become even as ye are, and perish with

From Equality *by Edward Bellamy. Copyright by D. Appleton and Co., 1897.*

you? But behold what we will do unto you. Be ye our servants and ye shall have water."

" 'And the people said, "Only give us to drink and we will be your servants, we and our children." And it was so.

" 'Now, the capitalists were men of understanding, and wise in their generation. They ordered the people who were their servants in bands with captains and officers, and some they put at the springs to dip, and others did they make to carry the water, and others did they cause to seek for new springs. And all the water was brought together in one place, and there did the capitalists make a great tank for to hold it, and the tank was called the Market, for it was there that the people, even the servants of the capitalists, came to get water. And the capitalists said unto the people:

" ' "For every bucket of water that he bring to us, that we may pour it into the tank, which is the Market, behold! we will give you a penny, but for every bucket that we shall draw forth to give unto you that ye may drink of it, ye and your wives and your children, ye shall give to us two pennies, and the difference shall be our profit, seeing that if it were not for this profit we would not do this thing for you, but ye should all perish."

" 'And it was good in the people's eyes, for they were dull of understanding, and they diligently brought water unto the tank for many days, and for every bucket which they did bring the capitalists gave them every man a penny; but for every bucket that the capitalists drew forth from the tank to give again unto the people, behold! the people rendered to the capitalists two pennies.

" 'And after many days the water tank, which was the Market, overflowed at the top, seeing that for every bucket the people poured in they received only so much as would buy again half of a bucket. And because of the excess that was left of every bucket, did the tank overflow, for the people were many, but the capitalists were few, and could drink no more than others. Therefore did the tank overflow.

" 'And when the capitalists saw that the water overflowed, they said to the people:

" ' "See ye not the tank, which is the Market, doth overflow? Sit ye down, therefore and be patient, for ye shall bring us no more water till the tank be empty."

" 'But when the people no more received the pennies of the capitalists for the water they brought, they could buy no more water from the capitalists, having naught wherewith to buy. And when the capitalists saw that they had no more profit because no man bought water of them, they were troubled. And they sent forth men in the highways, the byways, and the hedges, crying, "If any thirst let him come to the tank and buy water of us, for it doth overflow." For they said among themselves, "Behold, the times are dull; we must advertise."

" 'But the people answered, saying: "How can we buy unless ye hire us, for how else shall we have wherewithal to buy? Hire ye us, therefore, as before, and we will gladly buy water, for we thirst, and ye will have no need to advertise." But the capitalists said to the people: "Shall we hire you to bring water when the tank, which is the Market, doth already overflow? Buy ye, therefore, first water, and when the tank is empty, through your buying, will we hire you again." And so it was because the capitalists hired them no more to bring water that the people could not buy the water they had brought already, and because the people could not buy the water they had brought already, the capitalists no more hired them to bring water. And the saying went abroad, "It is a crisis."

" 'And the thirst of the people was great, for it was not now as it had been in the days of their fathers, when the land was open before them, for every one to seek water for himself, seeing that the capitalists had taken all the springs, and the wells, and the water wheels, and the vessels and the buckets, so that no man might come by water save from the tank, which was the Market. And the people murmured against the capitalists and said: "Behold, the tank runneth over, and we die of thirst. Give us, therefore, of the water, that we perish not."

" 'But the capitalists answered: "Not so. The water is ours. Ye shall not drink thereof unless ye buy it of us with pennies." And they confirmed it with an oath, saying, after their manner, "Business is business."

" 'But the capitalists were disquieted that the people bought no more water, whereby they had no more any profits, and they spake one to another, saying: "It seemeth that our profits have stopped our profits, and by reason of the profits we have made, we can make no more profits. How is it that our profits are become unprofitable to us, and our gains do make us poor? Let us therefore send for the soothsayers, that they may interpret this thing unto us," and they sent for them.

" 'Now, the soothsayers were men learned in dark sayings, who joined themselves to the capitalists by reason of the water of the capitalists, that they might have thereof and live, they and their children. And they spake for the capitalists unto the people, and did their embassies for them, seeing that the capitalists were not a folk quick of understanding neither ready of speech.

" 'And the capitalists demanded of the soothsayers that they should interpret this thing unto them, wherefore it was that the people bought no more water of them, although the tank was full. And certain of the soothsayers answered and said, "It is by reason of overproduction," and some said, "It is glut"; but the signification of the two words is the same. And the others said, "Nay, but this thing is by reason of the spots on the sun." And yet others answered, saying, "It is neither by reason of glut, nor yet of spots on the sun that this evil hath come to pass, but because of lack of confidence."

" 'And while the soothsayers contended among themselves, according to their manner, the men of profit did slumber and sleep, and when they awoke they said to the soothsayers: "It is enough. Ye have spoken comfortably unto us. Now go ye forth and speak comfortably likewise unto this people, so that they be at rest and leave us also in peace."

" 'But the soothsayers, even the men of the dismal science—for so they were named of some—were loath to go forth to the people lest they should be stoned, for the people loved them not. And they said to the capitalists:

" ' "Masters, it is a mystery of our craft that if men be full and thirst not but be at rest, then shall they find comfort in our speech even as ye. Yet if they thirst and be empty, find they no comfort therein but rather mock us, for it seemeth that unless a man be full our wisdom appeareth unto him but emptiness." But the capitalists said: "Go ye forth. And ye not our men to do our embassies?"

" 'And the soothsayers went forth to the people and expounded to them the mystery of overproduction, and how it was that they must needs perish of thirst because there was overmuch water, and how there could not be enough because there was too much. And likewise spoke they unto the people concerning the sun spots, and also wherefore it was that these things had come upon them by reason of lack of confidence. And it was even as the soothsayers had said, for the people their wisdom seemed emptiness. And the people reviled them, saying: "Go up, ye bald-heads! Will ye mock us? Doth plenty breed famine? Doth nothing come out of much?" And they took up stones to stone them.

" 'And when the capitalists saw that the people still murmured and would not give ear to the soothsayers, and because also they feared lest they should come upon the tank and take of the water by force, they brought forth to them certain holy men (but they were false priests), who spake unto the people that they should be quiet and trouble not the capitalists because they thirsted. And these holy men, who were false priests, testified to the people that this affliction was sent to them of God for the healing of their souls, and that if they should bear it in patience and lust not after the water, neither trouble the capitalists, it would come to pass that after they had given up the ghost they would come to a country where there should be no capitalists but an abundance of water. Howbeit, there were certain true prophets of God also, and these had compassion on the people and would not prophesy for the capitalists, but rather spake constantly against them.

" 'Now, when the capitalists saw that the people still murmured and would not be still, neither for the words of the soothsayers nor of the false priests, they came forth themselves unto them and put the ends of their fingers in the water that overflowed in the tank and wet the tips thereof, and they scattered the drops from the tips of their fingers abroad upon the people who thronged the tank, and the name of the drops of water was charity, and they were exceeding bitter.

" 'And when the capitalists saw yet again that neither for the words of the soothsayers, nor of the holy men who were false priests, nor yet for the drops that were called charity, would the people be still, but raged the more, and crowded upon the tank as if they would take it by force, then took they counsel together and sent men privily forth among the people. And these men sought out the mightiest among the people and all who had skill in war, and took them apart and spake craftily with them, saying:

" ' "Come, now, why cast ye not your lot in with the capitalists? If ye will be their men and serve them against the people, that they break not in upon the tank, then shall ye have abundance of water, that ye perish not, ye and your children."

" 'And the mighty men and they who were skilled in war hearkened unto this speech and suffered themselves to be persuaded, for their thirst constrained them, and they went within unto the capitalists and became their men, and staves and swords were put in their hands and they became a defense unto the capitalists and smote the people when they thronged upon the tank.

" 'And after many days the water was low in the tank, for the capitalists did make fountains and fish ponds of the water thereof, and did bathe therein, they and their wives and their children, and did waste the water for their pleasure.

" 'And when the capitalists saw that the tank was empty, they said, "The crisis is ended"; and they sent forth and hired the people that they should bring water to fill it again. And for the water that the people brought to the tank they received for every bucket a penny, but for the water which the capitalists drew forth from the tank to give again to the people they received two pennies, that they might have their profit. And after a time did the tank again overflow even as before.

" 'And now, when many times the people had filled the tank until it overflowed and had thirsted till the water therein had been wasted by the capitalists, it came to pass that there arose in the land certain men who were called agitators, for that they did stir up the people. And they spake to the people, saying that they should associate, and then would they have no need to be servants of the capitalists and should thirst no more for water. And in the eyes of the capitalists were the agitators pestilent fellows, and they would fain have crucified them, but durst not for fear of the people.

" 'And the words of the agitators which they spake to the people were on this wise:

" ' "Ye foolish people, how long will ye be deceived by a lie and believe to your hurt that which is not? for behold all these things that have been said unto you by the capitalists and by the soothsayers are cunningly devised fables. And likewise the holy men, who say that it is the will of God that ye should always be poor and miserable and athirst, behold! they do blaspheme God and are liars, whom he will bitterly judge though he forgive all others. How cometh it that ye may not come by the water in the tank? Is it not because ye have no money? And why have ye no money? Is it not because ye receive but one penny for every bucket that ye bring to the tank, which is the Market, but must render two pennies for every bucket ye take out, so that the capitalists may have their profit? See ye not how by this means the tank must overflow, being filled by that ye lack and made to abound out of your emptiness? See ye not also that the harder ye toil and the more diligently ye seek and bring the water, the worse and not the better it shall be for you by reason of the profit, and that forever?"

" 'After this manner spake the agitators for many days unto the people, and none heeded them, but it was so that after a time the people hearkened. And they answered and said unto the agitators:

" ' "Ye say truth. It is because of the capitalists and of their profits that we want, seeing that by reason of them and their profits we may by no means come by the fruit of our labor, so that our labor is in vain, and the more we toil to fill the tank the sooner doth it overflow, and we may receive nothing because there is too much, according to the words of the soothsayers. But behold, the capitalists are hard men and their tender mercies are cruel. Tell us if ye know any way whereby we may deliver ourselves out of our bondage unto them. But if ye know of no certain way of deliverance we beseech you to hold your peace and let us alone, that we may forget our misery."

" 'And the agitators answered and said, "We know a way."

" 'And the people said: "Deceive us not, for this thing hath been from the beginning, and none hath found a way of deliverance until now, though many have sought it carefully with tears. But if ye know a way, speak unto us quickly."

" 'Then the agitators spake unto the people of the way. And they said:

" ' "Behold, what need have ye at all of these capitalists, that ye should yield them profits upon your labor? What great thing do they wherefore ye render them this tribute? Lo! it is only because they do order you in bands and lead you out and in and set your tasks and afterward give you a little of the water yourselves have brought and not they. Now, behold the way out of this bondage! Do ye for yourselves that which is done by the capitalists—namely, the ordering of your labor, and the marshaling of your bands, and the dividing of your tasks. So shall ye have no need at all of the capitalists and no more yield to them any profit, but all the fruit of your labor shall ye share as brethren, every one having the same; and so shall the tank never overflow until every man is full, and would not wag the tongue for more, and afterward shall ye with the overflow make pleasant fountains and fish ponds to delight yourselves withal even as did the capitalists; but these shall be for the delight of all."

" 'And the people answered, "How shall we go about to do this thing, for it seemeth good to us?"

" 'And the agitators answered: "Choose ye discreet men to go in and out before you and to marshal your bands and order your labor, and these men shall be as the capitalists were; but, behold, they shall not be your masters as the capitalists are, but your brethren and officers who do your will, and they shall not take any profits, but every man his share like the others, that there may be no more masters and servants among you, but brethren only. And from time to time, as ye see fit, ye shall choose other discreet men in place of the first to order the labor."

" 'And the people hearkened, and the thing was very good to them. Likewise seemed it not a hard thing. And with one voice they cried out, "So let it be as ye have said, for we will do it!"

" 'And the capitalists heard the noise of the shouting and what the people said, and the soothsayers heard it also, and likewise the false priests and the mighty men of war, who were a defense unto the capitalists; and when they heard they trembled exceedingly, so that their knees smote together, and they said one to another, "It is the end of us!"

" 'Howbeit, there were certain true priests of the living God who would not prophesy for the capitalists, but had compassion on the people; and when they heard the shouting of the people and what they said, they rejoiced with exceeding great joy, and gave thanks to God because of the deliverance.

" 'And the people went and did all the things that were told them of the agitators to do. And it came to pass as the agitators had said, even according to all their words. And there was no more any thirst in that land, neither any that was ahungered, nor naked, nor cold, nor in any manner of want; and every man said unto his fellow, "My brother," and every woman said unto her companion, "My sister," for so were they with one another as brethren and sisters which do dwell together in unity. And the blessing of God rested upon that land forever.' "

NATURAL RIGHTS
William J. Wainwright

I

It may not be useful to distinguish natural rights from other rights. If one does choose to speak of natural rights (and many do), it is desirable to be as clear about them as possible. I propose to define natural rights as rights which meet three conditions. They must correspond to moral obligations, and these obligations must be both universal and important. Each of these conditions calls for some comment.

(A) Saying that natural rights correspond to obligations does not commit me to the view that wherever we have a right we have a corresponding obligation, but only to the view that wherever we have a natural right we have a corresponding obligation. Now am I maintaining that wherever we have an important and universal moral obligation we have a natural right, but only that wherever we have an important and universal moral obligation, then, if there is a corresponding right, that right is a natural right.

(B) The moral obligations which correspond to natural rights are universal. By definition any moral obligation is universal in the sense that it is *prima facie* binding on anyone who is in the appropriate situation. Thus the obligation to keep promises is *prima facie* binding on anyone who has freely made

From the *American Philosophical Quarterly.* Copyright by the American Philosophical Quarterly, *1967. Reprinted by permission of the publisher.*

a promise. Statements of moral obligation are universal or universalizable. We are not, however, interested in this sort of universality.

Someone who occupies a certain station in life may have moral obligations to those who stand in some special relation to him. Obligations of this sort are universal in the sense that anyone who occupies that station has certain definite obligations to anyone who stands in the special relation to him. But there are two senses in which these obligations are not universal. The obligations do not in fact fall on every man (or they fall on them only conditionally—*if* they ever occupy that station then they must . . .) and one has these obligations only toward certain persons (those who stand in the special relation). The demand that an obligation be universal may be, and I think sometimes is, a demand that it either fall on all men actually as well as conditionally (that it be universal with respect to its subject) or that it be an obligation of which all men are the object (that it be universal with respect to its object) or both.

1. What can it mean to say that an obligation actually falls on all men? It can mean at least two things: (a) That the obligation falls on man as man and not simply in so far as he plays a special role or enters into a special relation with someone, or (b) that the role or special relation which gives rise to the obligation is one which most men are likely to assume at one time or another, for example, by being a parent or entering into an agreement.

2. That an obligation is one of which all men are the object can also be understood in two ways. That is, (a) it can be understood as an obligation which we have toward a man simply because he is a man and not because, for example, he has merit or has entered into a contract with us. (The obligation to save a drowning man is, I suppose, universal in this sense.) Or (b) it can be understood as an obligation which is such that most men would at some time or other be the object of this obligation, for example, by being a child or the recipient of a promise.

We should notice that if an obligation is universal with respect both to its subject and its object, it is reasonable to suppose that it is one which actually and not simply conditionally applies in all societies (and this in the double sense that both subjects and objects of the obligation are to be met with in all societies).

If the obligation is one which falls on man as such, then it is an obligation which falls on men in all societies. If the obligation is universal with respect to its subject in the second sense, i.e., if it is an obligation which most men fall under at some time or other, then it is natural to expect that the obligation will fall on men in all societies. However, this is not necessarily the case, for it could be true of a given obligation both that it falls on most men at some time or other and that in some society it never falls on anyone. This observation suggests another sense in which an obligation could be universal with respect to its subject—viz., that it be an obligation which falls on most men at some time or other in *any* society. (Parental obligations or those arising from a promise *might* be obligations of this sort.) This in turn could be taken in at least two ways. "Any society" could be understood as meaning any actual society (past societies, present societies, and those which are likely to arise in the future) or it could be understood as meaning any possible society. Thus we have four senses in which any moral obligation is universal with respect to its subject. The four senses are:

i. that the obligation fall on man as man,
ii. that it fall on most men at some time or other,
iii. that it fall on most men at some time or other, in any actual society, and
iv. that it fall on most men at some time or other in any possible society.

Corresponding to the four senses in which an obligation may be universal with respect to its subject, we can distinguish four senses in which an obligation may be universal with respect to its object.

i. the obligation is to man as man,
ii. it is such that most men would at some time or other be the object of this obligation,
iii. it is such that in any actual society most men will at some time be its object, and
iv. it is such that in any possible society most men will at some time be its object.[1]

I have said that natural rights correspond to universal obligations. We are now in a position to spell this out more clearly.

Natural rights may be provisionally defined as rights which correspond to important moral obligations which are universal with respect to their object in either the first or fourth senses and which are universal with respect to their subject in either the first or fourth senses.

(C) By definition any moral obligation is important in the sense that it overrides (all?) non-moral obligations. Natural rights not only correspond to moral obligations, and thus share in the importance which is involved in any moral obligation, they correspond to the more important of these obligations. One obligation is more important than another if it generally overrides the other where there is a conflict between the two.

The universality of the corresponding obligation might be thought to be sufficient to distinguish natural rights from other rights, particularly in view of the fact that even the less important obligations are important in the sense that they override all non-moral obligations. Importance has been made a condition for the following reason. I am inclined to think that "Be polite" is a moral rule. It is possible that the ground for having a code of etiquette, and this rule, would be found in all possible societies. The obligation would then be universal in the required sense. Furthermore, there seems to be nothing improper in speaking of a right to be treated politely (e.g., not to be insulted).

A right, therefore, corresponds to the universal obligation. Nevertheless it seems a bit odd to speak of a natural right to be treated politely. If we introduce the notion of importance, we get out of this difficulty, for presumably politeness is not one of the more important obligations.

I would like to conclude this section of my paper by comparing my definition with two others with which it might be confused. The first is the notion that natural rights are those which must be respected if society is to endure. For an obligation to have subjects and objects in a possible society, all that is necessary is that the grounds occur in that society. It is not necessary that the obligation be respected or even recognized. Thus, even if there were a society which did not recognize the right to life, it could still be the case that the obligation has subjects and objects in that society and that it is important in that society, i.e., it could be true both that men in that society ought not to kill and that men in that society have a right to life, and that this obligation and right should be regarded as overriding in that society. From this it follows that an obligation can be important and universal in the required way (and thus that the corresponding right is a natural right) and yet not be recognized in some society. Now if a right is not recognized in some society, then respect for that right can hardly be a necessary condition of the survival of society. Therefore, if my definition of natural rights is correct, their recognition is not necessary for the survival of society. Furthermore, I do not think that the claim that natural rights are those which must be respected if society is to endure is at all plausible. Respect for a right cannot be a necessary condition of society if it is not recognized and more or less adhered to in all societies. To accept the claim would mean that nothing would count as a natural right which was not recognized in all societies and I do not believe that we wish to place this restriction on the notion of natural rights.

Margaret MacDonald suggests[2] that natural rights are the fundamental conditions of a good society. If taken literally, this is probably false. The fundamental conditions for a good society may well include many things other than the recognition and fulfillment of certain obligations. For example, certain material and historical conditions may be necessary for a good society. On the other hand, since natural rights correspond to important moral obligations which occur in any possible society, and since no society can—perhaps analytically—be a good one which does not respect the important obligations which occur in that society, it follows that no society can be a good society which does not respect natural rights. Respect for natural rights is a necessary condition for a good society.

II

I shall now examine some of the rights which Locke considers to be natural rights. The purpose of this discussion will be to sharpen and qualify the remarks made in Part I.

(A) The right to life and the obligation not to take a human life rest on the claim that each of us is God's property.[3] If this is true at all, then it is true of each man in any possible society and the obligation will presumable be universal with respect both to its subject and its object in the first sense.

Liberty is also a natural right. To enslave another is to exercise the power of life and death over him. But because I have no rights to take his life (he is God's property), I cannot have a right to enslave him.[4] Since the obligation not to kill another is universal with respect both to its subject and to its object in the first sense, it would seem that the obligation not to enslave another is also subject universal and object universal in the first sense.

But this will not do, for Locke says that men may forfeit their right to life and liberty if they unjustly attack another,[5] thereby cutting themselves off from the moral community.[6] This suggests that a necessary condition of the possession of the rights to life and liberty is membership in a community of rational beings who are governed by laws, either those of nature or those of political society.[7] If so, the ground for the right to life and liberty is not simply that one is God's property but also includes the fact that one is a member of a moral community in the sense required.[8] We have already seen that the first part of the ground will be found in all possible societies, but would the second part of the ground also be found in all possible societies?

A society most of whose members prey upon other communities is surely a possible society. In such a society most members would have unjustly resorted to violence and so would have forfeited (not have) the right to life and liberty. If my definition is correct, it would follow that life and liberty are not natural rights, for the corresponding obligations would not be object universal in either the first or fourth sense. We might conclude from this that my definition is inadequate. On the other hand, we might conclude that, contrary to Locke, refusing to resort to the unjust use of violence is not a ground for these rights. Or we might conclude that there is no natural right to life and liberty as such, but only a natural right to life and liberty in so far as one does not unjustly resort to violence. Members of a criminal society may well enjoy these rights.

(B) The primary ground for property rights is labor.[9] Locke also suggests gift,[10] bequest,[11] and exchange[12] as grounds for property rights. The obligations to respect property so acquired seem to be subject universal in the first sense. All men are obligated to respect property, i.e., one doesn't have to take up a special role or do something special or belong to a special society to come under this obligation. If gift, bequest, and exchange are sources of property rights, and labor is construed as broadly as Locke construes it (so as to include picking something up, gathering berries, etc.) then it is difficult to believe that there would be very many who would not have property in something in any possible society. If so, obligation will be object universal in the fourth sense.

(C) Parents have a right to exercise authority over their children during the minority of the child.[13] What obligation corresponds to this right? The right arises from the obligation to care for one's children, but this is not a corresponding obligation in the sense in question (where rights in one person correspond to obligations in another). If we take seriously the notion that one is under the natural law only if one has reason, and if children lack reason,[14] then the corresponding obligation is not the obligation to obey one's parents. The corresponding obligation will presumably be that of not interfering with the parents' direction of their children. The ground for this right and obligation is the obligation parents have to care for their children. This in turn is based on the fact that children lack reason and have been given by God to the parents as their responsibility.[15] (Freedom is justified only in so far as one is a full member of a community governed by laws, but full membership requires rationality which children lack.[16] Furthermore, since children lack reason, guidance is necessary for their own good.[17]) Would these grounds be found in any possible society?

There are two difficulties. In the first place, a society in which parents do not know their own children is a logically possible society. For example, the children are taken away at birth and raised in public institutions. No birth records are kept. In the second place, it is logically possible that there be a (human) society in which children have no parents. (They are raised in a test tube.) In either case, the obligation which corresponds to the right may still be subject universal in the first sense. All men may be obligated to refrain from interfering with a parent's direction of his children. On the other hand, in the first society parents do not direct their children and are unable to do so, except accidentally, because they do not know who their children are. It would, therefore, seem that the obligation has *no* objects in this society and is therefore not object universal in either the first or the fourth sense. It should be noticed, however, that the reason why the obligation has no objects in this society is to be found in the peculiar institutions of this society, and these institutions may be morally suspect. It is possible, though perhaps false, that wherever the grounds for this right and obligation do not occur, the absence of these grounds is itself a ground for moral criticism. In the second society there are no parents and hence no objects of the obligation in question. The obligation is not, then, object universal in either the first or fourth sense. But it should be noticed that it may still be true that the ground for the right and obligation will be found in any society which is at all likely to occur. (The notion of a society which is at all likely to occur is to be distinguished from that of an actual society mentioned in Part I. Actual societies include past and present societies, and those which will probably arise in the future. Societies which are at all likely to arise include not only actual societies, but also all those societies the occurrence of which is not highly improbable. The dividing line between the two conceptions is clearly not a sharp one.)

(D) Locke also asserts that children have an obligation to honor and assist their parents on the grounds that they have been begotten and nurtured by them.[18] Corresponding to this obligation, parents have a right to these things.[19] I am inclined to think that Locke would say that the obligation is object universal in the fourth sense. It arises from the fact that parents have begotten and nurtured children and this is something most, though not all, men will do in all possible societies. Whether this is true or not would depend on whether the ground is primarily the begetting or the nurture of children. If it is the former, then the ground of the obligation will occur in any society which is at all likely to occur (though not in all possible ones, since societies without parents are logically possible). If it is the latter, then it need not occur in any society which is at all likely to occur—whatever the concept of a society which is at all likely to occur includes, it surely includes a society where the children are nurtured by the community. But even though the obligation to honor and assist one's parents might not be object universal, either in the sense that it has objects in all possible societies or in the sense that it has objects in any society which is at all likely to occur, the individual's obligation to honor and respect the ones who have nurtured him may be, for presumably in any possible society there would be objects of this obligation.[20] At the same time, there could well be a society in which a relatively few people were involved in nurturing the children, and if this were the case it would not be true that *most* people in all possible societies were the object of this obligation.

If the primary ground for the obligation is that one has been begotten by one's parents, the right will not be subject universal in either the first sense or the fourth sense because of the possibility of a parentless society. However, all men will be under it in any society which is at all likely to occur. If the ground for the obligation is nurture, then it need not be subject universal in either the first or fourth sense nor in the sense that persons would be subject to this obligation in any society which is at all likely to occur, for there may be societies in which parents do not nurture their children. On the other hand, an obligation to honor and assist those who have nurtured you will be subject universal in the first sense (if we may suppose that all men must be nurtured to a greater or less degree by someone or other).

(E) Our discussion of Locke has suggested that there may be senses of universality other than those which were suggested in Part I. These senses are:

v. the obligation has (many) subjects and objects in any society which is at all likely to occur,
vi. the obligation has (only) some subjects and objects in any possible society.
vii. the obligation has (only) some subjects and objects in any society which is at all likely to occur, and
viii. any society in which the obligation does not have (many or some) subjects or objects is such that the features which constitute reasons why there are no subjects and objects are grounds for moral criticism.

Should we abandon our provisional definition and extend the notion of natural rights so as to include rights which correspond to important obligations which are universal in any or all of these senses? I am inclined not to do so, on the grounds that natural right theorists have had a very strong sort of universality in mind and that the provisional definition is therefore closer to what has traditionally been meant by "natural rights." However, it seems to me to make little difference whether or not we extend the notion of natural rights in the ways suggested, as long as we are clear as to just what we are doing.

(F) Are the obligations which correspond to the rights we have discussed important obligations? The obligations not to kill, enslave or steal from another are surely important. The obligation to assist, honor, and respect one's parents and the obligation not to interfere with a parent's direction of his children seem less important. In particular the last obligation seems to be one which could be easily overriden by other more important obligations. I am not sure whether it is more plausible to deny that the last is a natural right or to drop the notion that a natural right must correspond to a more important obligation.[21]

III

I should now like to say something about the connection between the notion of natural rights and the notion of a state of nature. The concept of a state of nature can be used in at least two ways. It can be used to argue for the necessity of political society by pointing out the disadvantages which men would suffer if there were no political society. The notion of a state of nature can also be used in another way, for it may be argued that by examining man in a state of nature we can discover natural rights and obligations in the defined sense. Locke uses the concept of a state of nature in both these ways.

If we look at our characterization of natural rights we can see the plausibility of the second move. Natural rights correspond to obligations which fall on men in any society and whose objects can be found in any society. The picture of a state of nature can (in part) be regarded as an attempt to sketch features common to all societies. (Examples of such features might be parental relationships, work, agreements entered into, etc.) If these features are the grounds of certain rights and obligations, one may conclude that these rights and obligations are universal in the required sense, that they will hold in any society. Furthermore, if these rights and obligations are overriding in the state of nature, we may expect them to be overriding in all societies. This is not, however, strictly necessary, for the special arrangements of some society could be such that the obligation or right arising from one of the common features was generally outweighed in that society though not in others.

For the purpose of determining natural rights in the defined sense it is not essential that the state of nature be a state without government. The picture will be drawn without government only if political society is considered to be adventitious, i.e., if political society is not considered necessary to human society. That the state of nature has in practice been pictured as a state without government is due both to the fact that political society was considered accidental or adventitious and to the fact that the examination of a state of nature was serving a double purpose—furnishing reasons for the necessity of government as well as a doctrine of natural rights.

When the state of nature is pictured as society with government abstracted, we have another meaning of "natural rights," viz., "natural rights" are those moral rights, perhaps the most important ones, which obtain in a state of nature whether or not these rights carry over into, or remain important in, political society. (The right to judge one's own case would be an example of a right which one has in the absence of judicial institutions and which does not carry over into political society.) It is to be noticed, however, that if a right does not carry over into political society or if it loses its importance in political society, then it is not a natural right in the defined and, I venture to say, important sense.

It is true that Locke is interested in drawing a distinction between those rights and obligations which arise in nonpolitical society and those which arise in political society. It is not clear that we should be interested in this. In the first place, it may well be that any possible society is a political society. (This of course does not imply that certain rights may not be grounded in the nonpolitical aspects of society.) In the second place, Locke is interested in natural rights largely because he is interested in showing that there are (should be) restraints on arbitary power. Yet the only rights which will function in this way are those which carry over into political society and are thus natural rights in my sense. Finally, natural rights are usually thought to be rights which all or most men have. If this is the case, rights which hold only in a state of nature cannot be natural rights.

NOTES

1. In saying that an obligation to do x is subject or object universal, I mean that (all or most) men are subjects or objects of a *prima facie* obligation to do x. I do not mean to deny that the obligation may be overridden by other obligations in certain circumstances.
2. Margaret MacDonald, "Natural Rights" in *Philosophy, Politics and Society,* ed. Peter Laslett (First Series, Oxford, Basil Blackwell, 1963), pp. 47–48.
3. John Locke, *Second Treatise on Civil Government,* para. 6.
4. *Ibid.,* paras. 22–24
5. *Ibid.,* paras. 16–18, 23, 85.
6. *Ibid.,* paras. 8, 10–11, 16.
7. Cf. *ibid.,* para. 57.
8. This is not quite right, for infants and madmen are not members of the moral community in any full sense (paras. 57, 60) and yet they have a right to life. They have no right to liberty—to act autonomously—but presumably they do have a right not to be enslaved. The difference is perhaps this: children and madmen are potentially full members of the moral community, but those who unjustly resort to violence have wilfully severed their connections with it.
9. Locke, *op. cit.,* paras. 27 ff.
10. *Ibid.,* para. 46.
11. *Ibid.,* para. 72.
12. *Ibid.,* paras. 14, 46.

13. *Ibid.*, para. 67.
14. *Ibid.*, para. 57.
15. *Ibid.*, para. 56.
16. *Ibid.*, para. 57.
17. *Ibid.*, para. 63.
18. *Ibid.*, para. 66.
19. *Ibid.*, para. 67.

20. One might object that the nurture of children is not a *logically* necessary condition of a human society. I am inclined to think that childhood (involving nurture and guidance of some sort) is (logically) necessary for a human existence in a way in which begetting children and being begotten by human parents is not. I am, however, by no means clear on this point.

21. We might have considered (putative) natural rights other than those mentioned by Locke. We might, for example, have considered the rights mentioned in the U.N. Declaration. I think that an examination of these rights would show that they correspond to important obligations which are subject and object universal in sense (i) or in one of the senses (iv) through (viii). It is difficult, however, to determine in just what senses a corresponding obligation is universal without determining what the grounds of the obligation are. In examining Locke, one has the advantage that the grounds are given.

BIBLIOGRAPHICAL NOTE

There is no elementary introduction to the natural law tradition in political thought. Unfortunately, the student must jump into these murky waters headfirst. But there are a number of general treatments of the subject. See: A. P. D'Entreves, *Natural Law: An Historical Survey;* Leo Strauss, *Natural Right and History;* Robert Oppenheimer, *Moral Principles in Political Philosophy;* Benjamin F. Wright, *American Interpretations of Natural Law.*

The political conflicts of the 1960s have made the abolitionists the subject of renewed interest. A useful collection of some of the results is Martin Duberman's *The Anti-Slavery Vanguard: New Essays on the Abolitionists.* Merton L. Dillon has catalogued these efforts and offered some remarks on the reasons for the alternating harsh and sympathetic treatments of the abolitionists by American historians in "The Abolitionists: A Decade of Historiography, 1959–1969," *Journal of Southern History* (1969). Representative tracts of both the abolitionists and defenders of slavery are now conveniently available in *Slavery Attacked: The Abolitionist Crusade,* ed. John L. Thomas, and *Slavery Defended: The Views of the Old South,* ed. Eric L. McKitrick. The student may also wish to analyze antislavery arguments cross nationally. See: Frank Tannenbaum, *Slave and Citizen: The Negro in the Americas;* Frank J. Klingberg, *The Anti-Slavery Movement in England;* Eric Williams, *Capitalism and Slavery.* On individual writers see: Joseph Harbutian, *Piety Versus Moralism;*

David P. Edgell, *William Ellery Channing: An Intellectual Portrait;* John L. Thomas, *The Liberator: William Lloyd Garrison* and Irving H. Bartlett, *Wendell Phillips: Brahmin Radical.*

For accounts of the concept of natural right to justify unregulated capitalism see Richard Hofstadter's *Social Darwinism in American Thought* and Robert G. McClosky's *American Conservatism in the Age of Enterprise.* The incorporation of laissez-faire capitalism into the constitution through the argument for "substantive" due process is most clearly presented (and attacked in Holmes' dissent) in *Lochner v. New York.*

Sumner's assertive writing style was well-suited for the short essay. See his "Earth Hunger," The Challenge of Facts," and "What Social Classes Owe to Each Other."

Edward Bellamy's major work, *Looking Backward,* is not only a delight to read but it is a major work of Utopian thought which ranks with Harrington's *Oceana* and More's *Utopia.* Yet there is little commentary on Bellamy. See Arthur E. Morgan's *Edward Bellamy* and *The Philosophy of Edward Bellamy.*

2. The Morality of Resistance

When does a man declare that he has exhausted all alternatives for peaceful reform and advocate rebellion? Moreover, what methods is he morally entitled to employ against what he regards as a corrupt government? The fact that America was a nation born in revolution has not made the problem of justifying resistance any less difficult.

Opposition to one's government can take a variety of forms and there is no universal agreement on either the desirability or effectiveness of any one of them. One avenue of opposition is, of course, dissent. Protected and encouraged at least formally by liberal democratic governments, dissent involves criticism of the government and even peaceful picketing. Many writers, however, have contended that dissent alone, even when it occurs in a system with competitive elections, may not be effective in altering the policies of government. It may be necessary to actually break a law, provided that this is done nonviolently, publicly, and with full acceptance of the consequences, in order to persuade one's fellow citizens that change is in order. This practice, referred to as civil disobedience, is the subject of the selection by the President's Commission on the Causes and Prevention of Violence. The majority report of the Commission argues against encouraging widespread use of civil disobedience in a democratic society. Their arguments are of varying plausibility and it is the task of the student to judge their worth.

Between dissent and even civil disobedience and revolution, one often finds violent opposition to the state. These acts, either of a small band of men or a group in society are acts of frustration and indignation. They are often ill-planned but are nevertheless destructive instances of rebellion. Historically, these acts have been associated with peasant uprisings. More recently, they have taken the form of the urban riot. There are several problems in justifying this sort of activity.

Robert Paul Wolff argues that this sort of rebellion must be evaluated on grounds other than the justification of violence since the concept of violence itself is merely "ideological rhetoric designed to advance the concrete interests of particular groups." A good portion of Wolff's position rests upon his new found commitment to anarchism.

Can one excuse the violence which is the result of spontaneous and confused acts of resistance? Jeffrie G. Murphy gives a qualified yes. Do these rebellions, as destructive as they are, contribute to social and political progress? Thoreau, in his analysis of John Brown's attempt to free slaves at Harpers Ferry, thinks they do.

The ultimate act of resistance to political authority is, of course, revolution. Aimed at overthrowing the existing government and altering the entire social, political, and economic structure of a society, the revolution is an awesome, and for many an exhilerating phenomenon. Thomas Jefferson offers a number of remarks on the subject. Like all of Jefferson's writings they are a curious combination of naivete and realism. Philip Abbott's analysis is critical of some of the tactics and justifications of revolutionaries themselves.

NOTES ON REVOLUTION
Thomas Jefferson

To John Adams, 1823

... The generation which commences a revolution rarely completes it. Habituated from their infancy to passive submission of body and mind to their kings and priests, they are not qualified when called on to think and provide for themselves; and their inexperience, their ignorance and bigotry make them instruments often, in the hands of the Bonapartes and Iturbides, to defeat their own rights and purposes. This is the present situation of Europe and Spanish America. But it is not desperate. The light which has been shed on mankind by the art of printing, has eminently changed the condition of the world. As yet, that light has dawned on the middling classes only of the men in Europe. The kings and the rabble, of equal ignorance, have not yet received its rays; but it continues to spread, and while printing is preserved, it can no more recede than the sun return on his course. A first attempt to recover the right of self-government may fail, so may a second, a third, &c. But as a younger and more instructed race comes on, the sentiment becomes more and more intuitive, and a fourth, a fifth, or some subsequent one of the ever renewed attempts will ultimately succeed. In France, the first effort was defeated by Robespierre, the second by Bonaparte, the third by Louis XVIII. and his holy allies: another is yet to come, and all Europe, Russia excepted, has caught the spirit; and all will attain representative government, more or less perfect. This is now well understood to be a necessary check on kings, whom they will probably think it more prudent to chain and tame, than to exterminate. To attain all this, however, rivers of blood must yet flow, and years of desolation pass over; yet the object is worth rivers of blood, and years of desolation. For what inheritance so valuable, can man leave to his posterity? The spirit of the Spaniard, and his deadly and eternal hatred to a Frenchman, give me much confidence that he will never submit, but finally defeat this atrocious violation of the laws of God and man, under which he is suffering; and the wisdom and firmness of the Cortes, afford reasonable hope, that that nation will settle down in a temperate representative government, with an executive properly subordinated to that. Portugal, Italy, Prussia, Germany, Greece, will follow suit. You and I shall look down from another world on these glorious achievements to man, which will add to the joys even of heaven.

To Colonel Smith, 1787

... The British ministry have so long hired their gazetteers to repeat, and model into every form, lies about our being in anarchy, that the world has at length believed them, the English nation has believed them, the ministers themselves have come to believe them, and what is more wonderful, we have believed them ourselves. Yet where does this anarchy exist? Where did it ever exist, except in the single instance of Massachusetts? And can history produce an instance of rebellion so honorably conducted? I say nothing of its motives. They were founded in ignorance, not wickedness. God forbid we should ever be twenty years without such a rebellion. The people cannot be all, and always, well informed. The part which is wrong will be discontented, in proportion to the importance of the facts they misconceive. If they remain quiet under such misconceptions, it is a lethargy, the forerunner of death to the public liberty. We have had thirteen States independent for eleven years. There has been one rebellion. That comes to one rebellion in a century and a half, for each State. What country before, ever existed a century and a half without a rebellion? And what country can preserve its liberties, if its rulers are not warned from time to time, that this people preserve the spirit resistance? Let them take arms. The remedy is to set them right as to facts, pardon and pacify them. What signify a few lives lost in a centruy or two? The tree of liberty must be refreshed from time to time, with the blood of patriots and tyrants. It is its natural manure.

A PLEA FOR CAPTAIN JOHN BROWN
Henry David Thoreau

I trust that you will pardon me for being here. I do not wish to force my thoughts upon you, but I feel forced myself. Little as I know of Captain Brown, I would fain do my part to correct the tone and the statements of the newspapers, and of my countrymen generally, respecting his character and actions. It costs us nothing to be just. We can at least express our sympathy with, and admiration of, him and his companions, and that is what I now propose to do. . . .

The newspapers seem to ignore, or perhaps are really ignorant, of the fact that there are at least as many as two or three individuals to a town throughout the North who think much as the present speaker does about him and his enterprise. I do not hesitate to say that they are an important and growing party. We aspire to be something more than stupid and timid chattels, pretending to read history and our Bibles, but desecrating every house and every day we breathe in. Perhaps anxious politicians may prove that only seventeen white men and five negroes were concerned in the late enterprise; but their very

From The Writings of Henry David Thoreau. *Copyright by Houghton Mifflin Co., 1893.*

anxiety to prove this might suggest to themselves that all is not told. Why do they still dodge the truth? They are so anxious because of a dim consciousness of the fact, which they do not distinctly face, that at least a million of the free inhabitants of the United States would have rejoiced if it had succeeded. They at most only criticise the tactics. . . . Though we wear no crape, the thought of that man's position and probable fate is spoiling many a man's day here at the North for other thinking. If any one who has seen him here can pursue successfully any other train of thought, I do not know what he is made of. If there is any such who gets his usual allowance of sleep, I will warrant him to fatten easily under any circumstances which do not touch his body or purse. I put a piece of paper and a pencil under my pillow, and when I could not sleep I wrote in the dark.

On the whole, my respect for my fellow-men, except as one may outweigh a million, is not being increased these days. I have noticed the cold-blooded way in which newspaper writers and men generally speak of this event, as if an ordinary malefactor, though one of unusual "pluck," as the Governor of Virginia is reported to have said, using the language of the cock-pit, "the gamest man he ever saw,"—had been caught, and were about to be hung. He was not dreaming of his foes when the governor thought he looked so brave. It turns what sweetness I have to gall, to hear, or hear of, the remarks of some of my neighbors. When we heard at first that he was dead, one of my townsmen observed that "he died as the fool dieth;" which, pardon me, for an instant suggested a likeness in him dying to my neighbor living. Others, craven-hearted, said disparagingly, that "he threw his life away," because he resisted the government. Which way have they thrown *their* lives, pray?—such as would praise a man for attacking singly an ordinary band of thieves or murderers. I hear another ask, Yankee-like, "What will he gain by it?" as if he expected to fill his pockets by this enterprise. Such a one has no idea of gain but in this worldly sense. If it does not lead to a "surprise" party, if he does not get a new pair of boots, or a vote of thanks, it must be a failure. "But he won't gain anything by it." Well, no, I don't suppose he could get four-and-sixpence a day for being hung, take the year round; but then he stands a chance to save a considerable part of his soul,—and *such* a soul!—when *you* do not. No doubt you can get more in your market for a quart of milk than for a quart of blood, but that is not the market that heroes carry their blood to.

Such do not know that like the seed is the fruit, and that, in the moral world, when good seed is planted, good fruit is inevitable, and does not depend on our watering and cultivating; that when you plant, or bury, a hero in his field, a crop of heroes is sure to spring up. This is a seed of such force and vitality, that it does not ask our leave to germinate.

The momentary charge at Balaklava, in obedience to a blundering command, proving what a perfect machine the soldier is, has, properly enough, been celebrated by a poet laureate; but the steady, and for the most part successful, charge of this man, for some years, against the legions of Slavery, in obedience to an infinitely higher command, is as much more memorable than that as an intelligent and conscientious man is superior to a machine. Do you think that that will go unsung?

"Served him right,"—"A dangerous man,"—"He is undoubtedly insane." So they proceed to live their sane, and wise, and altogether admirable lives, reading their Plutarch a little, but chiefly pausing at that feat of Putnam, who was let down into a wolf's den; and in this wise they nourish themselves for brave and patriotic deeds some time or other. The Tract Society could afford to print that story of Putnam. You might open the district schools with the reading of it, for there is nothing about Slavery or the Church in it; unless it occurs to the reader that some pastors are *wolves* in sheep's clothing. "The American Board of Commissioners for Foreign Missions," even, might dare to protest against *that* wolf. I have heard of boards, and of American boards, but it chances that I never heard of this particular lumber till lately. And yet I hear of Northern men, and women, and children, by families, buying a "life-membership" in such societies as these. A life-membership in the grave! You can get buried cheaper than that.

Our foes are in our midst and all about us. There is hardly a house but is divided against itself, for our foe is the all but universal woodenness of both head and heart, the want of vitality in man, which is the effect of our vice; and hence are begotten fear, superstition, bigotry, persecution, and slavery of all kinds. We are mere figure-heads upon a hulk, with livers in the place of hearts. The curse is the worship of idols, which at length changes the worshiper into a stone image himself; and the New-Englander is just as much an idolater as the Hindoo. This man was an exception, for he did not set up even a political graven image between him and his God.

A church that can never have done with excommunicating Christ while it exists! Away with your broad and flat churches, and your narrow and tall churches! Take a step forward, and invent a new style of outhouses. Invent a salt that will save you, and defend our nostrils.

The modern Christian is a man who has consented to say all the prayers in the liturgy, provided you will let him go straight to bed and sleep quietly afterward. All his prayers begin with "Now I lay me down to sleep," and he is forever looking forward to the time when he shall go to his *"long* rest." He has consented to perform certain old-established charities, too, after a fashion, but he does not wish to hear of any new-fangled ones; he doesn't wish to have any supplementary articles added to the contract, to fit it to the present time. He shows the whites of his eyes on the Sabbath, and the blacks all the rest of the week. The evil is not merely a stagnation of blood, but a stagnation of spirit. Many, no doubt, are well disposed, but sluggish by constitution and by habit, and they cannot conceive of a man who is actuated by higher motives than they are. Accordingly they pronounce this man insane, for they know that *they* could never act as he does, as long as they are themselves. . . .

I read all the newspapers I could get within a week after this event, and I do not remember in them a single expression of sympathy for these men. I have since seen one noble statement, in a Boston paper, not editorial. Some voluminous sheets decided not to print the full report of Brown's words to the exclusion of other matter. It was as if a publisher should reject the manuscript of the New Testament, and print Wilson's last speech. The same journal which contained this pregnant news was chiefly filled, in parallel columns, with the reports of the political conventions that were being held. But the descent to them was too steep. They should have been spared this contrast,—been printed in an extra, at least. To turn from the voices and deeds of earnest men to the *cackling* of political conventions! Office-seekers and speech-makers, who do not so much as lay an honest egg, but wear their breasts bare upon an egg of chalk! Their great game is the game of straws, or rather that universal aboriginal game of the platter, at which the Indians cried *hub, bub!* Exclude the reports of religious and political conventions, and publish the words of a living man. . . .

"All is quiet at Harper's Ferry," say the journals. What is the character of that calm which follows when the law and the slaveholder prevail? I regard this event as a touchstone designed to bring out, with glaring distinctness, the character of this government. We needed to be thus assisted to see it by the light of history. It needed to see itself. When a government puts forth its strength on the side of injustice, as ours to maintain slavery and kill the liberators of the slave, it reveals itself a merely brute force, or worse, a demoniacal force. It is the head of the Plug-Uglies. It is more manifest than ever that tyranny rules. I see this government to be effectually allied with France and Austria in oppressing mankind. There sits a tyrant holding fettered four millions of slaves; here comes their heroic liberator. This most hypocritical and diabolical government looks up from its seat on the gasping four millions, and inquires with an assumption of innocence: "What do you assault me for? Am I not an honest man? Cease agitation on this subject, or I will make a slave of you, too, or else hang you."

We talk about a *representative* government; but what a monster of a government is that where the noblest faculties of the mind, and the *whole* heart, are not *represented!* A semihuman tiger or ox, stalking over the earth, with its heart taken out and the top of its brain shot away. Heroes have fought well on their stumps when their legs were shot off, but I nver heard of any good done by such a government as that.

The only government that I recognize—and it matters not how few are at the head of it, or how small its army—is that power that establishes justice in the land, never that which establishes injustice. What shall we think of a government to which all the truly brave and just men in the land are enemies, standing between it and those whom it oppresses? A government that pretends to be Christian and crucifies a million Christs every day!

Treason! Where does such treason take its rise? I cannot help thinking of you as you deserve, ye governments. Can you dry up the fountains of thought? High treason, when it is resistance to tyranny here below, has its origin in, and is first committed by, the power that makes and forever recreates man. When you have caught and hung all these human rebels, you have accomplished nothing but your own guilt, for you have not struck at the fountain-head. You presume to contend with a foe against whom West Point cadets and rifled cannon *point* not. Can all the art of the cannon-founder tempt matter to turn against its maker? Is the form in which the founder thinks he casts it more essential than the constitution of it and of himself?

The United States have a coffle of four millions of slaves. They are determined to keep them in this condition; and Massachusetts is one of the confederated overseers to prevent their escape. Such are not all the inhabitants of Massachusetts, but such are they who rule and are obeyed here. It was Massachusetts, as well as Virginia, that put down this insurrection at Harper's Ferry. She sent the marines there, and she will have *to pay the penalty of her sin*. . . .

It was his peculiar doctrine that a man has a perfect right to interfere by force with the slaveholder, in order to rescue the slave. I agree with him. They who are continually shocked by slavery have some right to be shocked by the violent death of the slaveholder, but no others. Such will be more shocked by his life than by his death. I shall not be forward to think him mistaken in his method who quickest succeeds to liberate the slave. I speak for the slave when I say that I prefer the philanthropy of Captain Brown to that philanthropy which neither shoots me nor liberates me. At any rate, I do not think it is quite sane for one to spend his whole life in talking or writing about this matter, unless he is continuously inspired, and I have not done so. A man may have other affairs to attend to. I do not wish to kill nor to be killed, but I can foresee circumstances in which both these things would be by me unavoidable. We preserve the so-called peace of our community by deeds of petty violence every day. Look at the policeman's billy and handcuffs! Look at the jail! Look at the gallows! Look at the chaplain of the regiment! We are hoping only to live safely on the outskirts of *this* provisional army. So we defend ourselves and our hen-roosts, and maintain slavery. I know that the mass of my countrymen think that the only righteous use that can be made of Sharp's rifles and revolvers is to fight duels with them, when we are insulted by other nations, or to hunt Indians, or shoot fugitive slaves with them, or the like. I think that for once the Sharp's rifles and the revolvers were employed in a righteous cause. The tools were in the hands of one who could use them.

The same indignation that is said to have cleared the temple once will clear it again. The question is not about the weapon, but the spirit in which you use it. No man has appeared in America, as yet, who loved his fellow-man so well, and treated him so tenderly. He lived for him. He took up his life and he laid it down for him. What sort of violence is that which is encouraged, not by soldiers, but by peaceable citizens, not so much by laymen as by ministers of the Gospel, not so much by the fighting sects as by the Quakers, and not so much by Quaker men as by Quaker women? . . .

Any man knows when he is justified, and all the wits in the world cannot enlighten him on that point. The murderer always knows that he is justly punished; but when a government takes the life of a man without the consent of his conscience, it is an audacious government, and is taking a step towards its own dissolution. Is it not possible that an individual may be right and a government wrong? Are laws to be enforced simply because they were made? or declared by any number of men to be good, if they are *not* good? Is there any necessity for a man's being a tool to perform a deed of which his better nature disapproves? Is it the intention of law-makers that *good* men shall be hung ever? Are judges to interpret the law according to the letter, and not the spirit? What right have *you* to enter into a compact with yourself that you *will* do thus or so, against the light within you? Is it for *you* to *make up* your mind,—to form any resolution whatever,—and not accept the convictions that are forced upon you, and which ever pass your understanding? I do not believe in lawyers, in that mode of attacking or defending a man, because you descend to meet the judge on his own ground, and, in cases of the highest importance, it is of no consequence whether a man breaks a human law or not. Let lawyers decide trivial cases. Business men may arrange that among themselves. If they were the interpreters of the everlasting laws which rightfully bind man, that would be another thing. A counterfeiting law-factory, standing half in a slave land and half in a free! What kind of laws for free men can you expect from that?

I am here to plead his cause with you. I plead not for his life, but for his character,—his immortal life; and so it becomes your cause wholly, and is not his in the least. Some eighteen hundred years ago Christ was crucified; this morning, perchance, Captain Brown was hung. These are the two ends of a chain which is not without its links. He is not Old Brown any longer; he is an angel of light.

ON VIOLENCE
Robert Paul Wolff

Everything I shall say in this essay has been said before, and much of it seems to me to be obvious as well as unoriginal. I offer two excuses for laying used goods before you. In the first place, I think that what I have to say about violence is true. Now, there are many ways to speak falsehood and only one way to speak truth. It follows, as Kierkegaard pointed out, that the truth is likely to become boring. On a subject as ancient and much discussed as ours here, we may probably assume that a novel—and, hence, interesting—view of violence is likely to be false.

From the Journal of Philosophy, *Vol. LXVI, No. 19, (October 2, 1969). Reprinted by permission of publisher and author.*

But truth is not my sole excuse, for the subject before us suffers from the same difficulty that Kant discerned in the area of metaphysics. After refuting the various claims that had been made to transcendent rational knowledge of things-in-themselves, Kant remarked that the refutations had no lasting psychological effect on true believers. The human mind, he concluded, possessed a natural disposition to metaphysical speculation, which philosophy must perpetually keep in check. Somewhat analogously, men everywhere are prone to certain beliefs about the legitimacy of political authority, even though their beliefs are as groundless as metaphysical speculations. The most sophisticated of men persist in supposing that some valid distinction can be made between legitimate and illegitimate commands, on the basis of which they can draw a line, for example, between mere violence and the legitimate use of force. This lingering superstition is shared by those dissenters who call police actions or ghetto living conditions "violent"; for they are merely advancing competing legitmacy claims.

I shall set forth and defend *three* propositions about violence:

First: The concept of violence is inherently confused, as is the correlative concept of non-violence; these and related concepts depend for their meaning in political discussions on the fundamental notion of legitimate authority, which is also inherently incoherent.

Second: It follows that a number of familiar questions are also confusions to which no coherent answers could ever be given, such as: when it is permissible to resort to violence in politics; whether the black movement and the student movement should be non-violent; and whether anything good in politics is ever accomplished by violence.

Finally: The dispute over violence and non-violence in contemporary American politics is ideological rhetoric designed either to halt change and justify the existing distribution of power and privilege or to slow change and justify some features of the existing distribution of power and privilege or else to hasten change and justify a total redistribution of power and privilege.

Let us begin with the first proposition, which is essential to my entire discussion.

I

The fundamental concepts of political philosophy are the concepts of power and authority.[1] Power in general is the ability to make and enforce decisions. Political power is the ability to make and enforce decisions about matters of major social importance. Thus the ability to dispose of my private income as I choose is a form of power, whereas the ability to make and enforce a decision about the disposition of some sizable portion of the tax receipts of the federal government is a form of *political* power. (So too is the ability to direct the decisions of a large private corporation; for the exercise of political power is not confined to the sphere of government.) A complete analysis of the concept of political power would involve a classification both of the means employed in the enforcing of decisions and of the scope and variety of questions about which decisions can be made. It would also require an examination of the kinds of opposition against which the decision could be enforced. There is a very considerable difference between the ability a parliamentary majority has to enforce its decisions against the will of the minority and the ability of a rebel military clique to enforce its decisions against the Parliament as a whole.

Authority, by contrast with power, is not an ability but a right. It is the right to command and, correlatively, the right to be obeyed. Claims to authority are made in virtually every area of social life, and, in a remarkably high proportion of cases, the claims are accepted and acquiesced in by those over whom they are made. Parents claim the right to be obeyed by their children; husbands until quite recently claimed the right to be obeyed by their wives; popes claim the right to be obeyed by the laity and clergy; and of course, most notably, virtually all existing governments claim the right to be obeyed by their subjects.

A claim to authority must be sharply differentiated both from a threat or enticement and from a piece of advice. When the state commands, it usually threatens punishment for disobedience, and it may even on occasion offer a reward for compliance, but the command cannot be reduced to the mere threat or reward. What characteristically distinguishes a state from an occupying army or private party is its insistence, either explicit or implicit, on its *right* to be obeyed. By the same token, an authoritative command is not a mere recommendation. Authority says, "Do this!" not, "Let me suggest this for your consideration."

Claims to authority have been defended on a variety of grounds, most prominent among which are the appeal to God, to tradition, to expertise, to the laws of history, and to the consent of those commanded. We tend to forget that John Locke thought it worth while to devote the first of his *Two Treatises on Civil Government* to the claim that Europe's monarchs held their authority by right of primogenitural descent from Adam. It is common today to give lip service to the theory that authority derives from the consent of the governed, but most of us habitually accord *some* weight to any authority claim issuing from a group of men who regularly control the behavior of a population in a territory, particularly if the group tricks itself out with flags, uniforms, courts of law, and printed regulations.

Not all claims to authority are justified. Indeed, I shall suggest shortly that few if any are. Nevertheless, men regularly accept the authority claims asserted against them, and so we must distinguish a descriptive from a normative sense of the term. Let us use the term '*de facto* authority' to refer to *the ability to get one's authority claims accepted by those against whom they are asserted.* 'De jure authority', then, will refer to *the right to command and to be obeyed.* Obviously, the concept of *de jure* authority is primary, and the concept of *de facto* authority is derivative.

Thus understood, *de facto* authority is a form of power, for it is a means by which its possessor can enforce his decisions. Indeed, as Max Weber—from whom much of this analysis is taken—has pointed out, *de facto* authority is the *principal* means on which states rely to carry out their decisions. Threats and inducements play an exceedingly important role in the enforcement of political decisions, to be sure, but a state that must depend upon them entirely will very soon suffer a crippling reduction in its effectiveness, which is to say, in its political power. Modern states especially require for the coordination of the behavior of large numbers of individuals. The myth of legitimacy is the only efficient means available to the state for achieveing that coordination.

Force is the ability to work some change in the world by the expenditure of physical effort. A man may root up a tree, move a stalled car, drive a nail, or restrain another man, *by force.* Force, in and of itself, is morally neutral. Physically speaking, there may be very little difference between the physical effort of a doctor who resets a dislocated shoulder and that of the ruffian who dislocated it. Sometimes, of course, force is used to work some change in the body of another man—to punch him, shoot him, take out his appendix, hold his arms, or cut his hair. But there is in principle no significant distinction between these uses of force and those uses which involve changing some other part of the world about which he cares. A man who slips into a parking place for which I am heading inflicts an injury on me roughly as great as if he had jostled me in a crowd or stepped on my toe. If he destroys a work of art on which I have lavished my more intense creative efforts, he may harm me more than a physical assault would.

Force is a means to power, but it is not of course a guarantee of power. If I wish to elicit hard work from my employees, I can threaten them with the lash or tempt them with bonuses—both of which are employments of force—but if my workers prefer not to comply, my threats and inducements may be fruitless. It is a commonplace both of domestic and of international politics that the mere possession of a monopoly of force is no guarantee of political power. Those who fail to grasp this truth are repeatedly frustrated by the baffling inability of the strong to impose their will upon the weak.

There are, as far as I can see, *three* means or instruments by which power is exercised—three ways, that is to say, in which men enforce or carry out their social decisions. The first is *force,* the ability to rearrange the world in ways that other men find appealing or distasteful. In modern society, money is of course the principal measure, exchange medium, and symbol of force. The second instrument of power is *de facto* authority—the ability to elicit obedience, as opposed to mere compliance, from others. *De facto* authority frequently accrues to those with a preponderance of force, for men are fatally prone to suppose that he who can compel compliance deserves obedience. But *de facto* authority does not reduce to the possession of a preponderance of force, for men habitually obey commands they know could not effectively be enforced. The third instrument of power is social opinion, or what might be called the "symbolic" use of force. When a runner competes in a race, he may want the first-prize money or the commercial endorsements that will come to the winner, or he may even just like blue ribbons—but he may also want the acclaim of the fans. Now, that acclaim is expressed by certain uses of force—

by clapping of hands and cheering, which are physical acts. But its value to the runner is symbolic; he cherishes it as an expression of approval, not merely as a pleasing sound. To say that man is a social creature is not merely to say that he hangs out in groups, nor even to say that he engages in collective and cooperative enterprises for self-interested purposes; it is most important to say that he values symbolic interactions with other men and is influenced by them as well as by the ordinary exercise of force and by claims of authority. This point is important for our discussion, for, as we shall see, many persons who shrink from the use of force as an instrument of political power have no compunctions about the use of social opinion or what I have called the "symbolic" use of force. Anyone who has observed a progressive classroom run by a teacher with scruples of this sort will know that a day "in coventry" can be a far crueler punishment for an unruly ten-year old than a sharp rap on the knuckles with a ruler.

We come, finally, to the concept of violence. Strictly speaking, *violence is the illegitimate or unauthorized use of force to effect decisions against the will or desire of others.* Thus, murder is an act of violence, but capital punishment *by a legitimate state* is not; theft or extortion is violent, but the collection of taxes *by a legitimate state* is not. Clearly, on this interpretation the concept of violence is normative as well as descriptive, for it involves an implicit appeal to the principle of *de jure* legitimate authority. there is an associated sense of the term which is purely descriptive, relying on the descriptive notion of *de facto* authority. Violence in this latter sense is the use of force in ways that are proscribed or unauthorized by those who are generally accepted as the legitimate authorities in the territory. Descriptively speaking, the attack on Hitler's life during the second World War was an act of violence, but one might perfectly well deny that it was violent in the strict sense, on the grounds that Hitler's regime was illegitimate. On similar grounds, it is frequently said that police behavior toward workers or ghetto dwellers or demonstrators is violent even when it is clearly within the law, for the authority issuing the law is illegitimate.

It is common, but I think wrong-headed, to restrict the term 'violence' to uses of force that involve bodily interference or the direct infliction of physical injury. Carrying a dean out of his office is said to be violent, but not seizing his office when he is absent and locking him out. Physically tearing a man's wallet from his pocket is "violent," but swindling him out of the same amount of money is not. There is a natural enough basis for this distinction. Most of us value our lives and physical well-being above other goods that we enjoy, and we tend therefore to view attacks or threats on our person as different in kind from other sorts of harm we might suffer. Nevertheless, the distinction is not sufficiently sharp to be of any analytical use, and, as we shall see later, it usually serves the ideological purpose of ruling out, as immoral or politically illegitimate, the only instrument of power that is available to certain social classes.

In its strict or normative sense, then, the concept of political violence depends upon the concept of *de jure,* or legitimate authority. If there is no such thing as legitimate political authority, then it is impossible to distinguish between legitimate and illegitimate uses of force. Now, of course, under any circumstances, we can distinguish between right and wrong, justified and unjustified, uses of force. Such a distinction belongs to moral philosopny in general, and our choice of the criteria by which we draw the distinction will depend on our theory of value and obligation. But the distinctive political concept of violence can be given a coherent meaning *only* by appeal to a doctrine of legitimate political authority.

On the basis of a lengthy reflection upon the concept of *de jure* legitimate authority, I have come to the conclusion that philosophical anarchism is true. That is to say, I believe that there is not, and there could not be, a state that has a right to command and whose subjects have a binding obligation to obey. I have defended this view in detail elsewhere, and I can only indicate here the grounds of my conviction. Briefly, I think it can be shown that every man has a fundamental duty to be autonomous, in Kant's sense of the term. Each of us must make himself the author of his actions and take responsibility for them by refusing to act save on the basis of reasons he can see for himself to be good. Autonomy, thus understood, is in direct opposition to obedience, which is submission to the will of another, irrespective of reasons. Following Kant's usage, political obedience is heteronymy of the will.

Now, political theory offers us one great argument designed to make the autonomy of the individual compatible with submission to the putative authority of the state. In a democrary, it is claimed, the citizen is both law-giver and law-obeyer. Since he shares in the authorship of the laws, he submits to his own will in obeying them, and hence is autonomous, not heteronymous.

If this argument were valid, it would provide a genuine ground for a distinction between violent and nonviolent political actions. Violence would be a use of force proscribed by the laws or executive authority of a genuinely democratic state. The only possible justification of illegal or extralegal political acts would be a demonstration of the illegitimacy of the state, and this in turn would involve showing that the commands of the state were not expressions of the will of the people.

But the classic defense of democracy is *not* valid. For a variety of reasons, neither majority rule nor any other method of making decisions in the absence of unanimity can be shown to preserve the autonomy of the individual citizens. In a democracy, as in any state, obedience is heteronymy. The autonomous man is of necessity an anarchist. Consequently, there is no valid *political* criterion for the justified use of force. Legality is, by itself, no justification. Now, of course, there are all manner of utilitarian arguments for submitting to the state and its agents, even if the state's claim to legitimacy is unfounded. The laws may command actions that are in fact morally obligatory or whose effects promise to be beneficial. Widespread submission to law may bring about a high level of order, regularity, and predictability in social relationships which is valuable independently of the particular character of the acts commanded.

But in and of themselves, the acts of police and the commands of legislatures have no peculiar legitimacy or sanction. Men everywhere and always impute authority to established governments, and they are always wrong to do so.

II

The foregoing remarks are quite banal, to be sure. Very few serious students of politics will maintain either the democratic theory of legitimate authority or any alternatives to it. Nevertheless, like postheological, demythologized Protestants who persist in raising prayers to a God they no longer believe in, modern men go on exhibiting a superstitious belief in the authority of the state. Consider, for example, a question now much debated: When is it permissible to resort to violence in politics? If 'violence' is taken to mean an *unjustified* use of force, then the answer to the question is obviously *never*. If the use of force were permissible, it would not, by definition, be violence, and if it were violent, it would not, by definition, be permissible. If 'violence' is taken in the strict sense to mean "an illegitimate or unauthorized use of force," then *every* political act, whether by private parties or by agents of the state, is violent, for there is no such thing as legitimate authority. If 'violence' is construed in the restricted sense as "bodily interference or the direct infliction of physical harm," then the obvious but correct rule is to resort to violence when less harmful or costly means fail, providing always that the balance of good and evil produced is superior to that promised by any available alternative.

These answers are all trivial, but that is precisely my point. Once the concept of violence is seen to rest on the unfounded distinction between legitimate and illegitimate political authority, the question of the appropriateness of violence simply dissolves. It is mere superstition to describe a policeman's beating of a helpless suspect as "an excessive use of force" while characterizing an attack by a crowd on the policeman as a resort to violence." The implication of such a distinction is that the policeman, as the duly appointed representative of a legitimate government, has a right to use physical force, although no right to use "excessive" force, whereas the crowd of private citizens has no right at all to use even moderate physical force. But there are no legitimate governments, hence no special rights attaching to soldiers, policemen, magistrates, or other law-enforcement agents, hence no coherent distinction between violence and the legitimate use of force.

Consider, as a particular example, the occupation of buildings and the student strike at Columbia University during April and May of 1968. The consequences of those acts have not yet played themselves out, but I think certain general conclusions can be drawn. First, the total harm done by the students and their supporters was very small in comparison with the good results that were achieved. A month of classwork was lost, along with many tempers and a good deal of sleep. Someone—it is still not clear who—burned the research notes of a history professor, an act which, I am happy to say, produced a universal revulsion shared even by the SDS. In the following year, a number of classes were momentarily disrupted by SDS activists in an unsuccessful attempt to repeat the triumph of the previous spring.

Against this, what benefits flowed from the protest? A reactionary and thoroughly unresponsive administration was forced to resign; an all-university Senate of students, professors, and administrators was created, the first such body at Columbia. A callous and antisocial policy of university expansion into the surrounding neighborhood was reversed; some at least of the university's ties with the military were loosened or severed; and an entire community of students and professors were forced to confront the moral and political issues which till then they have managed to ignore.

Could these benefits have been won at less cost? Considering the small cost of the uprising, the question seems to me a bit finicky; nevertheless, the answer is clearly, No. The history of administrative intransigence and faculty apathy at Columbia makes it quite clear that nothing short of a dramatic act such as the seizure of buildings could have deposed the university administration and produced a university senate. In retrospect, the affair seems to have been a quite prudent and restrained use of force.

Assuming this assessment to be correct, it is tempting to conclude, "In the Columbia case, violence was justified." But this conclusion is *totally wrong,* for it implies that a line can be drawn between legitimate and illegitimate forms of protest, the latter being justified only under special conditions and when all else has failed. We would all agree, I think, that, under a dictatorship, men have the right to defy the state or even to attack its representatives when their interests are denied and their needs ignored—the only rule that binds them is the general caution against doing more harm than they accomplish good. My purpose here is simply to argue that a modern industrial democracy, whatever merits it may have, is in this regard no different from a dictatorship. No special authority attaches to the laws of a representative, majoritarian state; it is only superstition and the myth of legitimacy that invests the judge, the policeman, or the official with an exclusive right to the exercise of certain kinds of force.

In the light of these arguments, it should be obvious that I see no merit in the doctrine of nonviolence, nor do I believe that any special and complex justification is needed for what is usually called "civil disobedience." A commitment to nonviolence can be understood in two different senses, depending on the interpretation given to the concept of violence. If violence is understood in the strict sense as the political use of force in ways proscribed by a legitimate government, then of course the doctrine of nonviolence depends upon the assumption that there *are* or *could be* legitimate governments. Since I believe this assumption to be false, I can attribute no coherent meaning to this first conception of nonviolence.

If violence is understood, on the other hand, as the use of force to interfere with someone in a direct, bodily way or to injure him physically, then the doctrine of nonviolence is merely a subjective queasiness having no moral rationale. When you occupy the seats at a lunch counter for hours on end, thereby depriving the proprieter of the profits he would have made on ordinary sales during that time, you are taking money out of his pocket quite as effectively as if you had robbed his till or smashed his stock. If you persist in the sit-in until he goes into debt, loses his lunch counter, and takes a job as a day laborer, then you have done him a much greater injury than would be accomplished by a mere beating in a dark alley. He may deserve to be ruined, of course, but, if so, then he probably also deserves to be beaten. A penchant for such indirect coercion as a boycott or a sit-in is morally questionable, for it merely leaves the dirty work to the bank that forecloses on the mortgage or the policeman who carries out the eviction. Emotionally, the commitment to nonviolence is frequently a severely repressed expression of extreme hostility akin to the mortifications and self-flagellations of religious fanatics. Enough testimony has come from Black novelists and psychiatrists to make it clear that the philosophy of nonviolence is, for the American Negro, what Nietzsche called a "slave morality"—the principal difference is that, in traditional Christianity, God bears the guilt for inflicting pain on the wicked; in the social gospel, the law acts as the scourge.

The doctrine of civil disobedience is an American peculiarity growing out of the conflict between the authority claims of the state and the directly contradictory claims of individual conscience. In a futile attempt to deny and affirm the authority of the state simultaneously, a number of conscientious dissenters have claimed the right to disobey what they believe to be immoral laws, so long as they are prepared to submit to punishment by the state. A willingness to go to jail for one's beliefs is widely viewed in this country as evidence of moral sincerity, and even as a sort of argument for the position one is defending.

Now, tactically speaking, there is much to be said for legal martyrdom. As tyrannical governments are perpetually discovering, the sight of one's leader nailed to a cross has a marvelously bracing effect on the faithful members of a dissident sect. When the rulers are afflicted by the very principles they are violating, even the *threat* of self-sacrifice may force a government to its knees. But leaving tactics aside, no one has any moral obligation whatsoever to resist an unjust government openly rather than clandestinely. Nor has anyone a duty to invite and then to suffer unjust punishment. The choice is simple: if the law is right, follow it. If the law is wrong, evade it.

I think it is possible to understand why conscientious and morally concerned men should feel a compulsion to seek punishment for acts they genuinely believe to be right. Conscience is the echo of society's voice within us. The men of strongest and most independent conscience are, in a manner of speaking, just those who have most completely internalized this social voice, so that they hear and obey its commands even when no policeman compels their compliance. Ironically, it is these same men who are most likely to set themselves against the government in the name of ideals and principles to which they feel a higher loyalty. When a society violates the very principles it claims to hold, these men of conscience experience a terrible conflict. They are deeply committed to the principles society has taught them, principles they have truly come to believe. But they can be true to their beliefs only by setting themselves against the laws of the very society that has been their teacher and with whose authority they identify themselves. Such a conflict never occurs in men of weak conscience, who merely obey the law, however much it violates the moral precepts they have only imperfectly learned.

The pain of the conflict is too great to be borne; somehow, it must be alleviated. If the commitment to principle is weak, the individual submits, though he feels morally unclean for doing so. If the identification with society is weak, he rejects the society and becomes alienated, perhaps identifying with some other society. But if both conscience and identification are too strong to be broken, the only solution is to expiate the guilt by seeking social punishment for the breach of society's laws. Oddly enough, the expiation, instead of bringing them back into the fold of law-obeyers, makes it psychologically all the easier for them to continue their defiance of the state.

III

The foregoing conclusions seem to reach far beyond what the argument warrants. The classical theory of political authority may indeed be inadequate; it may even be that the concept of legitimate authority is incoherent; but surely *some* genuine distinction can be drawn between a politics of reason, rules, and compromise on the one hand, and the resort to violent conflict on the other! Are the acts of a rioting mob different only in degree from the calm and orderly processes of a duly constituted court of law? Such a view partakes more of novelty than of truth!

Unless I very much misjudge my audience, most readers will respond roughly in this manner. There may be a few still willing to break a lance for sovereignty and legitimate authority, and a few, I hope, who agree immediately with what I have said, but the distinction between violence and nonviolence in politics is too familar to be so easily discarded. In this third section of my essay, therefore, I shall try to discover what makes the distinction so plausible, even though it is—I insist—unfounded.

The customary distinction between violent and nonviolent modes of social interaction seems to me to rest on *two* genuine distinctions: the first is the *subjective* distinction between the regular or accepted and the irregular or unexpected uses of force; the second is the *objective* distinction between those interests which are central or vital to an individual and those which are secondary or peripheral.

Consider first the subjective distinction between regular and irregular uses of force in social interactions. It seems perfectly appropriate to us that a conflict between two men who desire the same piece of land should be settled in favor of the one who can pull more money out of his pocket. We consider it regular and orderly that the full weight of the police power of the state be placed behind that settlement in order to ensure that nothing upset it. On the other hand, we consider it violent and disorderly to resolve the dispute by a fist fight or a duel. Yet what is the difference between the use of money, which is one kind of force, and the use of fists, which is another? Well, if we do not appeal to the supposed legitimacy of financial transactions or to the putative authority of the law, then the principal difference is that we are accustomed to settling disputes with dollars and we are no longer accustomed to settling them with fists.

Imagine how barbaric, how unjust, how *violent,* it must seem, to someone unfamiliar with the beauties of capitalism, that a man's ability to obtain medical care for his children should depend solely on the contingency that some other man can make a profit from his productive labor! Is the Federal Government's seizure of my resources for the purpose of killing Asian peasants less violent than a bandit's extortion of tribute at gunpoint? Yet we are accustomed to the one and unaccustomed to the other.

The objective distinction between central and peripheral interests also shapes our conception of what is violent in politics. When my peripheral or secondary interests are at stake in a conflict, I quite naturally consider only a moderate use of force to be justified. Anything more, I will probably call "violence." What I tend to forget, of course, is that other parties to the conflict may find their primary interests challenged and, hence, may have a very different view of what is and is not violent. In the universities, for example, most of the student challenges have touched only on the peripheral interests of professors. No matter what is decided about ROTC, curriculum, the disposition of the endowment, or Black studies, the typical philosophy professor's life will be largely unchanged. His tenure, salary, working conditions, status, and family life remain the same. Hence he is likely to take a tolerant view of building seizures and sit-ins. Bue let a classroom be disrupted, and he cries out that violence has no place on campus. What he means is that force has been used in a way that touches one of his deeper concerns.

The concept of violence serves as a rhetorical device for proscribing those political uses of force which one considers inimical to one's central interests. Since different social groups have different central interests and can draw on different kinds of force, it follows that there are conflicting definitions of violence. Broadly speaking, in the United States today, there are four conceptions of violence corresponding to four distinct socioeconomic classes.

The first view is associated with the established financial and political interests in the country. It identifies the violent with the illegal, and condemns all challenges to the authority of the state and all assaults on the rights of property as beyond the limits of permissible politics. The older segments of the business community adopt this view, along with the military establishment and the local elites of middle America. Robert Taft was once a perfect symbol of this sector of opinion.

The second view is associated with the affluent, educated, technical and professional middle class in America, together with the new, rapidly growing, future-oriented sectors of the economy, such as the communications industry, electronics, etc. They accept, even welcome, dissent, demonstration, ferment, and—within limits—attacks on property in ghetto areas. They look with favor on civil disobedience and feel at ease with extralegal tactics of social change. Their interests are identified with what is new in American society, and they are confident of coming out on top in the competition for wealth and status within an economy built on the principle of reward for profitable performance.

The "liberals," as this group is normally called, can afford to encourage modes of dissent or disruption that do not challenge the economic and social arrangements on which their success is based. They will defend rent strikes, grape boycotts, or lunch-counter sit-ins with the argument that unemployment and starvation are a form of violence also. Since they are themselves in competition with the older elite for power and prestige, they tend to view student rebels and black militants as their allies, up to the point at which their own interests are attacked. But when tactics are used that threaten their positions in universities, in corporations, or in affluent suburbs, then the liberals cry *violence* also, and call for the police. A poignant example of this class is the liberal professor who cheers the student rebels as they seize the Administration building and then recoils in horror at the demand that he share his authority to determine curriculum and decide promotions.

The third view of violence is that held by working-class and lower-middle-class Americans, those most often referred to as the "white backlash." They perceive the principal threat to their interests as coming from the bottom class of ghetto dwellers, welfare, clients, and nonunionized laborers who demand more living space, admission to union jobs with union wages, and a larger share of social product. To this hard-pressed segment of American society, 'violence' means street crime, ghetto riots, civil-rights marches into all-white neighborhoods, and antiwar attacks on the patriotic symbols of constituted authority with which backlash America identifies. Studies of the petty bourgeoisie in Weimar Germany suggest, and George Wallace's presidential campaign of 1968 confirms, that the lower middle class, when it finds itself pressed between inflationary prices and demands from the lower class, identifies its principal enemy as the lower class. So we find the classic political alliance of old established wealth with right-wing populist elements, both of which favor a repressive response to attacks on authority and a strong governmental policy toward the "violence" of demands for change.

The fourth view of violence is the revolutionary counterdefinition put forward by the outclass and its sympathizers within the liberal wing of the established order. Two complementary rhetorical devices are employed. First, the connotation of the term 'violence' is accepted, but the application of the term is reversed: police are violent, not rioters; employers, not strikers; the American army, not the enemy. In this way, an attack is mounted on the government's claim to possess the right to rule. Secondly, the denotation of the term is held constant and the connotation reversed. Violence is good, not bad; legitimate, not illegitimate. It is, in Stokely Carmichael's great rhetorical flourish, "as American as cherry pie." Since the outclass of rebels has scant access to the instruments of power used by established social classes—wealth, law, police power, legislation—it naturally seeks to legitimize the riots, harassments, and street crime which are its only weapons. Equally naturally, the rest of society labels such means "violent" and suppresses them.

In the complex class struggle for wealth and power in America, each of us must decide for himself which group he will identify with. It is not my purpose here to urge one choice rather than another. My sole aim is to argue that the concept of violence has no useful role to play in the deliberations leading to that choice. Whatever other considerations of utility and social justice one appeals to, no weight should be given to the view that *some* uses of force are prima facie ruled out as illegitimate and hence "violent" or that other uses of force are prima facie ruled in as legitimate, or legal. Furthermore, in the advancement of dissenting positions by illegal means, no special moral merit attaches to the avoiding, as it were, of body contact. Physical harm may be among the most serious injuries that can be done to an opponent, but, if so, it differs only in degree and not in kind from the injuries inflicted by so-called "non-violent" techniques of political action.

IV

The myth of legitimate authority is the secular reincarnation of that religious superstition which has finally ceased to play a significant role in the affairs of men. Like Christianity, the worship of the state has its fundamentalists, its revisionists, its ecumenicists (or world-Federalists), and its theological rationale. The philosophical anarchist is the atheist of politics. I began my discussion with the observation that the belief in legitimacy, like the penchant for transcendent metaphysics, is an ineradicable irrationality of the human experience. However, the slow extinction of religious faith over the past two centuries may encourage us to hope that in time anarchism, like atheism, will become the accepted conviction of enlightened and rational men.

PUNISHMENT FOR LOOTERS?
Jeffrie G. Murphy

> *If society lets any considerable number of its members grow up mere children, incapable of being acted on by rational considerations of distant motives, society has only itself to blame for the consequences.*
>
> *John Stuart Mill*

For reasons that should be obvious, a society tends to accept as excuses only those conditions which it is possible for its more advantaged members to satisfy. Any of us, no matter how wellborn, can suffer mental disorder. And so it is common, once mental disorder of a certain sort has been established, to excuse or at least mitigate the moral or legal responsibility for actions performed under the influence of the disorder. Similarly, any of us can act in ignorance, and some kinds of ignorance can excuse or mitigate responsibility for consequences.

Many of us, however, have not been placed by our society in the position of being economically and culturally deprived or of risking such deprivation. And so we tend to take a tone of righteous indignation when it is even suggested that *social* (as opposed to psychological) disadvantage be considered a legitimate excuse for wrongdoing. Many well-intentioned liberals, for example, react in horror when representative members of a black community demand amnesty for crimes, like looting, which they judge to be substantial products of social disadvantage. Against such heretical suggestions, we might even be tempted to argue that being responsible is part of the meaning of human dignity, and to deprive members of the black community of the opportunity of being held responsible for what they do is to regard them as having no dignity—to treat them as animals or children rather than mature persons. There is something ironic, after years of systematic treatment of blacks as children or animals, in wanting them to have that one dignity (responsibility) which it is painful for them to have; but there is perhaps some point in the argument.

Unless this plea for social excuses is carefully specified (as it often is not by those who make it), there will be good grounds for resisting it. It is important to see, for example, that we cannot cite social disadvantage as an argument that looting is morally or legally *right*. For looting is, since prohibited by statute, quite clearly legally wrong; and it would appear to be, because probably productive of more evil than beneficent consequences, morally wrong

Reprinted from Dissent, *January-February 1969, by permission of the publishers and the author. The* Author's Postscript, 1971 *has been added for this volume.*

as well. But the issue that concerns me here is not the objective rightness or wrongness of looting. Rather it is, granting that looting is wrong, whether or not its practice is, under certain social circumstances, to be *excused*. And this is quite a different issue. To hurt my secretary's feelings by extreme rudeness is morally wrong, but surely I am to be at least partially excused for this if I am laboring under great mental strain. (Suppose, for example, I had recently leaned that my child had an incurable illness.) We tend to excuse men in such circumstances because, though we know the act was wrong, we are not sure that we could have exercised any better restraint if comparably placed. And so it seems only fair to take a tolerant line.

Such an appeal to fairness provides, I think, a good reason for at least partially excusing (and therefore not punishing, or punishing with reduced severity) those who engage in looting during the recurrent disturbances in oureblack ghettos. For consider how the world must look to those people. As they perceive our society, it surely presents little but a source of deep and destructive frustration. Our mass media make the ownership of gaudy and frivolous possessions into not just a condition for human happiness, but a condition even for the worth of a person. The value that one has in our society is made to depend upon the material goods that one can conspicuously display. Attainment of these goods, however, is systematically impossible for our disadvantaged minorities. Society, at least as they (not too inaccurately) see it, is structured to thwart all the expectations which that society simultaneously holds out to them. Many of them are neither given, nor do they have an opportunity to earn, income sufficient for such basic necessities as food, clothing, and shelter—much less for the frivolities that are a part of the American way of life. Unlike those self-made men who are always happy to remind us that *they* were able to make it into affluent society ("I fight poverty; I work"), black people are for the most part not members of a temporary minority. Rather they are among the ranks of the *permanently disadvantaged,* the permanently left out. It is some indication of how highly their interests are valued that they are drafted in great numbers to fight in a war which has, as a major side effect, the scrapping of those programs that might make a start toward lifting them from their misery. It is not enough that they be oppressed; they must even assist in their own oppression.

What happens when general disorder breaks out in a ghetto? As might be expected, some of these people take the opportunity (the first they have ever had) to cash in on the American Dream. Let us grant that what they are doing is legally and morally wrong. But the important question, surely, is the following: Should they be held fully responsible (and thus be fully punished) for what they do? (Such a sympathetic question is particularly appropriate when harsh cries of "respect law and order" and "end crime in the streets" are serving as the great national excuse for not doing anything about the real violence in our society.) And it seems to me that reasonable and fair men should consider this question and answer it with a *no*. For if sincere, none of us could confidently claim that we would exercise any better restraint if comparably placed; and it is unjust to demand of one man any greater restraint than it is reasonable to expect of *any* man in similar circumstances. If suddenly forced to change places with the ghetto black, we just might still exercise restraint. But if we did, this would no doubt be a residue of our respect for property and legal authority—a respect unreasonable to demand of the ghetto dweller since he can seldom have any of the former and quite plausibly regards the latter as an instrument of his oppression.

So it seems to me unreasonable because unfair to punish, or at least punish with full severity, those ghetto dwellers who loot in times of civil disorder. This is to demand of them a greater restraint than is reasonable to demand of any man in such circumstances. Note, for example, how sharply these people differ from those middle-class souls who, following a tornado or other disaster, begin to loot the scattered possessions of their neighbors. Note also how they differ from the police who, it is said, have on occasion joined in the looting.

These actions are not merely wrong but are *inexcusable* because it *is* reasonable to demand that these people, given *their* circumstances, exercise a greater restraint. This is particularly true of the police who have, in virtue of their office, a *duty* to refrain from such acts.

Now I have taken looting as an example because it seems to me that the case for tolerance is best made with respect to crimes against property. One must be careful about generalizing the argument to include crimes against persons (e.g. police); for these crimes are, Mayor Daley to the contrary, of a morally graver kind than crimes against property. Yet even here, though surely the violence is morally and legally wrong, there are at least some grounds for partially excusing its performance by the socially disadvantaged. For these people are not as inclined as their more advantaged fellow citizens to view legal authority as a bulwark *against* violence. Their perception of police and other legal authorities is rather different from that of the rest of us, for they see this authority (again not too inaccurately) as itself essentially violent.

As Newton Garver has observed ("What Violence Is," *Nation*, June 24, 1968, pp. 819–22), violence is often institutionalized into socially sanctioned forms. And this kind of violence, since it is accepted uncritically by most people, is the most dangerous of all. Most of the great atrocities of history have resulted from this kind of violence rather than from the violence of individuals. (And so no gun control bill, no matter how useful on other grounds, will even make a start toward rooting out the real violence and sickness of our society.) Once again, then, we must ask ourselves: If we perceived legal authorities (especially police) as themselves violently coercive against all our aspirations, would we really be able to exercise that kind of restraint we can manifest when viewing the police as protectors? I suspect not. For the disadvantaged are acting here either under extreme provocation or in a kind of excusable ignorance. The police may not in fact be as universally repressive and evil as ghetto dwellers believe. But then these people, given their experience, have little opportunity to come to know this.

Obviously some rioters, particularly those who engage in crimes against persons, will have to be institutionally restrained. This will be largely for protection of others rather than as deterrence, since penal sanctions tend to deter only those with something to lose. But we should view this restraint in part as a regrettable necessity and not as the righteous infliction of punishment. And in many circumstances, especially those involving crimes against poverty, society can well afford to seek mere recovery of property and abandon, through a tolerance motivated by fairness, most attempts at punishment. For as Mill reminds us, when we treat people as children or animals by controlling them violently and repressively, rather than treating them with sympathy and reason, we bear a part of the responsibility for what they do. Many of us in the white and satisfied majority have not heeded our own pious cries for an end to violence and a return to law and order. The only difference between us and the ghetto revolutionary is simply that the outlets for our violence are institutionally approved. This connotes a factual difference, but not a morally relevant difference.

In closing, I should mention that what I am suggesting is not paternalistic and is not, therefore, an inroad on the dignity of the people in question. I am not suggesting that, like animals or machines, they act by reflex or necessity without being able to help what they do. Rather I am suggesting that the pressures they face are more severe and the alternative channels for releasing those pressures more limited than is the case with most of the rest of us, and that tolerance demands that we take these pressures into account as mitigating circumstances. So I am suggesting that we consider social excuses, not out of charity or benevolence, but out of *justice*. For it is unjust (and not simply uncharitable) to demand of another man more than we could realize if comparably placed. If this is an attack on dignity, it is an attack on the dignity of us all. For if those of us who are white and wellborn were forced to change places with the urban blacks, I am inclined to think we would exercise *less* restraint. For we are accustomed to getting most of our whims satisfied, and such habits die hard. So rather than citing black rebellion as evidence of basic black immorality, we should remember how long it was in coming and how much more destructive of life it could have been. This might incline us to marvel at the restraint of these people and to draw a more sympathetic conclusion about their moral character.

AUTHOR'S POSTSCRIPT, 1971
Though I still agree with the major thrust of my paper, I should like to take this opportunity to state my argument with more caution and care than I did in 1969. I do not want to maintain that social disadvantages should excuse *simpliciter*. Many socially disadvantaged persons do exercise restraint and obey the law, and this is sufficient to show that disadvantage does not in

general necessitate antisocial or illegal action. Similarly, insanity is not (and should not be) a criminal defense *simpliciter*. For not all forms of insanity necessitate illegal conduct—e.g. we would be very suspicious of any argument of the form "Jones, who is a compulsive exhibitionist, should be excused on grounds of insanity for his act of tax fraud." Surely we would demand, and rightly so, that a plausible case be made out that his insanity stands in a close casual relation to the very act he is charged with. For I do not think we want a collective conception of excuse any more than we want a collection conception of guilt. One of the important contributions that liberalism has made to legal thinking is the idea that criminal (though not necessarily moral) guilt is to be individualized and that admissible evidence is to be about the man charged and not about the social group of which he is a member. However, sometimes a man's social disadvantage does seem to play a prominent role in explaining *his* conduct. And thus, though I do not think that the criminal law should have "social disadvantage" as a separate defense, I do think it would be reasonable to let such disadvantage be *evidentially relevant* with respect to current defenses and elements of criminal responsibility. For example, consider the defense of self-defense. A man is excused on grounds of self-defense if it is held that he used deadly force in the reasonable belief that his life was being wrongfully threatened. But what is a *reasonable* belief? On most current standards, the criterion is in terms of what the average jury (mostly white, middle-class people) regards as reasonable—the so-called "objective standard" of reasonableness. But once we consider the possibility that what appears reasonable to the average white, middle-class man (e.g. how he views the police and their potential for doing him illegal injury) may be very different indeed from what appears reasonable to the average black ghetto-dweller on the same issue, we have grounds for skepticism of prevailing standards and for the traditional liberal rhetoric about trial by a "jury of one's peers."

REVOLUTIONARY ETHICS
Philip Abbott

The tasks of the revolutionary are formidable; the temptations are great. He faces a Leviathan with terrifying brute force at its disposal, a consituency which is often indifferent, unreliable, and even hostile. Moreover, the very structure of language stifles his political imagination and is sure to force his actions into the most unflattering conceptual categories. If he loses he is certain to face a violent if not an ignominious death. If he wins he must deal with the incredible burdens of political and social consolidation and reconstruction. It is not surprising then that although revolution is invariably justified in moral terms, precious few revolutionaries can pass a test involving the most minimal ethical demands. Nevertheless, I shall argue that some tests must be administered by all of us and that we must insist that they be passed. If we tolerate less, we impugn the names of all those who have suffered from injustice and oppression. Regrettably, if we could tote up a list of promises unkept, the modern revolutionary fares rather badly. Let me illustrate by discussing two related revolutionary problems.

I

No matter how inefficient or corrupt a regime has become, it still possesses some repository of authority. The existing government does occupy the offices; it has the uniforms, ambassadors, tax collectors, even the postage stamps. Perhaps most important, since political legitimacy is always closely conceptually related to force, it has the guns. And although the question often has a hollow ring when the on-going government asks the revolutionaries "Who do you represent?", the revolutionary usually has trouble answering. First, and this is so obvious that it is rarely mentioned, the revolutionary simply cannot afford to be too explicit. If he is, he faces conspiracy charges, arrests, and imprisonment. It was this problem which led to Lenin's capitulation in *What Is To Be Done?*:

The more we restrict the membership of this organization to persons who are engaged in revolution as a profession and who have been professionally trained in the art of combatting the political police, the more difficult will it be to catch the organization . . . [1]

Yet despite these precautions the reprisals, harassment, mass arrests, and infiltration by the government force the revolutionary from contact with his constituency. When an FBI official was reported to have said that he wanted radicals to think there was an agent behind every mailbox, he was reflecting a strategy all governments use. Entrap, hire informers, survey the revolutionary's actions, and then when he goes underground challenge his knowledge of and connection with his constituency. But the revolutionary's response is nearly as predictable as the government's actions. At first he regards the attention as a backhanded compliment. He feels the movement is indeed a threat. But then a different clothing style, a raised eyebrow, an objection or hesitation become clues for the detection of a government informer. "Revolutionary justice" is the result: the oppressed torture, maim, and kill their own people. Although we can say that such suspicion is understandable, those reactions are not morally justifiable. While the failure to distinguish explanation and understanding from excuses and justifications may be tendency of liberal thought, we must realize that it becomes the core of the revolutionary position. The acceptance of the role of the revolutionary involves great risks not only for himself but to those he represents. It simply is not justifiable to torture or summarily shoot suspected informers. One need not be a pacifist to recognize that torture is torture no matter who commits it. Who can want—

or trust—a leader who ordered necks broken and skin scalded? If we take seriously the notion of the war criminal then we must accept the notion of revolutionary criminality.

But there is another problem that arises from revolutionary paranoia. In some respects the problem of the revolutionary as representative is not unlike those of any political official. Political scientists have documented the status differential that almost immediately accompanies the accession to political leadership. If a president can wrap himself in a cocoon of sycophants and self-serving memos from bureaucrats, the revolutionary faces the same possibility. Since he reads only sympathetic newspapers, speaks only to those with similar commitments, his capacity for self-delusion is nearly unlimited (regardless of the effects of political intimidation). However imperfect and even fixed an election might be, the governmental official faces the possibility of a confrontation with reality. For the revolutionary, his delusion is only realized, if at all, at that brief moment before the gallows.

If anyone needs to hold his grip on reality it is the revolutionary. But he begins to see agents at every turn. He mistakes what may well be only a precaution taken by the government for a last ditch life and death struggle for power. He exaggerates his own importance, appeals to a bewildered or indifferent people for aid and plunges into a reckless putsch. David Caute appreciated the self-serving character of these moments when he watched Czech students in 1968:

> ... these observations reveal to me a certain perversity in my own attitude. Nostalgia for student riots, clashes with the police, and totally exposed thighs suggests a false romanticism, an irritable desire to inflict on an ostensibly sane society a form of chaos which, as a way of life, is superficial and nihilistic. The manner in which the young Czechs are conducting themselves is really a model of civil control and enlightenment, whereas we have become alcoholic on sensation and violence.[2]

Part of this problem results from the revolutionary's attitude toward the existing system. Not only is the on-going society corrupt and inhumane, it is irrational. It misses opportunities for progress; it is based upon the wrong premises; the rhetoric of its leaders is absurd and futile. If the system is patently insane and the revolutionary thinks he clearly diagnosed it, the indifference of the oppressed becomes logically impossible and by definition any revolutionary action is rational.

The only hope that the revolutionary has for keeping his sanity, both moral and political, is to continue to see the world through the eyes of his constituency. There are two aspects of the consciousness of oppressed people which can work to the benefit of the revolutionary if he will only use them. One is that the political silence of people is not always the result of indifference. More often than not, it is because of fear. As social critics, we have become too sophisticated in our analyses and have underestimated the power of systematic intimidation in a political order. A generation of people may *silently* calculate the cost of open resistance and conclude that it is simply not worth the effort. This seems to be especially the case in the instance of oppressed minorities. Recent historical analysis indicates that American slavery can best be described in terms of enforced political acquiescence occasionally erupting into acts of petty resistance rather than the long political slumber that is the stock description of both many liberals and Marxists. On this point Richard Hofstadter's remarks are instructive:

> ... in explaining the relatively small number of overt rebellions one must reckon with a certain amount of common sense among the blacks, many of whom were familiar with warfare and most of whom may be imagined to have had a sense of the odds against them. Near the Guinea Coast, where it might be feasible to capture and direct a white pilot or simply to drift back to shore, blacks mounted many mutinies. But once on the American strand, and situated in communities where they were usually divided into small groups (the two big colonial revolts, significantly were urban), denied all communication and outnumbered, where every white man had the use of a gun and there were slave patrols on the roads, they seem to have understood the hopelessness of insurrection aimed at the capture or maintenance of independent power.[3]

Men are more Hobbesian in this respect than both ideologies choose to admit. What the revolutionary can do is by example serve to weight the calculus of resistance against the governments. His very existence can say to a people, injustice has a chance of being overcome, include my support for you in your calculations. But this is a limited role and revolutionaries have not generally been content with it.

The problem of what Marxists refer to as raising people's political consciousness is, however, a serious one and it does need some attention. The oppressed have been provided with symbols designed to legitimize their status and history has shown that an existing political order can use these with great, although not unlimited, success. The temptation is to take the position most recently advanced by Regis Debray.[4] He contends that the people have been so systematically downtrodden they will never revolt. The task of the revolutionary is to form a guerrilla army. The concern for the support of the people must wait until the revolutionary army has taken power. Debray's position is nothing more than an argument for a coup d'etat guerrilla style. It even goes beyond the recommendations of Lenin mentioned earlier. Lenin's argument for an autocratic revolutionary organization was based upon the assumption, not entirely unfounded, that the risks of revolutionary activity are so great that if a revolution is to have any chance of success it must be organized by a core of professionals. Debray not only gives the professional revolutionary unlimited political decision-making authority but unlimited military control as well. If the silence of the people before the revolution is taken as a sign of their oppression, then can we assume that the same silence after the revolution will be interpreted in the same manner? In short, revolutions are simply too important to be left to revolutionaries of Debray's sort. An ill-fated jacquerie would seem to be preferable to a successful Debrayan revolution.

Yet the silence of the people the revolutionary fights and dies for is not his only problem as a political representative. Occasionally the revolutionary may wish that his sympathizers were silent. He may find that while he wants a comprehensive social revolution, his supporters are content with the alleviation of immediate injuries and a promise of better treatment in the future. It is certainly proper for the revolutionary to argue that piecemeal reforms do not alter the basic causes of injustice in a society and ask for support to reject them. It is quite another for the revolutionary to work secretly to sabotage the success of reformist measures. Revolutionary leaders who work to deny people voting rights or modest economic benefits in the name of some future, vastly superior society are in reality indistinguishable from a ruling elite which had selfishly delayed reform. The effects are the same. Let the oppressed discover for themselves the adequacy of incremental change; the revolutionary need only say, "I will be here to help when you find these promises have been broken."

In sum, we find that the revolutionary confronts many of the problems of representation as does his counterpart in a stable political order. He must occasionally assume the role of the virtual representative who tries to determine what the people need when the people do not say what they need and he must occasionally work for what he believes they really need when it is different from what the people think they need. Yet because he has no formal elective relationship with the people and because he does believe he is working for *their liberation* as well as his own, the revolutionary must recognize that he is primarily a delegate for their wishes. If the people make mistakes, if they lack vision and miss opportunities, the duty of the revolutionary is to recognize that they are his mistakes as well. The people's risks should also be the revolutionary's risks and not vice versa. Engels once said that revolutions are the most authoritarian of political actions, and like so many statements it has been forged into a self-fulfilling prophecy.

II

No problem is more serious for the revolutionary than the use and justification of violence. If the existing political order is as self-serving, corrupt, and vicious as he believes it to be, there are precious few alternatives to the use of violence to overthrow it. Yet as pressing as this situation is, the larger task of the revolutionary with regard to violence is even more difficult. While the state may be systematically employing terror, murder, and threats, the revolutionary finds he must use precisely these activities himself and somehow manage to distinguish his actions from those of the state. His actions must be justified or at least excused; those of the government are an exercise of political authority. The benefit of the doubt in regard to the justifiability of violence has nearly always rested with the state. Perhaps this moral imbalance is essential to the political stability men have managed to enjoy. But if this is so, it comes with a very high price, and no one feels the burden more than the revolutionary. While some writers have argued that violence is a word with no fixed meaning that governments use as a self-serving taboo,[5] there is an incontestable truth in the dictionary definition of violence as the use of physical force to injure or abuse. The British philosopher G. E. Moore once said that no matter how many dissertations are devoted to the assertion that time is unreal, breakfast still comes before lunch. No matter how many times revolutionaries deny the validity of the concept of violence, men still lie dead from well-placed-bullets.

But let me note three representative positions which do confront the problem of the justification of violence:

A. Revolutionary Amorality

In *The Prince* Machiavelli observes that with politics in general one "will find things which, though seeming good, will lead to his ruin if pursued, and others which, though seeming evil, will result in his safety and well-being."[6] Machiavelli's advice is to reject the trappings of traditional morality in favor of political prudence. And while he is forced to admit a distinction between "proper" and "improper" uses of cruelty, the former are justified because they help the prince remain in power.

It has been unfortunate that so many ethical theorists have insisted that somehow being moral "pays off," because when it is clear that it does not, the temptation of men is to foresake it. The temptation has never been greater for the revolutionary. When, for instance, Karl Kautsky, the German Social Democrat questioned the Soviet Terror, Trotsky replied: "The problem of revolution, as of war consists in breaking the will of the foe, forcing him to capitulate and to accept the conditions of the conqueror."[7] For Trotsky, "The enemy must be made harmless and in wartime this means that he must be destroyed."[8] The form or degree of violence was not one of principle—"it is a question of expediency . . . War like revolution works the same way: it kills individuals, and intimidates thousands."[9] No one could object to revolutionary violence unless he condemned every form of violence whatsoever ("a hypocritical Quaker"). By this logic Trotsky was able to justify the shooting of "landlords, capitalists and generals" as well as the taking of hostages.

B. Revolutionary Utilitarianism

A position giving some credence to moral restrictions on the use of violence is the view that says, in effect, any violent act that can be seen to advance the causes of the Revolution is justified, an act that does not is to be rejected. Now this position does appear to hover dangerously near the argument above for the abeyance of moral concern in the course of revolution (Trotsky does, in fact, use it at times), but it is conceptually although probably not empirically different. The revolutionary academic, Herbert Marcuse, has developed this position in "Ethics and Revolution." He suggests that the revolutionary employ an "historical calculus"—which estimates "the chances of a future society as against the chances of the existing society with respect to human progress, that is to say, technical and material progress used in such a way that it increases individual freedom and happiness."[10] If an estimation of the likelihood of the latter is greater than the chances of the former the revolutionary is presumably morally permitted to act.

There are several serious problems with Marcuse's analysis, all of them related to Marcuse's orthodox Marxist insistence upon the primacy of material goods in analysis. While he admits that the inhumanity of a calculus is evident this is to be blamed upon "the inhumanity of history itself, a token of its empirical, rational foundation."[11] What is calculable are "the material and intellectual resources available . . . the productive and distributive facilities in a society . . . the quantity and size of the labor force and of the population as a whole."[12] And while Marcuse does insist that certain forms of violence (arbitrary violence, cruelty, and indiscriminate terror) can never be justified because they negate the very end for which the revolution is a means, it is not clear (and Marxists are, of course, never clear on this point) whether the ends of revolution are human liberation, per se or human liberation, *ceteris paribus*. The revolutionary calculus involves material estimates, not human lives. If as Marcuse says, the trials, permanent terror, concentration camps, and dictatorship of the Party over the working classes were unjustifiable means for the Bolshevik revolution, but that accelerated industrialization, elimination of noncooperative layers of the management from the economy, enforcement of work discipline, and suspension of civil liberties were appropriate, can we not imagine a set of circumstances in which the killing of hostages, torture and terror would be a defense against counterrevolutionary violence? Since human life is only an appendix to the revolutionary's calculations, subject as it is to "historical considerations," it serves as the first ballast to be discarded in turbulent waters: ". . . suppression and sacrifice are daily exacted by all societies, and one cannot start . . . becoming moral and ethical at an arbitrary but expedient point of cut off: the point of revolution. Who can quantify and who can compare the sacrifices exacted by an established society and those exacted by its subversion?"[13] For the Marxist, history is a guarantee of movement toward human dignity; he need only concern himself with the means to achieve the result. Yet one need not be a confirmed skeptic to doubt that the former will take care of itself.

C. Revolutionary Intuitionism

Despite the inadequacies of the positions discussed above, they do at least give lip service to restrictions upon the use of violence. Violence is to be employed only when other measures have been exhausted, and certain acts of violence should be avoided because of their effect on the character of the revolutionary hiimself. A recent position eliminates even these restrictions. The writings of Franz Fanon, the Algerian psychiatrist, have captured the imagination of American black revolutionaries, and it is not difficult to understand the nature of their devotion. Fanon graphically and ruthlessly chronicles the devastating psychological effects of colonialization upon the native population. In order to "cure" the native of this generational inferiority trauma, Fanon advocates naked violence: "Violence alone, violence committed by the people, violence organized and educated by its leaders, makes it possible for the masses to understand social truths and gives the key to them."[14] Only the oppressed will understand the need for violence and only engaging in violent acts will natives understand the nature of the sickness imposed upon them. For Fanon, violence is a "cleansing force," freeing the native from his inferiority complex and restoring his self-respect.

Fanon's position is a version of the "propaganda by deed" advanced by many nineteenth-century European revolutionaries. At one level it is a pitiful caricature of the jacquerie and glorifies the frenzy of a confused and irrational people. In point of fact, the advocacy of "educational" terror is a tactic of despair on the part of the revolutionary leader. He no longer talks but bombs buildings and hopes that the people will follow his example. Even more dangerous, however, is the glorification of violence. What most men would justify on the basis of a logic of excuses, the revolutionary intuitionist elevates to a moral principle. The personalities this position attracts and the destruction it encourages make Fanonite politics indistinguishable from fascism.

What are we left to say about the justification of revolutionary violence? If it were not for the responsibility of providing some sort of an answer, one would declare the problem an unsolvable dilemma and plead for a small place for sensitivity and caution in the revolutionary's world of brutality and daring. We have confronted an immensely difficult problem in these pages, and the following suggestion can only be considered as no more than a starting point. Most of the ethical systems men have devised are based upon some social requisites and some regularities in human relations. As such they advance notably complex rules involving individual calculations, assessments of the motivations of oneself and others as well as sets of excuses for failure, under relatively fixed circumstances, to do one's duty. Moreover, they are based upon the good faith of others. In a revolutionary situation none of these conditions exists. Men do not trust one another; they cannot take for granted existing social roles; they no longer know what actions are excusable and what ones are not. In this situation, what men need is a very elementary moral system to allow them to still distinguish right from wrong, self-interest from duty and excuses from condemnation. While his theory of human nature may have been unsound, Hobbes was correct when he suggested clear and simple rules for men in the state of nature. We must agree to condemn certain acts of violence categorically. The use of terror, and the torture and killing of hostages must be condemned regardless of an appreciation of the revolutionary's anger, or apparently uncontrollable revenge or military necessity. An outline for a revolutionary ethics has not yet been written but until it is, men will continue to suffer, both politically and psychologically, long after their "successful" revolutions.

NOTES

1. V. I. Lenin, *What Is To Be Done?* (New York: International Publishers, 1902).
2. Quoted in Irving Howe, "The New 'Confrontation Politics' is a Dangerous Game," *New York Times Magazine* (October 20, 1968).
3. Richard Hofstadter, *America at 1750: A Social Portrait* (New York: Alfred A. Knopf, 1971), p. 120.
4. Regis Debray, *Revolution in the Revolution* (New York: Grove Press, 1967).
5. One of the most adamant revolutionaries on this point is Georges Sorel, *Reflections on Violence* (New York: Collier, 1950).
6. Niccolo Machiavelli, *The Prince and the Discourses* (New York: Modern Library, 1950), p. 56.
7. Leon Trotsky, *Terrorism and Communism* (Ann Arbor, Michigan: University of Michigan, 1961), p. 58.
8. *Ibid.*
9. *Ibid.*
10. Herbert Marcuse, "Ethics and Revolution" in *Ethics and Society,* Richard T. DeGeorge, ed., (Garden City, New York: Doubleday and Company, 1966), p. 140.
11. *Ibid.*, p. 145.
12. *Ibid.*
13. *Ibid.*
14. Franz Fanon, *The Wretched of the Earth* (New York: Grove Press, 1963), p. 147.

CIVIL DISOBEDIENCE
National Commission on the Causes
and Prevention of Violence

In a Task Force Report, *Law and Order Reconsidered,* presented to our Commission, the authors found it impossible to present a discourse on law and law enforcement without including a discussion of civil disobedience as contemporarily practiced. We, too, regard the impact of civil disobedience practices so relevant to the problem of maintaining our society obedient to law, that, in addition to endorsing the Staff Report,[1] we feel impelled to add comments of our own.

Our concern with civil disobediences is not that they may involve acts

Copyright by U.S. Government Printing Office, 1969.

of violence *per se*. Most of them do not. Rather, our concern is that erosion of the law is an inevitable consequence of widespread civil disobediences.

As observed by a legal scholar, . . . it is necessary to persuade those bent on civil disobedience that their conduct is fraught with danger, that violation of one law leads to violation of other laws, and eventually to a climate of lawlessness that by easy stages leads to violence.[2]

Our Commission heard the testimony of a number of noted educators who described their experiences with and causes of campus disruptions. The head of one of the nation's largest universities summed up his views with this comment: "I think that civil disobediences are mainly responsible for the present lawbreaking on university campuses."

An analysis of widely publicized defiances of law antecedent to the eruption of campus disorders supports that conclusion. For several years, our youth has been exposed to dramatic demonstrations of disdain for law by persons from whom exemplary conduct was to be expected. Segregationist governors had disobeyed court orders and had proclaimed their defiance of judicial institutions; civil rights leaders had openly disobeyed court injunctions and had urged their followers to do likewise; striking teachers' union members had contemptuously ignored judicial decrees. It was not surprising that college students, following adult example, destroyed scientific equipment and research data, interfered with the rights of others by occupying laboratories and classrooms, and in several instances temporarily closed their colleges.

The cancerous growth of disobediences has now reached many high schools and junior high schools of the nation.

Pointing out that force and repression are not the only threats to the rule of law, the dean of one of the nation's largest law schools observed:

The danger also arises from those groups whose commitments to social reform and the eradication of injustices lead to the defiance of law and the creation of disorder. We are learning that the rule of law can be destroyed through lack of fidelity to the law by large numbers of citizens as well as through abuses of authority by governmental officials.[3]

In our democratic society, lawlessness cannot be justified on the grounds of individual belief. The spectrum of individual consciences encompasses social and political beliefs replete with discordant views. If, for example, the civil libertarian in good conscience becomes a disobeyer of law, the segregationist is endowed with the same choice of conscience, or vice versa. If this reasoning is carried to its logical conclusion, we must also make allowance for the grievances of numerous groups of citizens who regard themselves shackled by laws in which they do not believe. Is each group to be free to disregard due process and to violate laws considered objectionable? If personal or group selectivity of laws to be obeyed is to be the yardstick, we shall face nationwide disobedience of many laws and thus anarchy.

We regard the right of peaceful dissent to be fundamental, not only to the individual freedoms we enjoy, but to the social progress so essential to our nation. Yet, just as fundamental are the disciplines that must control our individual and group actions, without which individual freedoms would be threatened and social progress retarded.

The United States Supreme Court, in upholding convictions for contempt of court of civil rights leaders, admonished all our citizens in these words:

> ... no man can be judge in his own case, however exalted his station, however righteous his motives, and irrespective of his race, color, politics or religion. . . . One may sympathize with the petitioners' impatient commitment to their cause. But respect for judicial process is a small price to pay for the civilizing hand of law, which alone can give abiding meaning to constitutional freedom.[4]

Every time a court order is disobeyed, each time an injunction is violated, each occasion on which a court decision is flouted, the effectiveness of our judicial system is eroded. How much erosion can it tolerate? It takes no prophet to know that our judicial system cannot face wholesale violations of its orders and still retain its efficacy. Violators must ponder the fact that once they have weakened the judicial system, the very ends they sought to attain—and may have attained—cannot then be preserved. For the antagonist of the disobeyer's attained objectives most likely will proceed viciously to violate them and since judicial institutions would no longer possess essential authority and power, the "rights" initially gained could be quickly lost.

It is argued that in instances where disobeyers seek to test the constitutionality of a legislative enactment or a court decree, and are willing to accept punishment, their acts should be condoned. We suggest that if in good faith the constitutionality of a statute, ordinance or a court decree is to be challenged, it can be done effectively by one individual or a small group. While the judicial test is in progress, all other dissenters should abide by the law involved until it is declared unconstitutional.

We commend to our fellow citizens the words of Richard Cardinal Cushing:

> ... observance of law is the eternal safeguard of liberty, and defiance of law is the surest road to tyranny. . . . Even among lawabiding men, few laws are loved, but they are uniformly respected and not resisted.

If we are to maintain and improve our democratic society, the government, including the judiciary, must have the respect and the loyalty of its citizens.

II DISOBEDIENCE TO LAW[5]

Over the past two decades increasing numbers of people seem to have embraced the idea that active disobedience to valid law—perhaps even violent disobedience—is justified for the purpose of achieving a desirable political goal. This idea found widespread support in the South as the white majority in that region resisted enforcement of the constitutionally defined rights of Negroes, and some such notion was probably not far from the minds of the Alabama State Troopers when they attacked Dr. King's peaceful demonstration at Selma in 1965. No doubt it was also prominent in the thinking of the Chicago policemen who administered punishment to the demonstrators in Chicago during the Democratic Convention of 1968

The same idea—that disobedience to law is justified in a good cause which can be furthered in no other way—is also widely held by many students, black citizens and other groups pressing for social change in America today. It is the illegal and sometimes violent activities of these groups that have been most perplexing and disturbing to the great majority of Americans Their actions have prompted the most intense interest in the ancient philosophical question of man's duty of obedience to the state. Business lunches and suburban cocktail parties have come to sound like freshman seminars in philosophy, as an older generation has argued back and forth over the rightness and the wrongness of "what the kids and the Negroes are doing."

When deliberate, active disobedience to duly enacted, constitutionally valid law is widely engaged in as a political tactic, and when "civil disobedience" is a topic hotly debated on every side, it is impossible for a Task Force on Law and Law Enforcement to file a report that does not discuss this age-old subject, however briefly.

The American Ideal

In a democratic society, dissent is the catalyst of progress. The ultimate viability of the system depends upon its ability to accommodate dissent; to provide an orderly process by which disagreements can be adjudicated, wrongs righted, and the structure of the system modified in the face of changing conditions. No society meets all these needs perfectly. Moreover, political and social organizations are, by their nature, resistant to change. This is as it should be, because stability—order—is a fundamental aim of social organization. Yet stability must not become atrophy, and the problem is to strike the proper balance between amenability to change and social stability.

Every society represents a style of living. The style is represented by the way in which people relate to the social structure, the way in which social decisions are made, the procedures which govern the ways people in the society relate to each other. In a democratic society such as ours, the governing ideals are government by the rule of law, equality before the law, and ultimate control of the law-making process by the people. We depend upon these principles both to accommodate and to limit change, and to insure the style of living we prefer.

As Tocqueville observed, America is peculiarly a society of law. The law has played a greater part among us than is the case in any other social system— in our restless and jealous insistence on the utmost range of freedom for the individual; in our zeal to confine the authority of the state within constitutional dikes; and in our use of law as a major instrument of social change. The practice of judicial review in the United States has had an extraordinary development, with no real parallels elsewhere. It has kept the law a powerful and persistent influence in every aspect of our public life.

We believe with Jefferson that the just powers of government are derived— and can only be derived—from the consent of the governed. We are an independent, stiff-necked people, suspicious of power, and hardly docile before authority. We never hesitate to challenge the justness and the constitutional propriety of the powers our governments and other social institutions assert. In the robust and sinewy debates of our democracy, law is never taken for granted simply because it has been properly enacted.

Our public life is organized under the explicit social compact of the Constitution, ratified directly by the people, not the states, and designed to be enforced by the courts and by the political process as an instrument to establish and at the same time to limit the powers of government. As Justice Brandeis once observed, "[t]he doctrine of the separation of powers was adopted by the Convention of 1787, not to promote effiiency but to preclude the exercise of arbitrary power. The purpose was, not to avoid friction, but, by means of the inevitable friction incident to the distribution of the governmental powers among three departments, to save the people from autocracy. . . . And protection of the individual . . . from the arbitrary or capricious exercise of power . . . was believed to be an essential of free government."

The social contract of our Constitution goes beyond the idea of the separation of powers, and of enforceable limits on the competence of government. The governments established by the national and state constitutions of the United States are not omnipotent. A basic feature of the Constitution, made explicit in the Ninth and Tenth Amendments, is that rights not delegated to governments are reserved to the people. The Amendments may not be directly enforceable in the courts, but the idea they represent animates many judicial decisions, and influences the course of legislation and other public action.

In a multitude of ways, the Constitution assures the individual a wide zone of privacy and of freedom. It protects him when accused of crime. It asserts his political rights—his right to speak, to vote, and to assemble peaceably with his fellows to petition the government for a redress of his grievances. Freedom of speech and of the press are guaranteed. Religious liberty is proclaimed, and an official establishment of religion proscribed. And the Constitution seeks assurance that society will remain open and diverse, hospitable to freedom, and organized around many centers of power and influence, by making the rules of federalism and of liberty enforceable in the courts.

The unwritten constitution of our habits is dominated by the same concern for preserving individual freedom against encroachment by the state or by social groups. The anti-trust laws; the rights of labor; the growing modern use of state power to assure the equality of the Negro; the wide dispersal of power, authority, and opportunity in the hands of autonomous institutions of business, labor, and education—all bespeak a characteristic insistence that our social arrangements protect liberty, and rest on the legitimacy of consent, either through the Constitution itself, made by the people, and capable of change only by their will, or through legislation and other established methods of social action.

In broad outline, such is the pluralist social compact which has evolved out of our shared experience as a people. It has its roots in our history. And it grows and changes, in accordance with its own rules and aspirations, as every generation reassesses its meaning and its ideals.

Our Contemporary Discontents

Today there are many who maintain that these ideals, and the institutions established to maintain them, no longer operate properly. In recent years, increasing numbers of Americans have taken to the streets to express their views on basic issues. Some come to exercise their right to dissent by parades and picketing. Some dramatize their causes by violating laws they feel to be wrong. Some use the issues being protested as drums to beat in a larger parade. For example, the Vietnam war has been used on one side as a dramatic moment in the ubiquitous, always-evil Communist conspiracy; on the other as an exemplar of the fundamental diabolism of western capitalist nations. Some take to the streets in the belief that the public, if made aware of their grievances, will institute the necessary processes to correct them. Others come in anger; not hopeful, but insistent; serving notice, not seeking audience. Finally, there are even a few who take to the streets to tear at the fabric of society; to confront, to commit acts of violence, to create conditions under which the present system can be swept away.

Out of the widening protest, one disturbing theme has repeatedly appeared. Increasingly, those who protest speak of civil disobedience or even revolution as necessary instruments of effecting needed social change, charging that the processes of lawful change built into the system are inadequate to the task.

The American response to this disobedience to law—to events which are contrary to our fundamental beliefs about the mode of social and political change—has been ambivalent. The reason lies in the fact that the American people are going through a crisis of conscience. The issues in whose name violence has been committed have deeply disturbed and divided the American people. The tactics of the demonstrators have encountered angry opposition, but many Americans continue to sympathize with some or all of the goals sought by the demonstrators. After all, although one might argue that the Negro has advanced in the last ten years, few would maintain he has attained full first-class citizenship. And who would say the ghettos are not an agonizing disgrace? Similarly, Vietnam is hardly an open-and-shut case. The only point of view from which it is clearly praiseworthy is the self-interest of ourselves and our allies. The draft, another key issue, is at best a regrettable and clumsily administered system. Finally, when the young charge that our system—political and social—is shot through with hypocrisy, only the most fanatic feels no twinge.

We must, of course, realize that civil rights demonstrations arise from great suffering, disappointment and yearning. We must recognize the importance to the democratic process, and to the ultimate well-being of our nation, of young people combatting hypocrisy and indifference. But when these emotions become a basis for action and when that action creates social disorder, even the most sympathetic are forced to judge whether and to what extent the ends sought justify the means that are being used.

The difficult problem in this endeavor is to maintain perspective. The issues have reached a stage of polarization. Partisans on each side constantly escalate the rhetorical savagery of their positions, adding nothing but volume and abuse. There is a great temptation to take sides without thoughtful inquiry—if for no other reason than because it is simpler. What are some of the considerations which should guide us in this inquiry?

Moral Justifications for Disobedience to Law:
The Needs of the Individual

The idea that men have the right to violate the law under certain circumstances is not new. The oldest justification for such action seems to have been through appeal to a higher "natural law" which is the only proper basis of human law. This theory, which dates at least as far back as Plato, and which is in our own Declaration of Independence,[6] has recently found expression in the thought of Martin Luther King:

A just law is a man-made law of God. An unjust law is a code that is out of harmony with the moral law. To put it in the terms of Saint Thomas Aquinas, an unjust law is a human law that is not rooted in eternal and natural law.[7]

For St. Thomas political authority was derived from God and hence binding in conscience, but where authority was defective in title or exercise, there was no obligation of conscience.[8] Such a condition arose in the case of a ruler who had either usurped power or who, though legitimate, was abusing his authority by ruling unjustly. Indeed, when the ruler contravened the very purpose of his authority by ordering a sinful action, the subject was under an obligation *not* to obey. In the case of abuse of authority, St. Thomas apparently endorsed nothing more than passive resistance by the citizen; but where the ruler illegitimately possessed himself of power through violence, and there was no other recourse for the citizen, then St. Thomas allowed active resistance and even tyrannicide.

Later Catholic thinkers, such as the Jesuit, Francis Suarez, denied the divine right of kings, holding that the ruler derives his authority immediately from the people and only ultimately from God. These doctrines led logically to the conclusion that in any circumstances in which a ruler turns into a tyrant, whether originally a legitimate ruler or not, he may be deposed by the people, by force if necessary. This conclusion became, of course, the generally accepted view in the secular world, with the theories of Locke and Jefferson and the American and French Revolutions in the eighteenth century and the rise of liberal democracy in the nineteenth.

The notion of a "social compact" was always closely bound up with the emerging ideas of popular sovereignty.[9] This theory, especially prominent in John Locke, expresses the view that governments evolve by the consent of the governed and that the constitution establishing a government is a contract or agreement which, once it is established, is binding upon all men, both those opposed to it and those who favor it. When government's laws are consistent with terms of the covenant, then the people must obey them. But the people "are absolved from obedience when illegal attempts are made upon their liberties or properties, and may oppose the unlawful violence of those who were their magistrates when they invade their properties contrary to the trust put in them. . . ."[10]

Most of the unlawful opposition today to the Vietnam war is justified on the ground that the war is itself immoral and "unlawful" in various respects. Since it is immoral, the argument goes, there is no moral duty to obey those laws which are in the aid of the conduct of the war. Indeed, the argument continues, one's true moral duty is to resist the war and to take affirmative action to impede its prosecution. On theories of this kind, Americans have refused to be drafted; they have disrupted Selective Service facilities and destroyed Selective Service records; they have vilified the President, the Secretary of State and the Secretary of Defense and attempted to disrupt their public speeches; they have attempted to bar companies and governmental agencies participating in the war effort from university campuses and to disrupt the universities that refused to accede to that demand.

At the level of individual morality, the problem of disobedience to law is wholly intractable. One is tempted to suggest that even if the war is immoral, the general level of morality of the country is not much improved by the conduct described above. Moreover, if we allow individual conscience to guide obedience to the law, we must take all consciences. The law cannot distinguish between the consciences of saints and sinners. As Burke Marshall has said: "If the decision to break the law really turned on individual conscience, it is hard to see in law how Dr. King is better off than Governor Ross Barnett of Mississippi, who also believed deeply in his cause and was willing to go to jail."[11]

Where issues are framed in purely moral terms, they are usually incapable of resolution by substantially unanimous agreement. Moral decisions are reached by "individual prudential application of principle, with the principles so general as to be only of minimal assistance and with almost the whole field thus left to prudence."[12] This fact is illustrated by the story of the exchange that occurred between Emerson and Thoreau, the latter of whom had in 1845 personally seceded from the United States in protest against slavery. As part of his anti-slavery campaign, Thoreau was spending a night in jail. Emerson paid him a visit, greeting him by saying, "What are you doing in there, Henry?" Thoreau looked at him through the bars and replied, "What are you doing out there, Ralph?"[13]

But the issue raised by conscientious disobedience to law also has some more tractable social dimensions. What is the effect upon our society of this kind of conduct? For instance, how does it affect the people who engage in the disobedience? Does it have an effect upon other people? What does it do to our system of laws?

The Problem of Contagion: The Needs of Society

Although there are some who argue that tolerating any form of law violation serves as an encouragement of other forms of anti-social behavior by the violators, some research in this area suggests precisely the opposite. A series of studies of approximately 300 young black people who engaged in a series of acts of civil disobedience were undertaken in a western city. On the basis of their observations, the authors concluded: "[T]here have been virtually no manifestations of delinquency or anti-social behavior, no school drop-outs, and no known illegitimate pregnancies. This is a remarkable record for any group of teen-age children of any color in any community in 1964."[14]

In any event, the evidence is insufficient to demonstrate that acts of civil disobedience of the more limited kind inevitably lead to an increased disrespect for law or propensity toward crime. In fact, some experts have argued that engaging in disciplined civil disobedience allows people to channel resentment into constructive paths, thereby reducing the propensity for engaging in antisocial behavior.

But the fact that disobedience to law does not appear adversely to affect the attitudes of the people who engage in it is only one small part of the problem. For such conduct does have a serious adverse effect both upon other people in the society, and, most importantly of all, upon the system of laws upon which society must inevitably depend.

The effect of civil disobedience upon others in the community is clear. Except in the case of those acts designed solely to appeal to the conscience of the community, the purpose of much contemporary disobedience to law is to influence community action by harassing or intimidating the members of the community into making concessions to a particular point of view. In the case of the opposition to the Vietnam war, for example, those engaged in acts of disobedience are largely bent upon making miserable the lives of public officials who support the war, upon bringing economic pressure to bear on commercial enterprises participating in the war effort, and upon generally inconveniencing the public to dramatize a disaffection for war and convince others that the war is not worth the trouble it is causing. To the extent that these efforts succeed, others are obviously adversely affected.[15] But the most serious effect of all is suggested in the following question: "[W]hat lesson is being taught to the wider community by the precept and example of civil disobedience? It is tutelage in nonviolence or in defiance of authority, in rational confrontation of social ills or in undisciplined activism?"[16] There is every reason to believe that the lesson taught by much of the current disobedience to law is disastrous from the standpoint of the maintenance of a democratic society.

The experience of India in this regard is instructive because that country has had such a long and widespread familiarity with the practice of civil disobedience:

The fact is that the effect of protest behavior on the functioning of the political system has been palpable. We have already seen that Indians compel official attention and constrain decision-making by deliberately engaging in activities that threaten public order. Violence or the threat of violence has become an important instrument in Indian politics. Public protests involving a threat to public order and nonviolent civil disobedience have become habitual responses to alleged failures by government to do what a group of people want. While it is true that political accommodation is real in India, it is achieved at a higher level of political disorder than in any other of the world's democracies.[17]

The experience of India seems to indicate that civil disobedience has a strong tendency to become a pattern of conduct which soon replaces normal legal processes as the usual way in which society functions. Put in American terms, this would mean, once the pattern is established, that the accepted method of getting a new traffic light might be to disrupt traffic by blocking intersections, that complaints against businessmen might result in massive sit-ins, that improper garbage service might result in a campaign of simply dumping garbage into the street, and so on. Of course, these kinds of actions are not unknown in America today, but in India they have become a necessary part of the political system. Without a massive demonstration to support it, a grievance simply is not taken seriously because everyone knows that if the grievance were serious, there would be a demonstration to support it.

The adverse effect upon normal democratic processes is obvious. Though not intended to destroy democratic processes, civil disobedience tends plainly to impair their operation. This is a fact to which those who engage in civil disobedience should give consideration lest, in seeking to improve society, they may well seriously injure it.

This observation, however, will not answer the arguments of those who believe that the urgency of their message is so strong that illegal tactics are weapons that must be used—whatever the risks that such use may entail. But even urgent messages too frequently repeated lose their appeal. Where once people at least listened patiently, now only deaf ears are turned. Moreover, as Martin Luther King recognized, violence against an oppressor only tends in the long run to justify the oppression. Repeatedly putting one's body "on the line" does not enhance, but diminishes, the worth of that body to the dominant society. Those militants who now advocate revolution as the only alternative have recognized this truth.

The belief that a violent revolution is necessary to achieve social justice depends on the assumption that certain injustices are intrinsic to our system and therefore not amenable to change within the system. For revolution is justified only as a last resort, when justice is achievable by no other means.

We agree with the overwhelming majority of the people in this country that our problems, serious as they are, are not of the kind that make revolution even thinkable, let along justifiable. We believe that political and social mechanisms do exist and have produced significant change in recent years. The remedy for the discontented, we believe, is to seek change through lawful mechanisms, changes of the kind that other chapters of the Task Force report suggest.

But our beliefs and our words are really beside the point. What is important is rather the beliefs of those diverse, alienated groups in our society for whom the political and social mechanisms do not seem to work. We can only hope that the majority will respond convincingly to the needs of the discontented, and that the discontented will remain open to the possibility of achieving this response through peaceful means.

Conclusion

Official lawlessness—by some southern governors, by some policemen, by corrupt individuals in positions of public trust—is widely recognized as intolerable in a society of law, even if this recognition is too infrequently translated into the effective action to do something about the problem. We believe that the time has also come for those participating today in the various protest movements, on and off the college campuses, to subject their disobedience to law to realistic appraisal. The question that needs to be put to young people of generous impulses all over the country is whether tactics relying on deliberate, symbolic, and sometimes violent lawbreaking are in fact contributing to the emergency of a society that will show enhanced regard for human values— for equality, decency, and individual volition.

For some in the protest movement, this is not a relevant inquiry; their motivations are essentially illiberal and destructive. But this is not descriptive of most of those engaged today in social protest, including most who have violated the law in the course of their protest; their intention is to recall America to the ideals upon which she is founded.

We believe, however, that candid examination of what is occurring in the United States today will lead to the conclusion that disobedience to valid law as a tactic of protest by discontented groups is *not* contributing to the emergence of a more liberal and humane society, but is, on the contrary, producing an opposite tendency. The fears and resentments created by symbolic law violation have strengthened the political power of some of the most destructive elements in American society. Only naive and willful blindness can obscure the strength of these dark forces, which, but for the loosening of the bonds of law, might otherwise lie quiescent beneath the surface of our national life. An almost Newtonian process of action and reaction is at work, and fanaticism even for laudable goals breeds fanaticism in opposition. Just as "extremism in defense of liberty" does not promote liberty, so extremism in the cause of justice will extinguish hopes for a just society.

NOTES

1. Incorporated herein as Section II.
2. Norman Dorsen, Professor of Law and Director of the Authur Garfield Hays Liberties Program, New York University School of Law.
3. Francis A. Allen, Dean of the Law School and Professor of Law, University of Michigan.
4. *Walker v. City of Birmingham,* U.S. 307, 320-321.
5. This section reproduces Chapter 2 of the Report of our staff Task Force on Law and Law Enforcement, *Law and Order Reconsidered* (U.S. Government Printing Office: Washington, D.C., 1969). The chapter was prepared by the Directors of the Task Force, based in part on contributions by Francis A. Allen, Dean of the Law School, University of Michigan; Charles Monson, Associate Academic Vice President, University of Utah; and Eugene V. Rostow, Professor of Law, Yale University.
6. "We hold these truths to be self-evident, that all men are created equal, that they are endowed by their Creator with certain unalienable Rights, that among these are Life, Liberty and the pursuit of Happiness."
7. King, "Letter from the Birmingham Jail" (1963).
8. See generally the illuminating article by MacGuigan, "Civil Disobedience and Natural Law," 11 *Catholic Lawyer* 118 (1965).
9. See Copleston, *History of Philosophy,* vol. 3 (Westminster, Md., 1953), pp. 348–49.
10. Locke, *Second Treatise on Civil Government,* ch. 19, "Of the Dissolution of Government," sec. 228.
11. Burke Marshall, "The Protest Movement and the Law," 51 U. Va. L. Rev. 785, 800 (1965).
12. MacGuigan, *op. cit,* p. 125.
13. *Ibid.*
14. Pierce and West, "Six Years of Sit-Ins: Psychodynamics Causes and Effects," 12 *International Journal of Social Psychiatry* 30 (Winter 1966).
15. Even in the narrowly defined situation of acts designed solely to appeal to the conscience of the community, adverse effects frequently flow to others. Thus a refusal to accept induction into the armed services means that someone else must serve.
16. Allen, "Civil Disobedience and the Legal Order," Part 1, 36 *University of Cincinnati Law Review* 1, 30 (1967).
17. Bayley, *Non-violent Civil Disobedience and the Police: Lesson to be Learned from India* (consultant paper submitted to the Task Force), p. 15.

BIBLIOGRAPHICAL NOTE

Recent accounts of resistance are too numerous to permit a comprehensive bibliography. Fortunately for a reviewer, these works have been very uneven. One of the best sympathetic analyses of the past decade of protest is Staughton Lynd and Michael Ferber, *The Resistance.* For early accounts see Jack Newfield's *The Prophetic Minority* and Lynd's *S.N.C.C.: The New Abolitionists.* Two critical works are George Kennan, *Democracy and the Student Left,* and John Searle, *The Campus War.* Numerous journals devoted whole issues to the student movement: *Public Interest* (1968), *American Behavioral Scientist* (1968), *Daedalus* (1970). Since the pamphlets of a political movement are distributed hurriedly by basement printing machines (the modern counterpart is the mimeograph) or small ad hoc publishers, the records of protest, especially unsuccesful ones, are often lost to history. It is important that scholars compile what appear to be transitory period pieces for the evaluation of posterity. *The New Student Left,* ed. Mitchell Cohen and Dennis Hale, and *We Won't Go,* ed. Alice Lynd represent attempts to fill this need.

Julian Boyd has been compiling a fifty-volume collection of Jefferson's writings. Adrienne Koch and William Peden have produced a useful one-volume anthology. There are two standard biographies of Jefferson: Dumas Malone's multivolume *Jefferson and His Time,* and Gilbert Chinard, *Thomas Jefferson: Apostle of Americanism.* Adrienne Koch offers a consideration of the philosophical and ethical aspects of Jefferson's thought in *The Philosophy of Thomas Jefferson.* Also see Koch's *Jefferson and Madison* and Daniel Boorstin's *The Lost World of Thomas Jefferson.* Bernard Bailyn's very thorough *Pamphlets of American Revolution* reprints many valuable selections. Also see his fascinating interpretation of American revolutionary thought, *The Ideological Origins of the American Revolution.*

Thoreau's most famous essay, "Civil Disobedience" has not been reprinted here in order to provide his less well-known but more informative "A Plea for John Brown." There are many collections of Thoreau's writings. One interesting edition is *The Valorium Civil Disobedience,* ed. Walter Harding, since it includes the reactions of Thoreau's contemporaries.

Recent tracts on civil disobedience are legion. For representative works see *Civil Disobedience: Theory and Practice,* ed. Hugo Bedau; Charles E. Whittier and William Sloan Coffin, Jr., *Law, Order, and Civil Disobedience,* and Carl Cohen, *Civil Disobedience: Conscience, Tactics and the Law.* Also see *Conscience in America,* ed. Lillian Schissel, and *Protest: Pacifism and Politics,* ed. James Finn for two very able collections of pacifist writings.

Cleaver's major work is *Soul on Ice,* an autobiographical sketch of his road to political consciousness. Unmatched in this genre for its clarity and forcefulness, however, is *The Autobiography of Malcolm X*. Much has been written on the strategy and tactics of black protest. See Louis Lomax, *The Negro Revolt* and Harold Cruse, *The Crisis of the Negro Intellectual* on the problems which an oppressed minority confronts in devising a rational strategy of resistance.

A flood of books have been addressed to the general question of the sociological and psychological justification of violence. See Hugh Davies Graham's and Ted Robert Gurr's collection of essays prepared for the National Commission on the Causes and Prevention of Violence, *Violence in America: Historical and Comparative Perspectives.* Another report, *The Politics of Protest,* submitted to the Commission by Jerome Skolnick contends that what is puzzling about the protest of the sixties is that it was accompanied by so little violence. Edward Banfield's controversial, *The Unheavenly City* argues that explanations of civil disturbance have been over-intellectualized, that much of the rioting has been for "fun and profit". The opposite viewpoint is taken to its reductio ad absurdum by R.D. Laing, *The Politics of Experience.*

Robert Paul Wolff's intellectual movement toward anarchism can be seen by reading his *Poverty of Liberalism, In Defense of Anarchism* and his "Afterword" in *The Rule of Law.*

III. THE PROBLEMS OF SELF-GOVERNMENT

1. Class and Faction

All societies have some basic principle by which they organize themselves and continue to make decisions. In the United States this is accomplished through the mechanisms of majority rule. While the principle of majority rule has been often enunciated and rhetorically defended, Americans have generally imposed important qualifications on the power of electoral majorities.

In our political tradition, there has been present an acute sense of both the corrupting and the fleeting nature of power. Ethically, we realize that to give some men sway over others constitutes a grave responsibility which must be contained within formulae of tradition, law, and due process. Prudentially, we recognize that today's opposition may become tomorrow's majority. The rights and liberties which we may want to deny to others could later be just as easily denied to us.

The first five selections which follow examine the problems of factionalism and majority rule. The authors differ on many points, but all of them reject the populist view of democracy which was prominent at the turn of this century and which is being so often advocated today. Their proposals emphasize balance, countervailing forces, and even temporary deadlock to achieve checks on the exercise of political power. The last selection is a critique of the influence of interest groups on public policy.

James Madison argues that factional differences are inevitable. A stable republic can only be maintained when these factions are multiplied in order to prevent one from totally dominating the rest. When this multiplication occurs, interests are forced to tone down their demands and reach a compromise settlement. It should be noted that such a proliferation of interests also gives to political leaders some latitude in coalition-building and governing—a point probably not lost on Madison and his Federalist colleagues.

Calhoun is less concerned with the problems of factionalism than with the protection of minority and sectional rights. To some extent, his work has fallen into disrepute because he was mainly interested in establishing mechanisms to protect the slave-holding aristocracy. Yet his notion of the "concurrent majority" is one of the most original contributions to American political thought.

Recently, political scientists have also examined the complexities of majority rule. One of the most influential, Robert Dahl, has maintained that the United States is made up of a plurality of power centers and that considerable negotiation and persuasion are required to govern modern American society. In some ways, the America that Dahl describes is the type of political order that Calhoun had tried to create.

In this sort of pluralist society, there are elites divided by issues, not one cohesive ruling class. This development presents another problem for the advocate of majority rule. Kendall and Carey maintain that there are certain issues about which some people feel more intense than others. Should the political system take this "intensity factor" into account? Must it if that society is to survive? And does this consideration really negate the whole concept of majority rule?

These questions are by no means hypothetical. We can see how in the American experience rather small interest groups have assumed a virtual veto over whole areas of national policy, such as medicine, gun-control legislation, farm subsidies, housing, and even education. The proliferation of interests and factions has not led to the type of balanced polity Madison envisioned. In many areas of American life, powerful organized interests have worked out, with the blessings of government, a sort of feudalistic control at the expense of the unorganized. As Theodore Lowi indicates, we have come to regard government as being just an arena for interest group politics rather than as the manifestation of legitimate authority.

Such developments do not make the older debates on majority rule and factional power obsolete. They do, however, recast them in terms of twentieth-century America. It is an America in which the bureaucratic style has replaced the personal style and in which the traditional boundary between public authority and private activity will have to be thought out anew. We must ask ourselves to what extent are our eighteenth century modes of representation effective in ensuring majority rule? Equally important is the question which was originally raised: to what extent and for what purposes are we willing to see majority rule curtailed or ignored? These selections become a starting point for such an examination and evaluation.

THE FEDERALIST PAPERS
Number 10
James Madison

Among the numerous advantages promised by a well constructed union, none deserves to be more accurately developed than its tendency to break and control the violence of faction. The friend of popular governments, never finds himself so much alarmed for their character and fate, as when he contemplates their propensity to this dangerous vice. He will not fail, therefore, to set a due value on any plan which, without violating the principles to which he is attached, provides a proper cure for it. The instability, injustice, and confusion, introduced into the public councils, have, in truth, been the mortal diseases under which popular governments have everywhere perished; as they continue to be the favourite and fruitful topics from which the adversaries to liberty derive their most specious declamations. The valuable improvements made by the American constitutions on the popular models, both ancient and modern, cannot certainly be too much admired; but it would be an unwarrantable partiality, to contend that they have as effectually obviated the danger on this side, as was wished and expected. Complaints are everywhere heard from our most considerate and virtuous citizens, equally the friends of public and private faith, and of public and personal liberty, that our governments are too unstable; that the public good is disregarded in the conflicts of rival parties; and that measures are too often decided, not according to the rules of justice, and the rights of the minor party, but by the superior force of an interested and overbearing majority. However anxiously we may wish that these complaints had no foundation, the evidence of known facts will not permit us to deny that they are in some degree true. It will be found, indeed, on a candid review of our situation, that some of the distresses under which we labour, have been erroneously charged on the operation of our governments: but it will be found at the same time, that other causes will not alone account for many of our heaviest misfortunes; and, particularly, for that prevailing and increasing distrust of public engagements, and alarm for private rights, which are echoed from one end of the continent to the other. These must be chiefly, if not wholly, effects of the unsteadiness and injustice, with which a factious spirit has tainted our public administrations.

By a faction, I understand a number of citizens, whether amounting to majority or minority of the whole, who are united and actuated by some common impulse of passion, or of interest, adverse to the rights of other

From The Federalist. *Copyright by Masters and Co., 1857.*

citizens, or to the permanent and aggregate interests of the community.

There are two methods of curing the mischiefs of faction: The one, by removing its causes; the other, by controling its effects.

There are again two methods of removing the causes of faction: The one, by destroying the liberty which is essential to its existence; the other, by giving to every citizen the same opinions, the same passions, and the same interests.

It could never be more truly said, than of the first remedy, that it was worse than the disease. Liberty is to faction what air is to fire, an aliment, without which it instantly expires. But it could not be a less folly to abolish liberty, which is essential to political life, because it nourishes faction, than it would be to wish the annihilation of air, which is essential to animal life, because it imparts to fire its destructive agency.

The second expedient is as impracticable, as the first would be unwise. As long as the reason of man continues fallible, and he is at liberty to exercise it, different opinions will be formed. As long as the connection subsists between his reason and his self-love, his opinions and his passions will have a reciprocal influence on each other; and the former will be objects to which the latter will attach themselves. The diversity in the faculties of men, from which the rights of property originate, is not less an insuperable obstacle to an uniformity of interests. The protection of these faculties is the first object of government. From the protection of different and unequal faculties of acquiring property, the possession of different degrees and kinds of property immediately results; and from the influence of these on the sentiments and views of the respective proprietors, ensues a division of the society into different interests and parties.

The latent causes of faction are thus sown in the nature of man; and we see them everywhere brought into different degrees of activity, according to the different circumstances of civil society. A zeal for different opinions concerning religion, concerning government, and many other points, as well of speculation as of practice; an attachment to different leaders, ambitiously contending for preeminence and power; or to persons of other descriptions, whose fortunes have been interesting to the human passions, have, in turn, divided mankind into parties, inflamed them with mutual animosity, and rendered them much more disposed to vex and oppress each other, than to cooperate for their common good. So strong is this propensity of mankind, to fall into mutual animosities, that where no substantial occasion presents itself, the most frivolous and fanciful distinctions have been sufficient to kindle their unfriendly passions, and excite their most violent conflicts. But the most common and durable source of factions, has been the various and unequal distribution of property. Those who hold, and those who are without property, have ever formed distinct interests in society. Those who are creditors, and those who are debtors, fall under a like discrimination. A landed interest, a manufacturing interest, a mercantile interest, a moneyed interest, with many lesser interests, grow up of necessity in civilized nations, and divide them into different classes, actuated by different sentiments and views. The regulation of these various and interfering interests forms the principal task of modern legislation, and involves the spirit of party and faction in the necessary and ordinary operations of government.

No man is allowed to be a judge in his own cause; because his interest will certainly bias his judgment, and, not improbably, corrupt his integrity. With equal, nay, with greater reason, body of men are unfit to be both judges and parties at the same time; yet what are many of the most important acts of legislation, but so many judicial determinations, not indeed concerning the rights of single persons, but conerning the rights of large bodies of citizens? and what are the different classes of legislators, but advocates and parties to the causes which they determine? Is a law proposed concerning private debts? It is a question to which the creditors are parties on one side, and the debtors on the other. Justice ought to hold the balance between them. Yet the parties are, and must be, themselves the judges; and the most numerous party, or, in other words, the most powerful faction, must be expected to prevail. Shall domestic manufactures be encouraged, and in what degree, by restrictions on foreign manufactures? are questions which would be differently decided by the landed and the manfacturing classes; and probably by neither with a sole regard to justice and the public good. The apportionment of taxes, on the various descriptions of property, is an act which seems to require the most exact impartiality; yet there is, perhaps, no legislative act, in which greater opportunity and temptation are given to a predominant party, to trample on the rules of justice. Every shilling, with which they overburden the inferior number, is a shilling saved to their own pockets.

It is in vain to say, that enlightened statesmen will be able to adjust these clashing interests, and render them all subservient to the public good. Enlightened statesmen will not always be at the helm: nor, in many cases, can such an adjustment be made at all, without taking into view indirect and remote considerations, which will rarely prevail over the immediate interest which one party may find in disregarding the rights of another, or the good of the whole.

The inference to which we are brought is, that the *causes* of faction cannot be removed; and that relief is only to be sought in the means of controling its *effects*.

If a faction consists of less than a majority, relief is supplied by the republican principle, which enables the majority to defeat its sinister views, by regular vote. It may clog the administration, it may convulse the society; but it will be unable to execute and mask its violence under the forms of the constitution. When a majority is included in a faction, the form of popular government, on the other hand, enables it to sacrifice to its ruling passion or interest, both the public good, and private rights, against the danger of such a faction, and at the same time to preserve the spirit and the form of popular government, is then the great object to which our inquiries are directed. Let me add, that it is the great desideratum, by which alone this form of government can be rescued from the opprobrium under which it has so long laboured, and be recommended to the esteem and adoption of mankind.

By what means is this object attainable? Evidently by one of two only.

Either the existence of the same passion or interest in a majority, at the same time, must be prevented; or the majority, having such coexistent passion or interest, must be rendered, by their number and local situation, unable to concert and carry into effect schemes of oppression. If the impulse and the opportunity be suffered to coincide, we well know, that neither moral nor religious motives can be relied on as an adequate control. They are not found to be such on the injustice and violence of individuals, and lose their efficacy in proportion to the number combined together; that is, in proportion as their efficacy becomes needful.

From this view of the subject, it may be concluded, that a pure democracy, by which I mean a society consisting of a small number of citizens, who assemble and administer the government in person, can admit of no cure from the mischiefs of faction. A common passion or interest will, in almost every case, be felt by a majority of the whole; a communication and concert, results from the form of government itself; and there is nothing to check the inducements to sacrifice the weaker party, or an obnoxious individual. Hence it is, that such democracies have ever been spectacles of turbulence and contention; have ever been found incompatible with personal security, or the rights of property; and have, in general, been as short in their lives, as they have been violent in their deaths. Theoretic politicians, who have patronized this species of government, have erroneously supposed, that by reducing mankind to a perfect equality in their political rights, they would, at the same time, be perfectly equalized and assimilated in their possessions, their opinions, and their passions.

A republic, by which I mean a government in which the scheme of representation takes place, opens a different prospect, and promises the cure for which we are seeking. Let us examine the points in which it varies from pure democracy, and we shall comprehend both the nature of the cure and the efficacy which it must derive from the union.

The two great points of difference, between a democracy and a republic, are, first, the delegation of the government, in the latter, to a small number of citizens elected by the rest; secondly, the greater number of citizens, and greater sphere of country, over which the latter may be extended.

The effect of the first difference is, on the one hand, to refine and enlarge the public views, by passing them through the medium of a chosen body of citizens, whose wisdom may best discern the true interest of their country, and whose partiotism and love of justice, will be least likely to sacrifice it to temporary or partial considerations. Under such a regulation, it may well happen, that the public voice, pronounced by the representatives of the people, will be more consonant to the public good, than if pronounced by the people themselves, convened for the purpose. On the other hand the effect may be inverted. Men of factious tempers, of local prejudices, or of sinister designs, may by intrigue, by corruption, or by other means, first obtain the suffrages, and then betray the interests of the people. The question resulting is, whether small or extensive republics are most favourable to the election of proper guardians of the public weal; and it is clearly decided in favour of the latter by two obvious considerations.

In the first place, it is to be remarked, that however small the republic may be, the representatives must be raised to a certain number, in order to guard against the confusion of a multitude. Hence, the number of representatives in the two cases not being in proportion to that of the constituents, and being proportionally greatest in the small republic, it follows, that if the proportion of fit characters be not less in the large than in the small republic, the former will present a greater option, and consequently a greater probability of a fit choice.

In the next place, as each representative will be chosen by a greater number of citizens in the large than in the small republic, it will be more difficult for unworthy candidates to practise with success the vicious arts, by which elections are too often carried; and the suffrages of the people being more free, will be more likely to centre in men who possess the most attractive merit, and the most diffusive and established characters.

It must be confessed, that in this, as in most other cases, there is a mean, on both sides of which inconveniences will be found to lie. By enlarging too much the number of electors, you render the representative too little acquainted with all their local circumstances and lesser interests; as by reducing it too much, you render him unduly attached to these, and too little fit to comprehend and pursue great and national objects. The federal constitution forms a happy combination in this respect; the great and aggregate interests being referred to the national, the local and particular to the state legislatures.

The other point of difference is, the greater number of citizens, and extent of territory, which may be brought within the compass of republican, than of democratic government; and it is this circumstance principally which renders factious combinations less to be dreaded in the former, than in the latter. The smaller the society, the fewer probably will be the distinct parties and interests composing it; the fewer the distinct parties and interests, the more frequently will a majority be found of the same party; and the smaller the number of individuals composing a majority, and the smaller the compass within which they are placed, the more easily will they concert and execute their plans of oppression. Extend the sphere, and you take in a greater variety of parties and interests; you make it less probable that a majority of the whole will have a common motive to invade the rights of other citizens; or if such a common motive exists, it will be more difficult for all who feel it to discover their own strength, and to act in unison with each other. Besides other impediments, it may be remarked, that where there is a consciousness of unjust or dishonourable purposes, communication is always checked by distrust, in proportion to the number whose concurrence is necessary.

Hence, it clearly appears, that the same advantage, which a republic has over a democracy, in controlling the effects of faction, is enjoyed by a large over a small republic . . . is enjoyed by the union over the states composing it. Does this advantage consist in the substitution of representatives, whose enlightened views and virtuous sentiments render them superior to local prejudices, and to schemes of injustice? It will not be denied, that the representation of the union will be most likely to possess these requisite endowments. Does it consist in the greater security afforded by a greater variety of parties, against the event of any one party being able to outnumber and oppress the rest? In an equal degree does the increased variety of parties, comprised within the union, increase this security. Does it, in fine, consist in the greater obstacles opposed to the concert and accomplishment of the secret wishes of an unjust and interested majority? Here, again, the extent of the union gives it the most palpable advantage.

The influence of factious leaders may kindle a flame within their particular states, but will be unable to spread a general conflagration through the other states: a religious sect may degenerate into a political faction in a part of the confederacy; but the variety of sects dispersed over the entire face of it, must secure the national councils against any danger from that source: a rage for paper money, for an abolition of debts, for an equal division of property, or for any other improper or wicked project, will be less apt to pervade the whole body of the union, than a particular member of it; in the same proportion as such a malady is more likely to taint a particular county or district, than an entire state.

In the extent and proper structure of the union, therefore, we behold a republican remedy for the diseases most incident to republican government. And according to the degree of pleasure and pride we feel in being republicans, ought to be our zeal in cherishing the spirit, and supporting the character of federalists.

THE FEDERALIST PAPERS
Number 51
James Madison

To what expedient, then, shall we finally resort, for maintaining in practice the necessary partition of power among the several departments, as laid down in the constitution? The only answer that can be given is, that as all these exterior provisions are found to be inadequate, the defect must be supplied, by so contriving the interior structure of the government, as that its several constituent parts may, by their mutual relations, be the means of keeping each other in their proper places. Without presuming to undertake a full development of this important idea, I will hazard a few general observations, which may perhaps place it in a clearer light, and enable us to form a more correct

From The Federalist. *Copyright by Masters and Co., 1857*

judgment of the principles and structure of the government planned by the convention.

In order to lay a due foundation for that separate and distinct exercise of the different powers of government, which, to a certain extent, is admitted on all hands to be essential to the preservation of liberty, it is evident that each department should have a will of its own; and consequently should be so constituted, that the members of each should have as little agency as possible in the appointment of the members of the others. Were this principle rigorously adhered to, it would require that all the appointments for the supreme executive, legislative, and judiciary magistracies, should be drawn from the same fountain of authority, the people, through channels having no communication whatever with one another. Perhaps such a plan of constructing the several departments, would be less difficult in practice, than it may in contemplation appear. Some difficulties, however, and some additional expense would attend the execution of it. Some deviations, therefore, from the principle must be admitted. In the constitution of the judiciary department in particular, it might be inexpedient to insist rigorously on the principle; first, because peculiar qualifications being essential in the members, the primary consideration ought to be to select that mode of choice which best secures these qualifications; secondly, because the permanent tenure by which the appointments are held in that department, must soon destroy all sense of dependence on the authority conferring them.

It is equally evident, that the members of each department should be as little dependent as possible on those of the others, for the emoluments annexed to their offices. Were the executive magistrate, or the judges not independent of the legislature in this particular, their independence in every other would be merely nominal.

But the great security against a gradual concentration of the several powers in the same department, consists in giving to those who administer each department, the necessary constitutional means, and personal motives, to resist encroachments of the others. The provision for defence must in this, as in all other cases, be made commensurate to the danger of attack. Ambition must be made to counteract ambition. The interest of the man, must be connected with the constitutional rights of the place. It may be a reflection on human nature, that such devices should be necessary to control the abuses of government. But what is government itself, but the greatest of all reflections on human nature? If men were angels, no government would be necessary. If angels were to govern men, neither external nor internal controls on government would be necessary. In framing a government which is to be administered by men over men, the great difficulty lies in this: you must first enable the government to control the governed; and in the next place oblige it to control itself. A dependence on the people is, no doubt, the primary control on the government; but experience has taught mankind the necessity of auxiliary precautions.

This policy of supplying, by opposite and rival interests, the defect of better motives, might be traced through the whole system of human affairs, private as well as public. We see it particularly displayed in all the subordinate distributions of power; where the constant aim is, to divide and arrange the several offices in such a manner as that each may be a check on the other; that the private interest of every individual may be a sentinel over the public rights. These inventions of prudence cannot be less requisite in the distribution of the supreme powers of the state.

But it is not possible to give to each department an equal power of self-defence. In republican government, the legislative authority necessarily predominates. The remedy for this inconveniency is, to divide the legislature into different branches; and to render them by different modes of election, and different principles of action, as little connected with each other, as the nature of their common functions, and their common dependence on the society, will admit. It may even be necessary to guard against dangerous encroachments by still further precautions. As the weight of the legislative authority requires that it should be thus divided, the weakness of the executive may require, on the other hand, that it should be fortified. An absolute negative on the legislature, appears, at first view, to be the natural defence with which the executive magistrate should be armed. But perhaps it would be neither altogether safe, nor alone sufficient. On ordinary occasions, it might not be exerted with the requisite firmness; and on extraordinary occasions, it might be perfidiously abused. May not this defect of an absolute negative be supplied by some qualified connexion between this weaker department, and the weaker branch of the stronger department, by which the latter may be led to support the constitutional rights of the former, without being too much detached from the rights of its own department?

If the principles on which these observations are founded be just, as I persuade myself they are, and they be applied as a criterion to the several state constitutions, and to the federal constitution, it will be found, that if the latter does not perfectly correspond with them, the former are infinitely less able to bear such a test.

There are moreover two considerations particularly applicable to the federal system of America, which place that system in a very interesting point of view.

First. In a single republic, all the power surrendered by the people, is submitted to the administration of a single government; and the usurpations are guarded against, by a division of the government into distinct and separate departments. In the compound republic of America, the power surrendered by the people, is first divided between two distinct governments, and then the portion allotted to each subdivided among distinct and separate departments. Hence a double security arises to the rights of the people. The different governments will control each other; at the same time that each will be controled by itself.

Second. It is of great importance in a republic, not only to guard the society against the oppression of its rulers; but to guard one part of the society against the injustice of the other part. Different interests necessarily exist in different classes of citizens. If a majority be united by a common interest, the rights of the minority will be insecure. There are but two methods of providing against this evil: the one, by creating a will in the community independent of the majority, that is, of the society itself; the other, by comprehending in the society so many separate descriptions of citizens, as will render an unjust combination of a majority of the whole very improbable, if not impracticable. The first method prevails in all governments possessing an hereditary or self-appointed authority. This, at best, is but a precarious security; because a power independent of the society may as well espouse the unjust views of the major, as the rightful interests of the minor party, and may possibly be turned against both parties. The second method will be exemplified in the federal republic of the United States. Whilst all authority in it will be derived from, and dependent on the society, the society itself will be broken into so many parts, interests, and classes of citizens, that the rights of individuals, or of the minority will be in little danger from interested combinations of the majority. In a free government, the security for civil rights must be the same as that for religious rights. It consists in the one case in the multiplicity of interests, and in the other in the multiplicity of sects.

The degree of security in both cases will depend on the number of interests and sects; and this may be presumed to depend on the extent of country and number of people comprehended under the same government. This view of the subject must particularly recommend a proper federal system to all the sincere and considerate friends of republican government: since it shows, that in exact proportion as the territory of the union may be formed into more circumscribed confederacies, or states, oppressive combinations of a majority will be facilitated; the best security under the republican form, for the rights of every class of citizens, will be diminished; and consequently, the stability and independence of some member of the government, the only other security, must be proportionally increased. Justice is the end of government. It is the end of civil society. It ever has been, and ever will be pursued, until it be obtained, or until liberty be lost in the pursuit. In a society, under the forms of which the stronger faction can readily unite and oppress the weaker, anarchy may as truly be said to reign, as in a state of nature, where the weaker individual is not secured against the violence of the stronger: and as in the latter state, even the stronger individuals are prompted, by the uncertainty of their condition, to submit to a government which may protect the weak, as well as themselves: so in the former state, will the more powerful factions or parties be gradually induced, by a like motive, to wish for a government which will protect all parties, the weaker as well as the more powerful. It can be little doubted, that if the state of Rhode Island was separated from the confederacy, and left to itself, the insecurity of rights under the popular form of government within such narrow limits, would be displayed by such reiterated oppressions of factious majorities, that some power altogether independent of the people, would soon be called for by the voice of the very factions whose misrule had proved the necessity of it. In the extended republic of the United States, and among the great variety of interests, parties, and sects, which it embraces, a coalition of a majority of the whole society could seldom take place upon any other principles than those of justice and the general good: whilst there being thus less danger to a minor from the will of a major party, there must be less pretext also, to provide for the security of the former, by introducing into the government a will not dependent on the latter: or, in other words, a will independent of the society itself. It is no less certain than it is important, notwithstanding the contrary opinions which have been entertained, that the larger the society, provided it lie within a practical sphere, the more duly capable it will be of self-government. And happily for the *republican cause,* the practicable sphere may be carried to a very great extent, by a judicious modification and mixture of the *federal principle.*

THE CONCURRENT MAJORITY
John C. Calhoun

After observing that there are few protections offered a minority against the abuses of majority rule, Calhoun offers the following provision.

From what has been said, it is manifest, that this provision must be of a character calculated to prevent any one interest, or combination of interests, from using the powers of government to aggrandize itself at the expense of the others. Here lies the evil: and just in proportion as it shall prevent, or fail to prevent it, in the same degree it will effect, or fail to effect the end intended to be accomplished. There is but one certain mode in which this result can be secured; and that is, by the adoption of some restriction or limitation, which shall so effectually prevent any one interest, or combination of interests, from obtaining the exclusive control of the government, as to render hopeless all attempts directed to that end. There is, again, but one mode in which this can be effected; and that is, by taking the sense of each interest or portion of the community, which may be unequally and injuriously affected by the action of the government, separately, through its own majority, or in some other way by which its voice may be fairly expressed; and to require the consent of each interest, either to put or to keep the government in action. This, too, can be accomplished only in one way,—and that is, by such an organism of the government,—and, if necessary for the purpose, of the community also,— as will, by dividing and distributing the powers of government, give to each division or interest, through its appropriate organ, either a concurrent voice

From A Disquisition on Government and A Discourse on the Constitution and Government of the United States. *Copyright by A. S. Johnson, 1851.*

in making and executing the laws, or a veto on their execution. It is only by such an organism, that the assent of each can be made necessary to put the government in motion; or the power made effectual to arrest its action, when put in motion;—and it is only by the one or the other that the different interests, orders, classes, or portions, into which the community may be divided, can be protected, and all conflict and struggle between them prevented,—by rendering it impossible to put or to keep it in action, without the concurrent consent of all.

Such an organism as this, combined with the right of suffrage, constitutes, in fact, the elements of constitutional government. The one, by rendering those who make and execute the laws responsible to those on whom they operate, prevents the rulers from oppressing the ruled; and the other, by making it impossible for any one interest or combination of interests or class, or order, or portion of the community, or obtain exclusive control, prevents any one of them from oppressing the other. It is clear, that oppression and abuse of power must come, if at all, from the one or the other quarter. From no other can they come. It follows, that the two, suffrage and proper organism combined, are sufficient to counteract the tendency of government to oppression and abuse of power; and to restrict it to the fulfilment of the great ends for which it is ordained.

In coming to this conclusion, I have assumed the organism to be perfect, and the different interests, portions, or classes of the community, to be sufficiently enlightened to understand its character and object, and to exercise, with due intelligence, the right of suffrage. To the extent that either may be defective, to the same extent the government would fall short of fulfilling its end. But this does not impeach the truth of the principles on which it rests. In reducing them to proper form, in applying them to practical uses, all elementary principles are liable to difficulties; but they are not on this account, the less true, or valuable. Where the organism is perfect, every interest will be truly and fully represented, and of course the whole community must be so. It may be difficult, or even impossible, to make a perfect organism,—but, although this be true, yet even when, instead of the sense of each and of all, it takes that of a few great and prominent interests only, it would still, in a great measure, if not altogether, fulfil the end intended by a constitution. For, in such case, it would require so large a portion of the community, compared with the whole, to concur, or acquiesce in the action of the government, that the number to be plundered would be too few, and the number to be aggrandized too many, to afford adequate motives to oppression and the abuse of its powers. Indeed, however imperfect the organism, it must have more or less effect in diminishing such tendency.

It may be readily inferred, from what has been stated, that the effect of organism is neither to supersede nor diminish the importance of the right of suffrage; but to aid and perfect it. The object of the latter is, to collect the sense of the community. The more fully and perfectly it accomplishes this, the more fully and perfectly it fulfils its end. But the most it can do, of itself, is to collect the sense of the greater number; that is, of the stronger interests, or combination of interests; and to assume this to be the sense of the community. It is only when aided by a proper organism, that is can collect the sense of the entire community,—of each and all its interests; of each, through its appropriate organ, and of the whole, through all of them united. This would truly be the sense of the entire community; for whatever diversity each interest might have within itself,—as all would have the same interest in reference to the action of the government, the individuals composing each would be fully and truly represented by its own majority or appropriate organ, regarded in reference to the other interests. In brief, every individual of every interest might trust, with confidence, its majority or appropriate organ, against that of every other interest.

It results, from what has been said, that there are two different modes in which the sense of the community may be taken; one, simply by the right of suffrage, unaided; the other, by the right through a proper organism. Each collects the sense of the majority. But one regards numbers only, and considers the whole community as a unit, having but one common interest throughout; and collects the sense of the greater number of the whole, as that of the community. The other, on the contrary, regards interests as well as numbers;—considering the community as made up of different and conflicting interests, as far as the action of the government is concerned; and takes the sense of each, through its majority or appropriate organ, and the united sense of all, as the sense of the entire community. The former of these I shall call the numerical, or absolute majority; and the latter, the concurrent, or constitutional majority. I call it the constitutional majority, because it is an essential element in every constitutional government,—be its form what it may. So great is the difference, politically speaking, between the two majorities, that they cannot be confounded, without leading to great and fatal errors; and yet the distinction between them has been so entirely overlooked, that when the term *majority* is used in political discussions, it is applied exclusively to designate the numerical,—as if there were no other. Until this distinction is recognized, and better understood, there will continue to be great liability to error in properly constructing constitutional governments, especially of the popular form, and of preserving them when properly constructed. Until then, the latter will have a strong tendency to slide, first, into the government of the numerical majority, and, finally, into absolute government of some other form. To show that such must be the case, and at the same time to mark more strongly the difference between the two, in order to guard against the danger of overlooking it, I propose to consider the subject more at length.

The first and leading error which naturally arises from overlooking the distinction referred to, is, to confound the numerical majority with the people; and this so completely as to regard them as identical. This is a consequence that necessarily results from considering the numerical as the only majority. All admit, that a popular government, or democracy, is the government of the people; for the terms imply this. A perfect government of the kind would be one which would embrace the consent of every citizen or member of the community; but as this is impracticable, in the opinion of those who regard the numerical as the only majority, and who can perceive no other way by which the sense of the people can be taken,—they are compelled to adopt this as the only true basis of popular government, in contradistinction to governments of the aristocratical or monarchical form. Being thus constrained, they are, in the next place, forced to regard the numerical majority, as, in effect, the entire people; that is, the greater part as the whole; and the government of the greater part as the government of the whole. It is thus the two come to be confounded, and a part made identical with the whole. And it is thus, also, that all the rights, powers, and immunities of the whole people come to be attributed to the numerical majority; and, among others, the supreme, sovereign authority of establishing and abolishing governments at pleasure.

This radical error, the consequence of confounding the two, and of regarding the numerical as the only majority, has contributed more than any other cause, to prevent the formation of popular constitutional governments,— and to destroy them even when they have been formed. It leads to the conclusion that, in their formation and establishment, nothing more is necessary than the right of suffrage,—and the allotment to each division of the community a representation in the government, in proportion to numbers. If the numerical majority were really the people; and if, to take its sense truly, were to take the sense of the people truly, a government so constituted would be a true and perfect model of a popular constitutional government; and every departure from it would detract from its excellence. But, as such is not the case,—as the numerical majority, instead of being the people, is only a portion of them,— such a government, instead of being a true and perfect model of the people's government, that is, a people self-governed, is but the government of a part, over a part,—the major over the minor portion.

But this misconception of the true elements of constitutional government does not stop here. It leads to others equally false and fatal, in reference to the best means of preserving and perpetuating them, when, from some fortunate combination of circumstances, they are correctly formed. For they who fall into these errors regard the restrictions which organism imposes on the will of the numerical majority as restrictions on the will of the people, and, therefore, as not only useless, but wrongful and mischievous. And hence they endeavor to destroy organism, under the delusive hope of making government more democratic.

Such are some of the consequences of confounding the two, and of regarding the numerical as the only majority. And in this may be found the reason why so few popular governments have been properly constructed, and why, of these few, so small a number have proved durable. Such must continue to be the result, so long as these errors continue to be prevalent.

There is another error, of a kindred character, whose influence contributes much to the same results: I refer to the prevalent opinion, that a written constitution, containing suitable restrictions on the powers of government, is sufficient, of itself, without the aid of any organism,—except such as is necessary to separate its several departments, and render them independent of each other,—to counteract the tendency of the numerical majority to oppression and the abuse of power.

A written constitution certainly has many and considerable advantages; but it is a great mistake to suppose, that the mere insertion of provisions to restrict and limit the powers of the government, without investing those for whose protection they are inserted with the means of enforcing their observance, will be sufficient to prevent the major and dominant party from abusing its powers. Being the party in possession of the government, they will, from the same constitution of man which makes government necessary to protect society, be in favor of the powers granted by the constitution, and opposed to the restrictions intended to limit them. As the major and dominant party, they will have no need of these restrictions for their protection. The ballot-box, of itself, would be ample protection to them. Needing no other, they would come, in time, to regard these limitations as unnecessary and improper restraints;—and endeavor to elude them, with the view of increasing their power and influence.

The minor, or weaker party, on the contrary, would take the opposite direction;—and regard them as essential to their protection against the dominant party. And, hence, they would endeavor to defend and enlarge the restrictions, and to limit and contract the powers. But where there are no means by which they could compel the major party to observe the restrictions, the only resort left them would be, a strict construction of the constitution,—that is, a construction which would confine these powers to the narrowest limits which the meaning of the words used in the grant would admit.

To this the major party would oppose a liberal construction,—one which would give to the words of the grant the broadest meaning of which they were susceptible. It would then be construction against construction; the one to contract, and the other to enlarge the powers of the government to the utmost. But of what possible avail could the strict construction of the minor party be, against the liberal interpretation of the major, when the one would have all the powers of the government to carry its construction into effect,—and the other be deprived of all means of enforcing its construction? In a contest so unequal, the result would not be doubtful. The party in favor of the restrictions would be overpowered. At first, they might command some respect, and do something to stay the march of encroachment; but they would, in the progress of the contest, be regarded as mere abstractionist; and, indeed, deservedly, if they should indulge the folly of supposing that the party in possession of the ballot-box and the physical force of the country, could be successfully resisted by an appeal to reason, truth, justice, or the obligations imposed by the constitution. For when these, of themselves, shall exert sufficient influence to stay the hand of power, then government will be no longer necessary to protect society, nor constitutions needed to prevent government from abusing its powers. The end of the contest would be the subversion of the constitution, either by the undermining process of construction,—where its meaning would admit of possible doubt,—or by substituting in practice what is called party-usage, in place of its provisions;—or, finally, when no other contrivance would subserve the purpose, by openly and boldly setting them aside. By the one or the other, the restrictions would ultimately be annulled, and the government be converted into one of unlimited powers.

Nor would the division of government into separate, and, as it regards each other, independent departments, prevent this result. Such a division may do much to facilitate its operations, and to secure to its administration greater caution and deliberation; but as each and all the departments,—and, of course, the entire government,—would be under the control of the numerical majority, it is too clear to require explanation, that a mere distribution of its powers among its agents or representatives, could do little or nothing to counteract its tendency to oppression and abuse of power. To effect this, it would be necessary to go one step further, and make the several departments the organs of the distinct interests or portions of the community; and to clothe each with a negative on the others. But the effect of this would be to change the government from the numerical into the concurrent majority.

Having now explained the reasons why it is so difficult to form and preserve popular constitutional government, so long as the distinction between the two majorities is overlooked, and the opinion prevails that a written constitution, with suitable restrictions and a proper division of its powers, is sufficient to counteract the tendency of the numerical majority to the abuse of its power,—I shall next proceed to explain, more fully, why the concurrent majority is an indispensable element in forming constitutional governments; and why the numerical majority, of itself, must, in all cases, make governments absolute.

The necessary consequence of taking the sense of the community by the concurrent majority is, as has been explained, to give to each interest or portion of the community a negative on the others. It is this mutual negative among its various conflicting interests, which invests each with the power of protecting itself;—and places the rights and safety of each, where only they can be securely placed, under its own guardianship. Without this there can be no systematic, peaceful, or effective resistance to the natural tendency of each to come into conflict with the others: and without this there can be no constitution. It is this negative power,—the power of preventing or arresting the action of the government,—be it called by what term it may,—veto, interposition, nullification, check, or balance of power,—which, in fact, forms the constitution. They are all but different names for the negative power. In all its forms, and under all its names, it results from the concurrent majority. Without this there can be no negative; and, without a negative, no constitution. The assertion is true in reference to all constitutional governments, be their forms what they may. It is, indeed, the negative power which makes the constitution,—and the positive which makes the government. The one is the power of acting;

—and the other the power of preventing or arresting action. The two, combined, make constitutional governments.

But, as there can be no constitution without the negative power, and no negative power without the concurrent majority;—it follows, necessarily, that where the numerical majority has the sole control of the government, there can be no constitution; as constitution implies limitation or restriction,—and, of course, is inconsistent with the idea of sole or exclusive power. And hence, the numerical, unmixed with the concurrent majority, necessarily forms, in all cases, absolute government.

It is, indeed, the single, or *one power,* which excludes the negative, and constitutes absolute government; and not the *number* in whom the power is vested. The numerical majority is as truly a *single power,* and excludes the negative as completely as the absolute government of one, or of the few. The former is as much the absolute government of the democratic, or popular form, as the latter of the monarchical or aristocratical. It has, accordingly, in common with them, the same tendency to oppression and abuse of power.

Constitutional governments, of whatever form, are, indeed, much more similar to each other, in their structure and character, than they are, respectively, to the absolute governments, even of their own class. All constitutional governments, of whatever class they may be, take the sense of the community by its parts,—each through its appropriate organ; and regard the sense of all its parts, as the sense of the whole. They all rest on the right of suffrage, and the responsibility of rulers, directly or indirectly. On the contrary, all absolute governments, of whatever form, concentrate power in one uncontrolled and irresponsible individual or body, whose will is regarded as the sense of the community. And, hence, the great and broad distinction between governments is,—not that of the one, the few, or the many,—but of the constitutional and the absolute.

From this there results another distinction, which, although secondary in its character, very strongly marks the difference between these forms of government. I refer to their respective conservative principle;—that is, the principle by which they are upheld and preserved. This principle, in constitutional governments, is *compromise;*—and in absolute governments, is *force;*—as will be next explained.

It has been already shown, that the same constitution of man which leads those who govern to oppress the governed,—if not prevented,—will, with equal force and certainty, lead the latter to resist oppression, when possessed of the means of doing so peaceably and successfully. But absolute governments, of all forms, exclude all other means of resistance to their authority, than that of force; and, of course, leave no other alternative to the governed, but to acquiesce in oppression, however great it may be, or to resort to force to put down the government. But the dread of such a resort must necessarily lead the government to prepare to meet force in order to protect itself; and hence, of necessity, force becomes the conservative principle of all such governments.

On the contrary, the government of the concurrent majority, where the organism is perfect, excludes the possibility of oppression, by giving to each interest, or portion, or order,—where there are established classes,—the means of protecting itself, by its negative, against all measures calculated to advance the peculiar interests of others at its expense. Its effect, then, is, to cause the different interests, portions, or orders,—as the case may be,—to desist from attempting to adopt any measure calculated to promote the prosperity of one, or more, by sacrificing that of others; and thus to force them to unite in such measures only as would promote the prosperity of all, as the only means to prevent the suspension of the action of the government;—and, thereby, to avoid anarchy, the greatest of all evils. It is by means of such authorized and effectual resistance, that oppression is prevented, and the necessity of resorting to force superseded, in governments of the concurrent majority;—and, hence, compromise, instead of force, becomes their conservative principle.

It would, perhaps, be more strictly correct to trace the conservative principle of constitutional governments to the necessity which compels the different interests, or portions, or orders, to compromise,—as the only way to promote their respective prosperity, and to avoid anarchy,—rather than to the compromise itself. No necessity can be more urgent and imperious, than that of avoiding anarchy. It is the same as that which makes government indispensable to preserve society; and is not less imperative than that which compels obedience to superior force. Traced to this source, the voice of a people,— uttered under the necessity of avoiding the greatest of calamities, through the organs of a government so constructed as to suppress the expression of all partial and selfish intersts, and to give a full and faithful utterance to the sense of the whole community, in reference to its common welfare,—may, without impiety, be called *the voice of God.* To call any other so, would be impious.

AMERICAN PLURALISM
Robert A. Dahl

How can any government operate with "the consent of all"? This expression is one that Americans fell into the habit of using quite early in their national history.

Resolved (declared the First Continental Congress on October 14, 1774) *that the inhabitants of the English colonies in North America, by the immutable laws of nature . . . are entitled to life, liberty, and property: and they have never ceded to any, foreign power whatever, a right to dispose of either without their consent.*

We hold these truths to be self evident (declared the Second Continental Congress on July 14, 1776) *that all men are created equal, that they are endowed by their Creator with certain inalienable Rights, that among these are Life, Liberty, and the pursuit of Happiness.—That to secure these rights, Governments are instituted among men, deriving their just powers from the consent of the governed.*

By now the phrase comes so easily to the lips of an American that few ever pause to ask *why* governments should or *how* they can rest on the consent of all.

There are at least four reasons for insisting that governments ought, ideally, to derive their just powers from the consent of the governed. First, government without consent is inconsistent with personal freedom. To the extent that I am compelled to obey man-made rules that do not have my moral approval. I am not a free man. To be sure, personal freedom is an exacting demand; complete personal freedom is probably impossible to achieve. Nonetheless, one who believes in the value of individual freedom may reasonably hold that so far as possible no adult human being should ever be governed without his consent.

Second, government without one's consent can be an affront to human dignity and respect. We see this most vividly in extreme cases—the hapless victim in a concentration camp, who is subjected to the utmost humiliation, degradation, deprivation, and torture, loses thereby a part of his humanity.

Third, one may demand solely out of self-interest that a government rest on consent. For one might reason as follows: Certainly I do not want the government to act without *my* approval. But since I am not nor am I likely to be a dictator or even a member of a ruling oligarchy, perhaps the safest way to insure that the government will have *my* approval is to insist that it must

Reprinted by permission of the publisher from Robert A. Dahl, Pluralist Democracy in the United States, © *1967 by Rand McNally & Company, Chicago, pp. 14–24.*

have the approval of *everyone*. Reasoning from self-interest is not generally thought to be quite as noble as reasoning from general principles of freedom and dignity. Nonetheless we should rejoice, I believe, whenever freedom and dignity are supported by widespread self-interest; for nothing is quite so strong a buttress to social institutions as a firm foundation in self-interest.

Finally, one may insist on consent because one thinks that governments "deriving their just powers from the consent of the governed" are more likely to be stable and durable. There are innumerable reasons why one may want stable government, including the fact that revolutions are very uncertain affairs; with a few exceptions, among which, happily, the American Revolution may be counted, those who start the first fires of a revolution are consumed in the holocaust. To control the course of a revolution is almost as difficult as to direct the path of a tornado. Whatever the reasons why one may want stability in government, it is reasonable to suppose that a government is less likely to create hostility, frustration, and resentment—sentiments that breed revolution—if it acts with the approval of its citizens than if it does not. Common sense and modern history both lend substance to this judgment; in the past century the most durable governments in the world have rested on widespread suffrage and other institutions for popular control.

But if it is relatively easy to say *why* governments should derive their just powers from the consent of the governed, it is very much more difficult to say *how* they can do so. The difficulty stems from that inescapable element of conflict in the human condition: People living together simply will not always agree. When people disagree, how can a decision be based on the consent of all? Since political philosophers, like architects, sometimes conceal their failures behind a handsome facade, the unwary student may conclude that the solution would be clear if he only understood the philosophers better. In this case, however, modesty may be misplaced; although political philosophers have long wrestled with the problem, the disagreeable fact remains that they have not been able to prescribe a perfect solution except under certain highly improbable circumstances.

The obvious way out, of course, is to eliminate conflict. This happy solution is characteristic of many literary Utopias, where social life is downright inhuman in its lack of conflict. Utopianism of this genre appears in unsuspected places: Karl Marx was a militant critic of the Utopian socialists of an earlier generation, yet he evidently thought that his famous dialectic— "All history is the history of class conflict"—would for all practical purposes come to an end in a communist society: there would be no need for a state because there would be no significant conflicts.

If one concludes that complete agreement is a hopeless objective and not necessarily a very desirable one, then one must search elsewhere for a solution to the problem of consent. A second way out is to search for specific policies that every citizen approves of, even though he may have disagreed, initially, with his fellow citizens. It is not absurd, surely, to suppose that conflict can sometimes be transmuted into decisions that have the approval of everyone.

Perhaps all of us have had experiences of this kind, particularly when we try to arrive at decisions within some group where everyone else shares our fundamental values, even though we may differ on specific questions. There is something of this idea behind Rousseau's much disputed notion of a General Will that bespeaks more truly what we believe than we always do ourselves. Yet the difficulty with all solutions along these lines is that decisions rarely do receive unanimous approval. Do I consent to decisions with which I disagree? Who is a better judge than I of what my 'will', my policy, really is? Should anyone else have the authority to proclaim that a policy really has my consent? Although a distinction can be made between what I really believe is best and what I momentarily think or say is best, a good deal of experience suggests that to allow someone else to make this distinction for me is very dangerous. A tyrant might insist that he has my consent for all he does, though I deny it, because he knows better than I what I really want. When an individual says he disapproves of the policies of the government, even when they have the blessings of an enlightened dictator or an enlightened majority, the safest course in practise, I believe, is to postulate that he knows his own mind. Otherwise, government by consent is likely to degenerate into a mere ritualistic formula.

Even if people cannot always agree on specific policies, however, a third solution is to gain their consent for a *process*. It is perfectly reasonable of me to say that I approve of the process by which certain kinds of decisions are made, even if I do not always like the specific results. Thus the consent of the governed may be interpreted to mean their approval of the processes by which decisions are arrived at and their willingness to abide by these decisions even when these seem wrong.

But what kind of a process shall I require? If I hold that no one can, as a general matter, know my goals and values better than I myself, then no doubt I will insist that the process of making decisions must provide me with a full opportunity to make my views known; and even if I am willing to leave details to experts, I do not want anyone else to have more power over the decision, in the last say, than I do. A solution along these lines might well appeal to me as the best attainable, given the inescapable conditions mentioned earlier: that my need for human fellowship impels me to live in a society, that I cannot live with others without sometimes disagreeing with them, and that I must therefore find some way to adjust our conflicts that will appeal to all of us as fair.

This solution is, in fact, what links consent with democracy. In the real world, of course, democracies never quite satisfy all the conditions implied by this solution; but it serves as one standard against which to measure their success and failure.

But how is this solution to be applied? What kind of process will insure that I shall have a full opportunity to make my views known, and that no one else will have more power over decisions, in the last say, than I do?

There are a number of different answers to these questions, and it is with two of these that we are concerned. Purely as a matter of abstract theory, the one is admirably clear and explicit; this is decision-making by the sovereign majority. Yet no country seems to have adopted this method in entirety. The other is in greater or lesser degree the pattern that seems to have evolved in the countries we usually call 'democratic.' Yet the pattern is so blurred and chaotic—and there are so many variations from country to country—that it is difficult to describe.

Does the difference between these two kinds of answers reflect a conflict of ideals or only the familiar conflict between ideals and reality? Perhaps a bit of both. What an 'ideal democracy' would be is a subject of interminable dispute. One is tempted to say that there are as many different visions of what democracy ought to be as there are individuals who think about the matter. Because the advocates of each vision shape their definitions to fit their ideals, the world of political thought and political rhetoric is over-populated with definitions of the term 'democracy.'

I want to refrain here from adding to this definitional explosion. I shall speak of the American political system with terms that Americans themselves have used for generations—a democracy, a republic, or a democratic republic. One may if he chooses quarrel with my use of these terms, but he will find me an unwilling contestant, for I do not wish to argue overmuch about terms in this book. Without trying to decide, then, which of the different visions of democracy is more truly democratic, let me nonetheless describe two of these: decision-making by the sovereign majority, and pluralistic democracy.

In the vision of democracy as decision-making by the sovereign majority, the citizens of a given country all approve of the principle of majority rule, according to which all conflicts over the policies of government are settled, sooner or later, by a majority of citizens or voters—either directly in a public assembly or in a referendum, or indirectly through elected representatives. A person who approves of the principle of majority rule need not go so far as to assume, as Rousseau is often interpreted as saying, that a majority mysteriously reveals the 'real' will even of the minority who would prefer a different policy. Nor does one need to assume that every policy preferred by a majority is bound to be morally right. One need not even believe that the principle of majority rule is the best principle for every political system. Although people sometimes lay down these exaggerated requirements, none of them seems to be demanded either by strict logic or by interference from actual experience. To approve of a system that applies the principle of majority rule, evidently one needs only to believe that during this historical period and in this particular society the principle represents the fullest attainable achievement of one's values. An American is not logically inconsistent if he holds that majority rule is not the best principle to apply in the Congo. For it would be entirely consistent to argue that the workability and acceptability of majority rule depends upon the existence of conditions that may or may not be present in a specific society.

In fact, the straightforward application of the principle of the sovereign majority of all questions of public significance is, as a practical matter, not likely to receive everyone's continuing approval—except under unusual circumstances. While a citizen may make certain allowances for majority decisions that displease him, the more frequently he expects to be in a minority, the less likely he is to accept the principle of majority rule. One can, perhaps, accept calmly the prospect of being in a minority so long as the issues are trivial. But the more important the issues, the more difficult it is to accept defeat by a hostile majority. The more I expect that majorities are going to insist on policies that conflict with my most cherished values, the more likely I am to oppose the principle of majority rule. Surely few people would be so loyal to the abstract principle as to approve of it even if they expected it to lead regularly to repugnant policies. At some point even the most convinced adherent of majority rule will give up in despair. In a nation of convinced anti-Semites and religious bigots, a modern Jefferson might be compelled to oppose the principle of the sovereign majority. In short, continuing and universal approval of the principle of majority rule requires a high degree of consensus among all the citizens as to what the policies of government should be.

It seems reasonable to conjecture that the more diverse the beliefs held among a body of people, the less likely it is that they will approve of the idea of making decisions by majority rule. To the extent that this conjecture is valid, it is a severe restriction on the principle of rule by a sovereign majority, particularly in modern heterogeneous societies. For it seems entirely reasonable to hold that diversity of beliefs is likely to be greater the larger the number of citizens, the bigger the territory over which they are spread, and the greater the distinctions of race, ethnic group, regional culture, occupation, social class, income, property, and so on. Some advocates of rule by the sovereign majority have therefore argued, as Rousseau did, that majority decisions would be acceptable only among very small and highly homogeneous bodies of people, groups no larger perhaps than a town or a very small city. According to this view, nations even as small as Norway, and certainly as large as the United States, are unsuitable for democracy.

One possible way to maintain homogeneity would be to eliminate all dissenting minorities who would object to the decisions of a majority. In Athens the Ecclesia—the sovereign town meeting composed theoretically of all adult citizens—had the power of *ostracism,* by which it could banish an unpopular citizen from Athens for ten years. Rousseau evidently believed that homogeneity would be maintained if dissident citizens had the right to emigrate—presumably to a more sympathetic community. Another possibility, a painful one to Americans, is secession. Yet all of these solutions entail serious practical and moral difficulties, particularly in the modern world. Emigration, for example, can be a staggering price to pay simply for being in a minority; must the price of one's beliefs depend solely on the numbers who happen to share them? Yet if emigration is purely optional, who would emigrate? Many dissenters would remain to deny the legitimacy of majority rule as it applies to them. Shall we then expel these dissenters in order to maintain consensus? To expel an individual from a community is not difficult; American communities have often done so, sometimes with the aid of tar and feathers. But to expel a significant minority that does not chose to depart in peace can mean civil war. It might be said that a discontented minority can be permitted to separate amicably by the simple expedient of redrawing the boundary lines and thus creating a new and independent state. But should every minority that wishes to do so be allowed to secede in full possession of the territory in which they happen to reside, even if this has been so integrated into the economy, transportation system, defenses, and sense of nationhood of the larger country that its loss would be a serious blow? Such forbearance and generosity are unlikely. In any case, what is to be the fate of a minority within a minority, as in the case of Negroes in the South? And of minorities that are not geographically separated but intermixed, like Jehovah's Witnesses:

For Americans these questions are more than rhetorical; here, secession was proposed and rejected as a practical solution by a civil war. Lincoln's first inaugural address pierced the logic of secession:

Plainly, the central idea of secession is the essence of anarchy. A majority held in restraint by constitutional checks and limitations, and always changing easily with deliberate changes of popular opinions and sentiments, is the only true sovereign of a free people. Whoever rejects it does, of necessity, fly to anarchy or to depotism. Unanimity is impossible; the rule of a minority, as a permanent arrangement, is wholly inadmissible; so that, rejecting the majority principle, anarchy or depotism in some form is all that is left.

But even civil war did not finally settle the debate about the proper scope and limits of rule by majorities in the United States.

There is one further difficulty in the application of majority rule that is of special significance to Americans. That some people may have voted in the distant past to accept the Constitution of the United States—as a rather small proportion of the population did in 1787-8, and as the people or their representatives did in the territories prior to entering the Union—is surely no reason why we, today, should feel bound to accept their verdict: not, at any rate, if we demand continuing consent to the processes of government. Ideally, then, every new generation must be free to refuse its consent to the old rules and to make new ones. The Declaration of Independence contains these ringing phrases:

That whenever any Form of Government becomes destructive of these ends (Life, Liberty, and the pursuit of Happiness) *it is the Right of the People to alter or to abolish it, and to institute a new Government, laying its foundation on such principles and organizing its powers in such form, as to them shall seem most likely to effect their Safety and Happiness.*

Seventy years later, confronted by secession, and on the eve of war, in the inauguration speech from which I quoted a moment ago, Lincoln reaffirmed this principle:

> *This country, with its institutions, belongs to the people who inhabit it. Whenever they shall grow weary of the existing government, they can exercise their constitutional right of amending it, or their revolutionary right to dismember or overthrow it.*

But "the People" is an ambiguous phrase. Do these famous words mean that whenever a majority is discontented with the government it should be free to change it? If they are not permitted to do so, then can we say that they have given their approval, in any realistic sense, to the processes of government? Yet if every majority must be free to alter the rules of government, what is the significance of a "Constitution"? How can a constitution be more binding than ordinary law? Is there no legitimate way by which groups smaller than a majority can receive guarantees that the rules they agree to abide by will be more or less permanent and will not change at the whim of the next legislature?

These are difficult questions to answer, and no answers seem to command universal agreement. To gain "the consent of all" consistently applying the principle that the majority should be sovereign gives rise to serious problems, both logical and practical. Perhaps under certain unusual conditions, such as a very high degree of homogeneity, among a very small body of citizens, these problems could be solved.

In practise, however, popular governments have moved toward a rather different solution.

The practical solutions that democratic countries have evolved are a good deal less clear than a straightforward application of the principle of majority rule. These solutions seem less 'logical,' less coherent, more untidy, and a good deal more attainable. Patterns of democratic government do not reflect a logically conceived philosophical plan so much as a series of responses to problems of diversity and conflict, by leaders who have sought to build and maintain a nation, to gain the loyalty and obedience of citizens, to win general and continuing approval of political institutions, and at the same time to conform to aspirations for democracy. However, some common elements can be discovered.

For one thing, in practise, countries with democratic regimes use force, just as other regimes do, to repel threats to the integrity of the national territory. Consequently secession is, as a practical matter, usually either impossible or extremely costly. (Colonies thought to lie outside the territory of the 'nation' may, of course, be granted independence.) To a considerable extent, then, large minorities are virtually 'compelled' to remain within the territorial limits of the nation. To make compulsory citizenship tolerable, great efforts are made to create and sustain a common sense of nationhood, so that minorities of all kinds will identify themselves with the nation. Hence secession or mass emigration are not usually thought of as practical alternatives.

Second, many matters of policy—religious beliefs and practises, for example—are effectively outside the legal authority of any government. Often they are placed beyond the legal authority of government through understandings and agreements widely shared and respected. In many cases these understandings and agreements are expressed in written constitutions that cannot be quickly or easily amended. Such a constitution is regarded as peculiarly binding; and ordinary laws that run counter to the constitution will be invalid, or, at the very least, subject to special scrutiny.

Third, a great many questions of policy are placed in the hands of private, semi-public, and local governmental organizations such as churches, families, business firms, trade unions, towns, cities, provinces, and the like. These questions of policy, like those left to individuals, are also effectively beyond the reach of national majorities, the national legislature, or indeed any national policy-makers acting in their legal and official capacities. In fact, whenever uniform policies are likely to be costly, difficult, or troublesome, in pluralistic democracies the tendency is to find ways by which these policies can be made by smaller groups of like-minded people who enjoy a high degree of legal independence.

Fourth, whenever a group of people believe that they are adversely affected by national policies or are about to be, they generally have extensive opportunities for presenting their case and for negotiations that may produce a more acceptable alternative. In some cases, they may have enough power to delay, to obstruct, and even to veto the attempt to impose policies on them.

Now in addition to all these characteristics, the United States has limited the sovereignty of the majority in still other ways. In fact, the United States has gone so far in this direction that it is sometimes called a pluralistic system, a term I propose to use here.

The fundamental axiom in the theory and practise of American pluralism is, I believe, this: Instead of a single center of sovereign power there must be multiple centers of power, none of which is or can be wholly sovereign. Although the only legitimate sovereign is the people, in all perspective of American pluralism even the people ought never to be an absolute sovereign; consequently no part of the people, such as a majority, ought to be absolutely sovereign.

Why this axiom? The theory and practise of American pluralism tend to assume, as I see it, that the existence of multiple centers of power, none of which is wholly sovereign, will help (may indeed be necessary) to tame power, to secure the consent of all, and to settle conflicts peacefully:

- Because one center of power is set against another, power itself will be tamed, civilized, controlled, and limited to decent human purposes, while coercion, the most evil form of power, will be reduced to a minimum.

- Because even minorities are provided with opportunities to veto solutions they strongly object to, the consent of all will be won in the long run.

- Because constant negotiations among different centers of power are necessary in order to make decisions, citizens and leaders will perfect the precious art of dealing peacefully with their conflicts, and not merely to the benefit of one partisan but to the mutual benefit of all the parties to a conflict.

These are, I think, the basic postulates and even the unconscious ways of thought that are central to the American attempt to cope with the inescapable problems of power, conflict, and consent.

THE INTENSITY PROBLEM AND DEMOCRATIC THEORY
Willmore Kendall and George W. Carey

Dinner is over. Mr. and Mrs. Jones and Mr. and Mrs. Smith are having coffee. The question arises: What shall we do this evening? Play bridge? Go to the movies? Listen to some chamber music from the local FM station? Sit and chat? Each, in due course, expresses a "preference" among these four alternatives but with this difference: Mr. and Mrs. Jones and Mrs. Smith, though each has a preference, "don't much care." Their preferences are "mild" or "marginal." Not so Mr. Smith. His preference is "strong." He is tired, couldn't possibly get his mind on bridge, or muster the energies for going out to a movie. He has listened to chamber music all afternoon while working on an architectural problem, and couldn't bear any more. If the group does anything other than sit and chat, he at least will do it grudgingly. He "cares enormously" which alternative is chosen.

Now: which is the "correct" choice among the four alternatives? Which, "distributive justice" to one side, is the choice most likely to preserve good relations among the members of the group? Some theorists, it would seem, find these two questions easy to answer. Mr. Smith *ought* to have his way, and good relations are likely to be endangered if he does not; and these answers are equally valid whether the other three all prefer the same thing or prefer different things. Since, for the latter, the choice is a matter of indifference, it is both "more fair" and "more expedient" (less likely to lead to a quarrel) for the group to do what Mr. Smith prefers to do.

To another but highly related point. At the Philadelphia Convention, some of the delegates drew a distinction between "temporary" or "snap" or "frivolous" majorities on the one hand, and what we may call "serious" or "deliberate" majorities on the other. The Convention in consequence, wrote into the new Constitution severe limitations upon temporary majorities, and

From the American Political Science Review. *Copyright by the* American Political Science Review, *1968. Reprinted by permission of the publisher.*

left the path to the statute-book open only to serious, deliberate majorities—that is, majorities able to keep themselves in being long enough to gain control of both houses of Congress, of the Presidency, and of the Supreme Court. Why penalize the frivolous majorities? One possible answer seems to be this: Frivolous majorities will, in due course, prove to have been more or less indifferent on the policy-issue being decided because they will *not* remain in being long enough to gain mastery of the constitutional machinery. In other words, they will show, by their subsequent behavior, that they "didn't much care," in contrast to serious majorities which will, because their preferences are "strong," "stick to their guns."

The two situations sketched above, the one posing a problem in "moral" theory the other a problem in "political" theory, have not always been regarded as *in pari materia*. There is no evidence that the 55 at Philadelphia, though they certainly distinguished between frivolous and deliberate majorities, rested the distinction on the supposed relative strength of the preferences, or the opinions, of the individuals involved. They did not, on the record at least, go behind the distinction to ask, why does the frivolous majority turn out to be frivolous, while the serious or determined majority does not? But "we," in mid-Twentieth Century America, see at once the comparability, nay the identity, between the two situations. Because our "democratic theory" is more sophisticated than theirs, we readily bring the two situations together as illustrations of the "problem of intensity": Mr. Smith's "preference," being more "intense" than that of the others, should "weigh" more than theirs. Frivolous majorities, because they reflect "preferences" that are not "intense," must bide their time in favor of majorities that reflect "preferences" that are "intense. . . ."

All we are saying, up to this point, is a) that the theory of populistic democracy cannot, on its own basic premise, properly recognize it as a problem; and b) that, even if it could, it cannot, on its own basic premise, conceivably "do" anything about it (i.e., the only "principled" answer it can give to an outvoted "intense" minority in political society is, as indicated above, "So much the worse for you"). To those two points we may now add this one: contemporary democratic theory, because of the parochialism that lies at its very heart, has uncritically committed itself to the assumption that democratic theory and the theory of populistic democracy are one and the same thing—that, if you like, any theory that refuses to accept the populistic-democracy model, at least as a paradigm that all self-governing societies must seek to approximate at the earliest possible moment, is *ipso facto* anti-democratic, or if not that, non-democratic. One purpose of the present article, let us confess, is to combat that manifestation of parochialism.

With that in mind, let us approach our topic from another angle: The majority of the enfranchised in the self-governing society, we are told in a now vast corpus of political literature, might use its power to determine the result of an election as a means for writing rules into the statute-book (or even into the Constitution, if there be one), or for implementing policies, which violate the "rights" of "minorities" or of individuals; it might violate this or that allegedly indisputable principle of morality (or, what is equally reprehensible, perpetuate injustices); it might act foolishly, or out of ignorance, or out of momentary passion; and it might, all that entirely apart, ignore potential minority resistance to its legislation or policies and so produce defiance of the law, resistance to governmental action, and, at the margin, civil war. So the question gets itself asked: Is it possible, through the electoral process, to have it both ways, that is, somehow restrain the majority when, for any of the foregoing reasons, it "ought" to be restrained, and yet not challenge its "right" to "control" the government and, through the government, both legislation and policy-making? Much of the theory of the self-governing society handed down to us from the past (i.e., from the days before the advent of the theory of populistic democracy) insists, as is well known, that the correct answer to that question is "Yes, you can have it both ways." Calhoun's "concurrent majority" system, for example, says in effect, "Yes—by giving the minority the power to veto acts of the majority; that is, by letting the minority, any minority it would seem, decide when the majority 'ought' to be restrained." Similarly, John Adams' theory of the balanced constitution says in effect: "Yes, by giving the 'natural aristocracy' the power to veto acts of the majority and thus to decide when the majority 'ought' to be restrained." Clearly, however, neither succeeds in having it both ways, since neither is in the slightest concerned with the majority's "right" to control the government (though it is always amusing to remember that Calhoun appears to have had no quarrel with that right on the level of state government). Equally clearly, neither seems about to lose any sleep over the distinction between "intense" minorities and minorities that are something less than intense, or that between majorities that are "apathetic" and minorities that are something less than apathetic. Alike, Calhoun's veto and Adams' veto could be wielded by a minority only marginally concerned with the issue at stake. J. S. Mill, though he perhaps moves a trifle closer to the theory of populistic democracy, seeks a solution to the problem in an "artificial balance" between "classes," maintained through a system of "plural voting" which, again, reflects an indifference to the "right" of the merely numerical majority to control legislation and policy, and demands of the plural voters only that amount of "intensity" that will call them away from their normal pursuits, whether of foxes or of learning, long enough to cast their "extra" votes. Aristotle's polity, looking as it does to a "natural" rather than "artificial" balance, that is, to a situation in which the middle-class is as large as, or larger than, the poor class and the rich class, does depend upon the majority, that is, the middle class, conceived as possessing qualities that will dispose it to restrain itself, and therefore "saves" majority control of the government—though at the expense of any minority veto, and without regard (save as the majority itself may take it into account) to the "intensity" of the minority. (In the absence of such a natural balance, Aristotle is fully prepared to subordinate majority-rule to "justice" and "stability." Here, also, "intensity" figures in his formulations at most by implication, and of course even then only as bearing upon "stability," not "justice".) . . .

At least the following conditions, it seems to us, leap to the eye . . . as among those that a political system must meet if it is to handle the "intensity problem."

1. The system must have built-in facilities for *correct reciprocal anticipations,* on the part of groups and, ultimately, of individuals, of the intensity of each other's reactions, favorable or unfavorable, to the alternative courses of political behavior open to each. In our view, to the extent that the system fails to facilitate correct reciprocal anticipations, it is likely to encourage courses of action, on the part of groups and individuals, that will prove to be self-defeating, and that may easily lead to the breakdown of the system itself. And this applies equally to the "governors" and the "governed."

2. The condition just laid down does not mean, of course, that the system must never permit groups or individuals to take action that, because of the intensity of the reaction to it in this or that quarter or quarters, will deny them cooperation, or that it must never permit groups or individuals from attempting to exact, for their cooperation, or that it must never permit groups or individuals from attempting to exact, for their cooperation or compliance, a higher price than they can get. The important point is that groups and individuals shall not base their choice among various courses of action on *false* anticipations as to how others will respond; that, if you like, insofar as that is possible, they should not act in ignorance of foreseeable unfavorable reactions. The "governors" may well decide that they are *not* prepared to pay the price that this or that group will end up demanding for its cooperation or compliance. The "governed," on the other hand, may well decide to take, over against this or that legislative or policy *démarche,* retaliatory action that will bring down upon their heads disagreeable consequences. Our condition merely stipulates that such decisions must be taken, if the system is to work "rationally" from the standpoint of the participants, with the maximum possible knowledge of the consequences they will entail.

3. The condition does *not* require that a democratic system weigh "preferences" instead of counting them. As far as elections are concerned it can, in the end, do nothing *but* count, though democratic systems of course differ enormously as to who is counted, and how, and with respect to what. What it requires is merely that the "counted" shall, as they cast their votes in elections, be so situated as to be able to reckon, beforehand, with the intensity of the reaction in various quarters to the use they make of their votes. In other words, a democratic system does not fail to meet our major "condition" merely by not itself weighing preferences, but does fail to meet it when it affords groups and individuals insufficient opportunities, before their votes are cast, to do their own "weighing." Above all, our condition does not require that people be given their way on this or that issue because they happen to feel intensely about it. The decision as to when, and about what, to give them their way, is one that the "governors" must make according to their lights; it does

require that those lights, when issues are "up" about which some of the governed happen to feel strongly, be dimmed as little as possible by the system's machinery.

4. Correct reciprocal anticipation requires, clearly, a high degree of mutual knowledge and understanding among the participants. The science and technology of politics, despite its great leaps forward in recent decades, has yet to invent a thermometer-like device that can be inserted in people's heads, much less to their hearts, to "measure" the intensity of their preferences. The only preferences we actually "experience," and can calibrate with great accuracy, are our own; and there is indeed "no conceivable way" to "directly observe and compare the sensate intensities of preference of different individuals [or groups]," or even to correlate them with observable "changes in facial expression, words, posture, or even the chemistry of the body." Yet people do, and on our showing must if their political activity is to be other than counterproductive, attempt to make such correlations. The correlations they arrive at are often "proved out" by subsequent events, as, also, they are sometimes belied by them. All we are saying, for the moment, is that the critical variable here, the variable that results now in correct anticipations and now in incorrect ones, *must* be the knowledge-understanding the "anticipator" possesses as to what makes the other "tick." (The supreme example of the process at work, and the one most of us are likeliest to have experienced, or at least observed at first hand, is the smoothly-running family, in which each participant, husband or wife, brother or sister, parent or child, precisely because of the intimacy of their life together, can predict with a high degree of accuracy how the "others" will react to various alternative courses of action on his or her part). The successful politician, one might say, is, other things being equal, successful just to the extent that his anticipations in this regard approach the degree of accuracy achieved, day in day out, by the members of a smoothly-running family. And, from the standpoint of our overriding condition, a political system is to be judged "good" or "bad" according as it facilitates, or renders difficult, accurate anticipations of this kind.

5. A further corollary of the foregoing line of argument would be the following: The more "diverse" or "heterogeneous" the political society, the greater its need for elaborate and complex "machinery" to facilitate mutual knowledge and understanding of the kind here in question. Put otherwise: to the extent that a society is relatively homogeneous, so that people can safely assume that the "others" are pretty much like themselves, any given individual may fairly be expected to come up with fairly accurate forecasts as to the reactions of those others to any given political gambit he is contemplating. This for at least three basic reasons: First, the chances are greater, just to the extent that the society is homogeneous, that the legislative act or line of policy in question will affect oneself—that, if you like, the individual will possess first-hand personal knowledge as to the extent to which the contemplated step will or will not elicit cooperation. Second, and allowing now for the fact that a society can be highly homogeneous (non-diverse, in the sense of *Federalist* 10)

and still have in its bosom groupings that will be differently affected by a given policy decision, it remains true that the participants in a society have, to the extent that the latter is homogeneous, the greater opportunities to comprehend the composition and structure of the society, the "lay" of the potentially conflicting interests, goods, and "values." Third, just to the extent that the homogeneity of the homogeneous society is a matter of *shared* interests, goals, and values, we may fairly expect from the participants a higher degree of sympathetic "identification" with each other, thus a greater desire or willingness to understand beforehand the probable effects of the action contemplated, and thus, finally, a greater effort to feel the others out and seek some kind of accommodation with those who, predictably, will, if not accommodated, "cause trouble." The "extreme" case here, of course, is the "tightly-knit," "primitive" society which seeks, and obtains at whatever cost, unanimity, that is, does not submit issues to majority determination.

6. Having mentioned *Federalist* 10, with its emphasis on "diversity" as one of the two pre-conditions for a democratic republic that will not lead to tyranny, we must (a) say a word about the second of Publius' two pre-conditions, and (b) face the question whether, and to what extent, our own emphasis on mutual self-extent, our own emphasis on mutual self-knowledge places us (as at first blush it seems to) in opposition to Publius. As for (a), all that we have said about heterogeneity as an obstacle to successful handling of the "intensity problem" evidently applies, *mutatis mutandis,* to "extensiveness." An individual or group in, say, Florida, has scant opportunity, other things being equal, to make an accurate forecast concerning the reactions of an individual or group in, say, Washington (as we have largely been reminded by Watts, which seems to have surprised its neighbors in "extensive" Los Angeles hardly less rudely than it did its constructive neighbors in Portland, Maine). Distance, like diversity, is then a genuine obstacle to the kind of mutual knowledge and understanding that merges as desirable in the light of our analysis of the "intensity problem." And this analysis certainly appears to point to the thesis—a truism in much of what we call "traditional" political theory—that self-government can thrive only in the "small" state. Such, certainly, was the teaching of Aristotle, who, as every careful reader knows, is echoed on this point by Rousseau, with his insistence that in a true democracy each of the citizens must be so situated that he can come to know and understand the "others" whom he will encounter in the assembly. (Rousseau, we feel sure, would have construed "know" and "understand" to be a matter not merely of the "head," but also of the "heart.") We do not suggest, of course, that the traditional argument for the non-extensive republic necessarily rested, even in part, on considerations akin to our over-riding condition. Far from it; we suggest merely that the traditional argument would have been strengthened *had* it explicitly taken "intensity" into account, and that contemporary democratic theory would find itself less helpless, in the presence of the "intensity problem," had it given more weight to the considerations on which the traditional theorists did rest their argument. One might add . . . that democratic

societies have, in practice, departed notably less from the traditional teaching in this area than has democratic *theory*. As for (b), whether, on our showing here, we must end up taking issue with Publius in regard to his most celebrated doctrine, the answer is "No, indeed!" For our money, the case Publius makes out in *Federalist* 51 is, quite simply, unanswerable, and the conclusion at which he arrives beyond challenge:

In [an] . . . extended republic, and among the great variety of interests, parties, and sects which it embraces, a coalition of the majority of the whole society could seldom take place on any other principles than those of justice and the general good.

At worst, our analysis merely exposes a weakness of the *Federalist* 10 model, which Publius and his adepts must do something about lest their system come a cropper over the "intensity problem." (Again to anticipate a little: Publius, regardless of whether he had anything like the "intensity problem" in mind, *did* do something about it). In brief: just to the extent that a system does not meet Publius' two conditions, it will require special machinery to meet our condition, since mutual knowledge and understanding on the part of the participants, comprehension of the general workings of the system, sympathetic reciprocal identification, etc., will to that extent be, as a matter of course, the more difficult to achieve. For Publius' system. . . . does tend to generate intense competition among the "diverse" groups that it deploys over the "extensive" territory, thus increasing the danger that a group or combination of groups will, in the "heat of the battle" and with the righteous zeal that intense competition is likely to engender, try to ride rough-shod over intense preferences on the part of other groups.

7. It is impossible to mention the participants' attempts to calibrate the intensity of the preferences of the "others" by observing their behavior (the expression on their faces, the noises they make, etc.) without running hard up against this difficulty: The participants have nothing *except* observable behavior to go on in arriving at their anticipations. Yet the observable behavior may tell us more about the histrionic talents of the agonizer than about the intensity of his feelings on the issue that is up. (One thinks, as a matter of course, of Senator Dirksen, whose tear-glands would seem to be equipped with spigots.) The "others," in a word, may be bluffing about their intention to rock the boat if they can't get their way; may, for example, be using an issue about which they do not in fact feel strongly in order to gain this or that strategic advantage. And such bluffing is the more likely to be successful just to the extent that the participants have had insufficient opportunity to come to know and understand each other well. In order to meet our overriding condition, therefore, the system will require rules and procedures, analogous to those of a poker game, that impose potentially heavy penalties on the player who would like to win the pot with the weaker hand. To the extent that the system permits the bluffer to win the pot, it is unnecessarily exposed to varying degrees of instability; partly because it will run the danger of overlooking tomorrow's real boat-

rockers, and let itself in for trouble it might have avoided, and partly because it will run the danger of not mobilizing, behind the goals of the decision-makers, the maximum possible cooperation available to it given the "lay" of the "intensity problem" it faces. For the majority that can be bluffed will never be in position to make accurate forecasts as to the future reactions of the "others."

Can we conceive of rules and procedures that will minimize successful bluffing? Not easily, of course; but (a) the structure of the system can take into account the fact that X is likely to get by with his bluff just to the extent that Y and Z do not know and understand what kind of poker he plays, and (b) it can, through rules formal or informal, exact sacrifices from those who, in the course of playing out a political hand, demand that the intensity of their preferences be made a *ratio decidendi*—can, that is to say, put the costs of injecting such a demand so high that no one who does not have a genuinely intense preference will be willing to pay it. One possibility: give each member of the assembly *n* number of votes at the beginning of the session, and let him "spend" them as he sees fit—all of them if he likes, on a single issue, with the understanding that once they are gone he can cast no further votes. Another: encourage the "horse-trading" and "log-rolling" for which the Congress of the United States is so frequently denounced, thus maximizing the opportunity on the past of the participants to "trade" their votes on issues about which they do not feel intensely for votes of the others on issues about which they do. Viewed from the standpoint of our overriding condition, "log-rolling" may well play a beneficent role in the political system by helping to handle the "intensity problem. . . ."

PLURALISM AS AN IDEOLOGY
Theodore Lowi

Central capitalist theory is the belief that power and control are properties of the state and, therefore, should be feared and resisted. This proposition, while hard to deny, is patently one-sided; in fact it covers only one of at least three sides. It says nothing about who controls the state; and it says nothing about institutions other than the state that possesses the same properties of power and control.

The Marxist critique of capitalism is overwhelming on the question of control of the state, especially when applied to the very period of industrial growth when fear of the state was so pervasive in the U. S. Up to a point

From The End of Liberalism. *Copyright by W. W. Norton and Co., 1969. Reprinted by permission of the publisher.*

capitalist values were so directly expressed in the activities of Federal and State governments that it would have been impossible to say where the one ended and the other began. The very idea of capitalist public philosophy can be accurately termed a euphemism for capitalist political power during most of the nineteenth century. It was not a question of influence *on* the policy-maker; capitalism was so pervasive because it operated as an influence *in* the policy-maker.

Important as the Marxist analysis has been, American history suggests that it, like capitalist theory, presents one-sided truths. The side left untouched by capitalism and falsely treated by Marxism is that of the nature and significance of the institutions other than the state in an industrial civilization. Here the pluralist model is overwhelmingly superior, at least for American society.

Pluralist theory begins with recognition that there are many sources of power and control other than the state. In our differentiated society, there will be many basic interests represented by organizations able and willing to use power. This is why the pluralist can accept government expansion with equanimity. But the significance of the pluralistic organization of the society goes beyond that. Since there are so many well-organized interests, there is, in pluralist theory, no possibility that a unitary society, stratified in two or three simple, homogenized classes, could persist. The result, however, is not the Marxist revolution where the big class devours the small, but an evolution in which the unitary society becomes a pluralistic one—i.e., where the addition and multiplication of classes tends to wipe out the very notion of class stratification. Stratification in two simple classes, bourgeoisie and proletariat, seems to have been a passing phase of early industrialization. Perhaps that is the reason why it figured so large in the sociology of Marx.

Alexis de Tocqueville, over a decade before Marx, identified many of the fundamental features of the indistrial society. He expressed strikingly similar concern about the sort of society which was emerging. In his essay "How an Aristocracy May Be Created by Manufacturers," Tocqueville went to the core of the matter. He began by recognizing the importance of the division of labor and proceeded immediately to a consideration of what it does to human beings and social classes:

While the workman concentrates his faculties more and more upon the study of a single detail, the master surveys an extensive whole, and the mind of the latter is enlarged in proportion as that of the former is narrowed. . . . [I]n proportion as the mass of the nation turns to democracy, that particular class which is engaged in manufacturers becomes more aristocratic. Men grow more alike in the one, more different in the other; and inequality increases in the less numerous class in the same ratio in which it decreases in the community.

However, unlike Marx, Tocqueville provided more than a theory of alienation within simple social classes. He also paid attention to the composition of this industrial aristocracy. Tocqueville saw this new aristocracy as quite peculiar in comparison to its predecessors. While there are and will be extremes of wealth and poverty, the members of the new aristocracy do not constitute a unitary social class, for there develop no feelings of class, no consciousness of shared status:

> To tell the truth, though there are rich men, the class of rich men does not exist; for these rich individuals have no feelings or purposes, no traditions or hopes, in common; there are individuals, therefore, but no definite class. . . . [T]he rich [are] not compactly united among themselves. . . .

This was the very basis of James Madison's argument half a century before—and nothing had happened between Madison and Tocqueville to alter the fact—that industrialization produces social diversity along with extremes of wealth and poverty: "A landed interest, a manufacturing interest, a mercantile interest, a moneyed interest, with many lesser interests." Developments in the generations since Federalist 10 would only require that we lengthen Madison's list. Pluralists do not have to deny the Marxian proposition that there is a conflict between those who own and those who work for those who own. They need only answer by adding to Marx's the other equally intense conflicts. Exporters cannot love importers, except perhaps on the Fourth of July—and, in fact, many people may still have misgivings about the patriotism of importers. Renters cannot love owners. Borrowers cannot love lenders, nor creditors debtors, and this is particularly interesting in our day, when the biggest debtors are not the poor but the rich. Retailers cannot love wholesalers. The black middle class loves neither the black lower class nor the white sellers of middle-class housing.

In this context the existence of the administrative component merely confirms the reality of the pluralist model of society. Groups amount to far more than a facade for a class. Administration gives each basic interest an institutional core, renders each interest less capable of being absorbed or neutralized, gives each interest the capacity to articulate goals, integrate members, provide for leadership and succession, in short, to perpetuate itself. The organization of interests is the first step, but after rudimentary organization comes staff, procedures, membership service, internal propaganda, addition of more permanent personnel, salaried help, files—corporate existence, staying power.

As alluded to above, the pluralist model cuts equally against capitalist theory. It renders absurd the capitalist notion that government is the only source of power and control. It rightly rejects any and all notions of a natural distinction between the functions of government and the functions of nongovernmental institutions. Power and control are widely distributed. They are in fact ubiquitous.

Sayre and Kaufman introduce a useful game for pursuing the problem of government and nongovernment. Try to identify a governmental activity for which there is not an important counterpart in some private institution. The judiciary? Mediation and arbitration play a widespread and increasing role.

Police? Pinkertons are famous in our history; today every large company and school has its own security force, and private eyes continue to be hired for peephole duty; many highly innovating industries have their own secret service working in the world of industrial espionage. Welfare? Any listing of private, highly bureaucratized and authoritative welfare systems would be as long as it is unnecessary. Armies? It is difficult to overestimate the significance of private armies in the past, or such present private armies as those possessed by the Mafia and other syndicates, not to mention the neighborhood gangs and Minutemen. Society highly prizes the function they perform in administering the acceptable vices and keeping the violence associated with these vices subterranean. Obviously the game need not be carried into every realm.

Some activities may be found universally among modern governments; but they will not be found *only* in governments. Moreover, the complete pattern of functions associated with any given government is the result of time, chance, culture and politics. Government is only one institution of social control, as it was and always will be. Government is distinguishable from other institutions, as we shall soon see. But the distinction is not the one upon which the American Constitution and the nineteenth-century liberals erected their defenses.

This in turn reflects critically still further upon the Marxist model. Central to the pluralist model of power is the anti-Marxist hypothesis that with the flowering of the system of autonomous groups the monopoly hold of capitalism, or of any other class, passes. Control of the state does not pass from the capitalists to another class but rather is dispersed. This breaks the deterministic link between economics and politics: *In the pluralist system, modern developments have brought about a discontinuity between that which is socioeconomic and that which is political.* Politics in the pluralist model ceases to be an epiphenomenon of socioeconomic life. Politics becomes autonomous as the number of autonomous and competing social units multiplies.

In these simple propositions, reaching back to James Madison, lies the pluralist critique of capitalism and of Marxism. To summarize: (1) Groups, of which corporations are merely one type, possess power directly over a segment of society and also a share of control of the state. (2) Groups, rather than entrepreneurs and firms, are the dominant reality in modern life. (3) As long as even a small proportion of all interests remains strong and active, no unitary political class, or "power elite," will emerge. That is, in the pluralist system it is highly improbable that a consensus across a whole class can last long enough to institutionalize itself.

A good social theory is always but a step away from ideology. The better it is as theory, the more likely it is to become ideology. The bigger the scope of the theory the greater the likelihood of becoming the public philosophy. Pluralism became a potent American ideology. It did not become the public philosophy, but it is the principal intellectual member in a neocapitalistic public philosophy, interest-group liberalism.

Short and few are the steps in the reasoning procedure by which pluralist theory becomes pluralist ideology: (1) Since groups are the rule in markets and elsewhere, imperfect competition is the rule of social relations. (2) The method of imperfect competition is not really competition at all but a variant of it called bargaining—where the number of participants is small, where the relationship is face-to-face, and/or where the bargainers have "market power," which means that they have some control over the terms of their agreements and can administer rather than merely respond to their environment. (3) Without class solidarity, bargaining becomes the single alternative to violence and coercion in industrial society. (4) By definition, if the system is stable and peaceful it proves the self-regulative character of pluralism. It is, therefore, the way the system works and the way it ought to work.

A closer look will show how potent these principles are in a country so traditionally concerned about power. Most obviously they show pluralism to be very much in line with the realities of modern life. Groups and imperfect competition are impossible to deny. Second, the reasoning suggests that pluralism can be strongly positive toward government without relinquishing the traditional fear of government. Since the days of Madison the pluralist view has been that there is nothing to fear from government so long as many factions compete for its favor. Modern pluralism turned the Madisonian position from negative to positive; that is, government is good because many factions do compete for its favor. A third and obvious feature of pluralist reasoning is that with pluralism society remains automatic. Pluralism is just as mechanistic as orthodox Smithian economics, and since the mechanism is political it reinforces acceptance of government. Pluralists believe that pluralist competition tends toward an equilibrium, and therefore that its involvement with government can mean only good. Use of government is simply one of many ways groups achieve equilibrium. Pluralist equilibrium is really the public interest.

Pluralism's embrace of positive government first put it at an ideological pole opposite capitalism. This is the foundation of the liberal-conservative dialogue that bridged the gap between the old public philosophy and the new. On the basis of these opposing positions, debate over great issues took place in the United States, even without socialism, for many years following 1890. But this situation was only temporary. The two apparent anthitheses ultimately disappeared. The rhetoric continued, so that even today one may occasionally feel that the two poles represent substantial differences. But in reality they have come to represent a distinction without a difference. Capitalism and pluralism were not actually synthesized, however; in a sense, they absorbed each other.

The transformation, rather than the replacement, of capitalist public philosophy was made possible by two special features of pluralist ideology. First, pluralism shared the capitalist ideal of the automatic society. Second, the pluralist embrace of government turned out to be, in its own way, as antigovernmental as capitalism. Ultimately this shared mystique, despite differences along other lines, made some kind of fusion possible. The hidden hand of capitalist ideology could clasp the hidden hand of pluralism, and the two could shake affirmatively on the new public philosophy, interest-group liberalism. Here lies the foundation of the Consensus of 1937–67.

Here lies also the source of the weakness and eventual failure of interest-group liberalism, which has led us into a crisis of public authority in the United States more serious than any other in the twentieth century. Pluralism had helped bring American public values into the twentieth century by making the state an acceptable source of power in a capitalist society. Pluralism had also made a major contribution by helping to break down the Marxian notion of solidary classes and class-dominated government. But the zeal of pluralism for the group and its belief in a natural harmony of group competition tended to break down the very ethic of government by reducing the essential conception of government to nothing more than another set of mere interest groups.

The strength of pluralism rested in very great part upon the proposition, identified earlier, that a pluralist society frees politics by creating a discontinuity between the political world and the socioeconomic world. However, there is a related proposition that present pluralist theories either reject or miss altogether: *In a pluralist society there is also a discontinuity between politics and government.* The very same factors of competition and multiple power resources that frees politics from society also frees government from both society and politics. This is precisely why pluralism appealed to such constitutionalists as Madison. Group competition could neutalize many of the most potent power centers sufficiently to keep all of them within the formal structure of government. This was the Madisonian method of regulating groups and protecting the governmental authorities from control by any "majority," which could mean a class elite, a capitalist group, or a mass social movement. In contemporary pluralism this aspect of the pluralist argument has gone by the boards. Groups become virtuous; they must be accommodated, not regulated. Formalism in government becomes mere formality. Far from Madison, they could say, as the disappointed office-seeker is supposed to have said to President Cleveland, "What's a Constitution among friends?"

It should thus be evident that pluralist theory today militates against the idea of separate government. Separate government violates the basic principle of the automatic political society. This was reinforced by the scientific pluralist's scientific dread of such poetic terms as "public interest," "the state," and "sovereignty" that admittedly cannot be precisely defined and are closely associated aesthetically with the notion of separate government. But by such means pluralism gained a little and lost a lot. Only three of its losses are pursued here: (1) Pluralist theory achieved almost no additional scientific precision by insisting that government was nothing but an extension of the "political process." (2) It could maintain this fiction, and the fiction of the automatic political society, only by elimination of *legitimacy*. (3) It could maintain those fictions only by elimination of *administration*.

1. In 1908, Arthur F. Bentley fathered the scientific definition of the state as an interest that could be thought of "as an interest group itself." Despite preference for the immaculateness of the formulation, modern pluralists have ever since felt the tug of limitation more than the leverage of precision. Along the way concessions have been made, so that "we must reckon with the inclusive set of relationships that we call the state."[23] The fact that this institution did not seem to operate quite like a pressure group led Truman to the concept of a "potential interest group" whose interest is the "rules of the game."[24] These formulations did not introduce precision. They simply constituted an invitation to disregard those aspects of the political system not susceptible to group interpretation and the hypothesis of natural equilibrium. Even to the most sophisticated, government became "the political process. . . ."

2. Competition and its variant, bargaining, are types of conflict distinguishable by the existence of rules. Rules convert conflict into competition. But rules and their application imply the existence of a framework of controls and institutions separate from the competition itself. Whether we call this a *public* or not, *there is a political context that is not itself competition* within which political competition takes place.

A good way to approach the problem of the distinction is to return momentarily to the game of counterparts. It must have occurred to many already that something was missing. Once while participating in the exercise a student found the missing dimension by identifying prisons and imprisonment as a public activity without private counterpart. Leaving aside a quibble over the question of whether the Mafia has a prison system, it is easy to spot the essential point implied to the student in his choice of governmental activity. The practice of imprisonment suggests simply that the intrinsic governmental feature is *legitimate use of coercion.*

Legitimacy is not easy to operationalize, but its problems are actually easier to solve than those the pluralist solution offers, because our interest is not in measuring the behavioral attribute in question but only in using the fact of its existence as a criterion. It justifies our treating the state as a real thing apart and not merely a group or a poetic figment. Thus, while governments can rarely if ever perform any function that a nongovernmental institution cannot also perform, governmentalization of a function—that is, passing a public policy—is sought because the legitimacy of its sanctions makes its social controls more surely effective. This is what activates and motivates politics in the pluralist system, but it is far from being part and parcel of pluralism.

3. Finally, rules and their enforcement do not merely exist. They must be applied with regularity and some degree of consistency if pluralist competition is to exist at all. This is administration. Administration is necessary to construct and to change the system within which pluralism is to operate, yet pluralism presupposes the existence of that favorable structure, just as laissez faire presupposed a social system favorable to itself. To pluralists, social change in a pluralist system works in small increments. "Incrementalism" is what moves the successful polity, and by definition that is how the successful polity ought to be moved. This means that social oscillation in the pluralist

ideal is and ought to occur at a very narrow range around some point of equilibrium. But note how susceptible all of this is to the criticisms earlier heaped upon capitalist theory. First, it takes a certain predefined equilibrium as good and presupposes it in order to work the theory. Second, recall the problem of market perfection: Even if you get your economic equilibrium it may not be at anywhere near full employment. The political variant of this would be equilibrium at something far less than an acceptable level of participation, or satisfaction, or even "public interest." Let us take a simple dimension to illustrate both points: expansion of membership in the system. This usually comes from critical, as distinct from incremental, changes, and is usually imposed administratively. One need only ponder the case of the Negro, who was kept out of the pluralist system for ages, and who is being only now introduced into it not only by fiat but by a fiat with force, accompanied by intricate and authoritative processes of administration.

One of the most influential pluralist scholars, Robert A. Dahl, has made the following proposition about the political system: "When two individuals conflict with one another ... they confront three great alternatives: deadlock, coercion, or peaceful adjustment." Deadlock is "no deal"; there is no change of demands or behavior on either side. Coercion to Dahl means forcible change of behavior by physical imposition. This he feels is an extremely exceptional alternative, rarely involved even in governmental acts, all the more rarely involved in the affairs of popular governments. Everything else, including all other methods of government, comes under the rubric "peaceful adjustment," by which he means consultation, negotiation, and the search for mutually beneficial solutions. Obviously this cannot possibly exhaust the alternatives. It relies on an extremely narrow definition of coercion, giving one to believe that coercion is not involved if physical force is absent. And it depends on an incredibly broad and idealized notion of what is peaceful about peaceful adjustment. A slight readjustment of Dahl's categories will reveal what is missing. It will also reveal the ideological element just underneath the skin of pluralist theory. What Dahl is really dealing with here are the logical relations between two continua—the extent to which coercion is involved and the extent to which adjustment is involved in any response to conflicting interests. This slight formalizing of his scheme yields the following results:

TABLE 1. The Properties of Political Relationships

Likelihood of Coercion:	Likelihood of Peaceful Adjustment	
	Low	High
Remote	Deadlock	Negotiation
Immediate	"Coercion"	?

What goes in the fourth cell of the four-cell table of properties of political relationships? It is a vast category. It must include virtually all of the public and private "governmental processes" in which people have internalized the sanctions that might be applied. The element of coercion may seem absent when in actuality the participants are conducting themselves in a certain way largely because they do not feel they have any choice. Since it is well enough accepted to go unnoticed, this coercion can be called legitimate. Since it is regular and systematic, it can be called administration because an administrative component must be there if the conduct in question involves a large number of people making these peaceful adjustments. This immense fourth "great alternative" is missing from Dahl's scheme because it is beyond the confines of the theory of the perfect, self-regulating pluralist society. That fourth cell is actually the stable regime of legitimacy and effective administration without which neither the reality nor the theory of pluralism has any meaning.

Many social theorists earlier in the century stressed the distinction between nongovernment and government. Weber's definition of government is founded on the distinction. Mosca based his classification of modern and traditional systems upon the distinction. Robert McIver and many others based their liberal response to syndicalism upon the same distinction, passionately affirmed:

The extreme insistence of the guild socialists on functional representation becomes an attack on the state itself . . . A nation is not simply composed of crafts and professions. These might logically elect an economic "parliament," but if it possessed also political sovereignty it would be a denial of the whole process which has differentiated economic and political centres of power. The state is retained in name but disappears in fact . . . Political representation is real only because it is not based on any function but citizenship.

E. Pendleton Herring, although one of the key figures in developing pluralist political science, was still able to warn in the 1930's that while the "government of the democratic state reflects inescapably the underlying interest groups of society . . . the very fact that the state exists evinces a basic community of purpose."

These authors were defending the notion of a distinguishable government from the doctrines of fascists, syndicalists, corporativists, and guild socialists because it was these doctrines and experiments that sought to destroy the distinction. Not very much later American liberalism began to develop in the same direction, but these features of it tended to escape attention precisely because American pluralists had no explicit and systematic view of the state. They simply assumed it away. Such negative intellectual acts seldom come in for careful criticism.

Concern for government was an American culture trait. Yet, ironically, once the barriers to its expansion were broken, government ceased almost altogether to be a serious issue. Destruction of the principle of separate government, the coerciveness of government, the legitimacy of government, the administrative importance of government, was necessary if capitalist ideology was to be transformed rather than replaced. The fusion of capitalism and pluralism was a success; destruction of the principle of separate government was its secret.

As this aspect of pluralism becomes dominant in the new public philosophy its more repulsive features can more easily be seen. The new liberal public philosophy was corrupted by the weakness of its primary intellectual component, pluralism. The corrupting element was the myth of the automatic society granted us by an all-encompassing, ideally self-correcting, providentially automatic political process. This can hardly be more serviceable than the nineteenth-century liberal (now conservative) myth of the automatic society granted us by the total social equilibrium of freely contracting individuals in the market place. The pluralist myth helped bring about the new public philosophy, but the weakness of the myth made certain the degeneration of the public philosophy.

BIBLIOGRAPHICAL NOTE

There are many fine historical treatments of American liberal ideology. One of the best known is Richard Hofstadter, *The American Political Tradition.* Less critical are Louis Hartz, *The Liberal Tradition in America* and Daniel J. Boorstin, *The Genius of American Politics.* There have been a number of contemporary "revisionist" works; one interesting collection is *The Dissenting Past,* ed. Bernard Bernstein.

Several of the most important empirical studies of majority rule are Dahl's *Pluralist Democracy in America,* his *Preface to Democratic Theory;* William Riker, *The Theory of Political Coalitions;* and James M. Buchanan and Gordon Tullock, *The Calculus of Consent.* Besides Dahl's works, the intensity problem is explored in Kenneth Arrow, *Social Choice and Individual Values.*

The philosophical aspects of majority rule are examined in Henry Mayo, *Introduction to Democratic Theory;* Henry Steele Commager, *Majority Rule and Minority Rights;* Walter Lippman, *The Public Philosophy;* and Giovanni Sartori, *Democratic Theory.* Other works in this area are Willmore Kendall, *John Locke and the Doctrine of Majority Rule,* and Benjamin Barber, *Superman and Common Men.*

There are many studies of elites in the United States from a variety of perspectives. The power elite notion is presented by C. W. Mills in a book by that title and in Floyd Hunter's *Community Power Structure.* Dahl disputes this in his work, *Who Governs.* Also of interest in this area are Gabriel Kolko, *Wealth and Power in America,* and William Domhoff, *Who Rules America.*

2. The American as Citizen

Americans frequently attempt to analyze what it is that makes them unique when compared to other nationalities. In trying to explain this uniqueness, considerable attention has been focused on our political beliefs and attitudes. We try hard to impress foreign observers with what is termed, rather audaciously, "our way of life."

These four selections examine different aspects of our self-image and of our normative concepts of citizenship. In the first selection, Alexis de Tocqueville maintains that there is a distinctive American style of thinking which heavily relies on individual rationality. He also insists that religion plays a subtle, but nonetheless important role in our supposedly secular society. Tocqueville's description of American democracy and its citizenry remains one of the most perceptive portraits ever written by either a foreign or a domestic commentator.

A different aspect of American life is examined by Michael P. Riccards in his analysis of political socialization. Riccards maintains that there is a dominant motif in this socialization which places a premium on the moralistic, personal, and altruistic styles of politics. He further speculates that this dominant motif can become a powerful weapon when used by the discontented in attacking the inadequacies of American society.

The third selection is taken from V. O. Key's study of American public opinion. Key maintains that there is not any large scale commitment on the part of our citizenry to liberal values. The obvious question is: if the people do not preserve democracy, who does? Key concludes that it is the political elite which guards our basic liberties and upholds our institutions.

This sort of conclusion has tremendous import for any democratic philosopher. If Key is correct, then certain barriers must be established to protect not just these liberties, but also the very elite upon which so much depends. One problem, however, is that social scientists are uncertain to what extent and with what intensity the elite is commited to democratic values. Studies of political elites during the McCarthy period and during the formation and conduct of the Vietnamese war cast some doubt on the strength of that commitment.

The last selection deals with the problem of citizenship and political awareness. Michael Walzer maintains that the demand by radicals for total involvement in politics is unrealistic and undesirable. Instead he reminds us of the need to have some people who are nonparticipants, critics, and even kibbitzers. His argument leads to some interesting conclusions which are quite relevant to current discussions on participatory democracy.

In a society such as ours, there is a constant debate on what the proper role of the citizen is. His obligations, his activities, and his opinions take on an accentuated importance in explaining what type of politics we have and what type we may want. In quite different ways, these authors have addressed themselves to various aspects of these problems.

THE PHILOSOPHICAL METHOD AND BELIEFS OF AMERICANS
Alexis de Tocqueville

I think that in the civilized world, no country is less preoccupied with philosophy than the United States. The Americans have no school of philosophy of their own; and they have little concern for all the schools into which Europe is divided, the very names of which they hardly know. Nevertheless, it is easy to see that almost all the people of the United States have a common method and uniform rules for the conduct of intellectual inquiries. Although they have not taken the trouble to define the rules, they do have a common philosophical method shared by all.

To escape from traditional systems, the yoke of habit, family maxims, class opinions and to a certain extent national prejudices; to treat tradition as only a source of information and to accept existing facts as being no more than a sketch to show how things can be done better; to look for the reason for things within themselves; to observe the results without getting entangled in the means toward them and to see through forms to find the substance of things —such are the principal characteristics of what I would call the American philosophical method.

To carry this argument further and to select the trait which I consider most important, and the one which is all inclusive, I would say that in most mental operations each American relies on individual effort and judgment.

Therefore, of all the countries in the world, America is the one which least studies but best follows the precepts of Descartes. This should not be surprising. The Americans have never read the works of Descartes because their state of society distracts them from speculative studies, and yet they follow his precepts because this same state of society naturally leads them to adopt them.

The continuous activity which prevails in a democratic society results in the relaxation or the severing of ties between generations; thus each person loses track of the ideas of his ancestors or becomes unconcerned about them. Men living in such a society cannot derive their beliefs or opinions from their class, for, so to speak, there are no longer any classes and those which still do exist are composed of elements so mobile that they can never, as a body, exercise a real control over their members.

When it comes to the influence which one man's mind has on another's,

From De la democratie en Amerique. *Published by Michel Levy Freres, 1888. Translated by Barbara Riccards.*

this is necessarily limited in a country where the citizens, who are more or less similar, are all closely watched by each other. Since no signs of incontestable greatness or superiority can be seen in any one of them, they are continually taken back to their own reason as the most obvious source of truth. It is not only confidence in one's fellow man which is destroyed but also the willingness to accept any man's word as proof of anything.

Each man is shut up within himself and tries to judge the world from that vantage point. This American practice of relying only on oneself in making judgments leads to other mental habits as well. Since they can easily succeed in resolving all the little difficulties of life which they encounter, they quickly conclude that everything in the world can be explained, and that nothing in it exceeds the limits of their intelligence.

Thus, they begin to deny what they cannot understand. This leaves them with little use for the extraordinary and an extreme distaste for the supernatural. Since they are accustomed to relying on their own testimony, they like to see the object before them very clearly. They, therefore, take off all that covers it and remove anything in the way so that they can see it in broad daylight. This state of mind soon leads them to condemn forms which they see as being useless, hampering veils between them and the truth.

The Americans have no need to obtain their philosophical method from books. They have found it in themselves. Much the same can be said of what has happened in Europe. This same method has been established and popularized in Europe as the conditions of society have become more equal and men more like each other.

Let us consider for a moment the historical development of this. In the sixteenth century, reformers subjected some dogmas of the ancient faith to private scrutiny, but still refused to discuss the rest. In the seventeenth century, Bacon in the natural sciences and Descartes in philosophy abolished accepted formulas, destroyed the dominance of tradition, and upset the authority of the masters. The eighteenth century philosophers, using the same general principle, undertook to submit to the private judgment of each man the object of all of his beliefs. Is it not obvious that Luther, Descartes, and Voltaire all used the same method and that they differed only in the degree to which it should be applied?

Why did the reformers confine themselves so closely within the circle of religious ideas? Why did Descartes, who chose to apply his method only to certain matters although it could have been applied to all, say that men should judge for themselves philosophical questions but not political questions? Why did men in the eighteenth century suddenly draw general conclusions from this same method which Descartes and his predecessors has either not recognized or has rejected? What was the reason why this method suddenly emerged from the schools to penetrate society and become the common standard of intelligence during that period? Moreover, after it had become popular among the French, why was it openly adopted or secretly followed by all the people of Europe?

This philosophical method may have been born in the sixteenth century; it may have been more precisely defined and generally used in the seventeenth century; but in neither century could it have been commonly adopted. Political laws, the state of society, and the habits of thought which were all derived from causes of their own, were opposed to it. It was discovered at a time when men were beginning to grow more equal and more like each other. It could only be generally followed during those centuries when conditions had become more or less similar and people like each other.

Therefore, the philosophical method of the eighteenth century is not only French, but democratic. This explains why it was so readily adopted in Europe, where it contributed to altering society completely. It is not because the French have changed their ancient beliefs and modified their ancient opinions that they have upset the world. It is because they were the first to generalize and bring to light a philosophical method which made it easy to attack all that was old and to open a path to all that was new.

Nowadays, if I am asked why this same method is more often and more strictly applied by the French than by the Americans, though liberty is older and as complete among the latter, I reply that this is partly due to two circumstances which must be clearly understood.

It is religion which gave birth to the English colonies in America. It must never be forgotten that in the United States religion is intermingled with all the national customs and all the sentiments from which patriotism is born. For that reason it has a peculiar power.

To this powerful reason, another must be added which is no less important. In America, religion has set its own limits. The religious order is totally distinct from the political order so that old laws have been easily changed without changing old beliefs. In this way Christianity has kept a strong hold over the minds of Americans. More specifically, I would say that its power is not just that of a philosophy which has been examined and accepted but that of a religion which is believed in without discussion.

In the United States Christian sects are extremely diversified and are continually modified. But Christianity is so firmly established that no one tries to attack it or defend it. Since the Americans have accepted the main dogmas of the Christian religion without question, they are obliged to accept many moral truths originating from and connected to it in the same way. Thus, individual analysis is restricted within very narrow limits, and many important subjects about which men can have opinions are removed from the range of its influence.

The other circumstance which I referred to is this:

The state of society and the Constitution in America are democratic, but they have not had a democratic revolution. They arrived on the land which they now occupy in almost the same condition as they are today. This is a very important point.

Every revolution must shake old beliefs, change authority, and obscure common ideas. All revolutions have the effect of more or less throwing men back on themselves and of opening to each man's view an almost limitless empty space.

When standards of equality have resulted from a prolonged struggle between the different classes from which the older society was formed, envy, hatred and distrust of one's neighbor, together with pride and exaggerated self-confidence, seize the human heart and make it their domain for a while. This fact, without reference to equality, powerfully contributes to the division of men; it ensures that they will be distrustful of each other's judgment and that they will look for enlightenment only in themselves.

Everyone then attempts to be his own guide and form his own opinions on all subjects. Men are not linked by their ideas but by their interests and it could be said that human opinions form a sort of mental dust which is blown around on all sides, never being able to reassemble itself.

Thus the independence of mind which equality supposes to exist is never so great and excessive as when equality begins to establish itself. One should, therefore, distinguish between the intellectual liberty which can result from equality and the anarchy which revolution brings. Each of these two things must be considered separately in order not to conceive exaggerated hopes or fears for the future.

I believe that the men who live in new societies will often make use of their individual judgment, but I am far from believing that they will often abuse it. . . .

At different times, dogmatic beliefs are more or less numerous. They come about in various ways and may be changed in form or substance. But it can never happen that there are no dogmatic beliefs, that is to say, opinions which men take on trust without discussion.

If everyone undertook to form his own opinions and look for truth by way of only the isolated paths he made himself, it is unlikely that any large number of people would ever unite in any common belief.

It is easy to see that no society could prosper without such common beliefs or rather that there are no societies which manage in that way. For without common ideas, there is no common action, and without common action men might still exist but not as a social body. So for society to exist and, even more, for society to be prosperous, it is necessary that all the minds of its citizens should be similar and that all citizens should hold the same principal ideas. This could never happen unless each of them obtained his opinions from the same source and consented to receive a certain number of his beliefs from the community.

Moreover, considering each man by himself, dogmatic beliefs seem to be no less indispensible for living alone than for acting in common with his fellow man. If man had to prove to himself all the truths he uses, his job would never end. He would exhaust himself in proving preliminary points and make no progress. Since life is too short and human faculties too limited for such a course, man has to accept a number of facts and opinions which he has neither the leisure nor the power to examine and verify for himself, things which more able men have found out and which the world accepts. On this foundation he builds for himself the structure of his own thoughts. He does not proceed in this manner voluntarily; the inflexible laws of his existence compel him to do so.

There is no philosopher in the world, however great, who can help but believing a million things on the testimony of others or assuming the truth of many things which he himself has not established. This is not only necessary but desirable. Anyone who would examine everything for himself could not devote much time and attention to each question. This would keep his mental faculties in a state of perpetual excitement, which would prevent his going deeply into any truth or being firmly convinced of anything at all. His intellect would be both independent and powerless. Therefore, he must choose among the various things about which men have opinions, and he must adopt many beliefs without discussion in order to better investigate the small number he sets aside for examination. It is true that any man who receives his opinions from the word of others enslaves his mind, but it is a salutary servitude which permits him to make good use of freedom.

Somehow, authority is always bound to play a part in intellectual and moral life. Its role varies, but of necessity it has a place. The independence of the individual can be greater or less, but it can never be unlimited. Thus the question is not if intellectual authority exists in democratic ages, but only where it is and what its limits are.

I have shown before how the equality of conditions makes men instinctively incredulous of the supernatural, and gives them a very high and often exaggerated opinion of human reason. The men who live in these times of equality, therefore, do not easily place the intellectual authority to which they submit, beyond or outside humanity. Usually they seek the sources of truth in themselves or in those like themselves. This is enough to prove that no new religion could be established in such periods, and that all attempts to create one would not only be impious, but ridiculous and unreasonable. One can observe that democratic people would not easily believe in divine missions, that they would laugh at new prophets, and they would wish to find the chief arbiter of their beliefs within, and not beyond, the limits of their kind.

When conditions are unequal and men not alike, there are some very enlightened and learned individuals whose intelligence gives them great power, while the multitude is very ignorant and limited. Consequently, the men who live under an aristocracy allow the superior reasoning of a man or a class to guide their opinions, and they have little inclination to suppose the masses infallible.

During periods of equality, the opposite happens. The closer citizens come to being equal and alike, the less likely they are to believe blindly in a certain man or a certain class. The disposition to believe in the masses is strengthened, and public opinion becomes more and more the mistress of the world.

Not only is public opinion the only guide left to aid private judgment, but its power is infinitely greater in democracies than elsewhere. In times of equality, men have no faith in one another because of their likeness; but this same likeness gives them unlimited confidence in the judgment of the public. For they think it not unreasonable that, since they all have the same means of knowledge, truth will be found on the side of the majority.

The citizen of a democratic country, comparing himself with others who live with him, feels proud of his equality. But when he sees his fellow inhabitants as a group and begins to compare himself to such a large mass of people, he immediately realizes how insignificant and weak he is. This same equality, which makes him independent of each separate citizen, leaves him alone and defenseless to the actions of the majority.

In democracies, therefore, public opinion has a strange power unheard of in aristocratic nations. It uses no persuasion to forward its beliefs, but it enforces them, and infuses them into the faculties by a sort of enormous pressure of the minds of all upon the reason of each.

In the United States, the majority undertakes to furnish individuals with a multitude of ready-made opinions, thus relieving them of the necessity to form their own. There are a large number of theories on philosophy, morality, and politics that everyone adopts without examining, solely on the faith of public opinion. If one looks very closely one can see that religion itself is stronger as part of common opinion than as revealed doctrine.

I know that, with Americans, the political laws give the majority the sovereign right to rule society. This greatly increases the power which the majority anyhow has over men's minds. Nothing is more natural to man than to recognize superior intelligence in those who oppress him.

In effect, this political omnipotence of the majority in the United States augments the influence which public opinion would have had without it over each citizen, but it is not the foundation thereof. One must look to equality itself for the source of that influence and not in the more or less popular institutions that equal men have created for themselves. One may suppose that the intellectual domain of the greatest number would be less absolute in a democratic people governed by a king than in a pure democracy; but it will always be very nearly absolute. Whatever political laws govern men in times of equality, it can be foreseen that faith in public opinion will become a kind of religion and the majority will be its prophet.

Thus intellectual authority will be different, but it will not be diminished. I believe that it may acquire too much importance and confine the action of individual judgment within limits too narrow for the dignity and happiness of the human race. I clearly see two tendencies in equality: one turns each man's attention to new thoughts and the other keeps him from thinking at all. I can see how, aided by certain laws, democracy might extinguish that freedom of the mind which a democratic social condition favors. Thus it might happen that after having broken down all the bonds which classes or men imposed on it, the human spirit would be chained to the general will of the greatest number.

If democratic nations substituted this absolute power of the majority for all the various powers which checked or retarded individual thought, the evil itself would only change in character. Men would not have found the means for independence, but they would have succeeded in the very difficult task of giving servitude a new form. I cannot say too often that this is a matter for profound reflection for those who see intellectual liberty as being a sacred thing and who hate not only the despot but despotism. For myself, if I feel the hand of power lie heavy on my brow, I am little concerned about who oppresses me; I am no better inclined to pass my head under the yoke because a million men hold it for me.

THE SOCIALIZATION OF CIVIC VIRTUE
Michael P. Riccards

In his comparative study of developing countries, Seymour Martin Lipset has termed the United States, "the first new nation." As all new nations, the United States went through a difficult period of trying to assert its national identity and create a new citizenry from groups of foreign nationals. In the latter part of the nineteenth century, this country was faced with a similar problem but under far different circumstances—the assimilation of millions of immigrants into the American experience.

In assessing these periods of massive assimilation and acculturation, historians have generally found that the American political and social systems were remarkably effective. These systems instilled in the new young and the new old alike the values of liberalism and capitalism. The exact process of political socialization, however, has been and is still rather confusing. Like so much of our national life, it is quite informal and very diffuse. Generally, Americans have assumed that the schools were important agents in this socialization process, especially at the turn of the century. But the specific ways in which young Americans and older immigrants acquired their feelings and attitudes about the political system seems to have alluded systematic analysis.

Probably one reason why the political socialization process was historically considered to be so effective was that the economic and social frameworks reinforced it in a number of ways. To succeed in America, one had to learn the language, adopt Anglo-Saxon customs, and pay at least lip-service to its democratic ethos. Millions of Europeans quickly conformed to this formula because they wished to succeed in the new land which they had sacrificed so much to come to. It must be remembered that America was populated by the

Reprinted by permission of the author.

losers, the dreamers, and the schemers of other countries. They understood well the ideology of America: it was economic opportunity. They were willing to pay the price of acculturation. As a consequence, slowly, but irrevocably the manifestations of European culture were denigrated and subsumed into the American way of life.

Chroniclers of these events have not emphasized nearly enough the trauma which must have occured in all involved. They have not explored either the extent to which the life style of older America was changed by the massive infusion of foreign customs and ideologies. For as effective as the socialization process was, it could not totally assimilate these immigrants or even their descendents into a pre-arranged framework.

To a large extent this process of socialization is repeated for every generation and, here too, it is only partially successful. Each generation is a flood of foreigners which invades our society and changes it by their mere presence. Why this is so, one can not say for certain. Perhaps adults are poor teachers, or their children inattentive students. But in the end, each generation is only partially socialized into those patterns of the past meant to guide their lives in the future.

Political scientists have maintained that it is important that we realize how individuals are socialized, that is how they acquire their attitudes and beliefs about society in general and politics in particular. The assumption is that if one can understand the behavior and attitudes of a child during his formative years, it will be possible to predict the patterns of adult life. As this relates to politics, the feelings of trust, efficacy, and fairness which are inculcated in the young will be transposed onto the political world in which they will later participate.

Yet in examining the contemporary political socialization process, we are left with a variety of confusing statements and observations. First, the process itself is so informal and diffuse that it is quite difficult to understand what single agent of socialization is most important and which are of only secondary significance. In addition, if this process is so effective why is it that we are experiencing wide-spread alienation and dissent from the basic assumptions of our political life?

Any survey of political socialization must begin with questions of content: what specific values are being transmitted to the young? Socialization is an old field of inquiry for educators and philosophers, but a comparatively new one for political scientists. Most recently, David Easton, Jack Dennis, Fred Greenstein, and others have explored the socialization process by using the techniques of survey research. Their findings were rather similar; they concluded that children have a benevolent attitude toward authority, trust the government, and like the President and the policeman.

These studies were mostly done with white, middle class, and lower-middle class students and the results came as no surprise. Yet one did not experience from reading these works written in the 1960s that anything was happening in America. The bonds of trust, authority, and legitimacy were strongly interwoven in the hearts of our progeny. Somehow the society was undergoing severe convulsions at the same time the socialization process was being portrayed as being remarkably effective. Our experience contradicted our findings, or so it seemed.

There then came forays into the "other America" which produced quite different pictures. Dean Jaros and his associates at Kentucky found that in Appalacia, children were less likely to see authority as benevolent. A good proportion of them were cynical about politics and disliked the President. Edward Greenberg in his study of black children in Pittsburgh and Philadelphia found that they too did not share in the high positive orientation toward authority and trustfulness characteristic of earlier white samples.

Underlying these complications is a more basic question: are we interested in the values of children per se? As indicated before, the assumption underlying these studies is that early values are carried over to adulthood and help explain political behavior later on in life. However, this link between childhood socialization and adult behavior has never been conclusively demonstrated, only inferred. It does seem likely that in nonconflict situations, this transmital will be rather effective. One reason is that historically in the United States, politics has not been very visible or too important for the vast majority of the citizenry. Probably less than a tenth of the populace are really "political" in any intense meaning of the word. Most go about their lives, hoping only that taxes do not go too high or wars occur too frequently.

Apparently, this lack of interest has changed. Politics is more visible and social conflicts are more numerous. In this case, the political socialization-political behavior linkage becomes more complex to analyze. Many political scientists have argued that it is only in conflict situations that we can understand the true effectiveness of political inculcation. Since America is in a period of self-examination, perhaps it is possible to see how this socialization process does or does not function under considerable stress.

One observation which must be made at the start is that there is not one socialization process but many. In a society of 200-plus million people who rely on rather informal methods of inculcation, it is evident that a unitary process and result are not possible. Indeed each subculture in the United States has attitudes and beliefs which are in some way "politically" oriented.

While there is no unified process, there does appear to be a central or *dominant motif* which is to a large extent either accepted or rejected within its own terms. That dominant motif assumes that America is a democratic society in which individuals are more likely to be happy and well-off than in any other place on earth. In such a society, there is a specific network of political expectations prescribed for the individual which I have elsewhere termed "the Rousseauean model of citizenship." Within this conceptual framework, the American child is presented with the picture of a political world that is benevolent, trustworthy, harmonious, and tinted with moralistic hues. This model of citizenship emphasizes consensus, a discernible public interest, personal involvement, and even civic religion. The child is spared the need to consider the conflict aspect of collective living, the calculus of private interest, or the existence of pressure groups and political parties.

In order to examine more closely some of the subtleties of this model, I had conducted a simplified content analysis of the major third-grade textbooks sold in America. It is at the third grade that children are first exposed in a systematic way to politics and the life of the community.

These textbooks strongly emphasized the notion of "togetherness" and the necessity to be guided by the public interest in making decisions. In addition, these books stressed the importance of obedience with virtually no mention of the possibility or feasibility of disagreement. One of the most frequent and intriguing analogies is the comparison between law and the rules of the game. Children are told that they must obey the laws of the society because to do otherwise would lead to chaos. It would be like playing a game and not abiding by the rules.

Children are also taught to respect the government for the things that it does for them. Most especially, the government and its authority figures (the mayor, the policeman, the President) take a special interest in children and in the concerns that the children have about police and fire safety, education, parks, etc. In their role as citizens, children are familiarized with the procedure of voting for the right cause—not candidate. It is assumed that any representative will work for the public interest and the good of all.

The good citizen then is one who is loyal, altruistic, informed, and active. His participation is a further demonstration of his loyalty and this participation in turn reinforces his patriotism. The political ideals most often stressed are freedom and fairness; the notions of equality and toleration occur far less frequently.

In a more extensive impressionistic examination of ninety-three secondary school civics and American government textbooks, James Shaver found similar results. The textbooks which he examined did not indicate any awareness of the value conflicts inevitable in any modern society. None of the books in American government, for example, provided any methods by which one could assess factual claims that are so often made in political debates. The treatment of propaganda is brief; there is only cursory mention of public opinion, the sources of information, and the techniques for influencing opinion.

This tranquil world is the child's textbook democracy. It is the polity where the good man rises to address other good men about the great issues of the day. In making decisions, there is a public interest which can be ascertained by all rational men of good will. To do otherwise is to act against the moral canons of good citizenship. In addition, the child sees himself as being able to respond to the polity in a one-to-one relationship, highly personal and always rewarding. It is perhaps for this reason that most of these storybook towns are set within the suburbs—the symbol of a nostalgic return to small town life and village democracy.

It is this model of citizenship which is the dominant motif in American political socialization. It is this same model which also provides the vocabulary of obligation so often used by educators, politicians, and public information leaders when they address the populace. To a large extent, most of the debates on American citizenship have been cast within these terms by either accepting this model or by pointing up how it has been betrayed.

There are, of course, a variety of subcultures in which this dominant motif is not present or is consciously repudiated. As noted before, in studies of black children and poor white Appalacian children it has been found that they do not exhibit such strong feelings of trust, benevolence of authority, and personal efficacy. In other subcultures as the Amish or the Jehovah's Witnesses, government is regarded with extreme caution and deep suspicion.

These different kinds of political socialization are alternative or *secondary* motifs. However, they are secondary only in the sense that they affect fewer people than the dominant formalization and not in the sense that they do not command intense adherents. Very little work has been done by social scientists on these secondary motifs. Probably, one of the most interesting studies which has been done in this regard is Edgar Litt's examination of three secondary schools, each in different socioeconomic areas.

Litt first examined the civics textbooks used in an upper middle class, a lower middle class, and a working class community. He then interviewed civic and educational influentials to ascertain the intensity of their attitudes toward the proper orientation of the community school's civic education program. Lastly, he examined the overall effectiveness of exposure to a civics education course.

Litt found that generally there was no substantial difference in the content of these textbooks in their discussion of democracy or in their treatment of American procedures and institutions. With regard to the topic of participation, the texts used in the working class school contained fewer references to norms that encourage voting, feelings of political effectiveness, and a sense of civic duty. On the other hand, the texts in the upper middle class school emphasize more the view that politics is a process in which group struggle can be periodically ameliorated.

In all these communities, exposure to the courses seemed to strengthen support for the democratic process and negate political chauvinism. Community leaders supported these objectives in each case. However, it appears that students in the three communities were being trained to play different roles in the political system. In the working class community, students are taught about democratic procedures with much less emphasis on political participation or the importance of conflict. For them, politics is portrayed as a process whereby altruistic leaders carry out programs in the public interest.

In the second school, lower middle class students were trained in the elements of democratic government with some emphasis on the responsibilities of citizenship, but very little concern for the dynamics of public decision making. Only in the affluent community with a much more vibrant political life were the students given insights into the actual political process and the complex functions of politics. This is apparently a realization on the part of the community that they were training these students eventually for leadership positions. Thus one can see at work a very subtle but extremely important political recruitment process intertwined with political socialization. This development adds another complex aspect to the total picture; it indicates the important role of the subculture in reaffirming, altering, or discrediting formal civics training.

Political socialization has been portrayed up to now as a uniflow process—adult mentors forming new citizens. But it is equally possible that neophytes can socialize their elders. The most obvious example is political movements originated and sustained during their formative periods through youthful enthusiasm and dedication. The great movements of the sixties in civil rights, ecology, pacifism, and the McCarthy campaign are all illustrative of this social phenomenon.

More important than these, however, is the use of the dominant motif *as a weapon* by the recently socialized. This motif, or what has been termed the Rousseauean concept of citizenship, has had an unsettling influence on our social structures. Its basic vocabulary of personal involvement, public regardedness, and civic virtue forms the basis of self-accusation as well as of socialization. This motif is used to explain what the good citizen and the ideal polity should be like. But by its very persuasiveness, it holds up for continual scrutiny the deficiencies of the ongoing system.

All societies sanction some measure of institutionalized injustice. All leaders seek to solidify their positions and guarantee the viability of the coalition of interests they represent. In the process, access becomes more important than ability and tranquility is considered a greater public virtue than justice. The Rousseauean model of citizenship with its insistence on intense participation and its affirmation of egalitarianism runs head on into the bureaucratic and impersonal polity which characterizes most nation-states, including the United States.

Kenneth Keniston has shown that the new radicals of the 1960s came from the liberal, professional middle classes where involvement and efficacy are stressed. The best known young radical manifesto, the Port Huron Statement, throbs with a sense of personal betrayal by adult America of the ideals that the authors were brought up in. The dominant motif then becomes a yardstick by which the young can judge the citizenship of their elders. Consequently, this motif has become a weapon against what the newly socialized deem to be the moral deviation of their adult leaders.

This turn of events represents a confusing occurrence to most observers. The main purpose of socialization is to pass on present adult attitudes to future citizens, to get the young to believe in what their parents believed in. The process of socialization is supposed to be supportive of the political system, not disruptive of it. But if the above line of speculation is correct, then the present dominant motif of American political socialization produces undesirable consequences. It accentuates the trauma of social change and aggravates the "normal" attitudinal differences between generations. The past then becomes a constant wellspring of ideas for the future. It provides a host of historical examples and rhetorical devices which can be used in judging the failures of the present. The democratic, moralistic, and egalitarian aspects of this motif become the basis for social criticism and/or reform.

It is more difficult for a society to endure the charge of hypocrisy than injustice. Reformers over the years have argued with only limited success their rational case for social justice. But by holding up a commonly accepted ideal or set of ideals to that society and pointing up the discrepancies, social critics strengthen their initial position. The only response to genuine change then becomes repression which further aggravates the dissonance between the promise and the reality. It is at this junction that we find modern America. There is no consensus on whether the country should pay the cost of change or merely use the full power of the state to crush effective and prolonged dissent.

In the midst of this state of affairs criticism acclerates. The nonwhite minorities and professional women attack the society's claim to being egalitarian. The young argue that the society's democratic pretensions are a sham which cover up bureaucratic insolence and corporate ravishment.

From the point of view of political socialization, the problem is simple: either change the workings of the political and social order or alter the dominant motif describing normative citizenship. But for the society as an ongoing totality, the situation is more acute. Having uplifted the expectations of people, it must either make the sacrifices necessary to satisfy them or be willing to face the consequences of public disillusionment. America is learning all too well that while the socialization of civic virtue is an easy process to instill, it can be a frightening yardstick by which to be measured once school is out and events are in the saddle.

PUBLIC OPINION AND DEMOCRATIC POLITICS
V. O. Key, Jr.

The longer one frets with the puzzle of how democratic regimes manage to function, the more plausible it appears that a substantial part of the explanation is to be found in the motives that actuate the leadership echelon, the values that it holds, in the rules of the political game to which it adheres, in the expectations which it entertains about its own status in society, and perhaps in some of the objective circumstances, both material and institutional, in which it functions. Focus of attention on this sector of the opinion system contrasts with the more usual quest for the qualities of the people that may be thought to make democratic practices feasible. That focus does not deny the importance of mass attitudes. It rather emphasizes that the pieces of the puzzle are different in form and function, and that for the existence of a democratic opinion-oriented system each piece must possess the characteristics necessary for it to fit together with the others in a working whole. The superimposition over a people habituated to tyranny of a leadership imbued with democratic ideals probably would not create a viable democratic order.

VALUES AND MOTIVES OF THE ACTIVIST SUBCULTURE

The traits and characteristics of political activists assume importance in the light of a theory about why the leadership and governing levels in any society behave as they do. That theory amounts to the proposition that these political actors constitute in effect a subculture with its own peculiar set of norms of behavior, motives, and approved standards. Processes of indoctrination internalize such norms among those who are born to or climb to positions of power and leadership; they serve as standards of action, which are reinforced by a social discipline among the political activists. In some regimes the standards of the ruling groups prescribe practices of firmness toward the governed who are regarded as menials with no rights; they deserve no more than the rough and arbitrary treatment they receive. The rules of the game may prescribe that the proper practice for rulers is to maximize their own advantage as well as the correlative deprivations of the ruled. The ignorant, the poor, and the incompetent may be seen as entitled to what they get, which is very little. Or the rules of the game of a regime may mitigate the harshness of these outlooks

From Public Opinion and American Democracy. *Copyright by A. Knopf, 1961. Reprinted by permission of the publisher.*

by a compassionate attitude toward the wretched masses who cannot help themselves. Hence, we may have little fathers of the people. The point is that the politically active classes may develop characteristic norms and practices that tend to guide their behavior. In a loose sense these may be the norms of a subculture, that of the specialists in politics and government. Beliefs generally accepted among these persons tend to establish habits and patterns of behavior with considerable power of self-maintenance or persistence through time.

While the ruling classes of a democratic order are in a way invisible because of the vagueness of the lines defining the influentials and the relative ease of entry to their ranks, it is plain that the modal norms and standards of a democratic elite have their peculiarities. Not all persons in leadership echelons have precisely the same basic beliefs; some may even regard the people as a beast. Yet a fairly high concentration prevails around the modal beliefs, even though the definition of those beliefs must be imprecise. Fundamental is a regard for public opinion, a belief that in some way or another it should prevail. Even those who cynically humbug the people make a great show of deference to the populace. The basic doctrine goes further to include a sense of trusteeship for the people generally and an adherence to the basic doctrine that collective efforts should be dedicated to the promotion of mass gains rather than of narrow class advantage; elite elements tethered to narrow group interest have no slack for maneuver to accommodate themselves to mass aspirations. Ultimate expression of these faiths comes in the willingness to abide by the outcome of popular elections. The growth of leadership structures with beliefs including these broad articles of faith is probably accomplished only over a considerable period of time, and then only under auspicious circumstances.

If an elite is not to monopolize power and thereby to bring an end to democratic practices, its rules of the game must include restraints in the exploitation of public opinion. Dimly perceptible are rules of etiquette that limit the kinds of appeals to public opinion that may be properly made. If it is assumed that the public is manipulable at the hands of unscrupulous leadership (as it is under some conditions), the maintenance of a democratic order requires the inculcation in leadership elements of a taboo against appeals that would endanger the existence of democratic practices. Inflammation of the sentiments of a sector of the public disposed to exert the tyranny of an intolerant majority (or minority) would be a means of destruction of a democratic order. Or by the exploitation of latent differences and conflicts within the citizenry it may at times be possible to paralyze a regime as intense hatreds among classes of people come to dominate public affairs. Or by encouraging unrealistic expectations among the people a clique of politicians may rise to power, a position to be kept by repression as disillusionment sets in. In an experienced democracy such tactics may be "unfair" competition among members of the politically active class. In short, certain restraints on political competition help keep competition within tolerable limits. The observation of a few American political campaigns might lead one to the conclusion that there are no restraints on politicians as they attempt to humbug the people. Even so, admonitions ever recur against arousing class against class, against stirring the animosities of religious groups, and against demagoguery in its more extreme forms. American politicians manifest considerable restraint in this regard when they are tested against the standards of behavior of politicians of most of those regimes that have failed in the attempt to establish or maintain democratic practices.

The norms of the practice of politics in an order that has regard for public opinion include broad rules of etiquette governing relations among the activists, as well as rules governing the relations of activists with the public. Those rules, in their fundamental effect, assure the existence of a minority among the political activists; if those who control government can suppress opposition activists, an instrument essential for the formation and expression of public opinion is destroyed. A body of customs that amounts to a policy of "live and let live" must prevail. In constitutional democracies some of these rules are crystalized into fundamental law in guarantees such as those of freedom of speech, freedom of press, and the right to appeal to the electorate for power. Relevant also are procedures for the protection of property rights; a political opposition may be destroyed by expropriation as well as by execution. While such rules extend in their application to the entire population, one of their major functions is to prevent politicians from putting each other into jail or from destroying each other in the ordinary course of their competitive endeavors. All these elements of the rules of the game gain strength, not from their statement in the statutes and codes, but from their incorporation into the norms that guide the behavior of the political activists.

FORM AND STRUCTURE

Certain broad structural or organizational characteristics may need to be maintained among the activists of a democratic order if they are to perform their functions in the system. Fundamental is the absence of sufficient cohesion among the activists to unite them into a single group dedicated to the management of public affairs and public opinion. Solidification of the elite by definition forecloses opportunity for public choice among alternative governing groups and also destroys the mechanism for the unfettered expression of public opinion or of the opinions of the many subpublics. Maintenance of division and competition among political activists requires the kinds of etiquette that have been mentioned to govern their relations among themselves. Those rules, though, do not create the cleavages among the activists. Competitive segments of the leadership echelons normally have their roots in interests or opinion blocs within society. A degree of social diversity thus may be, if not a prerequisite, at least helpful in the construction of a leadership appropriate for a democratic regime. A series of independent social bases provide the foundations for a political elite difficult to bring to the state of unification that either prevents the rise of democratic processes or converts them into sham rituals.

At a more earthy level, maintenance of a multiplicity of centers of leadership and political activism requires arrangements by which men may gain a livelihood despite the fact that they are out of power. Consider the consequences for the structure of opinion leadership of a socioeconomic system in which those skilled in the arts of governance have open to them no way of obtaining a livelihood save by the exercise of those skills. In the United States the high incidence of lawyers among the politically influential provides a base of economic independence; the defeated politician can always find a few clients. Extensive reliance on part-time, amateur politicians in representative bodies and in many governing commissions has assured an economic cushion for many political activists. The custom of making many such offices economically unattractive has, in effect, required that they be filled by persons with an economic base independent of the public treasury. Opinion leaders and managers often find economic independence in posts with business associations and other voluntary societies. Communications enterprises, important in the operation of democracies, gain independence from government by their commercial position. The structure of government itself, through its many independent units and agencies, assures havens of some security for spokesmen for a variety of viewpoints. All this may boil down to the contention that development and maintenance of the type of leadership essential for the operation of a democratic political order is facilitated by the existence of a social system of some complexity with many centers that have some autonomy and economic independence. Perhaps a safer formulation would be that societies that do not meet these requisites may encounter difficult problems in the support of a fractionalized stratum of political activists; they need to construct functional equivalents of the means we have been describing to assure the maintenance of competing centers of leadership.

When viewed from another angle, these comments about the utility of independent foundations for competing sectors of the political elite relate to the more general proposition that regimes deferential to public opinion may best flourish when the deprivations contingent upon the loss of an election are limited. The structure of government itself may also contribute to that loss limitation. In federal regimes and in regimes with extensive devolution to elective local governmental authorities the prospect of loss of a national election may be faced with some equanimity, for the national minority may retain its position in many subordinate units of the nation and remain in a measure undisturbed by the alternations of control within the nation as a whole. The same function of loss limitation may be served by constitutional and customary expectations that limit the permissible range of governmental action.

Another characteristic may be mentioned as one that, if not a prerequisite to government by public opinion, may profoundly affect the nature of a democratic order. This is the distribution through the social structure of those persons highly active in politics. By various analyses, none founded on completely satisfactory data, we have shown that in the United States the political activists—if we define the term broadly—are scattered through the socioeconomic hierarchy. The upper-income and occupational groups, to be sure, contribute disproportionately; nevertheless, individuals of high political participation are sprinkled throughout the lesser occupational strata. Contrast the circumstances when the highly active political stratum coincides with the high socio-economic stratum. Conceivably the winning of consent and the creation of a sense of political participation and of sharing in public affairs may be far simpler when political activists of some degree are spread through all social strata. The alternative circumstance may induce an insensitivity to mass opinion, a special reliance on mass communications, and a sharpened sense of cleavage and separatism within the political order. The contention made here amounts to more than the axiom that democracies can exist only in societies that possess a well-developed middle class. In a modern industrial society with universal suffrage the chances are that a considerable sprinkling of political activists needs to exist in groups below the "middle class," however that term of vague referent may be defined. The correct general proposition may be that the operation of democratic processes may be facilitated by the distribution of persons participating in the order through all strata of the electorate. When the belief that democracy depended upon the middle class flourished, a comparatively narrow suffrage prevailed.

Allied with these questions is the matter of access to the wider circles of political leadership and of the recruitment and indoctrination of these political activists. Relative ease of access to the arena of active politics may be a preventive of the rise of intransigent blocs of opinion managed by those denied participation in the regularized processes of politics. In a sense, ease of access is a necessary consequence of the existence of a somewhat fragmented stratum of political activists. Systems built on rigid class lines or on the dominance of clusters of families may be especially prone to the exclusion of those not to the proper status born—or married. Yet ease of access does not alone suffice. It must be accompanied by means, either deliberate or informal, for the indoctrination of those admitted in the special mores and customs of the activist elements of the polity. Otherwise, ease of access may only facilitate the depredations of those alienated from the values of the political order. By their nature democratic political systems have large opportunity—if there is the necessary will—to extend widely opportunities for political participation in lesser capacities and thereby to sift out those capable of achieving access to the more restricted circles of influentials. Whether the builders of political orders ever set about deliberately and systematically to tackle such problems of recruitment and indoctrination may be doubtful. Those problems may be solved, when they are solved, by the unconscious and unwilled processes of evolutionary adaptation of social systems.

This discussion in terms of leadership echelons, political activists, or elites falls painfully on the ears of democratic romantics. The mystique of democracy has in it no place for ruling classes. As perhaps with all powerful systems of faith, it is vague on the operating details. Yet by their nature governing systems, be they democratic or not, involve a division of social labor.

Once that axiom is accepted, the comprehension of democratic practices requires a search for the peculiar characteristics of the political influentials in such an order, for the special conditions under which they work, and for the means by which the people keep them in check. The vagueness of the mystique of democracy is matched by the intricacy of its operating practices. If it is true that those who rule tend sooner or later to prove themselves enemies of the rights of man—and there is something to be said for the validity of this proposition—then any system that restrains that tendency however slightly can excite only awe. . . .

INEVITABILITY OF THE DECAY OF DEMOCRACIES?

Our exposition of the interactions between leadership and mass opinion enables us better to understand the argument that democracies, by their inner logic, tend toward decay. That in the long sweep of time all regimes tend toward decay is a proposition at least not negated by the annals of recorded history. Yet the contention, advanced by respectable authorities, is that democracies possess within themselves defects that inevitably lead to their decay in a manner peculiar to democracies.

The fatal weakness of modern mass democracies, so the argument goes, rests in the subjection of government to a public opinion whose mandates are certain to be destructive of the order. Implicit in that proposition is the assumption that mass opinion in the long run tends toward positions incompatible with the demands of the health of the order and that mass opinion tends to pull governments into harmony with those positions. Thus, we have the picture of a mass opinion animated by greed and by a disregard for the rights of man. Politicians must, the conclusion is, sooner or later adopt that view and in the process ultimately create a dictatorship of a majority dedicated to the reduction of all men to a drab equality, an action to be maintained only by a destruction of freedom. Or the argument is that governments accountable to democratic masses invariably tend to take the easy route, to dodge the hard decisions, to avoid at moments of crisis demands for the sacrifices by the populace necessary for the maintenance of the system. Governments, by their subjection to mass opinion, lose decisiveness and are bereft of the will to act, a condition creative of special dangers for the democracy that exists in a hostile international environment. All these consequences flow inevitably from the interaction between leadership and mass opinion as cliques of leaders seek power and, in so doing, are compelled to appeal to mass opinions that contain within themselves the seeds of national destruction. By a kind of Gresham's law, those leadership cliques with a wisdom greater than that of mass opinion either perish or embrace the follies of the mass.

What can we say about this melancholy hypothesis? For a certainty, there are democracies and democracies. Perhaps in some situations the hypothesis fits the facts, but our analyses of the American scene caution us against easy acceptance of so glib a theory of the dynamics of democratic self-destruction. We have pictured public opinion as the product of an interaction between political influentials and the mass of the people, an interaction that may produce alterations in mass opinion. In the course of time that interaction may also alter the modal position of the influentials as a novel doctrine asserted by one sector of the influentials gains acceptance among the masses. Mass opinion is not self-generating; in the main, it is a response to the cues, the proposals, and the visions propagated by the political activists.

If this conception of the formation of opinion has validity, democracies decay, if they do, not because of the cupidity of the masses, but because of the stupidity and self-seeking of leadership echelons. Politicians often make of the public a scapegoat for their own shortcomings; their actions, they say, are a necessity for survival given the state of public opinion. Yet that opinion itself results from the preachings of the influentials, of this generation and of several past generations.

Moreover, even if mass opinion assumes forms incompatible with the national interest, the articulation between government and mass opinion is so loose that politicians enjoy a considerable range of discretion within which to exercise prudence and good sense. Our explorations into the nature and form of mass opinion leave no doubt that its directives tend toward generality rather than specificity. Even on broad issues on which opinion becomes fairly well crystallized room may remain for choice among a variety of specific actions. Furthermore, translation of opinion into actions of electoral punishment or reward is a tortuous and uncertain procedure. The predictability of electoral response to a particular action remains so uncertain that the avoidance of a sensible decision because it will lose votes is usually the work of a man whose anxieties outweigh his capacities of prediction.

The argument amounts essentially to the position that the masses do not corrupt themselves; if they are corrupt, they have been corrupted. If this hypothesis has a substantial strain of validity, the critical element for the health of a democratic order consists in the beliefs, standards, and competence of those who constitute the influentials, the opinion-leaders, the political activists in the order. That group, as has been made plain, refuses to define itself with great clarity in the American system; yet analysis after analysis points to its existence. If a democracy tends toward indecision, decay, and disaster, the responsibility rests here, not in the mass of the people.

A DAY IN THE LIFE
OF A SOCIALIST CITIZEN
Michael Walzer

Imagine a day in the life of a socialist citizen. He hunts in the morning, fishes in the afternoon, rears cattle in the evening, and plays the critic after dinner. Yet he is neither hunter, fisherman, shepherd, nor critic; tomorrow he may select another set of activities, just as he pleases. This is the delightful portrait that Marx sketches in the *German Ideology* as part of a polemic against the division of labor. Socialists since have worried that it is not economically feasible; perhaps it isn't. But there is another difficulty that I want to consider: that is, the curiously apolitical character of the citizen Marx describes. Certain crucial features of socialist life have been omitted altogether.

In light of the recent discussions about participatory democracy, Marx's sketch needs to be elaborated. Before hunting in the morning, this unalienated man of the future is likely to attend a meeting of the Council on Animal Life, where he will be required to vote on important matters relating to the stocking of the forests. The meeting will probably not end much before noon, for among the many-sided citizens there will always be a lively interest even in highly technical problems. Immediately after lunch, a special session of the Fishermen's Council will be called to protest the maximum catch recently voted by the Regional Planning Commission. And the Marxist man will participate eagerly in these debates, even postponing a scheduled discussion of some contradictory theses on cattle-rearing. Indeed, he will probably love argument far better than hunting, fishing, or rearing cattle. The debates will go on so long that the citizens will have no rush through dinner in order to assume their roles as critics. Then off they will go to meetings of study groups, clubs, editorial boards, and political parties where criticism will be carried on long into the night.

Socialism, Oscar Wilde once wrote, would take too many evenings. This is, it seems to me, one of the most significant criticisms of socialist theory that has ever been made. The fanciful sketch above is only intended to suggest its possible truth. Socialism's great appeal is the prospect it holds out for the development of human capacities. An enormous growth of creative talent, a new and unprecedented variety of expression, a wild proliferation of sects, associations, schools, parties: this will be the flowering of the future society. But underlying this new individualism and exciting group life must be a broad,

Reprinted from Dissent, *May-June 1968, by permission of the author and publisher.*

self-governing community of equal men. A powerful figure looms behind Marx's hunter, fisherman, shepherd, and critic: the busy citizen attending his endless meetings. "Society regulates the general production," Marx writes, "and thus makes it possible for me to do one thing today and another tomorrow . . ." If society is not to become an alien and dangerous force, however, the citizens cannot accept its regulation and gratefully do what they please. They must participate in social regulation; they must be social men, organizing and planning their own fulfillment in spontaneous activity. The purpose of Wilde's objection is to suggest that just this self-regulation is compatible with spontaneity, that the requirements of citizenship are incompatible with the freedom of hunter, fisherman, and so on.

Politics itself, of course, can be a spontaneous activity, freely chosen by those men and women who enjoy it and to whose talents a meeting is so much exercise. But this is very unlikely to be true of all men and women all the time—even if one were to admit what seems plausible enough: that political life is more intrinsic to human nature than is hunting and cattle-rearing or even (to drop Marx's rural imagery) art or music. "Too many evenings" is a shorthand phrase that describes something more than the sometimes tedious, sometimes exciting business of resolutions and debates. It suggests also that socialism and participatory democracy will depend upon, and hence require, an extraordinary willingness to attend meetings, and a public spirit and sense of responsibility that will make attendance dependable and activity consistent and sustained. None of this can rest for any long period of time of among any substantial group of men upon spontaneous interest. Nor does it seem possible that spontaneity will flourish above and beyond the routines of social regulation.

Self-government is a very demanding and time-consuming business, and when it is extended from political to economic and cultural life, and when the organs of government are decentralized so as to maximize participation, it will inevitably become more demanding still. Ultimately, it may well require almost continuous activity, and life will become a succession of meetings. When will there be time for the cultivation of personal creativity or the free association of like-minded friends? In the world of the meeting, when will there be time for the tête-à-tête?

I suppose there will always be time for the tête-à-tête. Men and women will secretly plan love affairs even while public business is being transacted. But Wilde's objection isn't silly. The idea of citizenship on the Left has always been overwhelming, suggesting a positive frenzy of activity, and often involving the repression of all feelings except political ones. Its character can best be examined in the work of Jean-Jacques Rousseau, from whom socialists and, more recently, New Leftists directly or indirectly inherited it. In order to guarantee public-spiritedness and political participation, and as a part of his critique of bourgeois egotism, Rousseau systematically denigrated the value of private life:

The better the constitution of a state is, the more do public affairs encroach on private in the minds of the citizens. Private affairs are even of much less importance, because the aggregate of the common happiness furnishes a greater proportion of that of each individual, so that there is less for him to seek in particular cares.

Rousseau might well have written these lines out of a deep awareness that private life will not, in fact, bear the great weight that bourgeois society places upon it. We need, beyond our families and jobs, a public world where purposes are shared and cooperative activity is possible. More likely, however, he wrote them because he believed that cooperative activity could not be sustained unless private life were radically repressed, if not altogether eradicated. His citizen does not participate in social regulation as one part of a round of activities. Social regulation is his entire life. Rousseau develops his own critique of the division of labor by absorbing all human activities into the idea of citizenship: "Citizens," he wrote, "are neither lawyers, nor soldiers, nor priests by profession; they perform all these functions as a matter of duty." *As a matter of duty:* here is the key to the character of that patriotic, responsible, energetic man who has figured also in socialist thought, but always in the guise of a new man, freely exercising his human powers.

It is probably more realistic to see the citizen as the product of collective repression and self-discipline. He is, above all, *dutiful,* and this is only possible if he has triumphed over egotism and impulse in his own personality. He embodies what political theorists have called "republican virtue"—that means, he puts the common good, the success of the movement, the safety of the community, above his own delight or well-being, *always.* To symbolize his virtue, perhaps, he adopts an ascetic style and gives up every sort of self-decoration: he wears sans-culottes or unpressed khakis. More important, he foregoes a conventional career for the profession of politics; he commits himself entirely. It is an act of the most extreme devotion. Now, how is such a man produced? What kind of conversion is necessary? Or what kind of rigorous training?

Rousseau set out to create virtuous citizens, and the means he chose are very old in the history of republicanism: an authoritarian family, a rigid sexual code, censorship of the arts, sumptuary laws, mutual surveillance, the systematic indoctrination of children. All these have been associated historically (at least until recent times) not with tyrannical but with republican regimes: Greece and Rome, the Swiss Protestant city-states, the first French republic. Tyrannies and oligarchies, Rousseau argued, might tolerate or even encourage license, for the effect of sexual indulgence, artistic freedom, extravagant self-decoration, and privacy itself was to corrupt men and turn them away from public life, leaving government to the few. Self-government requires self-control: it is one of the oldest arguments in the history of political thought.

But if that argument is true, it may mean that self-government also leaves government to the few. For, if we reject the discipline of Rousseau's republicanism (as we have, and for good reasons), then only those men and women will be activists who volunteer for action. How many will that be? How many of the people you and I know? How many ought they to be? Certainly no radical movement or socialist society is possible without those every-ready participants, who "fly," as Rousseau said, "to the public assemblies."

Radicalism and socialism make political activity for the first time an option for all those who relish it and a duty—sometimes—even for those who don't. But what a suffocating sense of responsibility, what a plethora of virtue would be necessary to sustain the participation of everybody all the time! How exhausting it would be! Surely there is something to be said for the irresponsible nonparticipant and something also for the part-time activist, the half virtuous man (and the most scorned among the militants), who appears and disappears, thinking of Marx and then of his dinner? The very least that can be said is that these people, unlike the poor, will always be with us.

We can assume that a great many citizens, in the best of societies, will do all they can to avoid what Mel Tumin has nicely called "the merciless masochism of community-minded and self-regulating men and women." While the necessary meetings go on and on, they will take long walks, play with their children, paint pictures, make love, and watch television. They will attend sometimes, when their interests are directly at stake or when they feel like it. But they won't make the full-scale commitment necessary for socialism or participatory democracy. How are these people to be represented at the meetings? What are their rights? These are not only problems of the future, when popular participation has finally been established as the core of political and economic life. They come up in every radical movement; they are the stuff of contemporary controversy.

Many people feel that they ought to join this or that political movement; they do join; they contribute time and energy—but unequally. Some make a full-time commitment; they work every minute; the movement becomes their whole life and they often come to disbelieve in the moral validity of life outside. Others are established outside, solidly or precariously; they snatch hours and sometimes days; they harry their families and skimp on their jobs, but yet cannot make it to every meeting. Still others attend no meetings at all; they work hard but occasionally; they show up, perhaps at critical moments, then they are gone. These last two groups make up the majority of the people available to the movement (any movement), just as they will make up the majority of the citizens of any socialist society. Radical politics radically increases the amount and intensity of political participation, but it doesn't (and probably oughtn't to) break through the limits imposed on republican virtue by the inevitable pluralism of commitments, the terrible shortage of time, and the day-to-day hedonism of ordinary men and women.

Under these circumstances, words like citizenship and participation actually describe the enfranchisement of only a part, and not necessarily a large part, of the movement or the community. Participatory democracy means the sharing of power among the activists. Socialism means the rule of the men with the most evenings to spare. Both imply also an injunction to the others: join us, come to the meetings, participate!

Sometimes young radicals sound very much like old Christians, demanding the severance of every tie for the sake of politics. "How many Christian women are there," John Calvin once wrote, "who are held captive by their children!" How many "community people" miss meetings because of their families! But there is nothing to be done. Ardent democrats have sometimes urged that citizens be legally required to vote: that is possible, though the device is not attractive. Requiring people to attend meetings, to join in discussions, to govern themselves: that is not possible, at least not in a free society. And if they do not govern themselves, they will, willy-nilly, be governed by their activist fellows. The apathetic, the occasional enthusiasts, the part-time workers: all of them will be ruled by full-timers, militants, and professionals.

But if only some citizens participate in political life, it is essential that they always remember and be regularly reminded that they are . . . only some. This isn't easy to arrange. The militant in the movement, for example, doesn't represent anybody; it is his great virtue that he is self-chosen, a volunteer. But since he sacrifices so much for his fellowmen, he readily persuades himself that he is acting in their name. He takes their failure to put in an appearance only as a token of their oppression. He is certain he is their agent, or rather, the agent of their liberation.

He isn't in any simple sense wrong. The small numbers of participating citizens in the U.S. today, the widespread fearfulness, the sense of impotence and irrelevance: all these are signs of social sickness. Self-government is an important human function, an exercise of significant talents and energies, and the sense of power and responsibility it brings is enormously healthy. A certain amount of commitment and discipline, of not-quite-merciless masochism, is socially desirable, and efforts to evoke it are socially justifiable.

But many of the people who stay away from meetings do so for reasons that the militants don't understand or won't acknowledge. They stay away not because they are beaten, afraid, uneducated, lacking confidence and skills (though these are often important reasons), but because they have made other commitments; they have found ways to cope short of politics; they have created viable subcultures even in an oppressive world. They may lend passive support to the movement and help out occasionally, but they won't work, nor are their needs and aspirations in any sense embodied by the militants who will.

The militants represent themselves. If the movement is to be democratic, the others must *be represented*. The same thing will be true in any future socialist society: participatory democracy has to be paralleled by representative democracy. I'm not sure precisely how to adjust the two; I am sure that they have to be adjusted. Somehow power must be distributed, as it isn't today, to small groups of active and interested citizens, but these citizens must themselves be made responsible to a larger electorate. Nothing is more important than that responsibility; without it we will only get one or another sort of activist or *apparatchik* tyranny. And that we have already.

Nonparticipants have rights; it is one of the dangers of participatory democracy that it would fail to provide any effective protection for these rights. But nonparticipants also have functions; it is another danger that these would not be sufficiently valued. For many people in America today, politics is something to watch, an exciting spectacle, and there exists between the activists and the others something of the relation of actor and audience. Now for any democrat this is an unsatisfactory relation. We rightly resent the way actors play upon and manipulate the feelings of their audiences. We dislike the aura of magic and mystification contrived at on stage. We would prefer politics to be like the new drama with its alienation effects and audience participation. Fair enough.

But even the new drama requires its audience, and we ought not to forget that audiences can be critical as well as admiring, enlightened as well as mystified. More important, political actors, like actors in the theater, need the control and tension imposed by audiences, the knowledge that tomorrow the reviews will appear, tomorrow people will come or not come to watch their performance. Too often, of course, the reviews are favorable and the audiences come. That is because of the various sorts of collusion which presently develop between small and coopted cliques of actors and critics. But in an entirely free society, there would be many more political actors and critics than ever before, and they would, presumably, be self-chosen. Not only the participants, but also the nonparticipants would come into their own. Alongside the democratic politics of shared work and perpetual activism, there would arise the open and leisurely culture of criticism, second-guessing, and burlesque.

It would be a mistake to underestimate the importance of all these, even if they aren't marked, as they generally won't be, by responsibility and virtue. They are far more important in the political arena than in the theater. For activists and professionals in the movement or the polity don't simply contrive effects; their work has more palpable results. Their policies touch us all in material ways, whether we go or don't go to the meetings. And those who don't go may well turn out to be more effective critics than those who do: no one who was one of its first guessers can usefully second-guess a decision. That is why the best critics in a liberal society are men-out-of-office. In a radically democratic society they would be men who stay away from meetings, perhaps for months at a time, and only then discover that something outrageous has been prepetrated that must be mocked or protested. The proper response to such protests is not to tell the laggard citizens that they should have been active these past many months, not to nag them to do work that they don't enjoy and in any case won't do well, but to listen to what they have to say. After all, what would democratic politics be like without its kibbitzers?

BIBLIOGRAPHICAL NOTE

The attitudes and beliefs of the American people have been examined at length by social scientists. Of special interest is the cross-polity study done by Gabriel Almond and Sidney Verba, *The Civic Culture*. Also important are Samuel Stouffer, *Communism, Conformity and Civil Liberties;* S. M. Lipset, *Political Man;* and the works of Robert Lane, *Political Life; Political Ideology;* and *Political Thinking and Consciousness.*

Voting studies are also informative in assessing the attitudes of the citizenry. The most important studies are the Survey Research Center's *The American Voter* and *Elections and the Political Order*. Two older studies are Bernard Berlson et. al., *Voting,* and Paul Lazarsfeld, et. al., *The People's Choice.*

There has been a considerable amount of work on the political socialization process. The major volumes are: Richard E. Dawson and Kenneth Prewitt, *Political Socialization;* David Easton and Jack Dennis, *Children in the Political System;* Fred I. Greenstein, *Children and Politics;* Robert D. Hess and Judith V. Torney, *The Development of Political Attitudes in Children;* and *Learning About Politics,* ed. Roberta Sigel.

Changes in the American character have been examined by a variety of sources: David Reisman, *The Lonely Crowd;* Theodore Roszak, *The Making of a Counter Culture;* and Charles Reich's popular manifesto, *The Greening of America*. There have also been some studies of our concept of citizenship: Mark Roeloffs, *The Tension of Citizenship,* and Robert Pranger, *The Eclipse of Citizenship.*

IV. THE SEARCH FOR AUTHENTIC FREEDOM

1. Liberty and Political Restraint

The demands organizations make on the individual are extensive and pervasive. Many American theorists have sought to provide guidelines that would circumscribe the areas into which these organizations could protrude. As a whole, American political theorists have been more concerned with the power of the state than with the activities of economic organizations or the pressure of social conformity.

One of the earliest and most eloquent pleas for governmental restraint was Jefferson's First Inaugural Address. His address, with its emphasis on the dignity of the individual and the right of self-expression, is the classical liberal defense of toleration. Underlying Jefferson's thoughts on toleration was a simple faith that reason can effectively expose any falsehoods that may be brought into the public arena.

A more jaundiced view of American life and politics can be found in the writings of the great humorist and social critic, Mark Twain. Twain was a master of more than the simple narrative; he was also a sarcastic and biting commentator on the foibles of mankind. In his first essay, Twain points up the irrational nature of patriotism and how it is unconsciously inculcated in people. In his second essay, he much more pointedly deals with the strange, but common fusion of religion and war. His "War Prayer" has become a classic in American humor, and it is remarkably relevant to our modern experience. Like many American writers, Twain is suspicious of government and, indeed, of all social organization.

But pleas for toleration and recourse to humor are not enough; there must be laws that guarantee to all citizens some protection against the steady encroachment of both private inquiries and public authorities into their lives. The Brandeis-Warren doctrine on privacy is one such attempt to make the law grow to meet this problem. The great Supreme Court Justice and his law partner foresaw in the 1890s a situation that has become so vexing in our time. How can one prevent the systematic accumulation of data and the nightly news saturation from making every life and every activity a matter of public record? In this selection, two fine legal minds are actually seeking to make law. They argue from precedent and logical analogy in order to fashion a new doctrine which they maintain is implicit in the spirit of the old.

Another area where governmental restraint has been urged is in the economic sphere. Classical liberals have argued that it is only under the capitalist system that men can have maximum opportunity to express their desires and see their personal initiatives rewarded. One of the most articulate contemporary defenders of laissez-faire economics is Friedrich Hayek, who maintains that government planning leads to a totalitarian state. He argues that it is better to allow the unhampered functioning of the market place to sort out the desires and ambitions of people. No society can create and realize a collective goal without doing great harm to the liberties of its individual citizens.

Just what the proper dimensions of economic liberty are has been a continual topic of debate in America since the 1930s. It has been argued that such planning is done already in each area by large corporations that have little concern about their effect on society. Is not economic liberty meaningless without some guarantee of employment or some effective sanctions on shoddy merchandise or dangerous commodities? These issues and others must be considered when one is deciding the significance of tolerating certain economic activities in the United States.

THE FIRST INAUGURAL ADDRESS
Thomas Jefferson

Called upon to undertake the duties of the first executive office of our country, I avail myself of the presence of that portion of my fellow-citizens which is here assembled to express my grateful thanks for the favor with which they have been pleased to look toward me, to declare a sincere consciousness that the task is above my talents, and that I approach it with those anxious and awful presentiments which the greatness of the charge and the weakness of my powers so justly inspire. A rising nation, spread over a wide and fruitful land, traversing all the seas with the rich productions of their industry, engaged in commerce with nations who feel power and forget right, advancing rapidly to destinies beyond the reach of mortal eye—when I contemplate these transcendent objects, and see the honor, the happiness, and the hopes of this beloved country comittted to the issue, and the auspices of this day, I shrink from the contemplation, and humble myself before the magnitude of the undertaking. Utterly, indeed, should I despair did not the presence of many whom I here see remind me that in the other high authorities provided by our Constitution I shall find resources of wisdom, of virtue, and of zeal on which to rely under all difficulties. To you, then, gentlemen, who are charged with the sovereign functions of legislation, and to those associated with you, I look with encouragement for that guidance and support which may enable us to steer with safety the vessel in which we are all embarked amidst the conflicting elements of a troubled world.

During the contest of opinion through which we have passed the animation of discussions and of exertions has sometimes worn an aspect which might impose on strangers unused to think freely and to speak and to write what they think; but this being now decided by the voice of the nation, announced according to the rules of the Constitution, all will, of course, arrange themselves under the will of the law, and unite in common efforts for the common good. All, too, will bear in mind this sacred principle, that though the will of the majority is in all cases to prevail, that will to be rightful must be reasonable; that the minority possesses their equal rights, which equal law must protect, and to violate would be oppression. Let us, then, fellow-citizens, unite with one heart and one mind. Let us restore to social intercourse that harmony and affection without which liberty and even life itself are but dreary things. And let us reflect that, having banished from our land that religious intolerance under which mankind so long bled and suffered, we have yet gained little if we countenance a political intolerance as despotic, as wicked, and capable of as bitter and bloody persecutions. During the throes and convulsions of the ancient world, during the agonizing spasms of infuriated man, seeking through blood and slaughter his long-lost liberty, it was not wonderful that the agitation of the billows should reach even this distant and peaceful shore; that this should be more felt and feared by some and less by others, and should divide opinions as to measures of safety. But every difference of opinion is not a difference of principle. We have called by different names brethren of the same principle. We are all Republicans, we are all Federalists. If there be any among us who would wish to dissolve this Union or to change its republican form, let them stand undisturbed as monuments of the safety with which error of opinion may be tolerated where reason is left free to combat it. I know, indeed, that some honest men fear that a republican government can not be strong, that this Government is not strong enough; but would the honest patriot, in the full tide of successful experiment, abandon a government which has so far kept us free and firm on the theoretic and visionary fear that this Government, the world's best hope, may by possibility want energy to preserve itself? I trust not. I believe this, on the contrary, the strongest Government on earth. I believe it the only one where every man, at the call of the law, would fly to the standard of the law, and would meet invasions of the public order as his own personal concern. Sometimes it is said that man can not be trusted with the government of himself. Can he, then, be trusted with the government of others? Or have we found angels in the forms of kings to govern him? Let history answer this question.

Let us, then, with courage and confidence pursue our own Federal and Republican principles, our attachment to union and representative government. Kindly separated by nature and a wide ocean from the exterminating havoc of one quarter of the globe; too high-minded to endure the degradations of the others; possessing a chosen country, with room enough for our descendants to the thousandth and thousandth generation; entertaining a due sense of our equal right to the use of our own faculties, to the acquisitions of our own industry, to honor and confidence from our fellow-citizens, resulting not from birth, but from our actions and their sense of them; enlightened by a benign religion, professed, indeed, and practiced in various forms, yet all of them inculcating honesty, truth, temperance, gratitude, and the love of man; acknowledging and adoring an overruling Providence, which by all its dispensations proves that it delights in the happiness of man here and his greater happiness hereafter—with all these blessings, what more is necessary to make us a happy and a prosperous people? Still one thing more, fellowcitizens—a wise and frugal Government, which shall restrain men from injuring one another, shall leave them otherwise free to regulate their own pursuits of industry and improvement, and shall not take from the mouth of labor the bread it has earned. This is the sum of good government, and this is necessary to close the circle of our felicities.

About to enter, fellow-citizens, on the exercise of duties which comprehend everything dear and valuable to you, it is proper you should understand what I deem the essential principles of our Government, and consequently those which ought to shape its Administration. I will compress them within the narrowest compass they will bear, stating the general principle, but not all its limitations. Equal and exact justice to all men, of whatever state or persuasion, religious or political; peace, commerce, and honest friendship with all nations, entangling alliances with none; the support of the State governments in all their rights, as the most competent administrations for our domestic concerns and the surest bulwark against antirepublican tendencies; the preservation of the General Government in its whole constitutional vigor, as the sheet anchor of our peace at home and safety abroad; a jealous care of the right of election by the people—a mild and safe corrective of abuses which are lopped by the sword of revolution where peaceable remedies are unprovided; absolute acquiescence in the decisions of the majority, the vital principle of republics, from which is no appeal but to force, the vital principle and immediate parent of despotism; a well-disciplined militia, our best reliance in peace and for the first moments of war, till regulars may relieve them; the supremacy of the civil over the military authority; economy in the public expense, that labor may be lightly burthened; the honest payment of our debts and sacred preservation of the public faith; encouragement of agriculture, and of commerce as its handmaid; the diffusion of information and arraignment of all abuses at the bar of the public reason; freedom of religion; freedom of the press, and freedom of person under the protection of the habeas corpus, and trial by juries impartially selected. These principles form the bright constellation which has gone before us and guided our steps through an age of revolution and reformation. The wisdom of our sages and blood of our heroes have been devoted to their attainment. They should be the creed of our political faith, the text of civic instruction, the touchstone by which to try the services of those we trust; and should we wander from them in moments of error or of alarm, let us hasten to retrace our steps and to regain the road which alone leads to peace, liberty, and safety.

I repair, then, fellow-citizens, to the post you have assigned me. With experience enough in subordinate offices to have seen the difficulties of this the greatest of all, I have learnt to expect that it will rarely fall to the lot of imperfect man to retire from this station with the reputation and the favor which bring him into it. Without pretentions to that high confidence you reposed in our first and greatest revolutionary character, whose preeminent services had entitled him to the first place in his country's love and destined for him the fairest page in the volume of faithful history, I ask so much confidence only as may give firmness and effect to the legal administration of your affairs. I shall often go wrong through defect of judgment. When right, I shall often be thought wrong by those whose positions will not command a view of the whole ground. I ask your indulgence for my own errors, which will never be intentional, and your support against the errors of others, who may condemn what they would not if seen in all its parts. The approbation implied by your suffrage is a great consolation to me for the past, and my future solicitude will be to retain the good opinion of those who have bestowed it in advance, to conciliate that of others by doing them all the good in my power, and to be instrumental to the happiness and freedom of all.

Relying, then, on the patronage of your good will, I advance with obedience to the work, ready to retire from it whenever you become sensible how much better choice it is in your power to make. And may that Infinite Power which rules the destinies of the universe lead our councils to what is best, and give them a favorable issue for your peace and prosperity.

AS REGARDS PATRIOTISM
Mark Twain

It is agreed, in this country, that if a man can arrange his religion so that it perfectly satisfies his conscience, it is not incumbent upon him to care whether the arrangement is satisfactory to anyone else or not.

In Austria and some other countries this is not the case. There the state arranges a man's religion for him, he has no voice in it himself.

Patriotism is merely a religion—love of country, worship of country, devotion to the country's flag and honor and welfare.

In absolute monarchies it is furnished from the throne, cut and dried, to the subject; in England and America it is furnished, cut and dried, to the citizen by the politician and the newspaper.

The newspaper-and-politician-manufactured Patriot often gags in private over his dose; but he takes it, and keeps it on his stomach the best he can. Blessed are the meek.

Sometimes, in the beginning of an insane shabby political upheaval, he is strongly moved to revolt, but he doesn't do it—he knows better. He knows that his maker would find it out—the maker of his Patriotism, the windy and incoherent six-dollar subeditor of his village newspaper—and would bray out in print and call him a Traitor. And how dreadful that would be. It makes him tuck his tail between his legs and shiver. We all know—the reader knows it quite well—that two or three years ago nine tenths of the human tails in England and America performed just that act. Which is to say, nine tenths of the Patriots in England and America turned traitor to keep from being called traitor. Isn't it true? You know it to be true. Isn't it curious?

Yet it was not a thing to be very seriously ashamed of. A man can seldom—very, very seldom—fight a winning fight against his training; the odds are too heavy. For many a year—perhaps always—the training of the two nations had been dead against independence in political thought, persistently inhospitable

From Europe and Elsewhere *by Mark Twain. Copyright 1923, 1951 by The Mark Twain Company. Reprinted by permission of Harper & Row, Publishers, Inc.*

toward patriotism manufactured on a man's own premises, Patriotism reasoned out in the man's own head and fire-assayed and tested and proved in his own conscience. The resulting Patriotism was a shop-worn product procured at second hand. The Patriot did not know just how or when or where he got his opinions, neither did he care, so long as he was with what seemed the majority—which was the main thing, the safe thing, the comfortable thing. Does the reader believe he knows three men who have actual reasons for their pattern of Patriotism—and can furnish them? Let him not examine, unless he wants to be disappointed. He will be likely to find that his men got their Patriotism at the public trough, and had no hand in its preparation themselves.

Training does wonderful things. It moved the people of this country to oppose the Mexican War; then moved them to fall in with what they supposed was the opinion of the majority—majority Patriotism is the customary Patriotism—and go down there and fight. Before the Civil War it made the North indifferent to slavery and friendly to the slave interest; in that interest it made Massachusetts hostile to the American flag, and she would not allow it to be hoisted on her State House—in her eyes it was the flag of a faction. Then by and by, training swung Massachusetts the other way, and she went raging South to fight under that very flag and against that aforetime protected interest of hers.

There is nothing that training cannot do. Nothing is above its reach or below it. It can turn bad morals to good, good morals to bad; it can destroy principles, it can recreate them; it can debase angels to men and lift men to angelship. And it can do any one of these miracles in a year—even in six months.

Then men can be trained to manufacture their own Patriotism. They can be trained to labor it out in their own heads and hearts and in the privacy and independence of their own premises. It can train them to stop taking it by command, as the Austrian takes his religion.

THE WAR PRAYER
Mark Twain

It was a time of great and exalting excitement. The country was up in arms, the war was on, in every breast burned the holy fire of patriotism; the drums were beating, the bands playing, the toy pistols popping, the bunched firecrackers hissing and spluttering; on every hand and far down the receding and fading spread of roofs and balconies a fluttering wilderness of flags flashed in the sun; daily the young volunteers marched down the wide avenue gay and fine in their new uniforms, the proud fathers and mothers and sisters and sweethearts cheering them with voices choked with happy emotion as they swung by; nightly the packed mass meetings listened, panting, to patriot oratory which stirred the deepest deeps of their hearts, and which they interrupted at briefest intervals with cyclones of applause, the tears running down their cheeks the while; in the churches the pastors preached devotion to flag and country, and invoked the God of Battles, beseeching His aid in our good cause in outpouring of fervid eloquence which moved every listener. It was indeed a glad and gracious time, and the half dozen rash spirits that ventured to disapprove of the war and cast a doubt upon its righteousness straightway got such a stern and angry warning that for their personal safety's sake they quickly shrank out of sight and offended no more in that way.

Sunday morning came—next day the battalions would leave for the front; the church was filled; the volunteers were there, their young faces alight with martial dreams—visions of the stern advance, the gathering momentum, the rushing charge, the flashing sabers, the flight of the foe, the tumult, the enveloping smoke, the fierce purusit, the surrender!—them home from the war, bronzed heroes, welcomed, adored, submerged in golden seas of glory! With the volunteers sat their dear ones, proud, happy, and envied by the neighbors and friends who had no sons and brothers to send forth to the field of honor, there to win for the flag, or, failing, die the noblest of noble deaths. The service proceeded; a war chapter from the Old Testament was read; the first prayer was said; it was followed by an organ burst that shook the building, and with one impulse the house rose, with glowing eyes and beating hearts, and poured out that tremendous invocation—

God the all-terrible!   Thou who ordainest,
Thunder thy clarion and lightning thy sword!

Then came the "long" prayer. None could remember the like of it for passionate pleading and moving and beautiful language. The burden of its supplication was, that an ever-merciful and benignant Father of us all would watch over our noble young soldiers, and aid, comfort, and encourage them in their patriotic work; bless them, shield them in the day of battle and the hour of peril, bear them in His mighty hand, make them strong and confident, invincible in the bloody onset; help them to crush the foe, grant to them and to their flag and country imperishable honor and glory—

An aged stranger entered and moved with slow and noiseless step up the main aisle, his eyes fixed upon the minister, his long body clothed in a robe that reached to his feet, his head bare, his white hair descending in a frothy cataract to his shoulders, his seamy face unnaturally pale, pale even to ghastliness. With all eyes following him and wondering, he made his silent way; without pausing, he ascended to the preacher's side and stood there, waiting. With shut lids the preacher, unconscious of his presence, continued his moving prayer, and at last finished it with the words, uttered in fervent appeal, "Bless our arms, grant us the victory, O Lord our God, Father and Protector of our land and flag!"

The stranger touched his arm, motioned him to step aside—which the startled minister did—and took his place. During some moments he surveyed the spellbound audience with solemn eyes, in which burned an uncanny light; then in a deep voice he said:

"I come from the Throne—bearing a message from Almighty God!" The words smote the house with a shock; if the stranger perceived it he gave no attention. "He has heard the prayer of His servant your shepherd, and will grant it if such shall be your desire after I, His messenger, shall have explained to you its import—that is to say, its full import. For it is like unto many of the prayers of men, in that it asks for more than he who utters it is aware of—except he pause and think.

"God's servant and yours has prayed his prayer. Has he paused and taken thought? Is it one prayer? No, it is two—one uttered, the other not. Both have reached the ear of Him Who heareth all supplications, the spoken and the unspoken. Ponder this—keep it in mind. If you would beseech a blessing upon yourself, beware! lest without intent you invoke a curse upon a neighbor at the same time. If you pray for the blessing of rain upon your crop which needs it, by that act you are possibly praying for a curse upon some neighbor's crop which may not need rain and can be injured by it.

"You have heard your servant's prayer—the uttered part of it. I am commissioned of God to put into words the other part of it—that part which the pastor—and also you in your hearts—fervently prayed silently. And ignorantly and unthinkingly? God grant that it was so! You heard these words: 'Grant us the victory, O Lord our God!' That is sufficient. The *whole* of the uttered prayer is compact into those pregnant words. Elaborations were not necessary. When you have prayed for victory you have prayed for many unmentioned results which follow victory—*must* follow it, cannot help but follow it. Upon the listening spirit of God the Father fell also the unspoken part of the prayer. He commandeth me to put it into words. Listen!

"O Lord our Father, our young patriots, idols of our hearts, go forth to battle—be Thou near them! With them—in spirit—we also go forth from the sweet peace of our beloved firesides to smite the foe. O Lord our God, help us to tear their soldiers to bloody shreds with our shells; help us to cover their smiling fields with the pale forms of their patriot dead; help us to drown the thunder of the guns with the shrieks of their wounded, writhing in pain; help us to lay waste their humble homes with a hurricane of fire; help us to wring the hearts of their unoffending widows with unavailing grief; help us to turn them out roofless with their little children to wander unfriended the wastes of their desolated land in rags and hunger and thirst, sports of the sun flames of summer and the icy winds of winter, broken in spirit, worn with travail, imploring Thee for the refuge of the grave and denied it—for our sakes who adore Thee, Lord, blast their hopes, blight their lives, protract their bitter pilgrimage, make heavy their steps, water their way with the tears, stain the white snow with the blood of their wounded feet! We ask it, in the spirit of love, of Him Who is the Source of Love, and Who is the ever-faithful refuge and friend of all that are sore beset and seek His aid with humble and contrite hearts. Amen."

(After a pause.) "Ye have prayed it; if ye still desire it, speak! The messenger of the Most High waits."

It was believed afterward that the man was a lunatic, because there was no sense in what he said.

THE RIGHT TO PRIVACY
Louis D. Brandeis and Samuel D. Warren

That the individual shall have full protection in person and in property is a principle as old as the common law; but it has been found necessary from time to time to define anew the exact nature and extent of such protection. Political, social and economic changes entail the recognition of new rights, and the common law, in its eternal youth, grows to meet the demands of society. Thus, in very early times, the law gave a remedy only for physical interference with life and property, for trespasses *vi et armis.* Then the "right to life" served only to protect the subject from battery in its various forms; liberty meant freedom from actual restraint; and the right to property secured to the individual his lands and his cattle. Latter, there came a recognition of man's spiritual nature, of his feelings and his intellect. Gradually the scope of these legal rights broadened; and now the right to life has come to mean the right to enjoy life,— the right to be let alone; the right to liberty secures the exercise of extensive civil privileges; and the term "property" has grown to comprise every form of possession—intangible, as well as tangible. . . .

This development of the law was inevitable. The intense intellectual and emotional life, and the heightening of sensations which came with the advance of civilization, made it clear to men that only a part of the pain, pleasure, and profit of life lay in physical things. Thoughts, emotions, and sensations demanded legal recognition, and the beautiful capacity for growth which characterizes the common law enabled the judges to afford the requisite protection, without the interposition of the legislature.

Recent inventions and business methods call attention to the next step which must be taken for the protection of the person, and for securing to the individual what Judge Cooley calls the right "to be let alone." Instantaneous photographs and newspaper enterprise have invaded the sacred precincts of private and domestic life; and numerous mechanical devices threaten to make good the prediction that "what is whispered in the closet shall be proclaimed from the house-tops. . . ."

From Harvard Law Review, *1890.*

It is like the right not to be assaulted or beaten, the right not to be imprisoned, the right not to be maliciously prosecuted, the right not to be defamed. In each of these rights, as indeed in all other rights recognized by the law, there inheres the quality of being owned or possessed—and (as that is the distinguishing attribute of property) there may be some propriety in speaking of those rights as property. But, obviously, they bear little resemblance to what is ordinarily comprehended under that term. The principle which protects personal writings and all other personal productions, not against theft and physical appropriation, but against publicaiton in any form, is in reality not the principle of private property, but that of an inviolate personality. . . .

To determine in advance of experience the exact line at which the dignity and convenience of the individual must yield to the demands of the public welfare or of private justice would be a difficult task; but the more general rules are furnished by the legal analogies already developed in the law of slander and libel, and in the law of literary and artistic property.

1. The right to privacy does not prohibit any publication of matter which is of public or general interest.

In determining the scope of this rule, aid would be afforded by the analogy, in the law of libel and slander, of cases which deal with the qualified privilege of comment and criticism on matters of public and general interest. There are of course difficulties in applying such a rule; but they are inherent in the subject-matter, and are certainly no greater than those which exist in many other branches of the law,—for instance, in that large class of cases in which the reasonableness or unreasonableness of an act is made the test of liability. The design of the law must be to protect those persons with whose affairs the community has no legitimate concern, from being dragged into an undesirable and undesired publicity and to protect all persons, whatsoever; their position or station, from having matters which thy may properly prefer to keep private, made public against their will. It is the unwarranted invasion of individual privacy which is reprehended, and to be, so far as possible, prevented. The distinction, however, noted in the above statement is obvious and fundamental. There are persons who may reasonably claim as a right, protection from the notoriety entailed by being made the victims of journalistic enterprise. There are others who, in varying degrees, have renounced the right to live their lives screened from public observation. Matters which men of the first class may justly contend, concern themselves alone, may in those of the second be the subject of legitimate interest to their fellow-citizens. Peculiarities of manner and person, which in the ordinary individual should be free from comment, may acquire a public importance, if found in a candidate for political office. Some further discrimination is necessary, therefore, than to class facts or deeds as public or private according to a standard to be applied to the fact or deed *per se*. To publish of a modest and retiring individual that he suffers from an impediment in his speech or that he cannot spell correctly, is an unwarranted, if not an unexampled, infringement of his rights, while to state and comment on the same characteristics found in a would-be congressman could not be regarded as beyond the pale of propriety.

The general object in view is to protect the privacy of private life, and to whatever degree and in whatever connection a man's life has ceased to be private, before the publication under consideration has been made, to that extent the protection is to be withdrawn. Since, then, the propriety of publishing the very same facts may depend wholly upon the person concerning whom they are published, no fixed formula can be used to prohibit obnoxious publications. Any rule of liability adopted must have in it an elasticity which shall take account of the varying circumstances of each case,—a necessity which unfortunately renders such a doctrine not only more difficult of application, but also to a certain extent uncertain in its operation and easily rendered abortive. Besides, it is only the more flagrant breaches of decency and propriety that could in practice be reached, and it is not perhaps desirable even to attempt to repress everything which the nicest taste and keenest sense of the respect due to private life would condemn.

In general, then, the matters of which the publication should be repressed may be described as those which concern the private life, habits, acts, and relations of an individual, and have no legitimate connection with his fitness for a public office which he seeks or for which he is suggested, or for any public or quasi public position which he seeks or for which he is suggested, and have no legitimate relation to or bearing upon any act done by him in a public or quasi public capacity. The foregoing is not designed as a wholly accurate or exhaustive definition, since that which must ultimately in a vast number of cases become a question of individual judgment and opinion is incapable of such definition; but it is an attempt to indicate broadly the class of matters referred to. Some things all men alike are entitled to keep from popular curiosity, whether in public life or not, while others are only private because the persons concerned have not assumed a position which makes their doings legitimate matters of public investigation.

2. The right to privacy does not prohibit the communication of any matter, though in its nature private, when the publication is made under circumstances which would render it a privileged communication according to the law of slander and libel.

Under this rule, the right to privacy is not invaded by any publication made in a court of justice, in legislative bodies, or the committees of those bodies; in municipal assemblies, or the committees of such assemblies, or practically by any communication made in any other public body, municipal or parochial, or in any body quasi public, like the large voluntary associations formed for almost every purose of benevolence, business, or other general interest; and (at least in many jurisdictions) reports of any such proceedings would in some measure be accorded a like privilege. Nor would the rule prohibit any publication made by one in the discharge of some public or private duty, whether legal or moral, or in conduct of one's own affairs, in matters where his own interest is concerned.

3. The law would probably not grant any redress for the invasion of privacy by oral publication in the absence of special damage.

The same reasons exist for distinguishing between oral and written publication of private matters, as is afforded in the law of defamation by the restricted liability for slander as compared with the liability for libel. The injury resulting from such oral communications would ordinarily be so trifling that the law might well, in the interest of free speech, disregard it altogether.

4. The right to privacy ceases upon the publication of the facts by the individual, or with his consent.

This is but another application of the rule which has become familiar in the law of literary and artistic property. The cases there decided established also what should be deemed a publication,—the important principle in this connection being that a private communication of circulation for a registered purpose is not a publication within the meaning of the law.

5. The truth of the matter published does not afford a defence. Obviously this branch of the law should have no concern with the truth of falsehood of the matters published. It is not for injury to the individual's character that redress or prevention is sought, but for injury to the right of privacy. For the former, the law of slander and libel provides perhaps a sufficient safeguard. The latter implies the right not merely to prevent inaccurate portrayal of private life, but to prevent its being depicted at all.

6. The absence of "malice" in the publisher does not afford a defence.

Personal ill-will is not an ingredient of the offence, any more than in an ordinary case of trespass to person or to property. Such malice is never necessary to be shown in an action for libel or slander at common law, except in rebuttal of some defence, *e.g.*, that the occasion rendered the communication privileged, or, under the statutes in this State and elsewhere, that the statement complained of was true. The invasion of the privacy that is to be protected is equally complete and equally injurious, whether the motives by which the speaker or writer was actuated are, taken by themselves, culpable or not; just as the damage to character, and to some extent the tendency to provoke a breach of the peace, is equally the result of defamation without regard to the motives leading to its publication. Viewed as a wrong to the individual, this rule is the same pervading the whole law of torts, by which one is held responsible for his intentional acts, even though they are committed with no sinister intent; and viewed as a wrong to society, it is the same principle adopted in a large category of statutory offences.

The remedies for an invasion of the right of privacy are also suggested by those administered in the law of defamation, and in the law of literary and artistic property, namely:—

1. An action of tort for damages in all cases. Even in the absence of special damages, substantial compensation could be allowed for injury to feelings as in the action of slander and libel.
2. An injunction, in perhaps a very limited class of cases.

It would doubtless be desirable that the privacy of the individual should receive the added protection of the criminal law, but for this, legislation would be required. Perhaps it would be deemed proper to bring the criminal liability for such publication within narrower limits; but that the community has an interest in preventing such invasions of privacy, sufficiently strong to justify the introduction of such a remedy, cannot be doubted. Still, the protection of society must come mainly through a recognition of the rights of the individual. Each man is responsible for his own acts and omissions only. If he condones what he reprobates, with a weapon at hand equal to his defence, he is responsible for the results. If he resists, public opinion will rally to his support. Has he then such a weapon? It is believed that the common law provides him with one, forged in the slow fire of the centuries, and to-day fitly tempered to his hand. The common law has always recognized a man's house as his castle, impregnable, often, even to its own officers engaged in the execution of its commands. Shall the courts thus close the front entrance to constituted authority, and open wide the back door to idle or prurient curiosity?

PLANNING AND DEMOCRACY
Friedrich Hayek

The common features of all collectivist systems may be described, in a phrase ever dear to socialists of all schools, as the deliberate organization of the labors of society for a definite social goal. That our present society lacks such "conscious" direction toward a single aim, that its activities are guided by the whims and fancies of irresponsible individuals, has always been one of the main complaints of its socialist critics.

In many ways this puts the basic issue very clearly. And it directs us at once to the point where the conflict arises between individual freedom and collectivism. The various kinds of collectivism, communism, fascism, etc., differ among themselves in the nature of the goal toward which they want to direct the efforts of society. But they all differ from liberalism and individualism in wanting to organize the whole of society and all its resources for this

Reprinted from Friedrich Hayek, "Planning and Democracy" in The Road to Serfdom (Chicago: University of Chicago Press, 1944), Pp. 56–62, 68–71, by permission of the publisher and author.

unitary end and in refusing to recognize autonomous spheres in which the ends of the individual are supreme. In short, they are totalitarian in the true sense of this new word which we have adopted to describe the unexpected but nevertheless inseparable manifestations of what in theory we call collectivism.

The "social goal," or "common purpose," for which society is to be organized is usually vaguely described as the "common good," the "general welfare," or the "general interest." It does not need much reflection to see that these terms have no sufficiently definite meaning to determine a particular course of action. The welfare and the happiness of millions cannot be measured on a single scale of less and more. The welfare of a people, like the happiness of a man, depends on a great many things that can be provided in an infinite variety of combinations. It cannot be adequately expressed as a single end, but only as a hierarchy of ends, a comprehensive scale of values in which every need of every person is given its place. To direct all our activities according to a single plan presupposes that every one of our needs is given its rank in an order of values which must be complete enough to make it possible to decide among all the different courses which the planner has to choose. It presupposes, in short, the existence of a complete ethical code in which all the different human values are allotted their due place.

The conception of a complete ethical code is unfamiliar, and it requires some effort of imagination to see what it involves. We are not in the habit of thinking of moral codes as more or less complete. The fact that we are constantly choosing between different values without a social code prescribing how we ought to choose does not surprise us and does not suggest to us that our moral code is incomplete. In our society there is neither occasion nor reason why people should develop common views about what should be done in such situations. But where all the means to be used are the property of society and are to be used in the name of society according to a unitary plan, a "social" view about what ought to be done must guide all decisions. In such a world we should soon find that our moral code is full of gaps.

We are not concerned here with the question whether it would be desirable to have such a complete ethical code. It may merely be pointed out that up to the present the growth of civilization has been accompanied by a steady diminution of the sphere in which individual actions are bound by fixed rules. The rules of which our common moral code consists have progressively become fewer and more general in character. From the primitive man, who was bound by an elaborate ritual in almost every one of his daily activities, who was limited by innumerable taboos, and who could scarcely conceive of doing things in a way different from his fellows, morals have more and more tended to become merely limits circumscribing the sphere within which the individual could behave as he liked. The adoption of a common ethical code comprehensive enough to determine a unitary economic plan would mean a complete reversal of this tendency.

The essential point for us is that no such complete ethical code exists. This attempt to direct all economic activity according to a single plan would rasie innumerable questions to which the answer could be provided only by a moral rule, but to which existing morals have no answer and where there exists no agreed view on what ought to be done. People will have either no definite veiws or conflicting views on such questions, because in the free society in which we have lived there has been no occasion to think about them and still less to form common opinions about them.

Not only do we not possess such an all-inclusive scale of values: it would be impossible for any mind to comprehend the infinite variety of different needs of different people which compete for the available resources and to attach a definite weight to each. For our problem it is of minor importance whether the ends for which any person cares comprehend only his own individual needs, or whether they include the needs of his closer or even those of his more distant fellows—that is, whether he is egoistic or altruistic in the ordinary senses of these words. The point which is so important is the basic fact that it is impossible for any many to survey more than a limited field, to be aware of the urgency of more than a limited number of needs. Whether his interests center round his own physical needs, or whether he takes a warm interest in the welfare of every human being he knows, the ends about which he can be concerned will always be only an infinitesimal fraction of the needs of all men.

This is the fundamental fact on which the whole philosophy of individualism is based. It does not assume, as is often asserted, that man is egoistic or selfish or ought to be. It merely starts from the indisputable fact that the limits of our powers of imagination make it impossible to include in our scale of values more than a sector of the needs of the whole society, and that, since, strictly speaking, scales of value can exist only in individual minds, nothing but partial scales of values exist—scales which are inevitably different and often inconsistent with each other. From this the individualist concludes that the individuals should be allowed, within definied limits, to follow their own values and preferences rather than somebody else's; that within these spheres the individual's system of ends should be supreme and not subject to any dictation by others. It is this recognition of the individual as the ultimate judge of his ends, the belief that as far as possible his own veiws ought to govern his actions, that forms the essence of the individualist position.

This view does not, of course, exclude the recognition of social ends, or rather of a coincidence of individual ends which makes it advisable for men to combine for their pursuit. But it limits such common action to the instances where individual views concide; what are called "social ends" are for it merely identical ends of many individuals—or ends to the achievement of which individuals are willing to contribute in return for the assistance they receive in the satisfaction of their own desires. Common action is thus limited to the fields where people agree on common ends. Very frequently these common ends will not be ultimate ends to the individuals but means which different persons can use for different purposes. In fact, people are most likely to agree on common action where the common end is not an ultimate end to them but a means capable of serving a great variety of purposes.

When individuals combine in a joint effort to realize ends they have in common, the organizations, like the state, that they form for this purpose are given their own system of ends and their own means. But any organization thus formed remains one "person" among others, in the case of the state much more powerful than any of the others, it is true, yet still with its separate and limited sphere in which alone its ends are supreme. The limits of this sphere are determined by the extent to which the individuals agree on particular ends; and the probability that they will agree on a particular course of action necessarily decreases as the scope of such action extends. There are certain functions of the state on the exercise of whch there will be practical unanimity among its citizens; there will be others on which there will be agreement of a substantial majority; and so on, until we come to fields where, although each individual might wish the state to act in some way, there will be almost as many views about what the government should do as there are different people.

We can rely on voluntary agreement to guide the action of the state only so long as it is confined to spheres where agreement exists. But not only when the state undertakes direct control in fields where there is no such agreement is it bound to supress individual freedom. We can unfortunately not indefinitely extend the sphere of common action and still leave the individual free in his own sphere. Once the communal sector, in which the state controls all the means, exceeds a certain proportion of the whole, the effects of its actions dominate the whole system. Although the state controls directly the use of only a large part of the available resources, the effects of its decisions on the remaining part of the economic system become so great that indirectly it controls almost everything. Where, as was, for example, true in Germany as early as 1928, the central and local authorities directly control the use of more than half the national income (according to an official German estimate then, 53 per cent), they control indirectly almost the whole economic life of the nation. There is, then, scarcely an individual end which is not dependent for its achievement on the action of the state, and the "social scale of values" which guides the state's action must embrace practically all individual ends.

It is not difficult to see what must be the consequences when democracy embarks upon a course of planning which in its execution requires more agreement than in fact exists. The people may have agreed on adopting a system of directed economy because they have been convinced that it will produce great prosperity. In the discussions leading to the decision, the goal of planning will have been described by some such term as "common welfare," which only conceals the absence of real agreement on the ends of planning. Agreement will in fact exist only on the mechanism to be used. But it is a mechanism which can be used only for a common end; and the question of the precise goal toward which all activity is to be directed will arise as soon as the executive power has to translate the demand for a single plan into a particular plan. Then it will appear that the agreement on the desirability of planning is not supported by agreement on the ends the plan is to serve. The effect of the people's agreeing that there must be central planning, without agreeing on the ends, will be rather as if a group of people were to commit themselves to take a journey together without agreeing where they want to go with the result that they may all have to make a journey which most of them do not want at all. That planning creates a situation in which it is necessary for us to agree on a much larger number of topics than we have been used to, and that in a planned system we cannot confine collective action to the tasks on which we can agree but are forced to produce agreement on everything in order that any action can be taken at all, is one of the features which contributes more than most to determining the character of a planned system.

It may be the unanimously expressed will of the people that its parliament should prepare a comprehensive economic plan, yet neither the people nor its representatives need therefore be able to agree on any particular plan. The inability of democratic assemblies to carry out what seems to be a clear mandate of the people will inevitably cause dissatisfaction with democratic institutions. Parliaments come to be regarded as ineffective "talking shops," unable or incompetent to carry out the tasks for which they have been chosen. The conviction grows that if efficient planning is to be done, the direction must be "taken out of politics" and placed in the hands of experts—permanent officials or independent autonomous bodies. . . .

The argument by which the planners usually try to reconcile us with this development is that, so long as democracy retains ultimate control, the essentials of democracy are not affected. Thus Karl Mannheim writes:

"The only [sic] way in which a planned society differs from that of the nineteenth century is that more and more spheres of social life, and ultimately each and all of them, are subjected to state control. But if a few controls can be held in check by parliamentary sovereignty, so can many. . . . In a democratic state sovereignty can be boundlessly strengthened by plenary powers without renouncing democratic control."

This belief overlooks a vital distinction. Parliament can, of course, control the execution of tasks where it can give definite directions, where it has first agreed on the aim and merely delegates the working-out of the detail. The situation is entirely different when the reason for the delegation is that there no real agreement on the ends, when the body charged with the planning has to choose between ends of whose conflict parliament is not even aware, and when the most that can be done is to present to it a plan whch has to be accepted or rejected as a whole. There may and probably will be criticism; but as no majority can agree on an alternative plan, and the parts objected to can almost always be represented as essential parts of the whole, it will remain quite ineffective. Parliamentary discussion may be retained as a useful safety valve and even more as a convenient medium through which the official answers to complaints are disseminated. It may even prevent some flagrant abuses and successfully insist on particular shortcomings being remedied. But it cannot direct. It will at best be reduced to choosing the persons who are to have practically absolute power. The whole system will tend toward the plebiscitarian dictatorship in which the head of the government is from time to time confirmed in his position by popular vote, but where he has all the powers at his command to make certain that the vote will go in the direction he desires.

It is the price of democracy that the possibilities of conscious control are restricted to the fields where true agreement exists and that in some fields things must be left to chance. But in a society which for its functioning depends on central planning this control cannot be made dependent on a majority's being able to agree; it will often be necessary that the will of a small minority be imposed upon the people, because this minority will be the largest group able to agree among themselves on the question at issue. Democratic government has worked successfully where, and so long as, the functions of government were, by a widely accepted creed, restricted to fields where agreement among a majority could be achieved by free discussion; and it is the great merit of the liberal creed that it reduced the range of subjects on which agreement was necessary to one on which it was likely to exist in a society of free discussion; and it is the great merit of the liberal creed that it reduced the range of subjects on which agreement was necessary to one on which it was likely to exist in a society of free men. It is now often said that democracy will not tolerate "capitalism." If "capitalism" means here a competitive system based on free disposal over private property, it is far more important to realize that only within this system is democracy possible. When it becomes dominated by a collectivist creed, democracy will inevitably destroy itself.

We have no intention, however, of making a fetish of democracy. It may well be true that our generation talks and thinks too much of democracy and too little of the values which it serves. It cannot be said of democracy, as Lord Acton truly said of liberty, that it "is not a means to a higher political end. It is itself the highest political end. It is not for the sake of a good public administration that it is required, but for the security in the pursuit of the highest objects of a civil society, and of private life." Democracy is essentially a means, a utilitarian device for safeguarding internal peace and individual freedom. As such it is by no means infallible or certain. Nor must we forget that there has often been much more cultural and spiritual freedom under an autocratic rule than under some democracies—and it is at least conceivable that under the government of a very homogeneous and doctrinaire majority democratic government might be as oppressive as the worst dictatorship. Our point, however, is not that dictatorship must inevitably extirpate freedom but rather that planning leads to dictatorship because dictatorship is the most effective instrument of coercion and the enforcement of ideals and, as such, essential if central planning on a large scale is to be possible. The clash between planning and democracy arises simply from the fact that the latter is an obstacle to the suppression of freedom which the direction of economic activity requires. But in so far as democracy ceases to be a guaranty of individual freedom, it may well persist in some form under a totalitarin regime. A true "dictatorship of the proletariat," even if democratic in form, if it undertook centrally to direct the economic system, would probably destroy personal freedom as completely as any autocarcy has ever done.

The fashionable concentration on democracy as the main value threatened is not without danger. It is largely responsible for the misleading and unfounded belief that, so long as the ultimate source of power is the will of the majority, the power cannot be arbitary. The false assurance which many people derive from this belief is an important cause of the general unawareness of the dangers which we face. There is no justification for the belief that, so long as power is conferred by democratic procedure, it cannot be arbitrary; the contrast suggested by this statement is altogether false: it is not the source but the limitation of power which prevents it from being arbitrary, but it does not do so by its mere existence. If democracy resolves on a task which necessarily involves the use of power which cannot be guided by fixed rules, it must become arbitary power.

BIBLIOGRAPHICAL NOTE

The concept of toleration is dicussed in Benjamin Barber, *Superman and Common Men,* and Robert Paul Wolff, *The Poverty of Liberalism.* There have been many attempts to discuss toleration and civil liberties within a legal framework. Some of the best discussions of the classical liberal formulation on toleration are in the opinions of American jurists such as Oliver Wendell Holmes, Louis Brandeis, Benjamin Cardozo, Learned Hand, and Hugo Black. Some interesting scholarly studies are Carl Becker, *Freedom and Responsibility in the American Way of Life;* Zechariah Chaffee, *Free Speech in the United States;* Thomas I. Emerson, *Toward a General Theory of the First Amendment;* Leonard Levy, *Legacy of Suppression;* Alexander Meiklejohn, *Free Speech and Its Relation to Self-Government.* Criticisms of this approach are Walter Berns, *Freedom, Virtue and the First Amendment;* Harry Clor, *Obscenity and Public Morality;* and Abe Fortas, *Concerning Dissent and Civil Disobedience.*

The discussions on the proper domains of liberty are immense. One essential analytical discussion of liberty is Isaiah Berlin, *Two Concepts of Liberty.* Also important are Rousseau's *The Social Contract* and his *Discourses,* and John Stuart Mill's famous tract, *On Liberty.* Economic liberty is the central concern of most American conservatives; one popular work is William Buckley's *Up From Liberalism.* A more trenchant doctrine of laissez faire can be found in the numerous writings of Ayn Rand. The changing nature of the American economic system is examined in the works of John Kenneth Galbraith, especially his *New Industrial State.*

2. The Illusions of "Free" Men

Like all nations, the United States has engaged in the habit of self-congratulation. From the Founding Fathers to the present, Americans have emphasized their historical uniqueness and predestined good fortune. Indeed, we have even praised our way of life as being "the last great hope of mankind." The selections in this section force us to turn inward and reexamine our most treasured assumptions.

The first selection comes from the writings of Frederick Douglass. After being a slave for twenty-one years, Douglass escaped and became the best known Black orator during the Civil War period. The speech reprinted here was originally given in Rochester, New York, on the 5th of July, 1852.

With an eloquence rarely matched, Douglass sets forth his indictment of white America. In contrast to the usual pageantry and rhetoric of Independence Day, Douglass describes the plight of black slaves in the South. Although the evil of slavery has been abolished, Douglass' criticisms are still relevant today, for they describe what life is like in a country that one can never truly call his own.

The second selection, which is also critical of American political life, is the SDS's Port Huron Statement. This manifesto grew out of the disenchantment and discontent of white, middle-class students with what they see as being the barrenness of the American dream. In addition, the Statement is a critique of American foreign and domestic politicies which the authors contend are a betrayal of our historical ideals. In general, the students attack the illusion that we are what we think we are. We are not, they claim, defenders of freedom nor advocates of self-determination either at home or abroad.

In a different sort of prose, Seymour Martin Lipset comes to grips with an equally important American illusion: that we support liberal values. He finds strong evidence that a substantial number of the working class does not uphold basic liberal values. Instead they accept authoritarianism, political repression, and intolerance as desirable parts of our social life. His findings add further support to the contention made by V. O. Key that democracy is not preserved by the people but by the political elite.

The fourth view is more sweeping and more damaging to our self-image. This is Murray Edelman's contention that American politics is really a form of symbolic reassurance that gives the masses no effective say in the governance of America. Our so-called democratic institutions, our rituals, and our rhetoric are all instruments of deception calculated to mislead the people into thinking that the government is responsive to their wishes. In the long run, these instruments are manipulated by selfish interests and ambitious men who care little for our pretensions about self-government.

The last selection is both a critique and a exhortation. In his famous Letter from Birmingham Jail, Martin Luther King, Jr. documents the ways in which racial injustice and bigotry have been protected by law and custom. And yet with all this, the most eloquent leader of America's most oppressed group pleads for three of the rarest public virtues: reason, forgiveness, and charity.

The America which these selections describe is far different from the self-portrait we are used to. Even if we choose to deny the validity of these criticisms, we are forced to re-examine our basic assumptions and the present characteristics of our political life.

WHAT TO THE SLAVE IS THE FOURTH OF JULY?
Frederick Douglass

Fellow-citizens—Pardon me, and allow me to ask, why am I called upon to speak here to-day? What have I, or those I represent, to do with your national independence? Are the great principles of political freedom and of natural justice, embodied in that Declaration of Independence, extended to us? and am I, therefore, called upon to bring our humble offering to the national altar, and to confess the benefits, and express devout gratitude for the blessings, resulting from your independence to us?

Would to God, both for your sakes and ours, that an affirmative answer could be truthfully returned to these questions! Then would my task be light, and my burden easy and delightful. For who is there so cold that a nation's sympathy could not warm him? Who so obdurate and dead to the claims of gratitude, that would not thankfully acknowledge such priceless benefits? Who so stolid and selfish, that would not give his voice to swell the hallelujahs of a nation's jubilee, when the chains of servitude had been torn from his limbs? I am not that man. In a case like that, the dumb might eloquently speak, and the "lame man leap as an hart."

But, such is not the state of the case. I say it with a sad sense of the disparity between us. I am not included within the pale of this glorious anniversary! Your high independence only reveals the immeasurable distance between us. The blessings in which you this day rejoice, are not enjoyed in common. The rich inheritance of justice, liberty, prosperity, and independence, bequeathed by your fathers, is shared by you, not by me. The sunlight that brought life and healing to you, has brought stripes and death to me. This Fourth of July is *yours,* not *mine.* *You* may rejoice, *I* must mourn. To drag a man in fetters into the grand illuminated temple of liberty, and call upon him to join you in joyous anthems, were inhuman mockery and sacrilegious irony. Do you mean, citizens, to mock me, by asking me to speak to-day? If so, there is a parallel to your conduct. And let me warn you that it is dangerous to copy the example of a nation whose crimes, towering up to heaven, were thrown down by the breath of the Almighty, burying that nation in irrecoverable ruin! I can to-day take up the plaintive lament of a peeled and woe-smitten people.

"By the rivers of Babylon, there we sat down. Yea! we wept when we remembered Zion. We hanged our harps upon the willows in the midst thereof. For there, they that carried us away captive, required of us a song; and they who wasted us required of us mirth, saying, Sing us one of the songs of Zion. How can we sing the Lord's song in a strange land? If I forget thee, O

Jerusalem, let my right hand forget her cunning. If I do not remember thee, let my tongue cleave to the roof of my mouth."

Fellow-citizens, above your national, tumultuous joy, I hear the mournful wail of millions, whose chains, heavy and grievous yesterday, are to-day rendered more intolerable by the jubilant shouts that reach them. If I do forget, if I do not faithfully remember those bleeding children of sorrow this day, "may my right hand forget her cunning, and may my tongue cleave to the roof of my mouth!" To forget them, to pass lightly over their wrongs, and to chime in with the popular theme, would be treason most scandalous and shocking, and would make me a reproach before God and the world. My subject, then, fellow-citizens, is AMERICAN SLAVERY. I shall see this day and its popular characteristics from the slave's point of view. Standing there, identified with the American bondman, making his wrongs mine, I do not hesitate to declare, with all my soul, that the character and conduct of this nation never looked blacker to me than on this Fourth of July. Whether we turn to the declarations of the past, or to the professions of the present, the conduct of the nation seems equally hideous and revolting. America is false to the past, false to the present, and solemnly binds herself to be false to the future. Standing with God and the crushed and bleeding slave on this occasion, I will, in the name of humanity which is outraged, in the name of liberty which is fettered, in the name of the constitution and the bible, which are disregarded and trampled upon, dare to call in question and to denounce, with all the emphasis I can command, everything that serves to perpetuate slavery—the great sin and shame of America! "I will not equivocate; I will not excuse;" I will use the severest language I can command; and yet not one word shall escape me that any man, whose judgment is not blinded by prejudice, or who is not at heart a slaveholder, shall not confess to be right and just.

But I fancy I hear some one of my audience say, it is just in this circumstance that you and your brother abolitionists fail to make a favorable impression on the public mind. Would you argue more, and denounce less, would you persuade more and rebuke less, your cause would be much more likely to succeed. But, I submit, where all is plain there is nothing to be argued. What point in the anti-slavery creed would you have me argue? On what branch of the subject do the people of this country need light? Must I undertake to prove that the slave is a man? That point is conceded already. Nobody doubts it. The slaveholders themselves acknowledge it in the enactment of laws for their government. They acknowledge it when they punish disobedience on the part of the slave. There are seventy-two crimes in the state of Virginia, which, if committed by a black man, (no matter how ignorant he be,) subject him to the punishment of death; while only two of these same crimes will subject a white man to the like punishment. What is this but the acknowledgment that the slave is a moral, intellectual, and responsible being. The manhood of the slave is conceded. It is admitted in the fact that southern statute books are covered with enactments forbidding, under severe fines and penalties, the teaching of the slave to read or write. When you can point to any such laws, in reference to the beasts of the field, then I may consent to argue the manhood of the slave. When the dogs in your streets, when the fowls of the air, when the cattle on your hills, when the fish of the sea, and the reptiles that crawl, shall be unable to distinguish the slave from a brute, then will I argue with you that the slave is a man!

For the present, it is enough to affirm the equal manhood of the negro race. Is it not astonishing that, while we are plowing, planting, and reaping, using all kinds of mechanical tools, erecting houses, constructing bridges, building ships, working in metals of brass, iron, copper, silver, and gold; that, while we are reading, writing, and cyphering, acting as clerks, merchants, and secretaries, having among us lawyers, doctors, ministers, poets, authors, editors, orators, and teachers; that, while we are engaged in all manner of enterprises common to other men—digging gold in California, capturing the whale in the Pacific, feeding sheep and cattle on the hillside, living, moving, acting, thinking, planning, living in families as husbands, wives, and children, and, above all, confessing and worshiping the christian's God, and looking hopefully for life and immortality beyond the grave,—we are called upon to prove that we are men!

Would you have me argue that man is entitled to liberty? that he is the rightful owner of his own body? You have already declared it. Must I argue the wrongfulness of slavery? Is that a question for republicans? Is it to be settled by the rules of logic and argumentation, as a matter beset with great difficulty, involving a doubtful application of the principle of justice, hard to be understood? How should I look to-day in the presence of Americans, dividing and subdividing a discourse, to show that men have a natural right to freedom, speaking of it relatively and positively, negatively and affirmatively? To do so, would be to make myself ridiculous, and to offer an insult to your understanding. There is not a man beneath the canopy of heaven that does not know that slavery is wrong *for him*.

What! am I to argue that it is wrong to make men brutes, to rob them of their liberty, to work them without wages, to keep them ignorant of their relations to their fellow-men, to beat them with sticks, to flay their flesh with the lash, to load their limbs with irons, to hunt them with dogs, to sell them at auction, to sunder their families, to knock out their teeth, to burn their flesh, to starve them into obedience and submission to their masters? Must I argue that a system, thus marked with blood and stained with pollution, is wrong? No; I will not. I have better employment for my time and strength than such arguments would imply.

What, then, remains to be argued? Is it that slavery is not divine; that God did not establish it; that our doctors of divinity are mistaken? There is blasphemy in the thought. That which is inhuman cannot be divine. Who can reason on such a proposition! They that can, may; I cannot. The time for such argument is past.

At a time like this, scorching irony, not convincing argument, is needed. Oh! had I the ability, and could I reach the nation's ear, I would to-day pour out a fiery stream of biting ridicule, blasting reproach, withering sarcasm, and stern rebuke. For it is not light that is needed, but fire; it is not the gentle shower, but thunder. We need the storm, the whirlwind, and the earthquake. The feeling of the nation must be quickened; the conscience of the nation must be roused; the propriety of the nation must be startled; the hypocrisy of the nation must be exposed; and its crimes against God and man must be proclaimed and denounced.

What to the American slave is your Fourth of July? I answer, a day that reveals to him, more than all other days in the year, the gross injustice and cruelty to which he is the constant victim. To him, your celebration is a sham; your boasted liberty, an unholy license; your national greatness, swelling vanity; your sounds of rejoicing are empty and heartless; your denunciations of tyrants, brass-fronted impudence; your shouts of liberty and equality, hollow mockery; your prayers and hymns, your sermons and thanksgivings, with all your religious parade and solemnity, are to him mere bombast, fraud, deception, impiety, and hypocrisy—a thin veil to cover up crimes which would disgrace a nation of savages. There is not a nation on the earth guilty of practices more shocking and bloody, than are the people of these United States, at this very hour.

Go where you may, search where you will, roam through all the monarchies and despotisms of the old world, travel through South America, search out every abuse, and when you have found the last, lay your facts by the side of the every-day practices of this nation, and you will say with me, that, for revolting barbarity and shameless hypocrisy, America reigns without a rival.

PORT HURON STATEMENT
Students for a Democratic Society

We are people of this generation, bred in at least modest comfort, housed now in universities, looking uncomfortably to the world we inherit.

When we were kids the United States was the wealthiest and strongest country in the world; the only one with the atom bomb, the least scarred by modern war, an initiator of the United Nations that we thought would distribute Western influence throughout the world. Freedom and equality for each individual, government of, by, and for the people—these American values we found good, principles by which we could live as men. Many of us began maturing in complacency.

As we grew, however, our comfort was penetrated by events too troubling to dismiss. First, the permeating and victimizing fact of human degradation, symbolized by the Southern struggle against racial bigotry, compelled most of us from silence to activism. Second, the enclosing fact of the Cold War symbolized by the presence of the Bomb brought awareness that we ourselves, and our friends, and millions of abstract "others" we knew more directly because of our common peril, might die at any time. We might deliberately ignore, or avoid, or fail to feel all other human problems, but not these two, for these were too immediate and crushing in their impact, too challenging in the demand that we as individuals take the responsibility for encounter and resolution.

While these and other problems either directly oppressed us or rankled our consciences and became our own subjective concerns, we began to see complicated and disturbing paradoxes in our surrounding America. The declaration "all men are created equal . . ." rang hollow before the facts of Negro life in the South and the big cities of the North. The proclaimed peaceful intentions of the United States contradicted its economic and military investments in the Cold War status quo.

We witnessed, and continue to witness, other paradoxes. With nuclear energy whole cities can easily be powered, yet the dominant nation-states seem more likely to unleash destruction greater than that incurred in all wars of human history. Although our own technology is destroying old and creating new forms of social organization, men still tolerate meaningless work and idleness. While two-thirds of mankind suffers undernourishment, our own upper classes revel amidst superfluous abundance. Although world population is expected to double in forty years, the nations still tolerate anarchy as a major principle of international conduct and uncontrolled exploitation governs the sapping of the earth's physical resources. Although mankind desperately needs revolutionary leadership, America rests in national stalemate, its goals ambiguous and tradition-bound instead of informed and clear, its democratic system apathetic and manipulated rather than "of, by, and for the people."

Not only did tarnish appear on our image of American virtue, not only did disillusion occur when the hypocrisy of American ideals was discovered, but we began to sense that what we had originally seen as the American Golden Age was actually the decline of an era. The worldwide outbreak of revolution against colonialism and imperialism, the entrenchment of totalitarian states, the menace of war, overpopulation, international disorder, supertechnology—these trends were testing the tenacity of our own commitment to democracy and freedom and our abilities to visualize their application to a world in upheaval.

Our work is guided by the sense that we may be the last generation in the experiment with living. But we are a minority—the vast majority of our people regard the temporary equilibriums of our society and world as eternally functional parts. In this is perhaps the outstanding paradox: we ourselves are imbued with urgency, yet the message of our society is that there is no viable alternative to the present. Beneath the reassuring tones of the politicians, beneath the common opinion that America will "muddle through," beneath the stagnation of those who have closed their minds to the future, is the pervading feeling that there simply are no alternatives, that our times have witnessed the exhaustion not only of Utopias, but of any new departures as well. Feeling the press of complexity upon the emptiness of life, people are fearful of the thought that at any moment things might be thrust out of control. They fear change itself, since change might smash whatever invisible framework seems to hold back chaos for them now. For most Americans, all crusades are suspect, threatening. The fact that each individual sees apathy in his fellows perpetuates the common reluctance to organize for change. The dominant institutions are complex enough to blunt the minds of their potential critics, and entrenched enough to swiftly dissipate or entirely repel the energies of protest and reform, thus limiting human expectancies. Then, too, we are a materially improved society, and by our own improvements we seem to have weakened the case for further change.

Some would have us believe that Americans feel contentment amidst prosperity—but might it not better be called a glaze above deeply felt anxieties about their role in the new world? And if these anxieties produce a developed indifference to human affairs, do they not as well produce a yearning to believe there *is* an alternative to the present, that something *can* be done to change circumstances in the school, the workplaces, the bureaucracies, the government? It is to this latter yearning, at once the spark and engine of change, that we direct our present appeal. The search for truly democratic alternatives to the present, and a commitment to social experimentation with them, is a worthy and fulfilling human enterprise, one which moves us and, we hope, others today. On such a basis do we offer this document of our convictions and analysis: as an effort in understanding and changing the conditions of humanity in the late twentieth century, an effort rooted in the ancient, still unfulfilled conception of man attaining determining influence over his circumstances of life.

Making values explicit—an initial task in establishing alternatives—is an activity that has been devalued and corrupted. The conventional moral terms of the age, the politician moralities—"free world," "people's democracies"—reflect realities poorly, if at all, and seem to function more as ruling myths than as descriptive principles. But neither has our experience in the universities brought us moral enlightenment. Our professors and administrators sacrifice controversy to public relations; their curriculums change more slowly than the living events of the world; their skills and silence are purchased by investors in the arms race; passion is called unscholastic. The questions we might want raised—what is really important? can we live in a different and better way? if we wanted to change society, how would we do it?—are not thought to be questions of a "fruitful, empirical nature," and thus are brushed aside.

Unlike youth in other countries we are used to moral leadership being exercised and moral dimensions being clarified by our elders. But today, for us, not even the liberal and socialist preachments of the past seem adequate to the forms of the present. Consider the old slogans: Capitalism Cannot Reform Itself, United Front Against Fascism, General Strike, All Out on May Day. Or, more recently, No Cooperation with Commies and Fellow Travelers,

Ideologies are Exhausted, Bipartisanship, No Utopias. These are incomplete, and there are few new prophets. It has been said that our liberal and socialist predecessors were plagued by vision without program, while our own generation is plagued by program without vision. All around us there is astute grasp of method, technique—the committee, the *ad hoc* group, the lobbyist, the hard and soft sell, the make, the projected image—but, if pressed critically, such expertise is incompetent to explain its implicit ideals. It is highly fashionable to identify oneself by old categories, or by naming a respected political figure, or by explaining "how we would vote" on various issues.

Theoretic chaos has replaced the idealistic thinking of old—and, unable to reconstitute theoretic order, men have condemned idealism itself. Doubt has replaced hopefulness—and men act out of a defeatism that is labeled realistic. The decline of utopia and hope is in fact one of the defining features of social life today. The reasons are various: the dreams of the older left were perverted by Stalinism and never recreated; the congressional stalemate makes men narrow their view of the possible; the specialization of human activity leaves little room for sweeping thought; the horrors of the twentieth century, symbolized in the gas ovens and concentration camps and atom bombs, have blasted hopefulness. To be idealistic is to be considered apocalyptic, deluded. To have no serious aspirations, on the contrary, is to be "tough-minded."

In suggesting social goals and values, therefore, we are aware of entering a sphere of some disrepute. Perhaps matured by the past, we have no sure formulas, no closed theories—but that does not mean values are beyond discussion and tentative determination. A first task of any social movement is to convince people that the search for orienting theories and the creation of human values is complex but worthwhile. We are aware that to avoid platitudes we must analyze the concrete conditions of social order. But to direct such an analysis we must use the guideposts of basic principles. Our own social values involve conceptions of human beings, human relationships, and social systems.

We regard *men* as infinitely precious and possessed of unfulfilled capacities for reason, freedom, and love. In affirming these principles we are aware of countering perhaps the dominant conceptions of man in the twentieth century: that he is a thing to be manipulated, and that he is inherently incapable of directing his own affairs. We oppose the depersonalization that reduces human beings to the status of things—if anything, the brutalities of the twentieth century teach that means and ends are intimately related, that vague appeals to "posterity" cannot justify the mutilations of the present. We oppose, too, the doctrine of human incompetence because it rests essentially on the modern fact that men have been "competently" manipulated into incompetence—we see little reason why men cannot meet with increasing skill the complexities and responsibilities of their situation, if society is organized not for minority, but for majority, participation in decision-making.

Men have unrealized potential for self-cultivation, self-direction, self-understanding, and creativity. It is this potential that we regard as crucial and to which we appeal, not to the human potentiality for violence, unreason, and submission to authority. The goal of man and society should be human independence: a concern not with image of popularity but with finding a meaning in life that is personally authentic; a quality of mind not compulsively driven by a sense of powerlessness, nor one which unthinkingly adopts status values, nor one which represses all threats to its habits, but one which has full, spontaneous access to present and past experiences, one which easily unites the fragmented parts of personal history, one which openly faces problems which are troubling and unresolved; one with an intuitive awareness of possibilities, an active sense of curiosity, an ability and willingness to learn.

This kind of independence does not mean egotistic individualism—the object is not to have one's way so much as it is to have a way that is one's own. Nor do we deify man—we merely have faith in his potential.

Human relationships should involve fraternity and honesty. Human interdependence is contemporary fact; human brotherhood must be willed, however, as a condition of future survival and as the most appropriate form of social relations. Personal links between man and man are needed, especially to go beyond the partial and fragmentary bonds of function that bind men only as worker to worker, employer to employee, teacher to student, American to Russian.

Loneliness, estrangement, isolation describe the vast distance between man and man today. These dominant tendencies cannot be overcome by better personnel management, nor by improved gadgets, but only when a love of man overcomes the idolatrous worship of things by man. As the individualism we affirm is not egoism, the selflessness we affirm is not self-elimination. On the contrary, we believe in generosity of a kind that imprints one's unique individual qualities in the relation to other men, and to all human activity. Further, to dislike isolation is not to favor the abolition of privacy; the latter differs from isolation in that it occurs or is abolished according to individual will.

We would replace power rooted in possession, privilege, or circumstance by power and uniqueness rooted in love, reflectiveness, reason, and creativity. As a *social system* we seek the establishment of a democracy of individual participation, governed by two central aims: that the individual share in those social decisions determining the quality and direction of his life; that society be organized to encourage independence in men and provide the media for their common participation.

In a participatory democracy, the political life would be based in several root principles:

that decision-making of basic social consequence be carried on by public groupings;

that politics be seen positively, as the art of collectively creating an acceptable pattern of social relations;

that politics has the function of bringing people out of isolation and into community, thus being a necessary, though not sufficient, means of finding meaning in personal life;

that the political order should serve to clarify problems in a way instrumental to their solution; it should provide outlets for the expression of personal grievance and aspiration; opposing views should be organized so as to illuminate choices and facilitate the attainment of goals; channels should be commonly available to relate men to knowledge and to power so that private problems—from bad recreation facilities to personal alienation—are formulated as general issues.

The economic sphere would have as its basis the principles:

that work should involve incentives worthier than money or survival. It should be educative, not stultifying; creative, not mechanical; self-directed, not manipulated, encouraging independence, a respect for others, a sense of dignity and a willingness to accept social responsibility, since it is this experience that has crucial influence on habits, perceptions and individual ethics;

that the economic experience is so personally decisive that the individual must share in its full determination;

that the economy itself is of such social importance that its major resources and means of production should be open to democratic participation and subject to democratic social regulation.

Like the political and economic ones, major social institutions—cultural, educational, rehabilitative, and others—should be generally organized with the well-being and dignity of man as the essential measure of success.

In social change or interchange, we find violence to be abhorrent because it requires generally the transformation of the target, be it a human being or a community of people, into a depersonalized object of hate. It is imperative that the means of violence be abolished and the institutions—local, national, international—that encourage nonviolence as a condition of conflict be developed.

These are our central values, in skeletal form. It remains vital to understand their denial or attainment in the context of the modern world. . . .

WORKING CLASS AUTHORITARIANISM
S. M. Lipset

The gradual realization that extremist and intolerant movements in modern society are more likely to be based on the lower classes than on the middle and upper classes has posed a tragic dilemma for those intellectuals of the democratic left who once believed the proletariat necessarily to be a force for liberty, racial equality, and social progress. The Socialist Italian novelist Ignazio Silone has asserted that "the myth of the liberating power of the proletariat has dissolved along with that other myth of progress. The recent examples of the Nazi labor unions, like those of Salazar and Peron . . . have at last convinced of this even those who were reluctant to admit it on the sole grounds of the totalitarian degeneration of Communism."

At first glance the facts of a political history may seem to contradict this. Since their beginnings in the nineteenth century, workers' organizations and parties have been a major force in extending political democracy, and in waging progressive political and economic battles. Before 1914, the classic division between the working-class left parties and the economically privileged right was not based solely upon such issues as redistribution of income, status, and educational opportunities, but also rested upon civil liberties and international policy. The workers, judged by the policies of their parties, were often the backbone of the fight for greater political democracy, religious freedom, minority rights, and international peace, while the parties backed by the conservative middle and upper classes in much of Europe tended to favor more extremist political forms, to resist the extension of the suffrage, to back the established church, and to support jingoistic foreign policies.

Events since 1914 have gradually eroded these patterns. In some nations working-class groups have proved to be the most nationalistic sector of the population. In some they have been in the forefront of the struggle against equal rights for minority groups, and have sought to limit immigration or to impose racial standards in countries with open immigration. The conclusion of the anti-fascist era and the emergence of the cold war have shown that the struggle for freedom is not a simple variant of the economic class struggle. The threat to freedom posed by the Communist movement is as great as that once posed by Fascism and Nazism, and Communism, in all countries where it is strong, is supported mainly by the lower levels of the working class, or the rural popula-

From Political Man *by Seymour Martin Lipset. Copyright © 1959, 1960 by Seymour Martin Lipset. Reprinted by permission of Doubleday & Company, Inc.*

tion. No other party has been as thoroughly and completely the party of the working class and the poor. Socialist parties, past and present, secured much more support from the middle classes than the Communists have.

Some socialists and liberals have suggested that this proves nothing about authoritarian tendencies in the working class, since the Communist party often masquerades as a party seeking to fulfill the classic Western-democratic ideals of liberty, equality, and fraternity. They argue that most Communist supporters, particularly the less educated, are deceived into thinking that the Communists are simply more militant and efficient socialists. I would suggest, however, the alternative hypothesis that, rather than being a source of strain, the intransigent and intolerant aspects of Communist ideology attract members from that large stratum with low incomes, low-status occupations, and low education, which in modern industrial societies has meant largely, though not exclusively, the working class.

The social situation of the lower strata, particularly in poorer countries with low levels of education, predisposes them to view politics as black and white, good and evil. Consequently, other things being equal, they should be more likely than other strata to prefer extremist movements which suggest easy and quick solutions to social problems and have a rigid outlook.

The "authoritarianism" of any social stratum or class is highly relative, of course, and often modified by organizational commitments to democracy and by individual cross-pressures. The lower class in any given country may be more authoritarian than the upper classes, but on an "absolute" scale all the classes in that country may be less authoritarian than any class in another country. In a country like Britain, where norms of tolerance are well developed and widespread in every social stratum, even the lowest class may be less authoritarian and more "sophisticated" than the most highly educated stratum in an underdeveloped country, where immediate problems and crises impinge on every class and short-term solutions may be sought by all groups.

Commitments to democratic procedures and ideals by the principal organizations to which low-status individuals belong may also influence these individuals' actual political behavior more than their underlying personal values, no matter how authoritarian. A working class which has developed an early (prior to the Communists) loyalty to democratic political and trade-union movements which have successfully fought for social and economic rights will not easily change its allegiance.

Commitments to other values or institutions by individuals (cross-pressures) may also override the most established predispositions. For example, a French, Italian, or German Catholic worker who is strongly anticapitalist may still vote for a relatively conservative party in France, Italy, or Germany, because his ties to Catholicism are stronger than his resentments about his class status; a worker strongly inclined toward authoritarian ideas may defend democratic institutions against fascist attack because of his links to anti-fascist working-class parties and unions. Conversely, those who are not inclined toward extremist politics may back an extremist party because of certain aspects of its program and political role. Many persons supported the Communists in 1936 and 1943 as an anti-fascist internationalist party.

The specific propensity of given social strata to support either extremist or democratic political parties, then, cannot be predicted from a knowledge of their psychological predispositions or from attitudes inferred from survey data. Both evidence and theory suggest, however, that the lower strata are relatively more authoritarian, that (again, other things being equal) they will be more attracted to an extremist movement than to a moderate and democratic one, and that, once recruited, they will not be alienated by its lack of democracy, while more educated or sophisticated supporters will tend to drop away.

. . . The lower one goes on the socioeconomic ladder, the greater economic uncertainty one finds. White-collar workers, even those who are not paid more than skilled manual workers, are less likely to suffer the tensions created by fear of loss of income. Studies of marital instability indicate that this is related to lower income and income insecurity. Such insecurity will of course affect the individual's politics and attitudes. High states of tension require immediate alleviation, and this is frequently found in the venting of hostility against a scapegoat and the search for a short-term solution by support of extremist groups. Research indicates that the unemployed are less tolerant toward minorities than the employed, and more likely to be Communists if they are workers, or fascists if they are middle class. Industries which have a high rate of Communists in their ranks also have high economic instability.

The lower classes' insecurities and tensions which flow from economic instability are reinforced by their particular patterns of family life. There is a great deal of direct frustration and aggression in the day-to-day lives of members of the lower classes, both children and adults. A comprehensive review of the many studies of child-rearing patterns in the United States completed in the past twenty-five years reports that their "most consistent finding" is the "more frequent use of physical punishment by working-class parents. The middle class, in contrast, resorts to reasoning, isolation, and . . . 'love-oriented' techniques of discipline. . . . Such parents are more likely to overlook offenses, and when they do punish they are less likely to ridicule or inflict physical pain." A further link between such child-rearing practices and adult hostility and authoritarianism is suggested by the finding of two investigations in Boston and Detroit that physical punishments for aggression, characteristic of the working class, tend to increase rather than decrease aggressive behavior.

. . . Acceptance of the norms of democracy requires a high level of sophistication and ego security. The less sophisticated and stable an individual, the more likely he is to favor a simplified view of politics, to fail to understand the rationale underlying tolerance of those with whom he disagrees, and to find difficulty in grasping or tolerating a gradualist image of political change.

Several studies focusing on various aspects of working-class life and culture have emphasized different components of an unsophisticated perspective. Greater suggestibility, absence of a sense of past and future (lack of a prolonged time perspective), inability to take a complex view, greater difficulty in abstracting from concrete experience, and lack of imagination (inner "reworking" of experience), each has been singled out by numerous students of quite different problems as characteristic of low status. All of these qualities are part of the complex psychological basis of authoritarianism.

The psychologist Hadley Cantril considered suggestibility to be a major psychological explanation for participation in extremist movements. The two conditions for suggestibility are both typical of low-status persons: either the lack of an adequate frame of reference or general perspective, or a fixed, rigid one. A poorly developed frame of reference reflects a limited education, a paucity of the rich associations on a general level which provide a basis for evaluating experience. A fixed or rigid one—in a sense the opposite side of the same coin—reflects the tendency to elevate whatever general principles are learned to absolutes which even experience may fail to qualify and correct.

. . . One aspect of the lower classes' lack of sophistication and education is their anti-intellectualism (a phenomenon Engels long ago noted as a problem faced by working-class movements). While the complex esoteric ideology of Communism may have been one of the principal features attracting middle-class people to it, the fundamental anti-intellectualism which it shares with other extremist movements has been a source of strain for the "genuine" intellectuals within it. Thus it has been the working-class rank and file which has been least disturbed by Communism's ideological shifts, and least likely to defect. Their commitment, once established, cannot usually be shaken by a sudden realization that the party, after all, does not conform to liberal and humanistic values.

This helps to explain why socialist parties have been led by a high proportion of intellectuals, in spite of an original ideological emphasis on maintaining a working-class orientation, while the Communists have alienated their intellectual leaders and are led preponderantly by those with working-class occupations.[58] Almond's study concluded that ". . . while the party is open to all comers, working-class party members have better prospects of success in the party than middle class recruits. This is probably due both to party policy, which has always manifested greater confidence in the reliability of working-class recruits, and to the difficulties of assimilation into the party generally experienced by middle-class party members." . . .

To sum up, the lower-class individual is likely to have been exposed to punishment, lack of love, and a general atmosphere of tension and aggression since early childhood—all experiences which tend to produce deep-rooted hostilities expressed by ethnic prejudice, political authoritarianism, and chiliastic transvaluational religion. His educational attainment is less than that of men with higher socioeconomic status, and his association as a child with others of similar background not only fails to stimulate his intellectual interests but also creates an atmosphere which prevents his educational experience from increasing his general social sophistication and his understanding of different groups and ideas. Leaving school relatively early, he is surrounded on the job by others with a similarly restricted cultural, educational, and family background. Little external influence impinges on his limited environment. From early childhood, he has sought immediate gratifications, rather than engaged in activities which might have long-term rewards. The logic of both his adult employment and his family situation reinforces this limited time perspective. As the sociologist C. C. North has put it, isolation from heterogeneous environments, characteristic of low status, operates to "limit the source of information, to retard the development of efficiency in judgment and reasoning abilities, and to confine the attention to more trivial interests in life." . . .

THE SYMBOLIC NATURE OF POLITICS
Murray Edelman

Politics, like religion, love, and the arts, is a theme that men cannot leave alone: not in their behavior, nor in their talk, nor in their writing of history. In all countries and cultures men dwell on lore about the state: what it is and does and should be. The lore includes much that is vague, yet comes to have a powerful emotional pull. It includes much that is plainly contrary to what we see happen, yet the myth is all the more firmly believed and the more dogmatically passed on to others because men want to believe it and it holds them together. Sometimes politics is not myth or emotional at all, but a cool and successful effort to get money from others or power over them. Perhaps it can be cool and successful for some only because it is also obsessional, mythical, and emotional for some or for all. The symbolic side of politics calls for attention, for men cannot know themselves until they know what they do and what surrounds and nurtures them. Man creates political symbols and they sustain and develop him or warp him.

A man's relationship to the state is complicated. The state benefits and it threatens. Now it is "us" and often it is "them." It is an abstraction, but in its name men are jailed or made rich on oil depletion allowances and defense contracts, or killed in wars. For each individual the political constitution condenses all these things, in all their ambivalence and ambiguity. In doing so it symbolizes the complication that the individual is himself, for man is a political animal. This book examines politics as a symbolic form, but it can do so only by looking at man and politics as reflections of each other.

In their obsession with the state, men are of course obsessed with them-

Reprinted from Murray Edelman, Symbolic Uses of Politics *(Urbana: University of Illinois Press, 1964) by permission of the publisher.*

selves. If politics is as complicated and ambivalent as the men who create it, it is to be expected that its institutions and forms should take on strong meanings: meanings that men cue and teach each other to expect and that are vital for the acquiescence of the general public in the actions of elites and therefore for social harmony. Political forms thus come to symbolize what large masses of men need to believe about the state to reassure themselves. It is the needs, the hopes, and the anxieties of men that determine the meanings. But political forms also convey goods, services, and power to specific groups of men. There is accordingly no reason to expect that the meanings will be limited to the instrumental functions the political forms serve. The capacity of political forms both to serve as a powerful means of expression for mass publics and to convey benefits to particular groups is a central theme of this book.

The systematic research in political science of the last several decades has repeatedly called attention to wide gulfs between our solemnly taught, common sense assumptions about what political institutions do and what they actually do. The uses for the political system of both the common assumption and of the actual consequences are explored in detail later; but a few examples of the divergence are in point here.

Elections are an especially revealing example, for voting is the only form in which most citizens ever participate directly in government and is also the political behavior that has been most widely and most rigorously studied. School teachers, good government groups like the League of Women Voters, and candidates themselves never tire of repeating that voting gives the people control over their officials and policies, that the citizen who fails to vote should not complain if he gets poor government, and that elections are fundamental to democracy. But, rather paradoxically, the voting behavior studies have shown that issues are a minor determinant of how people cast their ballots, most voters being quite ignorant of what the issues are and of which party stands for what position. We also know from studies of legislative and administrative behavior that neither of these depends primarily upon election outcomes. So what people get does not depend mainly on their votes.

It does not follow that election campaigns are unimportant or serve no purpose. It is rather that the functions they serve are different and more varied than the ones we conventionally assume and teach. They give people a chance to express discontents and enthusiasms, to enjoy a sense of involvement. This is participation in a ritual act, however; only in a minor degree is it participation in policy formation. Like all ritual, whether in primitive or modern societies, elections draw attention to common social ties and to the importance and apparent reasonableness of accepting the public policies that are adopted. Without some such device no policy can survive and retain the support or acquiescence of its members. The key point is, however, that elections could not serve this vital social function if the common belief in direct popular control over governmental policy through elections were to be widely questioned. The insistence of the most involved upon general participation in the rite is both understandable and functional in this light. So is the impression individual voters have of the reasoned basis for their votes. One psychiatrist has written of voting that, "perhaps in no other area, save possibly that of religion, is the average person more convinced of the logical, defensible, and wholly rational nature of his decisions."

This conclusion raises the question of just how people's values do enter into the decisions of public organs and of the extent to which particular procedures make some groups' values carry more weight than others. This question is explored in the chapters that follow, with particular attention to the uses in public policy formation of myths, rites, and other symbolic forms.

Not only does systematic research suggest that the most cherished forms of popular participation in government are largely symbolic, but also that many of the public programs universally taught and believed to benefit a mass public in fact benefit relatively small groups. We can show that many business regulation and other law enforcement policies confer tangible benefits on the regulated businesses while conveying only symbolic reassurance to their ostensible beneficiaries, the consumers. . . .

Political scientists even more commonly recognize that the common and commonsense notions about the basically mechanical role of administrative agencies and courts in "carrying out" legislative or constitutional policy are gross distortions of the process that actually takes place. It is accordingly useful to look searchingly at every unquestioned or widely taught assumption about how government works, for it is a key characteristic of myth that it is generally unquestioned, widely taught and believed, and that the myth itself has consequences, though not the ones it literally proclaims.

If we are to make a start toward recognizing the symbolic elements in governmental proceedings and the impact of symbolic functions upon elite and mass behavior, it is necessary to consider some general characteristics of symbols and the conditions that explain their appearance and meanings. Fortunately, psychologists, anthropologists, and philosophers have learned a great deal about this subject, and the application of this body of knowledge to government leads to some exciting pathways, some fruitful speculations, and even a few firm conclusions.

Basic to the recognition of symbolic forms in the political process is a distinction between politics as a spectator sport and political activity as utilized by organized groups to get quite specific, tangible benefits for themselves. For most men most of the time politics is a series of pictures in the mind, placed there by television news, newspapers, magazines, and discussions. The pictures create a moving panorama taking place in a world the mass public never quite touches, yet one its members come to fear or cheer, often with passion and sometimes with action. They are told of legislatures passing laws, foreign political figures threatening or offering trade agreements, wars starting and ending, candidates for public office losing or winning, decisions made to spend unimaginable sums of money to go to the moon.

There is, on the other hand, the immediate world in which people make and do things that have directly observable consequences. In these activities men can check their acts and assumptions against the consequences and correct errors. There is feedback. Some men, relatively few, are involved in politics in this direct way.

Politics is for most of us a passing parade of abstract symbols, yet a parade which our experience teaches us to be a benevolent or malevolent force that can be close to omnipotent. Because politics does visibly confer wealth, take life, imprison and free people, and represent a history with strong emotional and ideological associations, its processes become easy objects upon which to displace private emotions, especially strong anxieties and hopes.

But it could not serve as conveyor of these fears and aspirations if it were simply a tool or mechanism which we all had the power and knowledge to manipulate for our own advantage. It is central to its potency as a symbol that it is remote, set apart, omnipresent as the ultimate threat or means of succor, yet not susceptible to effective influence through any act we as individuals can perform.

Research in a number of different sciences has pointed to the key function of remoteness as an influence upon symbolic meanings. One element involved here is the distinction between referential and condensation symbols. Every symbol stands for something other than itself, and it also evokes an attitude, a set of impressions, or a pattern of events associated through time, through space, through logic, or through imagination with the symbol. Students of this subject have noticed a fundamental distinction among symbols that groups them into two quite separate types. Referential symbols are economical ways of referring to the objective elements in objects or situations: the elements identified in the same way by different people. Such symbols are useful because they help in logical thinking about the situation and in manipulating it. Industrial accident statistics and cost figures in cost plus contracts are referential political symbols, though they may also be condensation symbols. Condensation symbols evoke the emotions associated with the situation. They condense into one symbolic event, sign, or act patriotic pride, anxieties, remembrances of past glories or humiliations, promises of future greatness: some one of these or all of them.

Where condensation symbols are involved, the constant check of the immediate environment is lacking. A traffic policeman at a busy corner may grow entranced momentarily with himself or his stick as representative of the august majesty of the state and indulge in the luxury of arbitrary power, perhaps by favoring traffic on one street; but the lengthening line of cars in front of him and some irate honking will soon remind him that he must face reality: drivers and a prosaic chief of police. There is no such check on the fantasies and conceptualizing of those who never can test objectively their conviction that the government and their home towns abound in communist spies and dupes and that John Birch symbolizes resistance to the threat. Nor is there the check of reality and feedback upon those to whom Adlai Stevenson or Barry Goldwater or Dwight Eisenhower are symbols of reason, intelligence, and virtue in public policy. Conclusive demonstrations that their heroes' policies may often be futile or misconceived are impossible simply because the link between dramatic political announcements and their impact on people is so long and so tangled. These people may be right or they may be wrong. The point is that there is no necessity, and often no possiblity, of continuously checking their convictions against real conditions.

No example can ever be wholly free of either referential or of condensation symbols; but the distinction between the two types of behavior is fundamental in realistic political analysis.

Practically every political act that is controversial or regarded as really important is bound to serve in part as a condensation symbol. It evokes a quiescent or an aroused mass response because it symbolizes a threat or reassurance. Because the meaning of the act in these cases depends only partly or not at all upon its objective consequences, which the mass public cannot know, the meaning can only come from the psychological needs of the respondents; and it can only be known from their responses.

One type of research that supports this view appears in the work of Smith, Bruner, and White, who have explored the tie between personality and opinions. They conclude that political opinions serve three different functions for the personality. One of these, object appraisal, or help in understanding the world, can only be performed by those political opinions that are fairly realistic: opinions which, in our terms, are based upon referential symbols and are constantly checked against the objects to which they refer. An opinion that the chief function of a party platform is to attract votes and not to forecast public policy would presumably further object appraisal.

Neither of the other functions our political opinions serve need meet the check of reality, however; and in both cases the functions are often best served by ignoring reality. Political opinions sometimes help in social adjustment, and this is the reason men are likely to talk politics with those who agree with them, avoid the subject with those who do not, and sometimes shade or change their opinions to create agreement. Finally, political opinions help "externalize" unresolved inner problems. In a time of depression or anxiety a large group of people may come to believe, for example, that Jewish or Communist or Catholic conspiracies in the government explain their business failures or their inability to realize other ambitions. It is important to notice that opinions developed to promote social adjustment or to project inner tensions will continue to be held and will even be strengthened so long as they really do help in social adjustment or in relieving anxieties, whether or not they are consistent with what is happening in the world.

Controversial political acts remote from the individual's immediate experience and which he cannot influence are highly available objects for such opinions. For much of the mass public, that is, they are bound to become condensation symbols, emotional in impact, calling for conformity to promote social harmony, serving as the focus of psychological tensions. The parade of "news" about political acts reported to us by the mass media and drunk up by the public as drama is the raw material of such symbolization. It has everything: remoteness, the omnipotent state, crises, and détentes. More than that, it has the blurring or absence of any realistic detail that might question or weaken the symbolic meanings we read into it. It is no accident of history or of culture that our newspapers and television present little news, that they overdramatize what they report, and that most citizens have only a foggy knowledge of public affairs though often an intensely felt one. If political acts are to promote social adjustment and are to mean what our inner problems require that they mean, then these acts have to be dramatic in outline and empty of realistic detail. In this sense publishers and broadcast licensees are telling the exact truth when they excuse their poor performance with the plea that they give the public what it wants. It wants symbols and not news.

The governments which most often outrage their citizens or force unwelcome changes in their behavior plainly have the greatest need for reassuring symbols. In this light it is no accident that all totalitarian states involve their populations intensively and almost constantly in discussion of public affairs. Mass meetings, political lectures, discussion groups, organizations for every age and occupational group have been the order of the day in all the fascist and communist dictatorships. The communist Chinese device of public self-criticism as a phase of political discussion is only the ad nauseam extension of this efficient device. It exhausts men's energies in passionate attachments to abstract and remote symbols rather than in private creative work. Such work brings the gratifications that come from planned manipulation of the environment: Veblen's "instinct of workmanship." In doing so it creates a personality resistant to manipulation.

Even without much encouragement by the government, obsessive involvement with verbal accounts of political acts occurs in democracies, too, and it has the same numbing impact upon the critical faculties. It can bring gratifications, looming threats, the appearance of victory and of defeat: in election campaigns and in policy battles elsewhere in the government or in international relations. A dramatic symbolic life among abstractions thereby becomes a substitute gratification for the pleasure of remolding the concrete environment.

Some political activity is quite concrete, of course: the work of the professional politician who uses politics to get jobs and votes; the maneuvers of the businessman who uses it to get profitable contracts or greater latitude in his economic activities; the activity of the local reform group out for better schools, playgrounds, and sewers. But a very small fraction of the population uses politics in this way. For most of the public it is a parade of abstractions, and this is as true of many good government and League of Women Voter types at the center as it is of the extremists well to their right and left. . . .

Our political institutions constitute, among other things, a device for providing symbolic reassurance to threatened groups, and the device works admirably for most issues. In the United States instances of direct extragovernmental mass action on political issues are much harder to find than examples of quiescence. We routinely institutionalize our symbolic reassurances in the form of constitutional or statutory guarantees and in the creation of administrative organizations. This contrasts with those political systems, such as the Latin American ones, in which the individual political figure or coterie pose as protectors. In the latter systems both the apparent absence of institutional protections and the vulnerability of the political leaders encourage extralegal collective action: vigilante movements and the coup d'état.

LETTER FROM BIRMINGHAM JAIL
Martin Luther King, Jr.

My Dear Fellow Clergyman:
    While confined here in the Birmingham city jail, I came across your recent statement calling my present activities "unwise and untimely." Seldom do I pause to answer criticism of my work and ideas. If I sought to answer all the criticisms that cross my desk, my secretaries would have little time for anything other than such correspondence in the course of the day, and I would have no time for constructive work. But since I feel that you are men of genuine good will and that your criticisms are sincerely set forth, I want to try to answer your statement in what I hope will be patient and reasonable terms.
    I think I should indicate why I am here in Birmingham, since you have been influenced by the view which argues against "outsiders coming in." I have the honor of serving as president of the Southern Christian Leadership Conference, an organization operating in every southern state, with headquarters in Atlanta, Georgia. We have some eighty-five affiliated organizations across the South, and one of them is the Alabama Christian Movement for Human Rights. Frequently we share staff, educational and financial resources with our affiliates. Several months ago the affiliate here in Birmingham asked us to be on call to engage in a nonviolent direct-action program if such were deemed necessary. We readily consented, and when the hour came we lived up to our promise. So I, along with several members of my staff, am here because I was invited here. I am here because I have organizational ties here.
    But more basically, I am in Birmingham because injustice is here. Just as the prophets of the eighth century B.C. left their villages and carried their "thus saith the Lord" far beyond the boundaries of their home towns, and just as the Apostle Paul left his village of Tarsus and carried the gospel of Jesus Christ to the far corners of the Greco-Roman world, so am I compelled to

From *Why We Can't Wait* by Martin Luther King Jr. Copyright © 1963 by Martin Luther King Jr. By permission of Harper and Row, Publishers, Inc.

carry the gospel of freedom beyond my own home town. Like Paul, I must constantly respond to the Macedonian call for aid.

Moreover, I am cognizant of the interrelatedness of all communities and states. I cannot sit idly by in Atlanta and not be concerned about what happens in Birmingham. Injustice anywhere is a threat to justice everywhere. We are caught in an inescapable network of mutuality, tied in a single garment of destiny. Whatever affects one directly affects all indirectly. Never again can we afford to live with the narrow, provincial "outside agitator" idea. Anyone who lives inside the United States can never be considered an outsider anywhere within its bounds.

You deplore the demonstrations taking place in Birmingham. But your statement, I am sorry to say, fails to express a similar concern for the conditions that brought about the demonstrations. I am sure that none of you would want to rest content with the superficial kind of social analysis that deals merely with effects and does not grapple with underlying causes. It is unfortunate that demonstrations are taking place in Birmingham, but it is even more unfortunate that the city's white power structure left the Negro community with no alternative.

In any nonviolent campaign there are four basic steps: collection of the facts to determine whether injustices exist; negotiation; self-purification; and direct action. We have gone through all these steps in Birmingham. There can be no gainsaying the fact that racial injustice engulfs this community. Birmingham is probably the most thoroughly segregated city in the United States. Its ugly record of brutality is widely known. Negroes have experienced grossly unjust treatment in the courts. There have been more unsolved bombings of Negro homes and churches in Birmingham than in any other city in the nation. These are the hard, brutal facts of the case. On the basis of these conditions, Negro leaders sought to negotiate with the city fathers. But the latter consistently refused to engage in good-faith negotiation.

Then, last September, came the opportunity to talk with leaders of Birmingham's economic community. In the course of the negotiations, certain promises were made by the merchants—for example, to remove the stores' humiliating racial signs. On the basis of these promises, the Reverend Fred Shuttlesworth and the leaders of the Alabama Christian Movement for Human Rights agreed to a moratorium on all demonstrations. As the weeks and months went by, we realized that we were the victims of a broken promise. A few signs, briefly removed, returned; the others remained.

As in so many past experiences, our hopes had been blasted, and the shadow of deep disappointment settled upon us. We had no alternative except to prepare for direct action, whereby we would present our very bodies as a means of laying our case before the conscience of the local and the national community. Mindful of the difficulties involved, we decided to undertake a process of self-purification. We began a series of workshops on nonviolence, and we repeatedly asked ourselves: "Are you able to accept blows without retaliating?" "Are you able to endure the ordeal of jail?" We decided to schedule our direct-action program for the Easter season, realizing that except for Christmas, this is the main shopping period of the year. Knowing that a strong economic-withdrawal program would be the by-product of direct action, we felt that this would be the best time to bring pressure to bear on the merchants for the needed change.

Then it occurred to us that Birmingham's mayoralty election was coming up in March, and we speedily decided to postpone action until after election day. When we discovered that the Commissioner of Public Safety, Eugene "Bull" Connor, had piled up enough votes to be in the run-off, we decided again to postpone action until the day after the run-off so that the demonstrations could not be used to cloud the issues. Like many others, we waited to see Mr. Connor defeated, and to this end we endured postponement after postponement. Having aided in this community need, we felt that our direct-action program could be delayed no longer.

You may well ask: "Why direct action? Why sit-ins, marches and so forth? Isn't negotiation a better path?" You are quite right in calling for negotiation. Indeed, this is the very purpose of direct action. Nonviolent direct action seeks to creat such a crisis and foster such a tension that a community which has constantly refused to negotiate is forced to confront the issue. It seeks so to dramatize the issue that it can no longer be ignored. My citing the creation of tension as part of the work of the nonviolent-resister may sound rather shocking. But I must confess that I am not afraid of the word "tension." I have earnestly opposed violent tension, but there is a type of constructive, nonviolent tension which is necessary for growth. Just as Socrates felt that it was necessary to create a tension in the mind so that individuals could rise from the bondage of myths and half-truths to the unfettered realm of creative analysis and objective appraisal, so must we see the need for nonviolent gadflies to create the kind of tension in society that will help men rise from the dark depths of prejudice and racism to the majestic heights of understanding and brotherhood.

The purpose of our direct-action program is to create a situation so crisis-packed that it will inevitably open the door to negotiation. I therefore concur with you in your call for negotiation. Too long has our beloved Southland been bogged down in a tragic effort to live in monologue rather than dialogue.

One of the basic points in your statement is that the action that I and my associates have taken in Birmingham is untimely. Some have asked: "Why didn't you give the new city administration time to act?" The only answer that I can give to this query is that the new Birmingham administration must be prodded about as much as the outgoing one, before it will act. We are sadly mistaken if we feel that the election of Albert Boutwell as mayor will bring the millennium to Birmingham. While Mr. Boutwell is a much more gentle person than Mr. Connor, they are both segregationists, dedicated to maintenance of the status quo. I have hope that Mr. Boutwell will be reasonable enough to see the futility of massive resistance to desegregation. But he will not see this without pressure from devotees of civil rights. My friends, I must say to you that we have not made a single gain in civil rights without determined legal and nonviolent pressure. Lamentably, it is an historical fact that privileged groups seldom give up their privileges voluntarily. Individuals may see the moral light and voluntarily give up their unjust posture; but, as Reinhold Niebuhr has reminded us, groups tend to be more immoral than individuals.

We know through painful experience that freedom is never voluntarily given by the oppressor; it must be demanded by the oppressed. Frankly, I have yet to engage in a direct-action campaign that was "well timed" in the view of those who have not suffered unduly from the disease of segregation. For years now I have heard the word "Wait!" It rings in the ear of every Negro with piercing familiarity. This "Wait" has almost always meant "Never." We must come to see, with one of our distinguished jurists, that "justice too long delayed is justice denied."

We have waited for more than 340 years for our constitutional and God-given rights. The nations of Asia and Africa are moving with jetlike speed toward gaining political independence, but we still creep at horse-and-buggy pace toward gaining a cup of coffee at a lunch counter. Perhaps it is easy for those who have never felt the stinging darts of segregation to say, "Wait." But when you have seen vicious mobs lynch your mothers and fathers at will and drown your sisters and brothers at whim; when you have seen hate-filled policemen curse, kick and even kill your black brothers and sisters; when you see the vast majority of your twenty million Negro brothers smothering in an airtight cage of poverty in the midst of an affluent society; when you suddenly find your tongue twisted and your speech stammering as you seek to explain to your six-year-old daughter why she can't go to the public amusement park that has just been advertised on television, and see tears welling up in her eyes when she is told that Funtown is closed to colored children, and see ominous clouds of inferiority beginning to form in her little mental sky, and see her beginning to distort her personality by developing an unconscious betterness toward white people; when you have to concoct an answer for a five-year-old son who is asking: "Daddy, why do white people treat colored people so mean?"; when you take a cross-country drive and find it necessary to sleep night after night in the uncomfortable corners of your automobile because no motel will accept you; when you are humiliated day in and day out by nagging signs reading "white" and "colored"; when your first name becomes "nigger," your middle name becomes "boy" (however old you are) and your last name becomes "John," and your wife and mother are never given the respected title "Mrs."; when you are harried by day and haunted by night by the fact that you are a Negro, living constantly at tiptoe stance, never quite knowing what to expect next, and are plagued with inner fears and outer resentments; when you are forever fighting a degenerating sense of "nobodiness"—then you will understand why we find it difficult to wait. There comes a time when the cup of endurance runs over, and men are no longer willing to be plunged into the abyss of despair. I hope, sirs, you can understand our legitimate and unavoidable impatience.

You express a great deal of anxiety over our willingness to break laws. This is certainly a legitimate concern. Since we so diligently urge people to obey the Supreme Court's decision of 1954 outlawing segregation in the public schools, at first glance it may seem rather paradoxical for us consciously to break laws. One may well ask: "How can you advocate breaking some laws and obeying others?" The answer lies in the fact that there are two types of laws: just and unjust. I would be the first to advocate obeying just laws. One has not only a legal but a moral responsibility to obey just laws. Conversely, one has a moral responsibility to disobey unjust laws. I would agree with St. Augustine that "an unjust law is no law at all."

Now, what is the difference between the two? How does one determine whether a law is just or unjust? A just law is a man-made code that squares with the moral law or the law of God. An unjust law is a code that is out of harmony with the moral law. To put it in the terms of St. Thomas Aquinas: An unjust law is a human law that is not rooted in eternal law and natural law. Any law that uplifts human personality is just. Any law that degrades human personality is unjust. All segregation statutes are unjust because segregation distorts the soul and damages the personality. It gives the segregator a false sense of superiority and the segregated a false sense of inferiority. Segregation, to use the terminology of the Jewish philospher Martin Buber, substitutes an "I-it" relationship for an "I-thou" relationship and ends up relegating persons to the status of things. Hence segregation is not only politically, economically and sociologically unsound, it is morally wrong and sinful. Paul Tillich has said that sin is separation. Is not segregation an existential expression of man's tragic separation, his awful estrangement, his terrible sinfulness? Thus it is that I can urge men to obey the 1954 decision of the Supreme Court, for it is morally right; and I can urge them to disobey segregation ordinances, for they are morally wrong.

Let us consider a more concrete example of just and unjust laws. An unjust law is a code that a numerical or power majority group compels a minority group to obey but does not make binding on itself. This is *difference* made legal. By the same token, a just law is a code that a majority compels a minority to follow and that it is willing to follow itself. This is *sameness* made legal.

Let me give another explanation. A law is unjust if it is inflicted on a minority that, as a result of being denied the right to vote, had no part in enacting or devising the law. Who can say that the legislature of Alabama which set up that state's segregation laws was democratically elected? Throughout Alabama all sorts of devious methods are used to prevent Negroes from becoming registered voters, and there are some counties in which, even though Negroes constitute a majority of the population, not a single Negro is registered. Can any law enacted under such circumstances be considered democratically structured?

Sometimes a law is just on its face and unjust in its application. For instance, I have been arrested on a charge of parading without a permit. Now, there is nothing wrong in having an ordinance which requires a permit for a parade. But such an ordinance becomes unjust when it is used to maintain segregation and to deny citizens the First-Amendment privilege of peaceful assembly and protest.

I hope you are able to see the distinction I am trying to point out. In no sense do I advocate evading or defying the law, as would the rabid segregationist. That would lead to anarchy. One who breaks an unjust law must do so openly, lovingly, and with a willingness to accept the penalty. I submit that an individual who breaks a law that conscience tells him is unjust, and who willingly accepts the penalty of imprisonment in order to arouse the conscience of the community over its injustice, is in reality expressing the highest respect for law.

Of course, there is nothing new about this kind of civil disobedience. It was evidenced sublimely in the refusal of Shadrach, Meshach and Abednego to obey the laws of Nebuchadnezzar, on the ground that a higher moral law was at stake. It was practiced superbly by the early Christians, who were willing to face hungry lions and the excruciating pain of chopping blocks rather than submit to certain unjust laws of the Roman Empire. To a degree, academic freedom is a reality today because Socrates practiced civil disobedience. In our own nation, the Boston Tea Party represented a massive act of civil disobedience.

We should never forget that everything Adolf Hitler did in Germany was "legal" and everything the Hungarian freedom fighters did in Hungary was "illegal." It was "illegal" to aid and comfort a Jew in Hitler's Germany. Even so, I am sure that, had I lived in Germany at the time, I would have aided and comforted my Jewish brothers. If today I lived in a Communist country where certain principles dear to the Christian faith are suppressed, I would openly advocate disobeying that country's antireligious laws.

I must make two honest confessions to you, my Christian and Jewish brothers. First, I must confess that over the past few years I have been gravely disappointed with the white moderate. I have almost reached the regrettable conclusion that the Negro's great stumbling block in his stride toward freedom is not the White Citizen's Counciler or the Ku Klux Klanner, but the white moderate, who is more devoted to "order" than to justice; who prefers a negative peace which is the absence of tension to a positive peace which is the presence of justice; who constantly says: "I agree with you in the goal you seek, but I cannot agree with your methods of direct action"; who paternalistically believes he can set the timetable for another man's freedom; who lives by a mythical concept of time and who constantly advises the Negro to wait for a "more convenient season." Shallow understanding from people of good will is more frustrating than absolute misunderstanding from people of ill will. Lukewarm acceptance is much more bewildering than outright rejection.

I had hoped that the white moderate would understand that law and order exist for the purpose of establishing justice and that when they fail in this purpose they become the dangerously structured dams that block the flow of social progress. I had hoped that the white moderate would understand that the present tension in the South is a necessary phase of the transition from an obnoxious negative peace, in which the Negro passively accepted his unjust plight, to a substantive and positive peace, in which all men will respect the dignity and worth of human personality. Actually, we who engage in nonviolent direct action are not the creators of tension. We merely bring to the surface the hidden tension that is already alive. We bring it out in the open, where it can be seen and dealt with. Like a boil that can never be cured so long as it is covered up but must be opened with all its ugliness to the natural medicines of air and light, injustice must be exposed, with all the tension its exposure creates, to the light of human conscience and the air of national opinion before it can be cured.

In your statement you assert that our actions, even though peaceful, must be condemned because they precipitate violence. But is this a logical assertion? Isn't this like condemning a robbed man because his possession of money precipitated the evil act of robbery? Isn't this like condemning Socrates because his unswerving commitment to truth and his philosophical inquiries precipitated the act by the misguided populace in which they made him drink hemlock? Isn't this like condemning Jesus because his unique God-consciousness and never-ceasing devotion to God's will precipitated the evil act of crucifixion? We must come to see that, as the federal courts have consistently affirmed, it is wrong to urge an individual to cease his efforts to gain his basic constitutional rights because the quest may precipitate violence. Society must protect the robbed and punish the robber.

I had hoped that the white moderate would reject the myth concerning time in relation to the struggle for freedom. I have just received a letter from a white brother in Texas. He writes: "All Christians know that the colored people will receive equal rights eventually, but it is possible that you are in too great a religious hurry. It has taken Christianity almost two thousand years to accomplish what it has. The teachings of Christ take time to come to earth." Such an attitude stems from a tragic misconception of time, from the strangely irrational notion that there is something in the very flow of time that will inevitably cure all ills. Actually, time itself is neutral; it can be used either destructively or constructively. More and more I feel that the people of ill will have used time much more effectively than have the people of good will. We will have to repent in this generation not merely for the hateful words and actions of the bad people but for the appalling silence of the good people. Human progress never rolls in on wheels of inevitability; it comes through the tireless efforts of men willing to be co-workers with God, and without this hard work, time itself becomes an ally of the forces of social stagnation. We must use time creatively, in the knowledge that the time is always ripe to do right. Now is the time to make real the promise of democracy and transform our pending national elegy into a creative psalm of brotherhood. Now is the time to lift our national policy from the quicksand of racial injustice to the solid rock of human dignity.

You speak of our activity in Birmingham as extreme. At first I was rather disappointed that fellow clergymen would see my nonviolent efforts as those of an extremist. I began thinking about the fact that I stand in the middle of two opposing forces in the Negro community. One is a force of complacency, made up in part of Negroes who, as a result of long years of oppression, are so drained of self-respect and a sense of "somebodiness" that they have adjusted to segregation; and in part of a few middle-class Negroes who, because of a degree of academic and economic security and because in some ways they profit by segregation, have become insensitive to the problems of the masses. The other force is one of bitterness and hatred, and it comes perilously close to advocating violence. It is expressed in the various black nationalist groups that are springing up across the nation, the largest and best known being Elijah Muhammad's Muslim movement. Nourished by the Negro's frustration over the continued existence of racial discrimination, this movement is made up of people who have lost faith in America, who have absolutely repudiated Christianity, and who have concluded that the white man is an incorrigible "devil."

I have tried to stand between these two forces, saying that we need emulate neither the "do-nothingism" of the complacent nor the hatred and despair of the black nationalist. For there is the more excellent way of love and nonviolent protest. I am grateful to God that, through the influence of the Negro church, the way of nonviolence became an integral part of our struggle.

If this philosophy had not emerged, by now many streets of the South would, I am convinced, be flowing with blood. And I am further convinced that if our white brothers dismiss as "rabble-rousers" and "outside agitators" those of us who employ nonviolent direct action, and if they refuse to support our nonviolent efforts, millions of Negroes will, out of frustration and despair, seek solace and security in black-nationalist ideologies—a development that would inevitably lead to a frightening racial nightmare.

Oppressed people cannot remain oppressed forever. The yearning for freedom eventually manifests itself, and that is what has happened to the American Negro. Something within has reminded him of his birthright of freedom, and something without has reminded him that it can be gained. Consciously or unconsciously, he has been caught up by the *Zeitgeist,* and with his black brothers of Africa and his brown and yellow brothers of Asia, South America and the Caribbean, the United States Negro is moving with a sense of great urgency toward the promised land of racial justice. If one recognizes this vital urge that has engulfed the Negro community, one should readily understand why public demonstrations are taking place. The Negro has many pent-up resentments and latent frustrations, and he msut releasusthem. So let him march; let him make prayer pilgrimages to the city hall; let him go on freedom rides—and try to understand why he must do so. If his repressed emotions are not released in nonviolent ways, they will seek expression through violence; this is not a threat but a fact of history. So I have not said to my people: "Get rid of your discontent." Rather, I have tried to say that this normal and healthy discontent can be channeled into the creative outlet of nonviolent direct action. And now this approach is being termed extremist.

But though I was initially disappointed at being categorized as an extremist, as I continued to think about the matter I gradually gained a measure of satisfaction from the label. Was not Jesus an extremist for love: "Love your enemies, bless them that curse you, do good to them that hate you, and pray for them which despitefully use you, and persecute you." Was not Amos an extremist for justice: "Let justice roll down like waters and righteousness like an ever-flowing stream." Was not Paul an extremist for the Christian gospel: "I bear in my body the marks of the Lord Jesus." Was not Martin Luther an extremist: "Here I stand; I cannot do otherwise, so help me God." And John Bunyan: "I will stay in jail to the end of my days before I make a butchery of my conscience." And Abraham Lincoln: "This nation cannot survive half slave and half free." And Thomas Jefferson: "We hold these truths to be self-evident, that all men are created equal . . ." So the question is not whether we will be extremists, but what kind of extremists we will be. Will we be extremists for hate or for love? Will we be extremists for the preservation of injustice or for the extension of justice? In that dramatic scene on Calvary's hill three men were crucified. We must never forget that all three were crucified for the same crime—the crime of extremism. Two were extremists for immorality, and thus fell below their environment. The other, Jesus Christ, was an extremist for love, truth and goodness, and thereby rose above his environment. Perhaps the South, the nation and the world are in dire need of creative extremists.

I had hoped that the white moderate would see this need. Perhaps I was too optimistic; perhaps I expected too much. I supposed I should have realized that few members of the oppressor race can understand the deep groans and passionate yearnings of the oppressed race, and still fewer have the vision to see that injustice must be rooted out by strong, persistent and determined action. I am thankful, however, that some of our white brothers in the South have grasped the meaning of this social revolution and committed themselves to it. They are still too few in quantity, but they are big in quality. Some—such as Ralph McGill, Lilliam Smith, Harry Golden, James McBride Dabbs, Ann Braden and Sarah Patton Boyle—have written about our struggle in eloquent and prophetic terms. Others have marched with us down nameless streets of the South. They have languished in filthy, roach-infested jails, suffering the abuse and brutality of policemen who view them as "dirty niggerlovers." Unlike so many of their moderate brothers and sisters, they have recognized the urgency of the moment and sensed the need for powerful "action" antidotes to combat the disease of segregation.

Let me take note of my other major disappointment. I have been so greatly disappointed with the white church and its leadership. Of course, there are some notable exceptions. I am not unmindful of the fact that each of you has taken some significant stands on this issue. I commend you, Reverend

Stallings, for your Christian stand on this past Sunday, in welcoming Negroes to your worship service on a nonsegregated basis. I commend the Catholic leaders of this state for integrating Spring Hill College several years ago.

But despite these notable exceptions, I must honestly reiterate that I have been disappointed with the church. I do not say this as one of those negative critics who can always find something wrong with the church. I say this as a minister of the gospel, who loves the church; who was nurtured in its bosom; who has been sustained by its spiritual blessings and who will remain true to it as long as the cord of life shall lengthen.

When I was suddenly catapulted into the leadership of the bus protest in Montgomery, Alabama, a few years ago, I felt we would be supported by the white church. I felt that the white ministers, priests and rabbis of the South would be among our strongest allies. Instead, some have been outright opponents, refusing to understand the freedom movement and misrepresenting its leaders; all too many others have been more cautious than courageous and have remained silent behind the anesthetizing security of stained-glass windows.

In spite of my shattered dreams, I came to Birmingham with the hope that the white religious leadership of the community would see the justice of our cause and, with deep moral concern, would serve as the channel through which our just grievances could reach the power structure. I had hoped that each of you would understand. But again I have been disappointed.

I have heard numerous southern religious leaders admonish their worshipers to comply with a desegregation decision because it is the law, but I have longed to hear white ministers declare: "Follow this decree because integration is morally right and because the Negro is your brother." In the midst of blatant injustices inflicted upon the Negro, I have watched white churchmen stand on the sideline and mouth pious irrelevancies and sanctimonious trivialities. In the midst of a mighty struggle to rid our nation of racial and economic injustice, I have heard many ministers say: "Those are social issues, with which the gospel has no real concern." And I have watched many churches commit themselves to a completely other-worldly religion which makes a strange, un-Biblical distinction between body and soul, between the sacred and the secular.

I have traveled the length and breadth of Alabama, Mississippi and all the other southern states. On sweltering summer days and crisp autumn mornings I have looked at the South's beautiful churches with their lofty spires pointing heavenward. I have beheld the impressive outlines of her massive religious-education buildings. Over an over I have found myself asking: "What kind of people worship here? Who is their God? Where were their voices when the lips of Governor Barnett dripped with words of interpositon and nullification? Where were they when Governor Wallace gave a clarion call for defiance and hatred? Where were their voices of support when bruised and weary Negro men and women decided to rise from the dark dungeons of complacency to the bright hills of creative protest?"

Yes, these qustions are still in my mind. In deep disappointment I have wept over the laxity of the church. But be assured that my tears have been tears of love. There can be no deep disappointment where there is not deep love. Yes, I love the church. How could I do otherwise? I am in the rather unique position of being the son, the grandson and the great-grandson of preachers. Yes, I see the church as the body of Christ. But, oh! How we have blemished and scarred that body through social neglect and through fear of being nonconformists.

There was a time when the church was very powerful—in the time when the early Christians rejoiced at being deemed worthy to suffer for what they believed. In those days the church was not merely a thermometer that recorded the ideas and principles of popular opinion; it was a thermostat that transformed the mores of society. Whenever the early Christians entered a town, the people in power became disturbed and immediately sought to convict the Christians for being "disturbers of the peace" and "outside agitators." But the Christians pressed on, in the conviction that they were "a colony of heaven," called to obey God rather than man. Small in number, they were big in commitment. They were too God-intoxicated to be "astronomically intimidated." By their effort and example they brought an end to such ancient evils as infanticide and gladiatorial contests.

Things are different now. So often the contemporary church is a weak, ineffectual voice with an uncertain sound. So often it is an archdefender of the status quo. Far from being disturbed by the presence of the church, the power structure of the average community is consoled by the church's silent—and often even vocal—sanction of things as they are.

But the judgment of God is upon the church as never before. If today's church does not recapture the sacrificial spirit of the early church, it will lose its authenticity, forfeit the loyalty of millions, and be dismissed as an irrelevant social club with no meaning for the twentieth century. Every day I meet young people whose disappointment with the church has turned into outright disgust.

Perhaps I have once again been too optimistic. Is organized religion too inextricably bound to the status quo to save our nation and the world? Perhaps I must turn my faith to the inner spiritual church, the church within the church, as the true *ekklesia* and the hope of the world. But again I am thankful to God that some noble souls from the ranks of organized religion have broken loose from the paralyzing chains of conformity and joined us as active partners in th struggle for freedom. They have left their secure congregations and walked the streets of Albany, Georgia, with us. They have gone down the highways of the South on tortuous rides for freedom. Yes, they have gone to jail with us. Some have been dismissed from their churches, have lost the support of their bishops and fellow ministers. But they have acted in the faith that right defeated is stronger than evil triumphant. Their witness has been the spiritual salt that has preserved the true meaning of the gospel in these troubled times. They have carved a tunnel of hope through the dark mountain of disappointment.

I hope the church as a whole will meet the challenge of this decisive hour.

But even if the church does not come to the aid of justice, I have no despair about the future. I have no fear about the outcome of our struggle in Birmingham, even if our motives are at present misunderstood. We will reach the goal of freedom in Birmingham and all over the nation, because the goal of America is freedom. Abused and scorned though we may be, our destiny is tied up with America's destiny. Before the pilgrims landed at Plymouth, we were here. Before the pen of Jefferson etched the majestic words of the Declaration of Independence across the pages of history, we were here. For more than two centuries our forebears labored in this country without wages; they made cotton king; they built the homes of their masters while suffering gross injustice and shameful humiliation—and yet out of a bottomless vitality they continued to thrive and develop. If the inexpressible cruelties of slavery could not stop us, the opposition we now face will surely fail. We will win our freedom because the sacred heritage of our nation and the eternal will of God are embodied in our echoing demands.

Before closing I feel impelled to mention one other point in your statement that has troubled me profoundly. You warmly commended the Birmingham police for keeping "order" and "preventing violence." I doubt that you would have so warmly commended the police force if you had seen its dogs sinking their teeth into unarmed, nonviolent Negroes. I doubt that you would so quickly commend the policemen if you were to observe their ugly and inhumane treatment of Negroes here in the city jail; if you were to watch them push and curse old Negro women and young Negro girls; if you were to see them slap and kick old Negro men and young boys; if you were to observe them, as they did on two occasions, refuse to give us food because we wanted to sing our grace together. I cannot join you in your praise of the Birmingham police department.

It is true that the police have exercised a degree of discipline in handling the demonstrators. In this sense they have conducted themselves rather "nonviolently" in public. But for what purpose? To preserve the evil system of segregation. Over the past few years I have consistently preached that nonviolence demands that the means we use must be as pure as the ends we seek. I have tried to make clear that it is wrong to use immoral means to attain moral ends. But now I must affirm that it is just as wrong, or perhaps even more so, to use moral means to preserve immoral ends. Perhaps Mr. Connor and his policemen have been rather nonviolent in public, as was Chief Pritchett in Albany, Georgia, but they have used the moral means of nonviolence to maintain the immoral end of racial injustice. As T. S. Eliot has said: "The last temptation is the greatest treason: To do the right deed for the wrong reason."

I wish you had commended the Negro sit-inners and demonstrators of Birmingham for their sublime courage, their willingness to suffer and their amazing discipline in the midst of great provocation. One day the South will recognize its real heroes. They will be the James Merediths, with the noble sense of purpose that enables them to face jeering and hostile mobs, and with the agonizing loneliness that characterizes the life of the pioneer. They will be old, oppressed, battered Negro women, symbolized in a seventy-two-year-old woman in Montgomery, Alabama, who rose up with a sense of dignity and with her people decided not to ride segregated buses, and who responded with ungrammatical profundity to one who inquired about her weariness: "My feets is tired, but my soul is at rest." They will be the young high school and college students, teh young ministers of the gospel and a host of their elders, courageously and nonviolently sitting in at lunch counters and willingly going to jail for conscience' sake. One day the South will know that when these disinherited children of God sat down at lunch counters, they were in reality standing up for what is best in the American dream and for the most sacred values in our Judaeo-Christian heritage, thereby bringing our nation back to those great wells of democracy which were dug deep by the founding fathers in their formulation of the Constitution and the Declaration of Independence.

Never before have I written so long a letter. I'm afraid it is much too long to take your precious time. I can assure you that it would have been much shorter if I had been writing from a comfortable desk, but what else can one do when he is alone in a narrow jail cell, other than write long letters, think long thoughts and pray long prayers?

If I have said anything in this letter that overstates the truth and indicates an unreasonable impatience, I beg you to forgive me. If I have said anything that understates the truth and indicates my having a patience that allows me to settle for anything less than brotherhood, I beg God to forgive me.

I hope this letter finds you strong in faith. I also hope that circumstances will soon make it possible for me to meet each of you, not as an integrationist or a civil-rights leader but as a fellow clergyman and a Christian brother. Let us all hope that the dark clouds of racial prejudice will soon pass away and the deep fog of misunderstanding will be lifted from our fear-drenched communities, and in some not too distant tomorrow the radiant stars of love and brotherhood will shine over our great nation with all their scintillating beauty.

Yours for the cause of Peace and Brotherhood,
Martin Luther King, Jr.

BIBLIOGRAPHICAL NOTE

There has been a large number of recent critiques of our public life. One of the most significant is Theodore Lowi, *The End of Liberalism*. The same line of thought is developed in Grant McConnell's *Private Power and American Democracy* and Thomas Dye and Harmon Ziegler, *The Irony of Democracy*.

Herbert Marcuse's *One Dimensional Man* and his *Eros and Civilization* present his forceful criticisms of the effects of present day technology on American life and politics. Another lucid philosophical examination is Robert Paul Wolff, *The Poverty of Liberalism* and its sequel, *In Defense of Anarchism*. Especially poignant is Philip Slater's discussion of America in *The Pursuit of Loneliness*.

There have been scores of books on the racial problem in America from Gunnar Myrdal, *The American Dilemma*, to George Jackson, *Soledad Brother*. One superb study of racial attitudes is Winthrop Jordon, *White Over Black* which can be well supplemented by the Report of the Kerner Commission done after the 1967 riots.

The political system and its problems is examined in Garry Wills' unsympathetic biography, *Nixon Agonistes* and Nick Kotz's study of the war on hunger, *Let Them Eat Promises*. The moral implications of that political system are discussed in Daniel Berrigan, *No Bar to Manhood* and Howard Zinn, *Disobedience and Democracy: Nine Fallacies on Law and Order*.

INDEX

Abbott, Philip, 38, 116
Adams, John, 8, 192
Aquinas, St. Thomas, 154, 282
Aristotle, 1, 4, 192, 195

Bellamy, Edward, 4, 86
Bentham, Jeremy, 52
Bentley, Arthur, 202
Boorstin, Daniel, 1, 3
Bourne, Randolph, 4
Brandeis, Louis D., 152, 237
Burke, Edmund, 52, 85

Calhoun, John C., 4, 5, 163, 192
Calvin, John, 234
Carey, George W., 164
Carlyle, Thomas, 32, 33
Channing, William, 85
Cotton, John, 7, 8

Dahl, Robert, 4, 8, 65, 163, 204, 205
Debray, Regis, 143
Dennis, Jack, 217
Descartes, Rene, 210, 211
Dewey, John, 4, 8
Douglass, Frederick, 257

Easton, David, 217
Edelman, Murray, 257
Emerson, Ralph Waldo, 4, 156

Fanon, Franz, 146, 147

Green, T. H., 4
Greenberg, Edward, 218
Greenstein, Fred I., 217

Harrington, James, 4
Hartz, Louis, 1, 2, 4
Hayek, Friederich, 238
Herring, E. Pendleton, 205
Hobbes, Thomas, 1, 30, 32, 37, 45, 49
Hofstadter, Richard, 143
Hume, David, 18, 54

Jaros, Dean, 218
Jefferson, Thomas, 20, 21, 37, 116, 152, 186, 237, 286

Kant, Immanuel, 24, 25, 124, 128
Kautsky, Karl, 145
Kendall, Willmore, 164
Keniston, Kenneth, 221
Key, V. O., 8, 208, 257
Kierkegaard, Soren, 123
King, Martin Luther, Jr., 151, 154, 155, 158, 258

Lenin, V. I., 141, 143
Lincoln, Abraham, 187, 286
Lipset, Seymour Martin, 8, 216, 257
Litt, Edgar, 220
Locke, John, 1, 4, 37, 49, 56, 57, 58, 59, 60, 61, 63, 65, 67, 68, 71, 72, 74, 75, 80, 108, 109, 110, 111, 112, 125

293

Lowi, Theodore, 164

MacDonald, Margaret, 107
Machiavelli, Niccolo, 145
Madison, James, 4, 163, 164, 199, 200, 202
Mannheim, Karl, 254
Marcuse, Herbert, 145, 146
Marx, Karl, 183, 197, 198, 199, 200, 230, 231
McIver, Robert, 205
Mill, John Stuart, 4, 136, 192
Milton, John, 4
Moore, G. E., 145
More, St. Thomas, 4
Murphy, Jeffrie G., 115

Niebuhr, Reinhold, 4, 8
Nietzsche, Friedrich, 131

Paine, Thomas, 8, 85
Paul, St., 52, 278, 286
Pitkin, Hanna, 38, 66, 70, 71
Plamenatz, John, 65, 67, 74, 75
Plato, 1, 29, 32, 154

Riccards, Michael P., 208

Rousseau, Jean Jacques, 1, 18, 49, 51, 184, 185, 186, 195, 218, 221, 231, 232, 233

Shaver, James, 219
Signey, Algernon, 4, 37
Smith, Adam, 24, 38
Spencer, Herbert, 86
Suarez, Francis, 155
Sumner, William Graham, 4, 85

Thoreau, Henry David, 4, 116, 156
Tocqueville, Alexis de, 2, 3, 152, 198, 199, 208
Trotsky, Leon, 145
Truman David, 203
Tussman, Joseph, 38, 50, 56, 59, 60, 61, 62, 63, 68, 69, 70, 71
Twain, Mark, 237

Wainwright, William J., 86
Walzer, Michael, 208
Weber, Max, 125, 205
Wilde, Oscar, 230
Williams, Roger, 4
Wolff, Robert Paul, 115